4TH EDITION

GLOBAL LOGISTICS and DISTRIBUTION PLANNING

strategies for management

4TH EDITION

GLOBAL LOGISTICS and DISTRIBUTION PLANNING

strategies for management

EDITED BY DONALD WATERS

The Institute of
Logistics and Transport

KOGAN
PAGE

First published in 1988
Revised edition 1990
Second edition 1994
Paperback edition published in 1995
Third edition 1999
Fourth edition 2003

Kogan Page Limited
120 Pentonville Road
London N1 9JN
United Kingdom
www.kogan-page.co.uk

British Library Cataloguing in Publication Data

A CIP record for this book is available from the British Library.

ISBN 0 7494 3930 0

Typeset by Saxon Graphics Ltd, Derby
Printed and bound in Great Britain by Biddles Ltd, Guildford and King's Lynn
www.biddles.co.uk

*This book is dedicated to the memory of
James Cooper and Marvin Manheim*

Contents

Figures

Tables

Contributors

Julian Allen is a Research Fellow at the Transport Studies Group, University of Westminster, where his major research interests are the market structure of the freight transport industry and the impact of manufacturing and retailing techniques on logistics and transportation systems. He lectures and conducts research on freight transport and logistics, and has published a number of papers, reports and chapters in books.

Grzegorz Augustyniak has an MA from the Warsaw School of Economics (SGH), where he is currently Assistant Professor in the Department of Management Theory. He is coordinator of a student exchange programme within the Community of European Management Schools, and is Deputy Director of the Polish-Japanese Management Center at SGH. Until 1998 he was a faculty member of the Department of Logistics at SGH and held visiting positions at Carleton University, the University of Calgary, the University of Minnesota and the University of British Columbia. He has been a consultant to many companies in manufacturing and distribution, and is currently working on improving productivity and quality in Poland.

Colin Bamford is Professor of Transport and Logistics at the University of Huddersfield. His interest in transport issues originated in the early 1970s when he was one of Ken Gwilliam's researchers at the University of Leeds. At Huddersfield he has been responsible for the development of a pioneering suite of undergraduate courses in transport and logistics management. More recently he has been involved in setting up a new distance-learning training programme for logistics managers in Hungary. He has written articles and supervised research on a variety of supply chain management topics, and published textbooks in the field of transport economics.

Adrian Beesley is currently Director of Consultancy with the Supply Chain Development Group, focusing on areas such as time compression and supply chain design. Before this he was Director of Client Operations at BAX Global, as part of their supply chain development

team. He has been a Senior Research Fellow with the University of Warwick's manufacturing group, where he worked on a number of projects for leading companies, often
based on time compression. During this time he developed time-based process mapping
for the supply chain. His other experiences include spells as Director of DLR Consulting in
the Far East, Senior Consultant at Price Waterhouse in London and Europe, Business
Development Manager for Interforward, and Company Logistics Manager for B&Q.

Alan Braithwaite is the Executive Chairman of LCP Consulting, which he founded in 1985.
In 17 years he has taken the company to the leading independent consultancy in supply
chain and logistics, working internationally and receiving world recognition in its specialization. He has worked with the LCP team to develop innovative new analytical and
design tools including Cost-to-Serve® and Time-to-Serve® to identify the value potential in
clients' supply chains. Alan is a visiting lecturer at Cranfield University in the UK, the
University of Ghent, and at Management Centre Europe. He is a regular speaker at conferences, and the author of many papers and articles. He holds an MSc in Business
Administration from the London Business School and a BSc in Chemical Engineering from
Birmingham University.

Michael Browne is the Exel Logistics Professor of Transport at the University of
Westminster, where he specializes in international logistics. He teaches freight transport
and logistics on the university's Master's programme in Transport Planning and
Management, and is responsible for directing research and consultancy activities in
logistics. His work has been published widely and presented at international conferences.
Michael is a member of the Research and Development Committee of the European
Logistics Association and has acted as a specialist adviser to the House of Commons
Transport Select Committee.

Ashok Chandrashekar is currently with the Software Services Group of IBM, working on
improving supply chain and related systems though effective process integration
strategies. Ashok has had wide-ranging experience in both industrial and academic
settings. In industry, he has designed, developed, implemented and operated international supply chains. He has also researched and taught extensively in the areas of supply
chain and operations management, and has several publications in leading journals. His
doctorate is from Arizona State University.

Garland Chow is an Associate Professor in the Faculty of Commerce and Business
Administration at the University of British Columbia. His interests span transport
economics, logistics, supply chain management and services management, and current
research includes work on the logistics services industry, prediction of bankruptcies in
transport firms and a book on motor carriers. His paper (co-authored with Trevor Heaver)
'Logistics performance, definition and measurement' in the *International Journal of Physical
Distribution and Logistics Management* was awarded that journal's best paper prize. Garland
is coordinator of the UBC supply chain specialization and a national Director of the
Canadian Association of Logistics Management.

Martin Christopher is Professor of Marketing and Logistics at Cranfield School of
Management. His work in the field of logistics and supply chain management has gained
international recognition. He has published widely and his recent books include *Logistics
and Supply Chain Management* and *Marketing Logistics*. Martin is also co-editor of the
International Journal of Logistics Management and is a regular contributor to conferences and
workshops around the world. At Cranfield, Martin chairs the Centre for Logistics and

Transportation, and is an Emeritus Fellow of the Institute of Logistics on whose council he sits. In 1988 he was awarded the Sir Robert Lawrence Gold Medal for his contribution to logistics education.

Jacques Colin is Professor of Management Science at the Université de la Méditerranée (Aix-Marseille 2, France). At the faculty of Economic Sciences and Business Administration, he is Director of CRET-LOG (Centre de REcherche sur le Transport et la LOGistique), which is the main French research centre devoted to logistics. He is a specialist in logistics and, more specifically, in the study of strategies developed by large companies, and in the effects of the development of logistics on land planning and the environment. He has carried out many research projects for government bodies, and is a consultant for major companies, such as IBM, SNCF, OTIS, SAGA, and ELF. He has widely published the results of this work.

Andrew Cox is Professor and Director of the Centre for Business Strategy and Procurement at Birmingham University's Business School. This centre undertakes research in all aspects of business strategy, supply chain management and procurement competence. Andrew has a major grant from the EPSRC to undertake a research project into critical assets in supply chain management. This involves working closely with a number of major UK companies on the development of audit tools for strategic and operational alignment. He has also worked as a consultant for the EU, HM Treasury, DTI, and for a range of multi-national firms based in Europe and the United States, emphasizing the evaluation of existing strategy, operational practice, procurement and supply competence. Andrew has written on a wide range of topics related to procurement and business strategy.

Robert Duncan is a Principal Consultant within PA Consulting Group's Manufacturing Industries Practice. He has over 30 years experience as both an executive and consultant in the field of supply chain management. His work has embraced many industry sectors and taken him all over the world. Robert's recent work has concentrated on the issues relating to order fulfilment for organizations trading over the Internet. He is a regular contributor to conferences and publications relating to supply chain management.

Dag Ericsson is professor of eLogistics at the University of Skovde in Sweden, where he specializes in the implementation of integrated logistics in manufacturing industry. He was the pioneer and developer of the Swedish concept of materials administration and supply chain management, and has written several books including *Purchasing: Concepts and tools*, *Materials Administration/Logistics*, *Supply Chain Management*, and the most recent, *Virtual Integration with IT as an Enabler*. In his recent research and consulting, Dag focuses on the interface between technology, management, organizational effectiveness and efficiency. He is especially concerned with renewal processes and organizational restructuring enabled by technological development. For this, he works with most of the global Swedish companies and with several international companies. His background as a professor and management consultant enables him to bridge the gaps between business, technology, and executive education.

Nathalie Fabbe-Costes is Professor of Management Science at the Université de la Méditerranée (Aix-Marseille 2, France) where she lectures on strategy, management information systems and logistics. She is also a senior researcher at CRET-LOG (Centre de REcherche sur le Transport et la LOGistique), which is the main French research centre devoted to logistics. Her major fields of interest are logistics as a global and complex inter-organizational management concept, a structured function within companies, and an increasing component of firms' strategy; and logistics information and communication systems: how to design and develop them, and their role in supply chain management and in the overall strategy of companies. She has written more than 100 publications since 1984, and has been co-author or editor of more than 10 books.

John Fernie is Professor of Retail Marketing and Head of School of Management at Heriot-Watt University, Scotland. He was previously Professor of Retailing and Logistics and Director of the Institute for Retail Studies at the University of Stirling. He has written and contributed to numerous textbooks and papers on retail management, especially in the field of retail logistics and the internationalization of retail formats. He is editor of the *International Journal of Retail and Distribution Management*, and received the prestigious award of Editor of the Year in 1997 in addition to Leading Editor awards in 1994, 1998 and 2000. He is on the editorial board of the *Journal of Product and Brand Management*, and is an active member of the Institute of Logistics and Transport, the Chartered Institute of Marketing, and the American Collegiate Retail Association. In 2001 he became a member of the Logistics Directors Forum, a group of leading professionals in logistics whose membership is limited to 150 invited senior executives.

Bill Galvin has more than 25 years of experience in logistics and supply chain management. This has covered most business sectors, including food and fashion retailing, consumer goods, industrials and utilities. He was recently Director of East Asia Practice at Kurt Salmon Associates, where his clients in Asia included Marks and Spencer, Jardine Matheson, Calvin Klein, Dairy Farm, First Pacific, Swire Group, Bristol-Myers Squibb, Kmart, IKEA, BAT and ICI. He is a Fellow of the Institute of Logistics, and of the Institute of Management Consultancy, both of the UK. Bill is also a founder member of the Hong Kong Logistics Association.

Derek Gittoes is the Vice President of Product Solutions at G-Log, where he is responsible for developing innovative solutions for the logistics challenges facing G-Log's customers. Derek has made significant contributions throughout his career in the interdisciplinary fields of logistics, operations research and computer science, in both the commercial and academic sectors. Prior to joining G-Log, he studied and worked at Princeton University, where he obtained his Master's degree in operations research. Derek also worked in Princeton's Computational and Stochastic Logistics and Transportation Engineering Laboratory (CASTLE Lab). Based on his research at Princeton, he co-founded an optimization software company that specializes in developing real-time optimization systems for large motor carriers and third-party logistics providers.

David Granville was educated at Heriot-Watt University, Edinburgh. Following a number of years in line management, he moved into training and development, and has spent 20 years working on assignments connected with logistics and supply chain management. He is currently Chief Executive of People Development Group plc (which incorporates Logistics Training International Limited and Direct Interaction Ltd). Since establishing this group in 1990 David has led its growth into the leading supplier of training and development services in the supply chain sector, providing training services on a global scale to many major companies. He has worked with governments, professional institutions, manufacturers, retailers and logistics service providers in over 50 countries across Europe, Asia, Southern Africa, the Americas and New Zealand. He is an enthusiastic contributor to the work of the Institute of Logistics and Transport, is a regular speaker at international conferences and seminars, and is an author of many articles and training courses.

David Hatherall has many years of experience as a senior manager of procurement and logistics. He was responsible for Hoechst UK procurement, warehousing, distribution and logistic functions, and frequently worked in Southeast Asia. He is currently a Director of Hatherall Associates, where he provides consultancy services and is increasingly involved with contractual, energy and strategic issues. David is a visiting examiner to several professional institutes, a regular speaker at seminars in Europe and Asia, and an associate lecturer for the Open University Business School. He is a fellow of the Chartered Institute of Purchasing and Supply, and works with the Institute of Logistics Transport Special Interest Group.

Trevor Heaver is Professor Emeritus at the Faculty of Commerce and Business Administration at the University of British Columbia. He is a past chairman of the World Conference on Transport Research and immediate Past President of the International Association of Maritime Economists. He specializes in transport policy, maritime economics, logistics and supply chain management. He still lectures at UBC but has been visiting professor recently at the University of Antwerp – UFSIA, the University of Sydney, Australia, and the University of Stellenbosch, South Africa. His current research and publications deal with issues of corporate strategy and service integration in international transport and logistics.

Peter Hines is Professor of Supply Chain Management and Director of the Lean Enterprise Research Centre at Cardiff Business School. He holds an MA in geography from Cambridge University and an MBA and PhD from the University of Cardiff. Peter followed a successful career in distribution and manufacturing industry before joining Cardiff Business School in 1992. He leads the 24-strong Lean Enterprise Research Centre. The Lean Enterprise Research Centre is the largest dedicated research centre in lean thinking in the world.

Chris Lonsdale first taught at the Department of Politics, University of Hull in 1992. In 1993 he moved to the University of Birmingham, teaching in the Department of Political Science and International Studies and the Institute for Local Government Studies. He moved to the Business School in 1994 and has worked since that time in the Centre for Business Strategy and Procurement, the School's supply chain management group. He received his PhD in 1995 and from 1997 to 2001 was the Programme Director of the MBA (Strategy and Procurement Management). In 2000, he was awarded honorary membership of the Chartered Institute of Purchasing and Supply.

Kirstie McIntyre has been successfully combining the fundamentals of sustainability with supply chain management and other business processes for several years now. Currently she is working with a range of clients in the public and private sectors via URS Corporate Sustainable Solutions. Previous to this, she spent seven years with the Xerox Corporation in a supply chain and manufacturing strategy development and environmental capacity. Kirstie has published widely in the areas mentioned above and can be contacted at: kirstie_mcintyre@urscorp.com

Alan McKinnon is Professor of Logistics in the School of Management at Heriot-Watt University, Edinburgh. A graduate of the universities of Aberdeen, British Columbia and London, he has been researching and teaching in the fields of freight transport and logistics management for over 20 years, and has published extensively on these subjects. He has also been an advisor to several government departments and committees, and consultant to numerous public and private sector organizations on a range of logistics-related topics. He is a Fellow of the Institute of Logistics and Transport.

Tim Randall is a Principal Consultant with LCP Consulting Limited. He has over 15 years of experience working with IT and business. For the past 12 years he has worked in the manufacturing, financial services and retail sectors, specializing in supply chain management, innovation management and performance improvement. Tim is a regular contributor to publications, and speaker at conferences, focusing on operations management issues. He is a Fellow of the Institute of Operations Management, the Royal Society for the Encouragement of Arts, Manufactures and Commerce, and a member of the Institute of Directors. He is a qualified engineer, has a postgraduate Diploma in Management Studies, and an MBA in Technology Management.

Joe Sanderson is a Research Fellow at the Centre for Business Strategy and Procurement at the University of Birmingham. He is currently working on a project to map the structural characteristics of supply and value chains in a range of service and industrial sectors. He has a BA in Politics from the University of Hull and is writing his doctoral thesis on the regulatory and organizational drivers of procurement efficiency in the UK utilities after privatization. His principal research interests are in international business and supply management, power in supply chains, and the impact of national, regional and international regulation on procurement practices.

Philip Schary is Professor Emeritus at the College of Business at Oregon State University, where he taught marketing and business logistics. He has been visiting professor at Cranfield School of Management, Copenhagen and Aarhus Schools of Business in Denmark, and the University of New South Wales in Australia. He has also lectured in Chile and China. He holds an MBA from UC Berkeley and a PhD from UCLA in business economics. He has written in professional journals and serves as editorial reviewer for two journals in logistics management. He has authored or co-authored several books, including *Managing the Global Supply Chain*, published by Copenhagen Business School Press.

Larry Simcox is the Director of Industry Performance at G-Log, where he is responsible for defining industry issues and best practices as they relate to logistics performance, processes and return on investment opportunities. Prior to this he spent five years with Moody's Investors Service as a Business Analyst and Associate Editor for their financial products, and was the Director of Industry Analysis and a Financial Product Consultant with Optum Inc, a supply chain execution software company that focuses on inventory, warehouse and transportation management. Larry was also a Value Proposition Analyst and Industry Financial Consultant with Manugistics, a provider of supply chain management optimization solutions. He obtained his Master's degree in business administration from Queens College in Charlotte, NC, and an undergraduate degree in business administration from Belmont Abbey College in Belmont, NC.

Lars Stemmler was born 1972 in Hamburg, Germany. Lars is a project manager with BLG Consult GmbH, a member of the BLG Logistics Group AG of Bremen, Germany. Prior to joining BLG he worked in various functions for Deutsche Schiffsbank AG, a leading ship finance institution, and for the Oldenburg Chamber of Industry and Commerce. He is also a guest lecturer in logistics at Oldenburg University and at the Bremen University of Applied Science. He holds a PhD in economics, received an MSc in logistics from Cranfield University in 1998 and also holds a Master's degree in business studies.

Remko van Hoek is a Professor in Supply Chain Management at the Cranfield School of Management, UK, and a managing director at the Corporate Executive Board, Washington DC. He also serves are European Editor of the *International Journal of Physical Distribution and Logistics Management* as well as on the editorial board of several other journals.

Donald Waters has degrees from Sussex, London and Strathclyde. He worked for a variety of organizations in the UK before moving to Canada to become Professor of Operations Management at the University of Calgary. In 1997 he returned to the UK to become Chief Executive of Richmond, Parkes and Wright, whose main interests are in management research, education and training. Donald continues to work for organizations around the world, using his specialist knowledge of operations and supply chain management. He has written a number of successful books in these areas.

Glyn Watson is a Research Fellow at the Centre for Business Strategy and Procurement at the University of Birmingham. His research interests include supply chain, supply chain typologies and supply chain management. Prior to joining the centre he did research in the broad area of European integration and on European business issues.

Tony Whiteing is a Senior Lecturer at the University of Huddersfield, where he manages the Transport and Logistics Research Unit. His interests in transport and logistics research go back some 25 years, having studied and worked at the University of Leeds Institute for Transport Studies before moving to Huddersfield in 1984. Tony is a member of the Institute of Logistics and Transport. He serves on their West and North Yorkshire Group Committee, and he is also a member of the Steering Group for the Logistics Research Network, an Institute of Logistics and Transport Special Interest Group which promotes collaborative research between academia and industry. His recent research has been in policy-related areas such as modal choice for freight transport and city logistics problems.

Introduction

The third edition of *Global Logistics and Distribution Planning: Strategies for management* appeared in 1999. Since then the whole field of logistics has continued to develop at a remarkable pace. Not long ago, logistics would hardly be mentioned in the long-term plans of even major companies; now its strategic role is recognized in almost every organization. There are many reasons for this change, ranging from improved communications to increasing concern for the environment. To a large extent, though, the current prominence of logistics comes from its development into a single, integrated function that is responsible for all aspects of material movement. With this broad view, logistics includes all the activities that are needed to ensure a smooth journey of materials from original suppliers, through supply chains and on to final customers.

This fourth edition of the book builds on the success of earlier editions and follows the same general format. It is not intended as an encyclopaedia of logistics including every topic that could be connected to this broad subject. Instead it is a forum in which a number of key issues are addressed. It focuses on areas that are of particular current interest, and emphasizes changes that have occurred in recent years. These areas include the wider integration of logistics, the growing importance of logistics strategies, improving communications and technology, the importance of global operations, and use of new management principles.

The contributors are acknowledged experts in their fields, and they give an authoritative view of current work from both academic and practical viewpoints. They describe contemporary thinking about a range of issues. This does not, of course, mean that they present the only view, and we hope that the material will promote informed discussion.

This new edition has been completely rewritten. Several of the previous chapters are still relevant to both the broad international readership and to contemporary issues in logistics, and these have been retained and updated. To keep the book's contemporary focus we have removed some of the previous chapters and replaced them by new ones. In this way, the book continues to evolve, discussing a broad range of current topics and views, but keeping within a reasonable length.

The book will appeal to everyone with an interest in the broader aspects of logistics. This includes logistics professionals, consultants, academics, and a variety of students. It also includes managers from different backgrounds who want an appreciation of current thinking about the supply chain. It is especially important for these non-specialists to realize the growing importance of logistics, and the way that it crosses organizational and disciplinary boundaries. The long-term success of every organization depends on its ability to deliver products to customers – and this is precisely the role of logistics.

James Cooper edited the first two editions of this book – and I have to agree with his summary of the pleasures of editing the contents:

> In my role as editor, I have already had the opportunity to read the thoughts and ideas expressed in each of the chapters. Indeed, one of the greatest pleasures of being editor was to be the first to enjoy the riches of the chapters as they converged into this book. I now leave it to new readers to explore the chapters that follow, in the anticipation that they too will benefit, both professionally and personally, from the wealth of knowledge and expertise that they contain.

Donald Waters
Penzance
February 2003

1

Development and trends in supply chain management

Donald Waters
Richmond, Parkes and Wright

INTRODUCTION

This chapter introduces some of the ideas discussed in the rest of the book. It outlines the reasons for rapid changes in logistics, and shows how it has matured into a single, integrated function that is responsible for the flow of materials throughout the supply chain. Logistics has an obvious strategic role, and the chapter mentions some options for the design of a logistics strategy. Organizations tend to adopt similar strategies, and this encourages wider trends, such as the continuing growth of global operations. The chapter finishes with some comments on performance measurement and improvement.

CHANGING VIEWS OF LOGISTICS

All organizations move materials to support their operations. These materials are both tangible (such as raw materials, components, finished goods, and spare parts) and intangible (predominantly information). Logistics is the function responsible for these movements; it manages the transport and storage of materials on their journey from original suppliers through supply chains and on to final customers. In practice, the terms 'logistics' and 'supply chain management' are used interchangeably, so the Institute of Logistics and Transport can give the following definitions.

Logistics is the time related positioning of resources or, the strategic management of the total supply-chain.

The **supply-chain** is a sequence of events intended to satisfy a customer. It can include procurement, manufacture, distribution and waste disposal, together with associated transport, storage and information technology.

[Institute of Logistics, 1998]

Unfortunately, people use many different terms to describe aspects of logistics. Even something as basic as a 'supply chain' may be called a 'process' when emphasizing operations, a 'marketing channel', 'logistics channel' or 'distribution channel' when emphasizing marketing, a 'value chain' (Porter, 1985) when considering added value, a 'demand chain' to show how customer demand is satisfied or a 'supply network' or 'supply web' to emphasize its complexity (Waters, 2003). The variety of terms can be confusing, but each gives a subtle difference in meaning.

Whatever names we give to different logistics activities, the important point is that they combine to form an essential function in every organization. Christopher (1986) emphasizes this broad importance by saying that 'Logistics has always been a central and essential feature of all economic activity.' Shapiro and Heskett (1985) agree, saying that 'There are few aspects of human activity that do not ultimately depend on the flow of goods from point of origin to point of consumption.'

Despite this importance, there is a long history of organizations paying little attention to their logistics. They traditionally put all their effort into making products, and then considered the movement and storage of materials as an uninteresting chore that formed part of the overheads of doing business. In 1962 Drucker described physical distribution as 'the economy's dark continent' and said that this formed 'the most sadly neglected, most promising area of... business' (Drucker, 1962).

After this, organizations began to realize that logistics can be expensive, and they gave it more attention. This was not easy, as Ray noted in 1976 that 'The whole area [of logistics costing] is clouded with ad hoc approaches and untidy accounting procedures, to which there appears little underlying systematic ideology.' At the same time Little (1977) said that 'Identifying logistics costs through accepted accounting statements in the firm is very misleading.' Many projects were started to find the 'total cost' of logistics, and by the 1980s surveys by, for example, McKibbin (1982), Ray, Gattorna and Allen (1980), Firth *et al* (1980) and Delaney (1986) suggested that logistics generally account for 15–20 per cent of costs. However, as late as 1994, Hill could still say that 'many distributors are unaware of the costs of the distribution service they provide'.

Taking overall figures for, say, the United States, the Gross Domestic Product (GDP) is $10 trillion, so $2 trillion dollars a year might be spent on logistics, with half of this for transport (US Statistical Abstract, 2001). We should, however, interpret such figures carefully as there are alternative views. The UK government, for example, says that 12 per cent of the GDP comes from wholesale and retail trades and 6 per cent comes from transport and storage (Office of National Statistics, 2001). This suggests that overall logistics costs are considerably higher – perhaps supporting an earlier estimate by Childerley (1980) that logistics accounted for 32.5 per cent of the UK GDP.

The status of logistics has continued to improve, and by 1996 a survey by Deloitte and Touche in Canada (Factor, 1996) showed that 98 per cent of companies considered supply chain management to be either 'critical' or 'very important'. The same survey emphasized the rate of change of logistics, with over 90 per cent of organizations either currently improving their supply chain or planning improvements within the next two years. The main pressures for this changing view of logistics can be summarized as follows:

- Recognition that logistics is an essential function in every organization, and that it directly affects overall performance.
- Realization that decisions about the supply chain can have a strategic significance.
- Appreciation of the high cost of logistics and the opportunity for major savings.
- Growing emphasis on customer service, and the way this depends on logistics.
- Increasing competition for both users and providers of logistics, who have to continually improve operations to remain competitive.
- New types of operations, which can force changes to logistics – such as just-in-time, total quality management, flexible operations, mass customization, lean operations and time compression.
- Improved communications allowing electronic data interchange (EDI), business to business (B2B), business to consumer (B2C) and other aspects of e-commerce.
- Improved technology such as item coding, electronic point of sales (EPOS) and global positioning for identifying, locating and tracking materials.
- A general trend towards integration of operations, including strategic alliances, partnerships and collaboration.
- More organizations concentrating on their core operations and outsourcing logistics to third parties.
- More organizations adopting a process focus, with logistics as an integral part of the whole process of satisfying customer demand.
- Changing patterns of power in the supply chain, with large organizations dominating some areas and setting prevailing standards.
- Growing concern for environmental damage, and changing attitudes towards pollution, waste, traffic congestion, road building and so on.

- Changing government policies on the ownership, regulation, use, responsibilities and cost of transport.
- Sustained growth of international trade, particularly through free trade areas such as the European Union and North American Free Trade Agreement.

INTEGRATION OF THE SUPPLY CHAIN

Initially, organizations responded to these pressures for change by looking for improvements to the separate activities of logistics – procurement, inventory control, warehousing, materials handling, packaging, transport and so on. It soon becomes clear, however, that these are not isolated activities, and changes in, say, transport have direct consequences for warehousing and other logistics operations. The best results clearly come from considering all aspects of material movement in a single, integrated function. This gives a broader and more inclusive view of logistics, with relevant activities coordinated under the umbrella of a unified function. The result is a more effective and efficient flow of materials, with lower overall costs.

One development from this view is 'quick response' or 'efficient customer response' (ECR), which links all the tiers of a supply chain so that a final customer buying a product from a retailer automatically sends a message back through the chain to trigger a response from upstream suppliers. When, for example, a customer buys a pair of jeans in a clothes shop, the EPOS (electronic point of sales) system sends a message back to the wholesaler to say that the stock needs replenishing, then back to the manufacturer to say that it is time to make another pair of jeans, then back to suppliers to say that they should deliver materials to the manufacturer, and so on. The result is 'a focus on the consumer, the development of partnership relationships between retailers and their suppliers, and an increased integration of the components of the supply-chain' (Szymankiewicz, 1997). Hutchinson (in O'Sullivan, 1997) says that, 'ECR means meeting consumer wishes better, faster and at less cost', and he adds, 'Is there anybody, wishing to remain in business, who believes that his or her company should not be striving to meet the wishes of the customer of their products and services better, faster and at less cost?'

The clear benefits from this integrated view include:

- common objectives for all parts of the supply chain;
- genuine cooperation to achieve these objectives;
- less uncertainty, errors and delays along the supply chain;
- less duplication of effort, information, planning, stocks, etc;
- elimination of operations that add no value for customers;
- improved efficiency and productivity, giving lower costs;
- lower stocks and shorter response times;

- actual demands triggering replenishments;
- faster and more flexible responses to customer demands;
- sharing information and highlighting important features such as costs;
- making planning easier;
- using available technology, such as EPOS, EDI and e-commerce;
- focusing on the importance of logistics.

By 1997 a survey by P-E Consulting found that 57 per cent of companies had moved to some form of integrated supply chain. Significantly, more than 90 per cent of companies expected an increase in integration over the next three years, with a quarter of companies moving to 'fully integrated' systems (although it was not clear what this actually meant). At the same time, though, Szymankiewicz (1997) noted that, 'In the grocery sector ECR is often regarded as an established way of doing business ... [but] overall there is more talk than action.' For a variety of reasons – ranging from an unwillingness to share information to a lack of appropriate technology – many organizations are still missing this opportunity to both raise customer service and lower costs.

LOGISTICS STRATEGY

A traditional view of the hierarchy of decisions within an organization starts with a mission to give an overall view of its purpose and aims. Then the corporate strategy and business strategy show, in general terms, how these aims will be achieved. Below this come the functional decisions – including logistics – which show exactly what is done to implement the higher strategies (shown in Figure 1.1).

Some of the decisions in logistics clearly have a strategic importance – such as the design of supply chains, sourcing policies, alliances with suppliers, methods of procurement, relations with customers, modes of transport, location of facilities, size of operations, levels of automation, recycling policies, and a whole range of other decisions. We can consider these in a 'logistics strategy', which consists of all the long-term decisions, policies, plans and culture relating to an organization's supply chains. This logistics strategy sets the context for all tactical and operational decisions about the supply chain, so it must be designed carefully, paying particular attention to the competing demands of:

- *higher strategies*, which set the organization's overall goals and context for logistics;
- the *business environment*, which includes all the factors that affect an organization, but that it cannot control, including customers, market conditions, technology, economic conditions, legal restraints, competitors, shareholders, interest groups, social conditions, and political conditions;

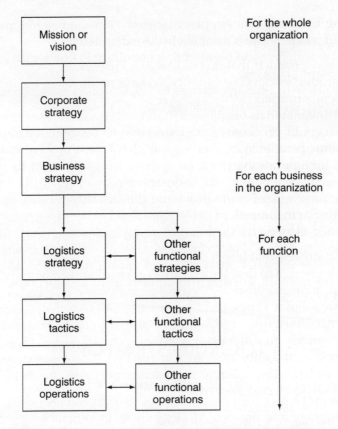

Figure 1.1 Place of logistics strategy in organizational decisions

- a *distinctive competence* that sets the organization apart from competitors, and is defined by the factors that are under the control of the organization, such as customer relations, employee skills, finances, products, facilities, technology used, suppliers, and resources available.

Each organization designs its own logistics strategy to balance these three factors, but they often follow similar paths. This allows us to describe some generic strategies. Porter (1985) suggested two basic strategies: cost leadership supplies the same, or comparable, products at a lower price; product differentiation gives products that customers cannot get anywhere else. In logistics, these two approaches are usually phrased in terms of terms of 'lean' and 'agile' strategies.

Organizations that adopt a lean strategy are aiming for the lowest possible costs. They organize efficient flows of materials to eliminate waste, minimize stocks, employ fewer people, use less materials, remove duplicated effort, eliminate non-value-adding operations, and so on. A typical analysis looks at the details of current operations, identifies any waste, and then looks for ways of removing it. Using this approach Toyota identified seven areas of the supply chain where waste is most likely (Monden, 1983).

- poor quality products that do not to satisfy customers;
- wrong production level or capacity, making products, or having capacity, not currently needed;
- transporting materials over long distances with complicated routes;
- badly designed processes with unnecessary, too complicated or time-consuming operations;
- waiting for operations to start or finish, for materials to arrive, for equipment to be repaired, and so on;
- too much movement during operations, with materials making unnecessary, long or inconvenient movements;
- too much stock, which increases complexity and raises costs.

Some people suggest that lean logistics puts too much emphasis on costs, and is not flexible enough to deal with rapidly changing conditions. They say that competition, more sophisticated customers, variable demand, unforeseen circumstances and a range of other considerations force a more flexible approach. An alternative agile strategy stresses customer satisfaction by responding quickly to different or changing circumstances. The two most common aspects of agility are speed of reaction (keeping a close check on conditions and reacting quickly to any changes) and the ability to tailor logistics to individual customer requirements.

At first sight it may seem difficult to reconcile the aims of lean and agile logistics. One looks to minimize costs, and sees customer service as a constraint; the other looks to maximize customer service, and sees costs as a constraint. In practice, the two policies are not necessarily distinct. If, for example, a supplier improves its EDI links with customers, it can both reduce costs and increase customer service – becoming both leaner and more agile. This means that organizations need not choose one strategy at the expense of the other, and Evans and Powell (2000) conclude that 'lean and agile are not mutually exclusive, they both have their merits, but also limitations, especially if an individual aspect is taken, in isolation, to the extreme'.

There are many other generic strategies for logistics, including time-based strategies (which deliver products quickly to customers), high-productivity strategies (which use resources as fully as possible), value-added strategies (which concentrate on adding customer value), diversification or specialization strategies (which set the width of product ranges), growth strategies (which aim for economies of scale and improved service of large operations), globalization strategies (which buy, store and move materials in a single, worldwide market), environmental protection strategies (which focus on sustainable operations, renewable resources, recycling, etc), and a whole range of others. As organizations adopt these strategies, they promote widespread trends within the industry. For example, organizations adopting lean strategies have encouraged a general lowering of logistics costs. These trends are very important for logistics, as they affect the general business environment and set the context in which all supply chains work.

TRENDS IN LOGISTICS

The following list outlines some of the most important current trends in logistics. Some of these have a fundamental impact on the way that organizations work, while others are fairly technical.

More collaboration along the supply chain

We have already seen that organizations now view logistics as a single integrated function. This integration does not just occur within each organization, but extends all along the supply chain. All the organizations along any particular supply chain share the same objective – satisfied final customers – and they should cooperate to achieve this aim. Their competitors are not other organizations within the same supply chain, but organizations in other supply chains. Christopher (1996) summarizes this by saying that 'supply chains compete, not companies'.

Improving communications

When a company wants to buy something, it typically has to generate a description of the product, request for price, purchase order, order confirmation, contract terms, shipping papers, financial arrangements, delivery details, special conditions, invoices and so on. In the past, all of this paperwork had to be printed and posted between organizations, making even the simplest transaction seem complicated and time-consuming. More recently, technology has revolutionized these communications. The first step came with fax machines, that could send electronic copies of documents between distant locations in seconds rather than days. By the 1990s EDI allowed remote computers to exchange data, and by 1997 about 2000 companies in the UK used EDI for trade (Stafford-Jones, 1997). Electronic trading mushroomed, with e-mail followed by e-business, e-commerce, e-trading – and soon 'e-anything'. It has been particularly useful for e-purchasing or e-procurement, which has developed in two main versions for B2B (business-to-business, where one business buys materials from another business) and B2C (business-to-customer, where a final customer buys from a business). By 2002 around 83 per cent of UK suppliers use B2B (MRO Software, 2001), with worldwide B2B trade valued at over US$2 trillion (Gartner Group, 2001).

Improvements in other technology

Improving technology has had widespread effects throughout logistics. For example, roadside detectors route lorries around traffic congestion and show the fastest journey to customers; warehouses use automatically guided vehicles and stacker cranes; vehicles are increasingly reliable and energy efficient; automatic transfer is making intermodal transport more efficient; new designs and materials improve the logistics infrastructure. It is difficult to find any area of logistics that is not affected by improving technology in some way, but there are two particularly important areas for e-business. The first is new tracking systems that use item coding to give each package an identifying tag (usually a bar code or magnetic stripe) which can be read to monitor all locations and movements. The second is EFT (electronic fund transfer) systems that acknowledge the receipt of materials and automatically transfer money from customers' bank accounts to the supplier's.

Reducing costs

Approaches such as lean logistics concentrate on reducing costs as much as possible. This normally benefits everyone, as logistics operators can offer competitive prices, and their customers are happy to pay as little as possible. Many organizations have reduced their logistics costs to levels that affect their whole operations. Lower transport costs, for example, allow organizations to work over a wider geographical area, which is why manufacturers in Asia can deliver goods anywhere in the world at prices that compare with domestic companies.

Shorter lead times

It is normally in everyone's interest to have the delay between ordering materials and having them delivered as short as possible. When customers decide to buy something they usually want it delivered immediately (or maybe at some specific time), while suppliers do not want products hanging around and clogging the supply chain.

There are many ways of reducing lead times, often based on flexible operations and convenient locations for facilities. One approach uses 'synchronized material movement', which makes information available to all parts of the supply chain at the same time so that there is no waiting for messages to move up and down.

Fewer suppliers

Traditionally, organizations have used a large number of suppliers. This encouraged competition, ensured that they got the best deal, and allowed deliveries to continue if one supplier ran into difficulties. However, the trend towards cooperation within a supply chain encourages organizations to look for the best suppliers and work exclusively – or largely – with them. This inevitably reduces the number of suppliers used, as illustrated by, say, Rank Xerox which reduced its suppliers from 5000 to 300, or Ford moving from 4000 to 350 (Lamming, 1993).

Concentration of ownership

Because large companies can get economies of scale and efficient operations, they dominate many supply chains. There are, for example, many supermarkets and transport companies, but the biggest ones continue to grow at the expense of small ones. The result is a continuing concentration of ownership, with large organizations setting standards that all operations must match.

Outsourcing

Organizations can often benefit from concentrating on their core operations and using specialized companies to take over peripheral activities. These peripheral activities might be anything from cleaning and catering through to accounting and information processing. Logistics is a particularly popular function for outsourcing, with expert third parties taking over part, or all, of the material movement and storage. Surveys suggest that around 30 per cent of logistics expenditure is outsourced in the EU (Marketline, 1993), and this is steadily growing.

Mass customization

This is the ability to personalize products to individual customer demands – and combines the benefits of mass production with the flexibility of customized products. It relies on B2C to give direct communications between a final customer and a manufacturer, and supply chains that can move materials reliably and quickly. Dell Computers were a pioneer of mass customization, as the company does not build standard computers, but waits until a customer places an order on its Web site and then builds a computer for the specific order. Dell works so closely with its suppliers that 'virtual integration' gives the impression that they are all part of the same company. Similar approaches in a 'Three-day car programme' suggest 'that 80 per cent of cars in the UK could be built to order by 2010' (3DayCar Programme, 2001; Holweg et al, 2001).

Postponement

Traditionally, manufacturers moved finished goods out of production and stored them in the distribution system until they were needed. When there are many variations on a basic product, this gives high stocks of similar products. Postponement moves almost-finished products into the distribution system, and delays final modifications or customization until the last possible moment. You can imagine this with 'package to order', where a company keeps a product in stock, but only puts it in a box written in the appropriate language when it is about to ship an order. Similarly, postponement allows manufacturers of electrical equipment to keep stocks of standard products, and only add the transformers and cables needed for different markets at the last minute.

Cross-docking

Traditional warehouses move materials into storage, keep them until needed, and then move them out to meet demand. Cross-docking coordinates the supply and delivery, so that goods arrive at the receiving area, and are immediately transferred to the loading area and put onto delivery vehicles. There may be some sorting, breaking of bulk and consolidation of materials at the warehouse, but no long-term storage. The basic activities can be done at a simple transfer point, so the ultimate aim is to remove the warehouse completely and have 'stock on wheels'. A related arrangement uses 'drop-shipping', where warehouses do not keep stock themselves, but coordinate the movement of materials directly from upstream suppliers to downstream customers.

Direct delivery

More customers are buying through the Web or finding other ways – such as mail order or catalogues – of buying directly from manufacturers or earlier tiers of the supply chain. This has the benefits of reducing lead times, reducing costs to customers, having manufacturers talking directly to their final customers, allowing customers access to a wider range of products, and so on. It also means that logistics has to move small deliveries quickly to final customers, often through parcel delivery services such as FedEx, UPS and DHL.

Increasing environmental concerns

There is growing concern about air and water pollution, energy consumption, urban development, waste disposal and other aspects of environmental damage. It is fair to say that logistics does not have a good reputation for environmental protection – demonstrated by the emissions from heavy lorries, use of greenfield sites for warehouses, calls for new road building, use of extensive packaging, oil spillage from tankers, and so on. On the positive side, however, logistics managers are clearly moving towards greener practices. Operators use more energy-efficient vehicles, control exhaust emissions, reuse packaging, switch to environmentally friendly modes of transport, increase recycling through reverse logistics, add safety features to ships, develop brownfield sites, and so on. There is a growing recognition that careful management can bring both environmental protection and lower costs.

GLOBAL LOGISTICS

One obvious trend that we have mentioned only in passing is the growth of international or global logistics. Improved communications and better transport mean that physical distances are less significant, and organizations can become global in outlook. They can effectively buy, transport, store, manufacture, sell and distribute products in a single worldwide market. Leontiades (1985) says that, 'One of the most important phenomena of the 20th century has been the international expansion of industry. Today, virtually all major firms have a significant and growing presence in business outside their country of origin.' Perhaps half of the trade between industrialized countries is accounted for by transfers between subsidiaries of the same company (Julius, 1990). In the United States, for example, a third of exports are sent by American companies to their overseas subsidiaries, and another third are sent by foreign manufacturers back to their home market.

There are many factors that encourage international operations, including the following:

- *Growing demand in new markets.* As developing regions become more prosperous, foreign companies recognize the opportunities for selling their products in new markets.
- *Manufacturers aiming for economies of scale.* Many manufacturing operations depend on – or work best with – stable, large-scale production. The best size for this is often larger than demand from a single market.
- *Greater demands on suppliers.* As customers become more demanding, local suppliers may not be able to meet their requirements, and organizations have to look further afield to find the best sources.
- *Convergence of market demands.* Different markets are increasingly accepting the same products – or at least, products with minor differences in finishing. This effect, which Ohmae (1985) calls 'Californianization', allows Coca-Cola, McDonald's, Toyota and Sony to sell the same products in virtually any country.

- *Removal of trade barriers.* There are many free trade areas that specifically encourage international operations, including the European Union and the North American Free Trade Agreement area.
- *Changing operations in logistics.* Better logistics makes international trade easier. Containerization and associated inter-modal transport, for example, make the movement of goods easier, faster and cheaper.
- *Specialized support operations.* Many organizations concentrate on their core competencies and outsource logistics to third parties. The outsourced operations are in locations determined by other organizations, and may not be in the same country.
- *Improved communications among consumers.* Satellite television, the Web and other communication channels have made customers more aware of products from outside their local regions.
- *Improved communications in business.* Developments in information systems mean that it is as easy to do business on the other side of the world as it is in the next town.

Because there are such benefits, many people think that global operations are inevitable. In practice, of course, there can be serious barriers and difficulties. Sometimes there may be problems with product design – with different regions demanding different types of product, products not lending themselves to global operations, or customers simply not viewing them favourably. Sometimes there is a demand for products but practical difficulties make it impossible to deliver them – such as problems at national frontiers, inadequate infrastructure, missing technical resources or human skills, or other cultural and economic differences.

One common problem is finding an appropriate organizational structure to deal with international trade, with the main choice between working nationally, internationally, multi-nationally or globally. Essentially, a national company only works within its home market and exports to other organizations in foreign countries; an international company has a centre in one country, from which it controls the activities of subsidiary divisions in other countries; a multi-national consists of connected, but largely independent companies in different countries; a global company sees the world as a single market, and works in the locations that are most effective and efficient. These descriptions are really too rigid, and organizations are generally more flexible in responding to local conditions, practices and demands. This gives a looser 'transnational' structure that can include many different types of operation and still give a unified culture for the overall organization.

MEASURING PERFORMANCE

A logistics strategy sets the overall aims and objectives for logistics, and decisions on a lower level work towards achieving these. The implication is that managers need some ways of monitoring progress, and these must include reliable performance measures. Similarly, when an organization looks for ways of improving logistics it must use appropriate measures to judge any change in performance. Unfortunately, it can be quite difficult to find meaningful measures. Logistics essentially offers an intangible service, and its quality depends to a large extent on subjective evaluation and customer perception. There are, of course, many possible measures, but we have to be careful that these relate to significant factors and give useful results. It is easy to measure, say, the annual cost of rail freight, but this may not be relevant for an insurance company. Rushton (1994) gives a list of measures that are used by grocery retailers, ranging from cost as a percentage of company sales to overtime hours as a percentage of total hours. Lennox (1995) reports a survey by KPMG that lists the most widely used measures of customer service, starting with the proportion of items supplied at first demand, the number of order-pick errors, availability of back orders, proportion of orders satisfied in full, amount of damage – and continuing down to lead time, courtesy of staff and ease of ordering.

Another problem with finding useful measures is the difficulty of separating the performance of logistics from both other internal operations and external influences. Late deliveries to customers, for example, might be caused by poor logistics – but they might also be caused by poor demand forecasts, or production problems, road works, traffic congestion, ferry operators on strike, or a whole range of other factors which logistics managers cannot control or even influence. As logistics provides the final link between suppliers and customers, it often gets the blame for faults in other parts of the system.

Whichever measures we take, we have to relate them to predefined targets. There are some absolute targets – such as no accidents or no customer complaints – but managers usually set arbitrary goals that are demanding but achievable. These take into account the overall context of logistics, and are generally based on comparison. If, for example, we met 94 per cent of demand from stock this month, we can judge this performance by comparing it with our last month's performance, or that of a competitor, the industry standard, or some other performance measure. The most widely used sources for these comparisons are actual performance achieved in the past, performance achieved by comparable operations within the organization, performance achieved by other organizations, benchmarks (giving comparisons with the industry's best performers), agreed targets given in the logistics strategy, absolute standards (such as zero defects) and accepted industry standards.

Once we have valid measures of performance and relevant targets, we can use them for a variety of purposes. If, for example, we are looking for improvements, we can use performance measures in the following procedure. This assumes that the main aim of logistics is to contribute to the accomplishment of the mission and corporate strategy, and it does this by designing an appropriate logistics strategy and making lower level decisions to support this.

1. Analyse the mission, corporate and business strategies from a logistics perspective.
2. Use these analyses to design a logistics strategy and set the overall objectives and goals for logistics.
3. Expand the logistics strategy to give more detailed plans, including standards and performance targets.
4. Monitor actual performance over time and compare this with the targets.
5. Analyse the differences between targets and achievements, identify the reasons for these differences and look for ways of improving performance.
6. Adjust operations, revise plans and take any other action necessary.

IMPROVING PERFORMANCE

A fundamental use of performance measures is to judge and encourage the improvements that are needed to remain competitive. But where should logistics managers look for improvements? Guy (1997) suggested that they should focus on internal comparisons to get value for money by:

- having a continual, long-term reduction in costs;
- avoiding complacency and reviewing operations regularly to make sure that they are still competitive;
- always considering the whole supply chain;
- allowing flexibility and necessary movement away from plans;
- making sure that logistics meets needs and not desires;
- making sure that logistics is fully integrated into overall operations;
- continually emphasizing the importance of logistics.

Such guidelines give general advice, but managers really need something more specific. Thankfully, there is no shortage of suggestions. All managers face a constant stream of 'new ideas' for improving operations, and the main difficulty is sifting through these to see which might bring real benefit, which are old ideas disguised in new words, and which are – at best – a waste of time. Most of the suggestions are supported by anecdotal evidence to show how the ideas have improved the performance of particular companies. Unfortunately, this evidence is presented to support a specific viewpoint and is not based on objective analyses. It is often difficult for managers to identify ideas that will work in their own organization. There is no doubt that TQM (total quality management), for example, has brought huge benefits to many organizations (Demming, 1986) – but it might not work in a particular company. In the same way, Hammer (1996) says that 75 per cent of organizations using re-engineering do not get the benefits they expect. Even well-established methods can be questioned, with Braithwaite (1996) describing MRP (material requirements planning) as, 'Too big, too slow and too inflexible … it is essentially obsolete and waiting to die.'

The best advice is to take a rational approach to improvement, perhaps using the following steps.

1. Make everyone aware that for the organization to remain competitive, changes are continually needed to the supply chain.
2. Examine current operations, identify their aims, see how well they achieve these, and identify problem areas and weaknesses.
3. Use benchmarking and other comparisons to identify potential improvements.
4. Design better procedures using the knowledge, skills and experience of everyone concerned.
5. Discuss the proposals widely and get people committed to the new methods.
6. Design a detailed plan for implementing the improvements.
7. Make any necessary changes to the organization's structure, systems, facilities, etc.
8. Give appropriate training to everyone involved.
9. Set challenging, but realistic, goals for everyone, and make it clear how these can be achieved.
10. Have a specific event to start the new methods.
11. Establish milestones and monitor progress to make sure they are achieved.
12. Give support and encouragement to everyone concerned.
13. Have continuing discussions about progress, problems, adjustments, etc.
14. Monitor and control progress, updating plans as necessary.
15. Accept that the new methods are only temporary, and continually look for further improvements.

Such formal approaches to improvement can bring significant results. If we just take one example, the Institute of Grocery Distribution (1998) found that stock levels in retail distribution centres fell by 8.5 per cent in the year to 1998. This is one illustration of the long-term trend for lower stocks that can clearly be seen at a national scale (Waters, 1989a, 1989b).

CONCLUSIONS

- In recent years organizations have begun to appreciate the importance of logistics, and recognize that it is an essential function which clearly affects wider performance. It is now viewed as a single, integrated function that is responsible for all the movements of materials through supply chains.
- Logistics has a clear strategic role in organizations. A logistics strategy shows how logistics supports the higher strategies, and sets the context for all other

decisions about the supply chain. There are several generic logistics strategies, with two common ones based on lean or agile operations.

- Logistics strategies lead to obvious trends, including more integration along supply chains, improving communications, use of new technology, lower costs, shorter lead times, fewer suppliers, concentration of ownership, outsourcing, and mass customization.
- One dominant trend has been the growth of international trade. A range of different factors encourages – and even forces – organizations to work internationally. Many are moving towards global operations that see the world as a single market.
- It can be difficult to get measures of logistics performance that give meaningful results. There are many possible measures, but they are often influenced by outside activities or include subjective views. The measures are usually used in some kind of comparison, and form part of a broader process.
- There are many suggestions for improving logistics, but managers have to be careful in adopting these. The best advice is to use a formal approach to improvement.

REFERENCES

3DayCar Programme (2001) [Online] www.cf.ac.uk/3DayCar

Braithwaite, A (1996) MRP: partially discredited solution in decline, *Logistics Focus*, **4** (4), pp 5–6

Childerley A (1980) The importance of logistics in the UK economy, *International Journal of Physical Distribution and Materials Management*, **10** (8)

Christopher, M (1986) *The Strategy of Distribution Management*, Heinemann, Oxford

Christopher M (1996) Emerging issues in supply chain management, *Proceeding of the Logistics Academic Network Inaugural Workshop*, Logistics Research Network, Warwick University, Warwick

Delaney, R V (1986) Managerial and financial challenges facing transport leaders, *Transportation Quarterly*, **40** (1), p 35

Demming W E (1986) *Out of the Crisis*, MIT Centre for Advanced Engineering, Cambridge, Mass

Drucker P (1962) The economy's dark continent, *Fortune,* (April), p 103

Evans, B and Powell, M (2000) Synergistic thinking: a pragmatic view of 'lean' and 'agile', *Logistics and Transport Focus*, **2** (10), pp 26–32

Factor, R (1996) Logistics trends, *Materials Management and Distribution*, (June), pp 17–21

Firth, D, Denham, F R, Griffin, K R, Heffernan, J *et al* (eds) (1980) *Distribution Management Handbook*, McGraw-Hill, London

Gartner Group (2001) [Online] www.gartner.com

20 ∎ Global logistics and distribution planning

Guy, B (1997) Logistics efficiency, *Logistics Focus*, **5** (10), p 15

Hammer, M (1996) *Beyond Reengineering*, Harper Collins, New York

Hill, G V (1994) Assessing the cost of customer service, in *Logistics and Distribution Planning*, 2nd edn, ed J Cooper, Kogan Page, London

Holweg, M, Judge, B and Williams, G (2001) The 3DayCar challenge: cars to customer orders, *Logistics and Transport Focus*, **3** (9), pp 36–44

Institute of Grocery Distribution (1998) *Retail Distribution 1998*, IGD, Herts

Institute of Logistics (1998) *Members' Directory*, p 8, Institute of Logistics and Transport, Corby

Julius, D A (1990) *Global Companies and Public Policy*, Royal Institute of International Affairs, London

Lamming, R (1993) *Beyond Partnership: Strategies for innovation and lean supply*, Prentice-Hall, London

Lennox, R B (1995) Customer service reigns supreme, *Materials Management and Distribution*, (Jan), pp 17–22

Leontiades, J E (1985) *Multinational Business Strategy*, DC Heath, Lexington, Mass

Little, W I (1977) The cellular flow logistics costing system, *International Journal of Physical Distribution and Materials Management*, **7** (6), pp 305–29

Marketline (1997) *EU Logistics*, Marketline International, London

McKibbin, B N (1982) Centre for Physical Distribution Management national survey of distribution costs, *Focus on Physical Distribution*, **1** (1), pp 16–18

Monden, Y (1983) *Toyota Production System*, Industrial Engineering and Management Press, Atlanta, Georgia

MRO Software (2001) *Supplying the Goods*, MRO Software, London

Office of National Statistics (2001) *Annual Abstract of Statistics*, HMSO, London

Ohmae, K (1985) *Triad Power: The coming shape of global competition*, Free Press, New York

O'Sullivan, D (1997) ECR – will it end in tears (quoting P Hutchinson), *Logistics Focus*, **5** (7), pp 2–5

P-E Consulting (1997) *Efficient Customer Response: Supply chain management for the new millennium?* P-E Consulting, Surrey

Porter, M E (1985) *Competitive Advantage*, Free Press, New York

Ray, D (1976) Distribution costing, *International Journal of Physical Distribution and Materials Management*, **6** (2), pp 73–107

Ray, D, Gattorna, J, and Allen, M (1980) Handbook of distribution costing and control, *International Journal of Physical Distribution and Materials Management*, **10** (5), pp 211–429

Rushton, A (1994) Monitoring logistics and distribution operations, in *Logistics and Distribution Planning*, 2nd edn, ed J Cooper, Kogan Page, London

Shapiro, R D and Heskett, J L (1985) *Logistics Strategy*, West Publishing, St Paul, Minn

Stafford-Jones, A (1997) Electronic commerce: the future with EDI, *Logistics Focus*, **5** (9), pp 9–10

US Statistical Abstract (2001) *Survey of Current Business*, Department of Commerce, Washington, DC

Szymankiewicz, J (1997) Efficient customer response – supply chain management for the new millennium? *Logistics Focus*, **5** (9), pp 16–22

Waters, C D J (1989a) Stock holding of manufacturing industry within the United Kingdom, *Engineering Costs and Production Economics*, vol 15, pp 127–32

Waters, C D J (1989b) The long term response of inventory holdings to technological developments and economic influence, *10th International Conference on Production Research*, Nottingham

Waters, D (2003) *Logistics: An introduction to supply chain management*, Palgrave Macmillan, Basingstoke

2

New directions in logistics

Martin Christopher
Cranfield School of Management

In recent years there has been a growing recognition that the processes whereby we satisfy customer demands are of critical importance to any organization. These processes are the means whereby products are developed, manufactured and delivered to customers and through which the continuing service needs of those customers are met. The logistics concept is the thread that connects these crucial processes and provides the basis for the design of systems that will cost-effectively deliver value to customers.

Accompanying this recognition of the importance of process has been a fundamental shift in the focus of the business towards the marketplace and away from the more inwardly oriented production and sales mentality that previously dominated most industries. This change in orientation has necessitated a review of the means whereby customer demand is satisfied – hence the dramatic upsurge of interest in logistics as a core business activity.

THE EMERGENCE OF THE VALUE-CONSCIOUS CUSTOMER

Recession in many markets, combined with new sources of competition, has raised the consciousness of customers towards value. 'Value' in today's context does not just mean value for money, although that is certainly a critical determinant of purchase for many buyers; it also means perceived benefits. Customers increasingly are demanding products with added value, but at lower cost, hence the new competitive imperative is to seek out ways to achieve precisely that.

Michael Porter (1980, 1985) was one of the first commentators to highlight the need for organizations to understand that competitive success could only come through cost-leadership or through offering clearly differentiated products or services. The basic model is illustrated in Figure 2.1. Porter's argument was that a company with higher costs and no differential advantage in the eyes of the customer was in effect a commodity supplier with little hope of long-term success unless it could find a way out of the box. His prescription was that the organization should seek to become either a low-cost producer or a differentiated supplier.

However, in reality it is not sufficient to compete only on the basis of being the lowest-cost supplier. The implication of this is that a competitor in the bottom right-hand corner has to compete on price – if a company is only a cost leader, how else can it compete? Competing solely in terms of price will merely reinforce the customer's view that the product is a commodity – the very thing the company wishes to avoid. On the other hand, a strategy based upon differentiation will make it possible to compete on grounds other than price. While value for money will always be an issue, the aim is to increase the customers' perception of the values they are receiving and hence their willingness to pay a higher price.

Organizations create value for their customers either by increasing the level of 'benefit' they deliver or by reducing the customers' costs. In fact customer value can be defined as follows:

$$\text{Customer value} = \frac{\text{Perceived benefits}}{\text{Total cost of ownership}}$$

Perceived benefits include both the tangible, product-related aspects and the less tangible, service-related elements of the relationship.

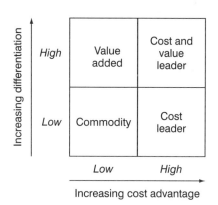

Figure 2.1   The competitive options

The key point to note is that these benefits are essentially perceptual and that they will differ by customer. The 'total cost of ownership' reflects all the costs associated with the relationship, not just the price of the product. Hence the customers' cost of carrying inventory, their ordering costs and other transactions costs all form part of this total cost concept. Because logistics management, perhaps uniquely, can impact upon both the numerator and the denominator of the customer value equation, it can provide a powerful means of enhancing customer value.

An argument that is being heard more frequently is that logistics is a core capability which enables the firm to gain and maintain competitive advantage. More and more the view is expressed (eg by Stalk, Evans and Shulman, 1992) that it is through capabilities that organizations compete. These capabilities include such processes as new product development, order fulfilment, marketing planning and information systems. There can be little doubt that companies that in the past were able to rely upon product superiority to attain market leadership can no longer do so, as competitive pressure brings increasing technological convergence. Instead these companies must seek to develop systems that enable them to respond more rapidly to customer requirements at ever lower costs.

LOGISTICS AND SUPPLY CHAIN MANAGEMENT

Logistics management is essentially an integrative process that seeks to optimize the flow of materials and supplies through the organization and its operations to the customer. It is essentially a planning process and an information-based activity. Requirements from the marketplace are translated into production requirements and then into materials requirements through this planning process.

It is now being recognized that for the real benefits of the logistics concept to be realized, there is a need to extend the logic of logistics upstream to suppliers and downstream to final customers. This is the concept of supply chain management.

Supply chain management is a fundamentally different philosophy of business organization, and is based upon the idea of partnership in the marketing channel and a high degree of linkage between entities in that channel. Traditional models of business organization were based upon the notion that the interests of individual firms are best served by maximizing their revenues and minimizing their costs. If these goals were achieved by disadvantaging another entity in the channel, then that was the way it was. Under the supply chain management model the goal is to maximize profit through enhanced competitiveness in the final market – a competitiveness which is achieved by a lower cost to serve, in the shortest time-frame possible. Such goals are only attainable if the supply chain as a whole is closely coordinated in order that total channel inventory is minimized, bottlenecks eliminated, time-frames compressed and quality problems eliminated.

This new model of competition suggests that individual companies compete not as company against company, but rather as supply chain against supply chain. Thus the successful companies will be those whose supply chains are more cost-effective than those of their competitors.

What are the basic requirements for successful supply chain management? Figure 2.2 outlines the critical linkages that connect the marketplace to the supply chain. The key linkages are between procurement and manufacturing, and between manufacturing and distribution. Each of these three activities, while part of a continuous process, has a number of critical elements.

Procurement

Typically in the past, supply management has been paid scant attention in many companies. Even though the costs of purchases for most businesses are the largest single cost, procurement has not been seen as a strategic task. That view is now changing, as the realization grows that not only are costs dramatically impacted by procurement decisions and procedures, but innovation and response-to-market capability are profoundly affected by supplier relationships.

The philosophy of co-makership is based upon the idea of a mutually beneficial relationship between supplier and buyer, instead of the more traditional adversarial stance that is so often encountered. With this partnership approach, companies will identify opportunities for taking costs out of the supply chain instead of simply pushing them upstream or downstream. Paperwork can be eliminated, problems jointly solved, quality improved and information shared. By its very nature, co-makership will normally involve longer-term relationships, based upon single-sourcing rather than multiple supply points. Xerox in Europe has adopted the co-makership philosophy, which has resulted in their supplier base falling from 5,000 to 300.

A fundamental feature of this integrated approach to supply chain management is the adoption of some form of materials requirements planning linked to schedule coordination. Basically, materials requirements planning (MRP) is a time-phased approach to managing the inbound flow of

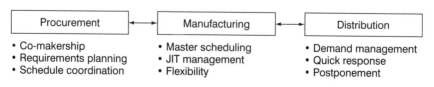

Figure 2.2   Critical linkages in the supply chain

materials, which potentially has the capability to link the factory to its suppliers. By itself, however, it lacks the connections to the customer in that it is a 'push' system rather than a 'pull' system. More recently there have been a number of developments to the concept which have enabled a more flexible demand-based approach to be adopted (Martin, 1983).

Beyond the idea of requirements planning is something much more fundamental that requires the linking of suppliers' production schedules with those of their customers. The aim should be to view your suppliers' operations as merely an extension of your own. Companies like Nissan, in their UK manufacturing facility, have developed closely linked systems with all of their suppliers so that those suppliers have full visibility not only of the production schedule at Nissan's Washington plant, but also of the real-time sequence in which cars are moving down the assembly line. By the use of electronic data interchange (EDI) and open communications, Nissan has been able to reduce lead times, eliminate inventories and take costs out of the supply chain. Other companies may have introduced similar just-in-time (JIT) systems, but often in so doing they have added to their suppliers' costs, not reduced them.

Manufacturing

There has been much talk of 'lean' manufacturing over the last decade (Womack, Jones and Roos, 1990). The idea of leanness in this sense is that wasteful activities are reduced or eliminated and that value-creating processes are performed more quickly. However, more important than leanness is agility. Agility is a wider supply chain concept that is more concerned with how the firm responds to changes in marketplace requirements – particularly requirements for volume and variety. Leanness is undoubtedly a desirable feature of a supply chain, unless it leads to a misplaced emphasis on manufacturing costs. It may be preferable, for example, to incur a cost penalty in the unit cost of manufacture if it enables the company to achieve higher levels of customer response at less overall cost to the supply chain.

The key word in manufacturing in today's environment is flexibility. Flexibility in terms of the ability to produce any variant in any quantity, without significant cost penalty, has to be the goal of all manufacturing strategies. In the past, and even still today, much of the thinking in manufacturing was dominated by the search for economies of scale. This type of thinking led to large mega-plants, capable of producing vast quantities of a standardized product at incredibly low unit costs of production. It also has led many companies to go for so-called 'focused factories' which produce a limited range of products for global consumption.

The downside of this is in effect the possibility of hitting diseconomies of scale: in other words, a build-up of large inventories of finished product ahead of demand, an inability to respond rapidly to changed customer requirements, and a limited variety that can be offered to the customer. Instead of economies of scale, the search is now on for strategies that will reduce total supply chain costs, not just manufacturing costs, and that will offer maximum flexibility against customer requirements. The goal must be 'the economic batch quantity of one', meaning that in the ideal world we would make things one at a time against known customer demands.

One of the lessons that the Japanese have taught us is that the route to flexibility in manufacturing does not necessarily lie through new technology, such as robotics, although that can help. A lot can be achieved instead through focusing upon the time it takes to plan, to schedule, to set up, to change over and to document. These are the classic barriers to flexibility, and if they can be removed then manufacturing can respond far more rapidly to customer requirements. In a factory with zero lead times, total flexibility is achieved with no forecasts and no inventory! Whilst zero lead times are clearly an impossibility, the Japanese have shown that impressive reductions in such lead times can be achieved by questioning everything we do and the way in which we do it.

Distribution

The role of distribution in the supply chain management model has extended considerably from the conventional view of the activity as being concerned solely with transport and warehousing. The critical task that underlies successful distribution today is demand management.

Demand management is the process of anticipating and fulfilling orders against defined customer service goals. Information is the key to demand management: information from the marketplace in the form of medium-term forecasts; information from customers, preferably based upon actual usage and consumption; information on production schedules and inventory status; and information on marketing activities such as promotions that may cause demand to fluctuate from the norm.

Clearly, while forecasting accuracy has always to be sought, it must be recognized that it will only rarely be achieved. Instead the aim should be to reduce our dependence upon the forecast by improved information on demand and by creating systems capable of more rapid response to that demand. This is the principle that underlies the idea of quick response logistics.

Quick response logistics has become the aim for many organizations, enabling them to achieve the twin strategic goals of cost reduction and service enhancement. In essence, the idea of quick response is based upon a replenishment-driven model of demand management. In other words, as items are consumed or purchased, this information is transmitted to the supplier, and this immediately triggers a response. Often more rapid, smaller consignment deliveries will be made; the trade-off being that any higher transport costs will be more than covered by reduced inventory in the pipeline and at either end of it, yet with improved service in terms of responsiveness. Clearly information technology has been a major enabling factor in quick response logistics, linking the point of sale or consumption with the point of supply.

A further trend that is visible in distribution is the search for postponement opportunities. The principle of postponement is that the final configuration or form of the product should be delayed until the last possible moment. In this way maximum flexibility is maintained, but inventory minimized. The distribution function takes on a wider role as the provider of the final added value. For example, at Xerox the aim is not to hold any inventory as finished product, but only as semi-finished, modular work in progress, awaiting final configuration once orders are received. Similarly at Hewlett Packard products are now designed with 'localization' in mind. In other words, products will be designed for modular manufacture, but with local assembly and customization to meet the needs of specific markets. In this way economies of scale in manufacturing can be achieved by producing generic products for global markets while enabling local needs to be met through postponed configuration.

'What is apparent is that distribution in the integrated supply chain has now become an information-based, value-added activity, providing a critical link between the marketplace and the factory.

THE NEW COMPETITIVE FRAMEWORK: THE THREE RS

We began this chapter with a brief review of how today's customer is increasingly seeking added value and how logistics management can provide that value. In the past, the primary means of achieving competitive advantage were often summarized as the 'four Ps' – product, price, promotion and place. These should now be augmented with the 'three Rs'– reliability, responsiveness and relationships – and logistics strategies need to be formulated with these as the objectives. Let us briefly examine each in turn.

Reliability

In most markets and commercial environments today, customers are seeking to reduce their inventory holdings. Just-in-time practices can be found in industries as diverse as car assembly and retailing. In such situations it is essential that suppliers can guarantee complete order-fill delivered at agreed times. Hence a prime objective of any logistics strategy must be reliability.

Making logistics systems more reliable means that greater emphasis must be placed upon process design and process control. The processes that are particularly generic to logistics are those to do with order fulfilment and supply chain management. Because traditionally these processes have been managed on a fragmented, functional basis, they tend to have a higher susceptibility to variability. These processes are typified by multiple 'hand-offs' from one area of functional responsibility to another, and by bottlenecks at the interfaces between stages in the chain. One of the benefits of taking a process view of the business is that it often reveals opportunities for simplification and the elimination of non-value-adding activities, so that reliability inevitably improves.

Responsiveness

Very closely linked to customers' demands for reliability is the need for responsiveness. Essentially this means the ability to respond in ever-shorter lead times with the greatest possible flexibility. Quick response, as we have seen, is a concept and a technology that is spreading rapidly across industries. For the foreseeable future, speed will be a prime competitive variable in most markets. The emphasis in logistics strategy will be upon developing the means to ship smaller quantities, more rapidly, direct to the point of use/consumption.

The key to time compression in the logistics pipeline is through the elimination or reduction of time spent on non-value-adding activities. Hence, contrary to a common misconception, time compression is not about performing activities faster, but rather performing fewer of them. The old cliché 'work smarter, not harder' is particularly relevant in this context.

As Hammer and Champy (Hammer, 1990) have pointed out, many of the processes used in our organizations were designed for a different era. They tend to be paper-based, with many – often redundant – manual stages. They are sequential and batch-oriented rather than parallel and capable of changing quickly from one task to another. Even though eliminating or reducing such activities may increase cost, the end result will often be more cost-effective. For example, shipping direct from factories to end-customers may be more expensive in terms of the unit cost of transport than shipping via a regional distribution centre, but time spent in the distribution centre is usually non-value-adding time.

Relationships

The trend towards customers seeking to reduce their supplier base has already been commented upon. The concept of 'single sourcing' has now received widespread support. The benefits of such an approach include improved quality, innovation sharing, reduced costs and integrated scheduling of production and deliveries. Underlying all of this is the idea that buyer/supplier relationships should be based upon partnership. More and more companies are discovering the advantages that can be gained by seeking out mutually beneficial, long-term relationships with suppliers. From the suppliers' point of view, such partnerships can prove formidable barriers to entry to competitors. Once again, companies are finding that logistics provides a powerful route to the creation of partnerships in the marketing channel. Logistics management should be viewed as the thread that connects the inbound and outbound flows of channel partners.

A good example of logistics partnership is the growing use of 'vendor managed inventory' (VMI). The underlying principle of VMI is that the supplier rather than the customer assumes responsibility for the flow of product into the customer's operations. Thus instead of the customer placing orders with the vendor – often at short notice – the vendor can directly access information relating to the rate of usage or sale of the product by the customer. With this information the supplier can better plan the replenishment of the product with less need to carry safety stock. In effect VMI enables the substitution of information for inventory in the supply chain.

The challenge to marketing and strategic planning in any business is to construct a corporate strategy that specifically builds upon logistics as a means to achieving competitive advantage through a much stronger focus on the three Rs. It is still the case that many organizations have not fully understood the strategic importance of logistics, and hence have not explicitly tailored logistics into their corporate strategies and their marketing plans.

THE ORGANIZATIONAL CHALLENGE

One of the most significant changes in recent years has been the way in which we think of organization structures. Conventionally, organizations have been 'vertical' in their design. In other words, businesses have organized around functions such as production, marketing, sales and distribution. Each function has had clearly identified tasks, and within these functional 'silos' or 'stovepipes' (as they have been called) there is a recognized hierarchy, up which employees might hope to progress. Figure 2.3 illustrates this type of functionally oriented business.

The problem with this approach is that it is inwardly focused and concentrates primarily on the use of resources rather than upon the creation of outputs. The outputs of any business can only be measured in terms of customer satisfaction achieved at a profit. Paradoxically, these outputs can only be realized through coordination and cooperation horizontally across the organization.

These horizontal linkages mirror the materials and information flows that link the customer with the business and its suppliers. They are in fact the core processes of the business. Figure 2.4 highlights the fundamental essence of the horizontal organization.

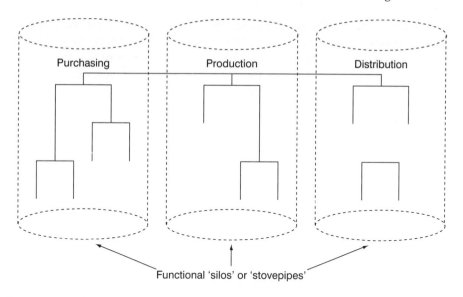

Figure 2.3 The vertical/functional organization

In the horizontal organization, the emphasis is upon the management of processes. These processes, by definition, are cross-functional and include new product development, order fulfilment, information management, profitability analysis and marketing planning.

The justification for this radically different view of the business is that these processes are in effect 'capabilities' and, as we have observed, it is through capabilities that the organization competes. In other words, the effectiveness of the new product development process, the order fulfilment process and so on determine the extent to which the business will succeed in the marketplace.

How does a conventionally organized business transform itself into a market-facing, process-oriented organization? One of the major driving forces for change is the revolution that has taken place in information technology

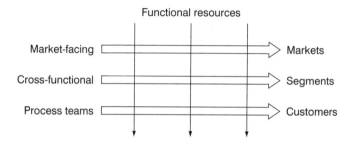

Figure 2.4 The horizontal/process organization

and systems, enabling the supply chain linkage to become a reality. More and more, the business will find itself organizing around the information system. In other words the processes for capturing information from the marketplace (forecasts, anticipated requirements, customer schedules and orders) will be linked to the processes for meeting that demand.

It is no coincidence that companies that have installed the new generation of 'enterprise resource planning' (ERP) systems have also been at the fore-front of the change from vertical to horizontal organizational structures. These systems enable entire supply chains to become truly demand-driven through the use of shared information. They open up new and exciting opportunities to create true end-to-end pipeline management and the achievement of the ultimate business goal of high service to customers at less cost.

SUMMARY

- Businesses in all types of industries are placing far greater emphasis on the design and management of logistics processes, and the integration of those processes upstream and downstream with those of suppliers and customers.
- The business of the future will undoubtedly be market-driven, with logistics processes providing a critical means for achieving corporate goals.
- It will be a highly coordinated network of outsourced flows of materials and supplies, integrated through an information system that reaches from the ultimate consumer to the far end of the supply chain.
- The era of logistics and supply chain management, which many have predicted for some time, seems finally to have arrived.

REFERENCES

Hammer, M (1990) Re-engineering work: don't automate, obliterate, *Harvard Business Review* (July/Aug)

Martin, A (1983) *Distribution Resource Planning*, Oliver Wight, Williston, VT

Porter, M (1980) *Competitive Strategy*, Free Press, New York

Porter, M (1985) *Competitive Advantage*, Free Press, New York

Stalk, G, Evans, P and Shulman, L E (1992) Competing on capabilities: the new rules of corporate strategy, *Harvard Business Review* (March/April)

Womack, J, Jones, D and Roos, D (1990) *The Machine that Changed the World*, Macmillan, New York

3

Future trends in supply chain management

Peter Hines
Lean Enterprise Research Centre, Cardiff

ABSTRACT

This chapter is conceptual in nature and is designed to take a review of the supply chain management field of study. This review is undertaken through the vantage of lean thinking (Womack and Jones, 1996). The chapter attempts to draw together traditional views of logistics and supply chain management before describing four key areas of present and future development which help to define the future logistics five 'rights' as well as an agenda for survival in the 21st century.

INTRODUCTION

One of the greatest difficulties in working within the area of logistics and supply chain management is in making clear what your area of research, education or practice is. Indeed, when the subject is written about there is rarely a clarity of definition, and most writers appear to take it for read that their audience automatically understands their implicit definition and agrees with it. In order to try to put some limits around the subject, a few more commonly used definitions are given below.

Christopher (1993: 2) employs a marketing-oriented definition of logistics:

The process of strategically managing the procurement, movement and storage of materials, parts and finished inventory (and the related information flows) through the organization and its marketing channels in such a way that current and future profitability are maximized through the cost-effective fulfilment of orders.

The Council of Logistics Management (cited in Blanchard, 1992: 3) provide a similar definition, somewhat broadened and hinting at a wider process including more upstream areas:

Logistics is the process of planning, implementing and controlling the efficient, cost-effective flow and storage of raw materials, in-process inventory, finished goods and related information from point of origin to point of consumption for the purpose of conforming to customer needs.

The Institute of Logistics (1997a: 8, 1997b: 5) again broadens this definition and combines other elements such as the introduction of a human aspect, as well as the term 'supply chain', in a definition which could be felt to encompass the whole of business management:

Logistics is the time related positioning of resource or the strategic management of the total supply-chain. The supply-chain is a sequence of events intended to satisfy a customer. It can include procurement, manufacture, distribution, and waste disposal, together with associated transport, storage and information technology. Logistics relates to goods, people, manufacturing capacity, information being: in the RIGHT place, at the RIGHT time, in the RIGHT quantity, at the RIGHT quality, at the RIGHT price.

Kotler (1997), describing supply chain management, refers to it as a broader concept than logistics management in that it integrates the entire value-adding process from procurement, conversion to dispatch to the final customer, in a definition that appears no wider than those given above.

At this juncture the reader may well be concerned that those working within the subject of logistics (or supply chain management) cannot really agree on what area they are addressing and what process or processes are covered. However, in spite of this concern many writers have attempted to elicit key points or future directions within the logistics/supply chain area. Christopher (1996), for instance, defines five emerging issues within supply chain management as:

- Supply chains compete, not companies.
- Most opportunities for cost reduction and/or value enhancement lie at the interface between supply chain partners.
- Supply chain competitiveness is based upon the value-added exchange of information.
- Supply chain integration implies process integration.

- Supply chain competitiveness requires the collective determination of strategy.

This definition suggests that supply chains may be more than the linear links of three or four companies, and also that the buyer–supplier or seller–buyer interface is of critical importance to improvement of the flow of goods and information.

In 1993 the Council of Logistics Management (CLM, 1993) established six key issues expected to be 'potentially important in the future logistics directions' as:

- environmental pressures;
- shifting power in the logistics channel;
- technology;
- the global marketplace;
- outsourcing options;
- cycle time to market.

Within the Logistics Research Network (LRN) there is also some debate about what the subject is and what the important areas are. Naslund (1997) defined logistics as being boundary-spanning, culturally specific and process oriented. In the 1998 LRN conference three sets of the authors coincidentally raised four particular aspects within the supply chain that they wished to explore. Decker and van Goor (1998) introduce a supply chain management hierarchy involving:

- physical integration;
- information integration;
- control integration;
- infrastructure integration.

Simons and Kiff (1998) describe their conceptual framework for supply chain improvement involving:

- control;
- time;
- centralization;
- structure.

In a similar vein, Taylor (1998) in describing his PITS approach recognizes four dimensions within supply chains that impact upon and complicate the planning and improvement task:

- time lags;
- geographical separation;
- functional silos;
- hierarchical structures.

In order to attempt to make some sense of these works and to put them within a logistics, or supply chain, frame of reference it is necessary to delimit what an individual author is referring to and whether there is comparability between different pieces of work. This is the first element of this chapter's review of supply chain management.

KEY AREA 1: MORE THAN JUST LORRIES AND BUYERS

A supply chain management typology

The first observation on the above discussion is that the terms 'logistics' and 'supply chain management' appear to be used interchangeably, particularly within the traditional logistics community. Unfortunately, as the term 'supply chain management' is gaining wider credence elsewhere, those dealing with other supply chain members, such as writers on purchasing, are attempting to claim the high ground and link the term to them rather than the logisticians. This can be seen by the usage of the term at a recent major purchasing conference, the Second Worldwide Symposium on Purchasing and Supply Chain Management, where the term 'logistics' failed to be found in any of the 28 papers, and traditional logistics people would have found little that they would term supply chain management.

This school of thought is perhaps typified by the functional imperialism of writers such as Cox (1999), whose attempt to 'Think strategically about supply chain management' starts in the strategic dictionary at 'procurement' and covers all the important subject areas right up to 'purchasing'. For the purposes of this first key area we will continue to use the terms 'logistics' and 'supply chain management' interchangeably, but we will demonstrate the difference in the next 'key area' discussion below.

Various evolutionary models have been presented in the recent past to describe logistics and supply chain management. Among the most important contributions are those of Coyle, Bardi and Langley (1996) and Stevens (1989). Coyle *et al* demonstrate an evolutionary logistics model (shown in Figure 3.1), primarily based on physical product movement, which mirrors the developments within the UK Institute of Logistics: a merger occurred in 1993 between the Institute of Materials Management and the Institute of Logistics and Distribution Management to create a body interested in the 'total supply-chain' (Institute of Logistics, 1997a: 8). The Stevens supply chain evolutionary model shows how individual departments integrate internally and then integrate externally to provide for an holistic flow of materials to the customer (see Figure 3.2).

However, both of these approaches suffer from an over-simplification of reality, and they still focus, even at their higher levels, on the physical movement of goods. Thus they are not totally adequate. Indeed, it is arguable whether an evolutionary model can indeed be adequate, as such an approach

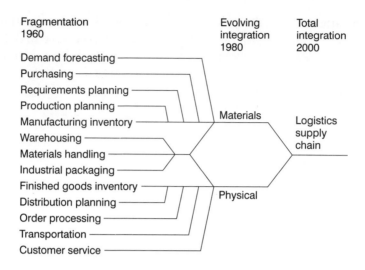

Figure 3.1 Coyle *et al*'s logistics evolutionary model

presupposes that there is one best way towards which all industries and levels of a supply chain are evolving. It would be more useful to have a typology or framework in which to place different logistics or supply chain systems, which does not presuppose that one type of logistics or supply chain research is more valuable than any other. The supply chain framework model presented in Figure 3.3 borrows from the Coyle *et al* and Stevens models as well as the Harland (1998) 'levels of supply chain' and Nassimbeni (1998) 'network structure' approaches.

The supply chain framework model provides a typology for researchers and writers within the field of logistics and supply chain management to delimit the type of supply chain they are describing. The model is made up of five distinct types of supply chains that are not evolutionary and not mutually exclusive, but are of increasing complexity and holism. Thus research may be carried out at each or every stage of the model.

The simplest stage, that of the intra-functional supply chain, involves work carried out within one particular element or functional area of a particular company. Within the logistics area this type of research might concentrate on the purchasing or distribution department, for instance. Reference to Table 3.1 and Figure 3.4 will show that of the 68 papers submitted for the 1996–98 Logistics Research Conferences, where a definable scale existed, 18 fell into this category. Of these, 15 were concerned with transport/distribution and 3 with purchasing, Thus, approximately 26 per cent of recorded papers addressed the supply chain from a single function or department perspective. A similar percentage split between distribution/transport and purchasing, but the opposite way around, might be expected at a similar purchasing-related conference such as the IPSERA annual conference.

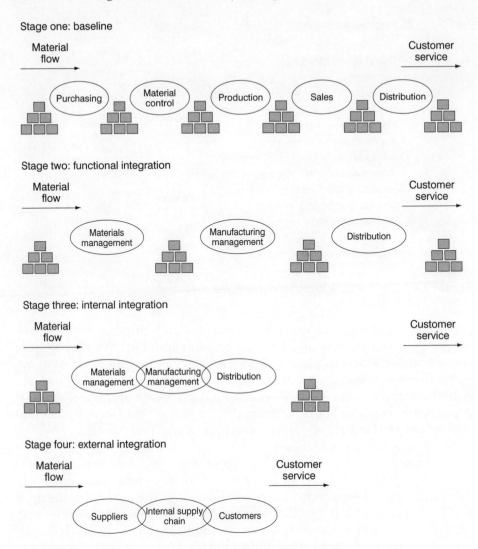

Figure 3.2 Steven's supply chain evolutionary model

These figures are based on those papers where it was possible to delimit the type of logistics or supply chain scale that was being addressed. The total number of full papers analysed was 11 for 1996, 34 for 1997 and 41 (based on abstracts received by 1 June 1998) for 1998.

The second type of supply chain research described in the supply chain framework model (Figure 3.3) is that concerned with inter-functional research. This is where research is carried out within a single organization involving two or more functions or departments. An example of this may be the application of internal change, for instance as described by Taylor (1998) in

1. Intra-functional supply chain

2. Inter-functional supply chain

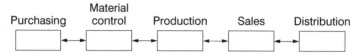

3. Inter-organizational supply chain

4. Network supply chain

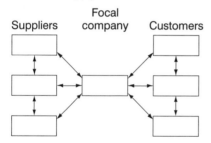

5. Regional clustering supply chains

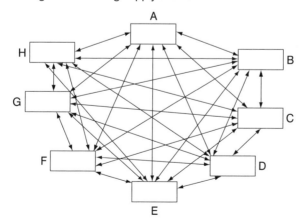

Figure 3.3　The supply chain framework model

Table 3.1 Distribution of supply chain research for 1996–98 LRN conferences

Model level	1996 conference	1997 conference	1998 conference	1996–98 total	1996–98 percentage
1. Intra-functional	3	5	10	18	26%
2. Inter-functional	1	1	6	8	12%
3. Inter-organizational	3	10	14	27	40%
4. Network	0	9	6	15	22%
5. Regional cluster	0	0	0	0	0%
Total	7	25	36	68	100%

his PITS approach in transforming a footwear manufacturer. Reference to Table 3.1 shows that this type of research accounted for around 12 per cent of work reported at the 1996–98 LRN conferences.

The third type of supply chain research features inter-organizational research where research is carried out across a company boundary. Although this type of work could be subdivided into what Harland (1998) calls dyadic (one buyer–one seller) and external chain (more than two elements of a linear supply chain), this distinction is not of major moment in the present classification. This type of inter-company research represented the largest part of research reported at recent LRN conferences, accounting for 40 per cent of papers.

The last decade has seen a great increase in this type of research. This is partly the result a fashionable move away from the first two types of work,

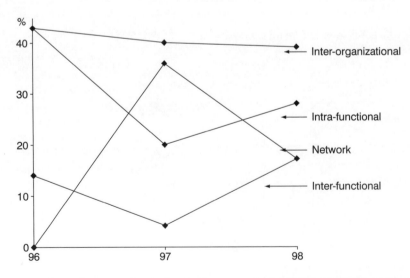

Figure 3.4 Distribution of supply chain research for 1996–98 LRN conferences

and partly because of the greater quantity of research being undertaken and a greater concern for holistic or (inter-organizational) supply chain management. This is certainly the level that has attracted most attention in the academic press over the last decade, and to a large degree it is the area on which the definitions of logistics and supply given above are based. As a result the majority of recent models and theories have been concentrated on this area. Such work would include just-in-time (JIT), efficient consumer response (ECR) and quick response (QR) (see discussions of these areas in, for instance, Christopher (1993); Kurt Salmon (1993); Peck (1998)). However, this 'holistic vision' should only be considered as about halfway along the total supply chain continuum.

The fourth level of supply chain research is that concerned with networks. This is an area that had attracted very little attention until the late 1980s (Thorelli, 1986; Jarillo, 1988). However, it was not until the early 1990s that any quantity of research was carried out in this area. This tends to give a more real-world feel to the research, but at the expense of adding greater complexity. This more recent work included the network sourcing model (Hines, 1994), network structures (De Toni and Nassimbeni, 1995), network strategy (Harland, 1998) and supplier associations (Hines, 1994; Aitken, 1997; Gullander, 1997). However, because this area has not received nearly as much of the research effort as the inter-organizational area (although it accounts for over 20 per cent of LRN papers), this element of supply chain management still lacks rigour. Jarillo noted in his 1988 work that although networking is fashionable, it 'lacks a generally accepted framework, with enough theoretical depth to help understand the plentiful anecdotal evidence'. To a large degree this still remains true today in spite of the contributions of Hines (1997), Harland (1998) and Nassimbeni (1998). There is a clear need for more research in this area.

The fifth element of the supply chain framework model is that of regional cluster supply chains, an area yet to be reported at a Logistics Research Network conference. This last area involves taking the network supply chains logic stage further and addressing their impact on particular regions where a cluster of firms exist (Hall and Andriani, 1998). Clearly a supply chain does not have to be linear, and indeed it can take a very complex form, such as many regional industrial systems (Nassimbeni, 1998), industry-based supplier associations (Esain and Hines, 1997a) or industrial network groups (Samuel, 1994; Esain and Hines, 1997b). As these regional clusters are very dynamic in nature and typically involve many dozens of firms, they are very difficult to study, except for simple case studies or the most crude questionnaire-based research. Clearly there exists here a very major research opportunity, particularly if such research can include meaningful theoretical discussion and modelling. However, such research will be of great importance both because this element of supply chain research is so heavily under-researched, and because it comes closest to the real world. If it can be carried out successfully it may yield the greatest benefit to industry, government and regions.

The above typology has been presented in order to aid clarity in discussions about logistics and supply chain management. However, the second key area to be addressed by this chapter is that of the difference between logistics and supply chain management. This is considered in the next section.

KEY AREA 2: MORE THAN JUST ORDERS AND INFORMATION

Supply chain policies and processes

Central to the definitions of logistics and supply chain management in the section above is the flow of goods from some type of supplier through an organization, possibly involving some conversion, to some type of customer. In addition, the definitions tend to suggest some type of information and cash flow, and in other cases involve a feedback loop or reverse logistics for recycled product. A typical example of this is provided by Figure 3.5, drawn from Coyle, Bardi and Langley (1996). In essence, Figure 3.5 describes the key activities required in a number of linked companies to fulfil the customer's requirements or in other words the order fulfilment process. Although the authors describe this as Supply Chain processes, for the present writer this may be best described as the central logistics process of order fulfilment.

In some cases when logistics is referred to, other functional or cross-functional areas are included, as in the case of the flowchart description of logistics provided by the Institute of Logistics (Institute of Logistics, 1997a, 1997b) and reproduced in Figure 3.6. In this case other areas such as human relations, safety, health and environment as well as training and education are brought in to the logistics field. In essence this definition of logistics covers the central order fulfilment process together with a number of other major or supporting

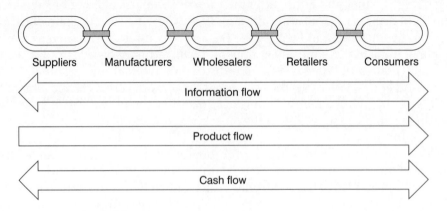

Figure 3.5 Integrated supply chain processes

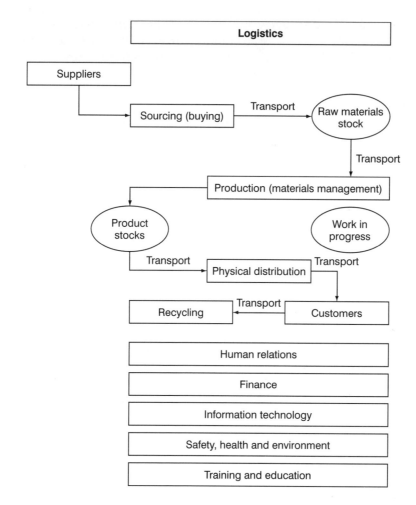

Figure 3.6 The Institute of Logistics flowchart description of logistics

processes. For the present author this view has moved away from just the central logistics (order fulfilment) process and is now encompassing other processes that may exist in a supply chain. Thus, the key difference between logistics and supply chain management is not that they cover a different collection of firms (as discussed in the section above), but that supply chain management encompasses a range of other major or support processes as well as order fulfilment.

This point can be illustrated by examples from present research projects in which the author is involved. The first point to make is that it is not possible categorically to define a small number of generic processes that apply in equal importance to all companies: processes will vary as a result of industrial sector, historical legacy and management style (Dimancescu, Hines and Rich, 1997; Hines *et al*, 1998). Taking one example from the fast-moving consumer goods (FMCG) sector (see Figure 3.7), a range of different processes may be seen, in this case over a typical product lifecycle (Hines *et al*, 2000). In this food-based supply chain there are a range of companies involved in the different processes illustrated in Figure 3.7, including a supermarket (retailer), a number of finished product food manufacturers (manufacturers), food producers (farmers) and other supporting firms such as transport providers, packaging manufacturers and raw material producers (eg steel, board, plastics) as well as more specialist suppliers such as design houses.

The central activity within this supply chain is encompassed within the order-fulfilment process. This activity involves the ordering of product, manufacture and delivery of product, and the accompanying cash transactions. This is the central logistics task of this supply chain. In addition, and closely associated with the logistics task, are the introduction of new products (after they have been either specially developed or introduced into the particular supply chain for the first time) and retirement of old products (Hines *et al*, 2000). In addition, and also closely associated with the central logistics task, is the promotion of products during the normal order fulfilment timescale (James and Jones, 1999).

The other two central processes being managed within this supply chain are new product development (the development of a new product from concept to point of introduction) and research and development (the development of new technologies or generic approaches that are unrelated to any particular new product). In this case the research and development process is completely 'offline' as it is not directly linked to particular products. In contrast the new product development process predates but leads to the new product introduction process.

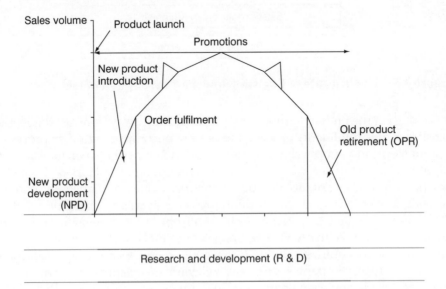

Figure 3.7 Key business processes in an FMCG environment within a product lifecycle (the Batman diagram)

Table 3.2 A correlation of business functions with key processes within an FMCG environment

Process Department/ Company	Order fulfilment	Old product retirement	New product introduction	Promotions	New product development	Research & development
Retailer: purchasing	***	**	***	***	***	
Retailer: stock control	***	***	***	***		
Retailer: store	***	***	*	***		
Retailer: marketing	*	*	***	***	***	***
Retailer: finance	***	*	**	**	**	
Retailer: food technology			**		***	***
Third-party distributor	***	*				
Manufacturer: distribution	***	**				
Manufacturer: manufacturing	***	*	**	**	*	
Manufacturer: purchasing	***		**	**		
Farmer: farming	***		*	*		
Packaging suppliers	***		***	***		
Raw material suppliers	***		*	*		
Design house			***	***		

*** Key player
** Important role
* Involved in process
No involvement

The distinction between the different processes and the key players involved in this particular example is shown in Table 3.2. However, it should be noted that other cases may be completely different, as the processes and people involved differ between food retailers and indeed between different product categories.

Applying this process-based logic to different environments will reveal a range of contingent processes. For instance, within an electrical distributor four key processes were found:

- order fulfilment (the central logistics process);
- supplier integration;
- sales order acquisition;
- new product introduction.

In a chemical manufacturing environment that the writer is involved in researching, the company involved has identified eight central processes:

- strategic management;
- new business development;
- customer support;
- traded order fulfilment (for factored goods) (one of the two central logistics processes);
- manufactured order fulfilment (the other central logistics process);
- cost management;
- quality and environmental management;
- continuous improvement.

With reference to papers presented at Logistics Research Network events between 1996 and 1998, nearly all can be regarded as logistics papers – using the above distinction between logistics and supply chain management – as they are broadly concerned with the order fulfilment process, but at the differing scales described within the supply chain framework model. However, there are a small number that, although still addressing processes in the supply chain, cannot be considered as logistics, such as the Riahi and Pawar (1997) paper.

KEY AREA 3: MORE THAN JUST FAST AND EFFICIENT

The tortoise and the hare

The third key area is a concern to move away from faster and more efficient thinking to a leaner approach, or to put it another way, to move away from thinking and acting like a hare when acting like a tortoise will almost certainly be more effective. Whether one is addressing manufacturing, materials handling or transportation issues, there is always the latest, faster and more efficient approach being put forward. Examples include:

- faster food canning lines that have even less flexibility for changeover;
- smarter automatic guided vehicles (AGVs) which are often less flexible on the shop floor;
- computer controlled hi-tech warehouses that encourage stock to be stored unnecessarily and for longer;
- centralized national distribution centres that dramatically increase transport distances and times;
- larger, faster and more powerful lorries that encourage more inventory, but often travel at slower speeds due to speed restrictions and congestion.

The type of 'efficient' thinking that has often been applied within logistics has in many cases led to little real improvement. Why is it that the total stock-holding figures issued by government yearly never seem to fall, or that trains take longer to travel from Cardiff to London than in the 1950s? The answer is that academics and firms often are misled into thinking faster is better, just like the hare in the famous tale. The reason for the problem is that lean thinking has not been applied. This way of thinking often concentrates on slowing point velocity and maximizing total system velocity. An example is operating a simpler and more flexible food packing line that enables more products to be made in each of perhaps 10 factories in the UK, with products distributed in small quantities more frequently from a larger number of manufacturing sites. This has not happened in many cases as it would require full logistics (order fulfilment) coordination, the waste to become visible and the application of an holistic lean logistics approach (Womack and Jones, 1996; Jones, Hines and Rich, 1997).

Fundamental to this would be that a product's true value is decided by the end-consumer and the total quantity and value is also defined at this point.

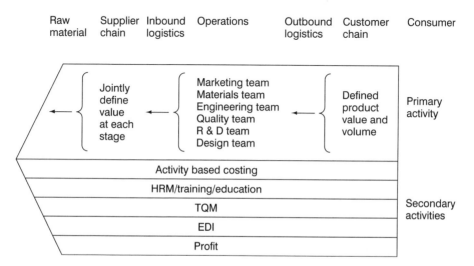

Figure 3.8 The integrated logistics value pipeline

This value definition is then translated along a supply chain or particular channels, or in the lean lexicon, value streams employing cross-functional teams at each supply tier pull product, with a group of key supporting processes aiding this central logistics process, as illustrated in Figure 3.8 (Hines, 1993).

After a number of specific value streams have been identified, products (and information) should be made to flow. Past research carried out within the Lean Enterprise Research Centre has found that for flows of physical goods in general, it is rare that any value is being added to the product for more than 5 per cent of its transition along a supply chain, with the information flow rarely reaching 1 per cent (Hines *et al*, 2000). Indeed, the physical delivery of a can of soft drink to a UK supermarket was found to have around three hours of value added to it over the span of 319 days (Jones *et al*, 1997)! This was a result of frequent attempts over the years to improve point velocity, but at the expense of total time: a true tortoise and hare example.

> Optimizing each piece of the supply chain in isolation does not lead to the lowest-cost solution. In fact it is necessary to look at the whole sequence of events, from the customer order right back to the order given to the raw materials producer, and forward through all successive firms making and delivering the product to the customer. In trying to identify possibilities for eliminating waste this makes most sense if it is done for one particular product or product family – and for all the tributaries that flow into this stream of value creation.
>
> (Jones *et al*, 1997:154–55)

A move to map out where the waste is occurring is the first step towards its removal, as it involves a move towards *managing by fact* from managing by guesswork. The mapping of different value streams has taken up a significant amount of the work time at the Lean Enterprise Research Centre, and a whole series of mapping approaches and methods have been collected and applied (Hines and Rich, 1998; Hines *et al*, 1998; Hines *et al*, 2000). Although the details of how to undertake such mapping are beyond the scope of this chapter, a list of the more frequently used tools is given in Table 3.3.

Table 3.3 Frequently used value stream mapping tools

1. Process activity mapping
2. Supply chain response matrix
3. Production variety tunnel
4. Quality filter mapping
5. Demand amplification mapping
6. Decision point analysis
7. Physical structure mapping
8. Value analysis time profile
9. Overall supply chain effectiveness mapping
10. Supply chain relationship mapping

Source: Hines *et al* (1998)

Once a particular value stream has been mapped, the work of academics and practitioners is to make products and information flow, but this requires them to find a way of communicating and working together in the change process. Commenting on this issue, Jones (1997) references an earlier writer on the subject:

> There is nothing more difficult to handle, more doubtful of success, and more dangerous to carry through than initiating change...The innovator makes enemies of all those who prospered under the old order, and only lukewarm support is forthcoming from those who would prosper under the new. Their support is lukewarm ... because men are generally incredulous, never trusting new things unless they have tested them by experience.
>
> (Machiavelli, 1514)

KEY AREA 4: MORE THAN JUST TEXTBOOKS AND TOTEBINS

Integrating theory and practice

In order to involve, encourage and allow experimentation within a beneficial transformation process, the Lean Enterprise Research Centre team devote a large amount of effort to action-based research which is carried out closely with companies and wider supply chains, whether within logistics or other areas. The research team starts by understanding the process as discussed above by using the value stream mapping toolkit. This team is multi-functional and, although it does not possess the full range of functional expertise, members are drawn from a wide range, including purchasing, distribution, manufacturing, marketing, information technology, maintenance and product development.

The second element of bringing theory and practice together is by working with companies or supply chains within the so-called AEIS cycle. This cycle involves:

- Raising *awareness* of what needs to be done (generally through the use of value stream mapping (Hines and Rich, 1998));
- Providing *education* in tools and methods that can be employed (through the application of a lean toolkit (Bicheno, 1998));
- Facilitating *implementation* of change on site; and then
- Helping to *standardize* the new working practices across the company or supply chain.

This type of practical research activity often requires the application of AEIS in several managerial levels across an enterprise, as illustrated in Figure 3.9 by the lean processing programme of the UK upstream automotive industry (Brunt, Rich and Hines, 1998; Hines *et al*, 1998). In addition, this practical

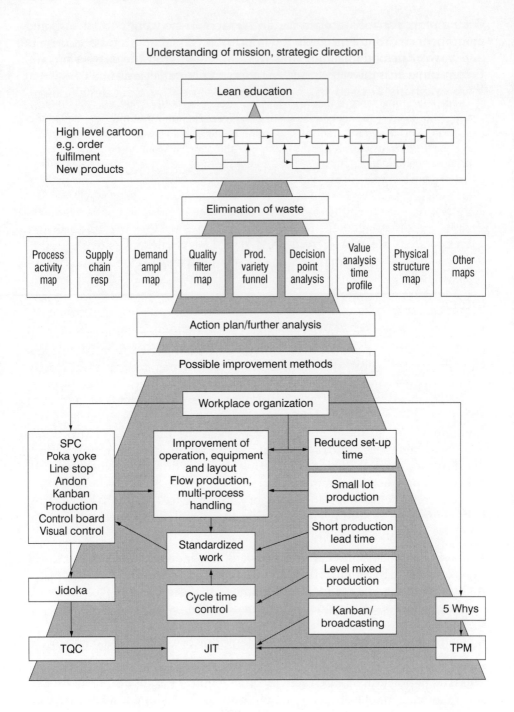

Figure 3.9 Outline steps of the LEAP programme (value stream management method)

partnership between academics and practitioners needs to be within a contingent environment, as what works in the automotive industry does not always work in food retailing. Thus, it is necessary to provide frameworks and principles such as the value stream analysis tool (Samuel and Hines, 1998) that were originally devised for another process (new product development) within shipbuilding, but can be applied successfully to make improvements in a logistics setting.

SUMMARY AND CONCLUSION

This chapter has attempted to review some of the trends and issues relating to supply chain management from a lean thinking perspective. In particular, four key areas have been addressed. The first of these was to show that logistics and supply chain management are more than just lorries and buyers. Instead a non-evolutionary five-phase model was presented that can be used for delimiting and defining research areas in order to aid clarity. The second key area discussed under the title 'more than just orders and information' discussed the difference between logistics and supply chain management. The section concluded by suggesting that both of these subjects could span any and all of the different subject scales, but that logistics is concerned with the order fulfilment process, while supply chain management is concerned not only with order fulfilment, but with a range of other processes such as product development or environmental management.

The third key area discussed was the move away from 'fast and efficient' thinking towards lean thinking based on faster total velocity but not necessarily faster point velocity. Some key principles of lean thinking were addressed such as value, value streams, pull and flow that would allow companies and supply chains to think more like a tortoise than a hare. A first stage in going lean that was discussed was the mapping of one or more value streams. It was also suggested, as a fourth key area, that in order to make lean thinking work in the real world it would be necessary for academics and practitioners to work more closely together. Examples from the work of the Lean Enterprise Research Centre were given to show how this might be achieved.

In conclusion, it is possible to say that in order to move the logistics and supply chain areas forward a number of key messages should be learnt. These can be put in the context of a reworking of the Institute of Logistics' five rights to:

- undertake the right research with gaps presented at the network and regional clustering levels;
- understand and focus on the right supply chain processes, with more work called for outside the order fulfilment process, for instance in environmental management, new product development and quality management, but especially in the more complex supply chain settings;

- undertake research with the right team of cross-functional members, with a view to practicality and making a real difference;
- undertake the right education programmes, addressing lean approaches to the supply chain and addressing key processes;
- share the research and applications at the right conferences, journals and texts.

ACKNOWLEDGEMENT

An earlier version of this chapter was presented as a keynote speech at the 1998 Logistics Research Network Conference, 10–11 September, 1998 at Cranfield University, UK under the title Supply chain management: from lorries to macro-economic determiner.

REFERENCES

Aitken, J (1997) Knowledge transfer within a supplier association, *Proceedings of the 1997 Logistics Research Network Conference*, University of Huddersfield
Bicheno, J (1998) *The Lean Toolbox*, Picsie Books, Buckingham
Blanchard, B (1992) *Logistics Engineering and Management,* Prentice-Hall, Englewood Cliffs, NJ
Brunt, D, Rich, N and Hines, P (1998) Aligning continuous improvement along the value chain, *Proceedings of the 7th International Annual IPSERA Conference*, pp 80–88, IPSERA, London
Christopher, M (1993) *Logistics and Supply Chain Management: Strategies for reducing costs and improving service*, Pitman , London
Christopher, M (1996) Emerging issues in supply chain management, *Proceedings of the Logistics Academic Network Inaugural Workshop*, Logistics Research Network, Warwick University, Warwick, 1996
Council of Logistics Management (1993) *Future Logistics Directions Questionnaire*, CLM, Oak Brook, IL
Cox, A (1999) Thinking strategically about supply chain management, in *Global Logistics and Distribution Planning*, 3rd edn, ed D Waters, Kogan Page, London
Coyle, J, Bardi, E and Langley, C (1996) *The Management of Business Logistics*, 6th edn, West Publishing, Minneapolis/St Paul
Decker, H and van Goor, A (1998) Applying activity-based costing to supply chain management, *Proceedings of the 1998 Logistics Research Network Conference*, Cranfield University
De Toni, A and Nassimbeni, G (1995) Supply networks: genesis, stability and logistics implications, *OMEGA*, **23** (4), pp 403–18

Dimancescu, D, Hines, P and Rich, N (1997) *The Lean Enterprise: Designing and managing strategic processes for customer-winning performance*, Amacom, New York

Esain, A and Hines, P (1997a) Regional innovation through inter-company networking: evidence from Wales, *Proceedings of the 3rd International Symposium on Logistics*, pp 87–96, University of Padua

Esain, A and Hines, P (1997b) Profit from regional value stream networks, *Institute of Logistics Members Directory 1997/8*, pp 20–26, Institute of Logistics, Corby

Gullander, S (1997) Effective partnership in product development in buyer/supplier networks, *Proceedings of the 1997 Logistics Research Network Conference*, University of Huddersfield

Hall, R and Andriani, P (1998) Developing inter-organisational strategy, *Proceedings of the 2nd Worldwide Symposium on Purchasing and Supply Chain Management*, pp 229–247, IPSERA, London

Harland, C (1998) Supply network strategy: observations on structure, infrastructure and operations performance, *Proceedings of the 2nd Worldwide Symposium on Purchasing and Supply Chain Management*, pp 248–267, IPSERA, London

Hines, P (1993) Integrated materials management: the value chain redefined, *International Journal of Logistics Management*, **4** (1), pp 13–22

Hines, P (1994) *Creating World Class Suppliers: Unlocking mutual competitive advantage*, Pitman, London

Hines, P (1997) A comparative typology of inter-company networking, in *Advanced Supply Management: The best practice debate*, ed A Cox and P Hines, Earlsgate Press, Boston, MA

Hines, P and Rich, N (1998) Outsourcing competitive advantage, *Proceedings of the 2nd Worldwide Symposium on Purchasing and Supply Chain Management*, pp 268–294, IPSERA, London

Hines, P, Rich, N, Bicheno, J, Brunt, D, Taylor, D, Butterworth, C and Sullivan, J (1998) Value stream management, *International Journal of Logistics Management*, **9** (2)

Hines, P, Esain, A, Francis, M and Jones, O (2000) Managing new product introduction and new product development, in *Value Stream Management*, ed P Hines, R Lamming, D Jones, P Cousins, and N Rich, Financial Times/Prentice-Hall, London

Institute of Logistics (1997a) *Members Directory 1997/98*, Institute of Logistics, Corby

Institute of Logistics (1997b) *1998 Diary*, Institute of Logistics, Corby

James, R and Jones, D (1999) Managing promotions within the value stream, in *Supply Chain Development*, ed P Hines, P Cousins, D Jones R Lamming and N Rich

Jarillo, J (1988) On strategic networks, *Strategic Management Journal*, **9**, pp 31–41

Jones, D, Hines, P and Rich, N (1997) Lean logistics, *International Journal of Physical Distribution and Logistics Management*, **27** (3/4), pp 153–73

Jones, O (1997) Optimising the supply chain: information or inventory, *Proceedings of the 1997 Logistics Research Network Conference*, University of Huddersfield

Kotler, P (1997) *Marketing Management: Analysis, planning, implementation and control*, 9th edn, Prentice Hall, New Jersey

Kurt Salmon (1993) *Efficient Consumer Response*, Kurt Salmon Associates, Washington, DC

Naslund, D (1997) Process logistics – to manage and improve processes, *Proceedings of the 1997 Logistics Research Network Conference*, University of Huddersfield

Nassimbeni, G (1998) Network structures and co-ordination mechanisms: a taxonomy, *International Journal of Operations and Production Management*, **18** (6), pp 538–54

Peck, H (1998) The development and implementation of co-managed inventory agreements in the UK brewing industry, *International Journal of Logistics: Research and Applications*, **1** (3)

Riahi, H and Pawar, K (1997) The development of a methodology to re-engineer communication patterns in a design and development environment, *Proceedings of the 1997 Logistics Research Network Conference*, University of Huddersfield

Samuel, D (1994) A local initiative for encouraging co-operation and improvements in the supply chain: SWIMM, *3rd International IPSERA Conference*, pp 515–34, University of Glamorgan

Samuel, D and Hines, P (1998) Designing a supply chain process: a food distribution case, *Proceedings of the 1998 Logistics Research Network Conference*, Cranfield University

Simons, D and Kiff, J (1998) Automotive after-sales distribution analysed within a conceptual framework for supply chain improvement, *Proceedings of the 1998 Logistics Research Network Conference*, Cranfield University

Stevens, G (1989) Integrating the supply chain, *International Journal of Physical Distribution and Materials Management*, **19** (8)

Taylor, D (1998) Redesigning an elephant: parallel incremental transformation strategy – an approach to the application of value stream management, *Proceedings of the 1998 Logistics Research Network Conference*, Cranfield University

Thorelli, H (1986) Networks, between hierarchies and markets, *Strategic Management Journal*, **7**, pp 37–51

Van Hoek, R (1998) *Postponed Manufacturing in European Supply Chains: A triangular approach*, Nederlandse Geografische Studies, University of Utrecht
Wilding, R (1997) Chaos theory and the supply chain, *Proceedings of the 1997 Logistics Research Network Conference*, University of Huddersfield
Womack, J and Jones, D (1996) *Lean Thinking*, Simon and Schuster, New York

4

Agile supply chain operating environments

Remko van Hoek
Cranfield School of Management

SUMMARY

Agile capabilities in the supply chain are needed now more than ever before. Lean capabilities – as a sole answer – fall fundamentally short because of their focus on optimizing internal supply chain operations, rather than creating the basic capabilities to respond to what matters to the customer. This chapter develops a categorization for operating environments, and shows how this can be used to assess the viability of an agile supply chain for meeting contingencies in supply and demand.

INTRODUCTION

In light of the economic slowdown and post 11 September 2001, supply chains are in a state of flux. Companies experience many potential breaking points in their supply chains. To name just a few areas of concern, global sourcing and distribution arrangements are at risk of disruption, customer bases are at risk because of cancelled orders, and there is significant additional uncertainty in forecasts. These factors are forcing companies and supply chain partners to be more flexible and responsive to demand and supply uncertainties. We now know that the market turbulence of the 1990s was only a start, and that continuing uncertainty makes the responsiveness that comes from agile supply chains a more valuable consideration than ever before.

The key word here is 'consideration'. If there is one rule in supply chain management, it is that 'there is no universal solution to all operating circumstances'. Lean manufacturing and lean value stream are known for their ability to streamline operations, eliminate waste, and support efficiency of response. This is a very valid set of capabilities in cost-centred operating environments, and a very valid approach to achieving internal efficiency. If there is one key to successful operations in today's environment, however, it is the need to move beyond internal optimization and into external effectiveness, as defined from the customers' point of view. The basis of the 'lean principles' is value. This is operationalized primarily through other principles and procedures that focus on some kind of optimization of internal operations. The fundamental lean 'pull' principle aims to trigger all operational activities by final work orders, and this holds significant potential to tie operations to customer demand. In practice, however, it is most often operationalized around kanbans (part-ordering cards) and other internally generated orders upstream in the supply chain, rather than true end-customer demand. Its focus is also on avoiding unnecessary movement and work in progress, so it is driven by efficiency rather than aiming to increase rapid response.

The key to agility is to let customers define their own preferred size and type of service window. This requires, first and foremost, the ability for an organization to structure fluid supply chains that can deal with dynamic and varied demand. Then key questions for supply chain management are how to create this agile capability, and where to implement it.

These questions are based on the notion that no single design or capability is appropriate for all operating environments. The key question in this chapter is 'Which operating environment most favours an agile supply chain?' The rest of the chapter will introduce contingencies or operating factors that help answer this question. It incorporates these factors into a more comprehensive description that shows when a supply chain should focus on agility, leanness and other options. First, though, the next section briefly introduces some principles of agile supply chains.

AGILE SUPPLY CHAIN PRINCIPLES

The 'agile supply chain' is not a philosophy or just a vision, it is much more a practical approach to organizing supply chain operations through the use of practices that enhance a supply chain's ability to be structured around individual end-customer demand. It is about moving away from supply chains in which one focal company directs supply chain operations around its own practices and procedures, and towards supply chains that work for each individual customer. The key here is organizing from the customer order backwards, or 'outside in', as opposed to creating product–service offerings and then pushing them into the market, or 'inside out'. Crucial requirements for this include:

- a relentless focus on drivers of customer value in all operations;
- responsiveness and flexibility capabilities;
- the ability to align supply chains operations in a dynamic manner.

Many authors have considered the way that agility can be achieved. Van Hoek (2001) offered a diagnostic questionnaire and benchmark that supports broader organizational assessment of agile capabilities in the areas of market sensitivity, process, information and network integration. Mason-Jones *et al* (2000) develop a contrasting comparison of agile and lean supply, which is helpful in characterizing the operations in which each is more appropriate (summarized in Table 4.1). Christopher and Towill (2001) offer a three-level model that specifies programmes that can support the realization of agile principles, and actions that can support these programmes (see Figure 4.1).

Both these latter authors implicitly assume the overwhelming benefits of creating an agile supply chain. In practice, of course, agile capabilities are not universally relevant or even desirable. For this reason, the rest of this chapter will focus on the development of a categorization for operating environments to show where an agile supply chain is appropriate, and where it is not.

OPERATING CIRCUMSTANCES REQUIRING AGILITY

Table 4.1, Christopher and Towill (2001) and the recently published special issue of the *International Journal of Physical Distribution and Logistics*

Table 4.1 Comparison of lean supply with agile supply: the distinguishing attributes

Distinguishing attributes	Lean supply	Agile supply
Typical products	Commodities	Fashion goods
Marketplace demand	Predictable	Volatile
Product variety	Low	High
Product life cycle	Long	Short
Customer drivers	Cost	Availability
Profit margin	Low	High
Dominant costs	Physical costs	Marketability costs
Stockout penalties	Long-term contractual	Immediate and volatile
Purchasing policy	Buy materials	Assign capacity
Information enrichment	Highly desirable	Obligatory
Forecasting mechanism	Algorithmic	Consultative

Source: Mason-Jone, Naylor and Towill (2000)

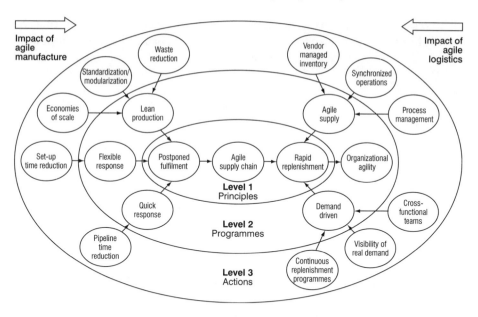

Figure 4.1 Three-level model for enabling the agile supply chain

Management (vol 31, no 4, 2001) do offer factors that impact the viability and relevance of agility. Factors previously introduced include demand volatility, product variety, forecastability and 'fashion-type' short lifecycles and fast delivery. Van Hoek and Harisson (2001) capture this in Figure 4.2. In this table, volatility, variety and forecastability are imbedded in market predictability, and time pressure is included as a separate dimension.

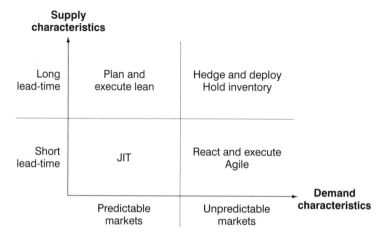

Figure 4.2 Leanness and agility under demand and supply

The relevance of factoring in demand and supply characteristics lies in the notion that creating the agile supply chain is about linking supply capabilities to demand requirements. In this respect, demand and supply 'characteristics' may be too general a term. There is an underlying dynamic between the two dimensions; supply abilities are to be created in response to demand requirements. Then one may think of the two dimensions as 'demand', indicating the viability of agility, and 'supply', indicating the feasibility of agility.

Responding to demand with a short lead time is a relevant feature of responsiveness to demand – but it also is a relatively basic one. It certainly does not capture the comprehensive set of responsiveness enhancers that are suggested by Figure 4.1. When relevant agile capabilities are considered, additional operating contingencies should be included. The remainder of this section will discuss demand and supply contingencies to be included in the categorization for operating environments.

Demand contingencies

To return to lead times, the length of response time is predominantly a relative measure; when a cross-industry categorization is developed for operating environments, the absolute length in weeks, days or hours may be less relevant than the relative length. Lead-time tolerance is often the most relevant factor, as it captures leeway that supply chains have in responding to demand. It also incorporates the fact that reliability of delivery may be more important than absolute lead time. A lead-time tolerance, therefore, contains both a speed and a reliability element.

'Forecastability' of demand is a better measure than predictions of market conditions because it is more closely linked to supply chain management capabilities. Market conditions are generally very difficult to predict at the detailed level (of individual stock-keeping units (SKUs) for example), but that does not mean that companies cannot forecast demand relatively accurately. More importantly from the contingency point of view is the fact that forecastability includes a supply chain management requirement of aligning mid- to longer-term capacity decisions to demand, rather than the hard to predict-market conditions. Of course, one might argue that an ultimately responsive system removes the need to forecast, but this is more of a theoretical perspective than a realistic one. Irrespective of the supply chain's responsiveness to actual orders, companies still have to forecast for mid- to longer-term factors, including advanced orders to suppliers, long cycle time production processes and capacity building plans.

Demand for a product is rarely stable, but contains spikes and valleys. It is traditionally difficult to accommodate this variance in demand across a given time period, because every supply chain has a limited capacity and other constraints, such as maximum order volumes or limits on the availability of expensive slack capacity. However, there are two underlying features here:

the difference between peak and valley of demand, and the frequency with which upswings and downswings occur.

For the latter, a standard seasonal pattern may have just one peak (in the summer for garden furniture, for example), whereas the fashion industry may have a minimum of six or eight seasons. Retail promotions may have peaks every other week. These seasonal swings in demand may be significant, with peak demands often accounting for 60 to 70 per cent of total demand.

Figure 4.3 shows an operationalization of the above three demand contingencies – lead-time tolerance, forecastability and variance in volume.

Supply contingencies

What are the key supply contingencies that impact the feasibility of creating an agile supply chain? It is in this area that most gaps in current knowledge exist, as most of the publications on agile supply chains focus on the relevance of the approach itself in modern markets. Given the strength of this argument in favour of agility, and its importance in the current uncertain economic landscape, it is time to move beyond this basic view and consider the four layers (at least) of supply contingencies or requirements for an agile supply chain.

'Postponement' has been identified widely as a mechanism that can support the creation of responsive supply (as shown in Figure 4.1). Delaying inventory allocation in the supply chain creates hedging options for responding to demand. This logistics postponement (delaying time and place functionality decisions) is helpful in the distribution segment of the supply chain, but ultimately only offers partial responsiveness. It still assumes that stocks of finished goods build in anticipation of unknown demand, with all the risks of stock outs still largely in place. Table 4.1 suggests that stock outs

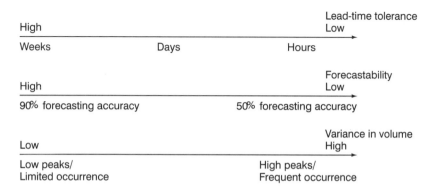

Figure 4.3   Demand contingencies impacting the viability of an agile supply chain

generally have a very high cost in agile environments. It is for this reason that 'form postponement' is used – to delay the specification of final form and function of products until the last moment. Many companies do this by delaying packaging, labelling, adding documentation or product peripherals. Extending postponement into manufacturing, assembly, module manufacturing and so on may help create the greater flexibility required for agility.

Associated with the need for form and function customization is the manufacturing and engineering principle of 'design variance' across products and product lines. In order to achieve levels of customization beyond the appearance of products, designs may have to vary beyond packaging, and even beyond modules, and into components and more basic features of design. This creates obvious design, manufacturing, sourcing and inventory complexities which have to be dealt with in agile operating environments. This contingency also shows how creating an agile supply chain requires more than revising logistics and distribution management, and can have an impact all the way back to product design. The impact on suppliers and trading partners is discussed in the next contingency.

'Supply chain partner modularity' specifies the extent to which individual companies participating in the creation of an agile supply chain will have to align operations through the redesign of management practices and interfaces for the flow of goods and information. Some examples may help clarify this. Traditional sourcing and contract logistics has a buy–sell approach that suggests interfaces limited to a transactional level; just-in-time (JIT) sourcing has more extensive interfaces, with sharing of demand data and alignment of operations. Integrated contract manufacturing, in which a third party controls the majority of build and make operations, extends the interface beyond aligned supply into integrated form and functionality creation. Fourth-party logistics is similar to this, with a third party taking over the organization and coordination of the entire flow of goods, information and management for the entire logistics function, based around tightly structured interfaces. These approaches lead to a modular supply chain in which boundaries between partners are blurred, and players are all orchestrated around real demand and service to the end-customer.

It is important to note here that this contingency is not limited to upstream suppliers, but also involves the downstream trading partners between the company and end-customer. This is traditionally a hard set of interfaces, compared with upstream suppliers who are paid for their supply efforts, giving companies an obvious lever in the structuring of these interfaces. The implication of agile reasoning, however, is that downstream partners and direct customers can also encourage alignment around this approach. Then channel interfaces should be structured around end-customer demand contingencies. Service to the end-customer gives the key to this; it is an objective that all supply chain players share, and where there is significant unification in purpose and objectives.

This brings us a final contingency, which is the 'supply chain scope'. In order to completely meet the standards demanded for customization, modularity and partner integration, the scale or scope of supply chain involvement may be significant. It goes far beyond traditional views, and develops one-to-one interfaces which extend into a 'value chain'. A value chain is a sequence of one-to-one interfaces leading up to a customer, while a supply chain has many-to-many interfaces and interconnections which must be rearranged dynamically around key processes and players in response to real demand. A network approach is far more appropriate here.

Figure 4.4 shows an operationalization of the above four supply contingencies – postponement, design variance, partner modularity and supply chain scope.

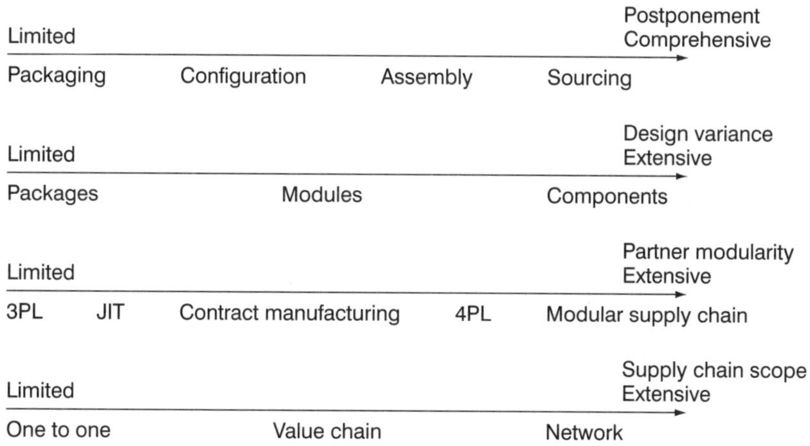

			Postponement
Limited			Comprehensive
Packaging	Configuration	Assembly	Sourcing
			Design variance
Limited			Extensive
Packages		Modules	Components
			Partner modularity
Limited			Extensive
3PL JIT	Contract manufacturing	4PL	Modular supply chain
			Supply chain scope
Limited			Extensive
One to one	Value chain		Network

Figure 4.4 Supply contingencies impacting the feasibility of an agile supply chain

THE CATEGORIZATION FOR OPERATING ENVIRONMENTS

Figure 4.5 shows a categorization for operating environments based on the contingency factors introduced in the previous section. In the categorization a number of alternative approaches to agility are mentioned. The first consideration is to distinguish A, B, C products – based on Pareto analysis (see also Christopher and Towill, 2001). Here A products (accounting for 80 per cent of volume and 20 per cent of orders) are more standardized, and the greater forecastability, lower volume variance and less customization make them more suited to lean approaches. B products are more variable and more suited to agility.

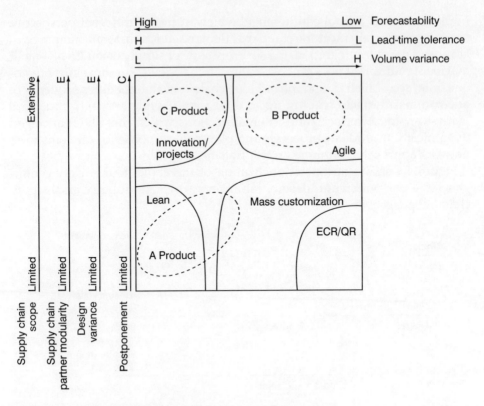

Figure 4.5 Categorization of operating environments

ECR and quick response are generally better in environments where demand requirements particularly impact delivery and distribution, but have less effect on upstream operations. Mass customization is generally better in environments with modest to significantly challenging demand, that can be met with medium postponement and customization.

Agility has been positioned in project environments. This is the right place from a supply contingency point of view, but is not so good from a demand contingency point of view. For example, in environments of innovation and single projects, lead-time leeway is often significantly greater.

CONCLUSION AND REFLECTIONS

This chapter has attempted to offer additional insight into the question of when and where to consider using agile capabilities in supply chain management. The identification of operating environments that favour – or disfavour – agile supply chains gives a more realistic chance of successful implementation. This question must be viewed from a different perspective from that taken in traditional companies, and should consider a range of broader issues.

For individual companies participating in supply chains, agility is not necessarily a universal answer, but may depend on the different types of product/market combinations. These can give different features, which need different solutions. Companies often find, for example, that about one-third of their products are most suited to agile logistics, while the remainder are more suited to other approaches.

Hopefully, this chapter will encourage support for further developments and ideas about the responsiveness to markets which is needed so much in the uncertain economic landscape that we face.

REFERENCES

Christopher, M and Towill, D (2001) An integrated model for the design of agile supply chains, *International Journal of Physical Distribution and Logistics Management*, **31** (4), pp 235–46

Mason-Jones, R, Naylor, J B and Towill, D (2000) Engineering the agile supply chain, *International Journal of Agile Management Systems*, **1**

Van Hoek, R (2001) Epilogue, Special issue on *Creating the Agile Supply Chain, International Journal of Physical Distribution and Logistics Management*, **31** (4), pp 290–300

Van Hoek, R and Harisson, A (2001) Editorial, Special issue on *Creating the Agile Supply Chain, International Journal of Physical Distribution and Logistics Management*, **31** (4), pp 231–34

5

Time compression in the supply chain

Adrian Beesley
Supply Chain Development Group

This chapter explores the 'time compression' approach to business process improvement in the supply chain. The concept and strategic relevance of this approach was first published in the West in the early 1990. However, it is an approach that still offers good potential and a fresh approach to achieving competitiveness through re-engineering. The rate of adoption of time compression has been slow, and part of the reason is that the approach requires the total commitment of the whole business from the top of the organization down. In addition, change within any organization has always been challenging, particularly when it involves making difficult decisions in one department or function to benefit another, for the good of the whole company or even supply chain. Supply chain objectives and their relation to time compression implementation strategies will be touched on, coupled with explanations of achievable benefits and case study examples.

Over 200 years ago Benjamin Franklin stated that 'time is money', and this was reiterated in 1990 by Stalk and Hout, claiming 'time is the last exploitable resource'. Today 'time' is still largely ignored by many companies, because of enduring approaches that create inertia in organizational structures and associated business processes. Managers have always used time to manage their operations, but control has usually been limited to a segment, or business function, within the supply chain. For example, in the past 'time' has been used for 'work study' and human performance measurement, but this approach is based on the use of past observations in relation to operations usually associated with long-established and outdated business processes.

Moreover this approach, and even some modern-day approaches, focuses on purely the value-adding elements of business process that often only account for 5 per cent (sometimes referred to as the business process velocity) of total process time. This emphasis on just the value-added time tends to be focused around making people work faster, often with a risk to quality, safety and ultimately livelihoods, as competitiveness starts to become an issue.

Another problematical dimension to these approaches is that the time-based implications of individual actions only recognized one side of a trade-off that may have holistic implications in a much broader supply chain context. Examples include companies who manage capacity and cost through applications and frameworks such as enterprise resource planning (ERP), manufacturing resource planning (MRPII), traditional accounting and functional budgeting. The resultant scope of thinking is usually constrained by not recognizing how time, stock, resource and service interrelate with each other along the supply chain. Using 'time' as a measure holistically creates a deeper understanding of the total business process, and therefore provides scope for optimization and also a pragmatic approach to change. The use of time in this context is directly linked with competitiveness, and will be referred to as the 'time compression' approach.

TIME COMPRESSION AND COMPETITION

Womack, Jones and Roos' landmark work within the automotive sector (1990) pointed out that competition had become more aggressive and customers were more demanding, so there is a constant need for a new source of competitiveness. Reich (1991) went further, showing the general applicability of this statement in a global context across many industrial sectors. He implied that competitive forces around the world are placing increasing pressures on markets and their supply chains. These comments are valid today, with, for example, low-cost producers able to compete on factors such as product quality and offer good levels of variety and service. The more established supply chains, typically operating in more developed countries and using a significant proportion of high-cost labour, must find new ways to compete. The time compression approach is one route to optimizing cost and service. If this approach is combined with a focus on customers, in markets that are time-sensitive, then a further dimension is added to it. Stalk and Hout (1993) make the comment that 'the world is moving to increased variety with better levels of service and faster levels of innovation. For the suppliers that operate and service these sectors, time based competition is of significant advantage.'

Cooper's 1994 European Survey illustrated industrialists' views on the importance of time as a future source of competitiveness. The survey represented a variety of industrial sectors with a mix of good and average companies. The results showed that within 10 years the companies anticipated that cycle times would be reduced by an average of 20 per cent. These results have today become manifest, with cycle times being a key consideration for most companies in Europe. However, the more holistic approach offered by time compression remains an opportunity for many companies, as borne out by the content of numerous industrial RFQs (requests for quotation) for third-party logistics over the past five years. The majority tend to focus on cost reduction, with often little or no consideration for the attainment of holistic supply chain benefits.

Some commentators such as Lamming (2002) consider that the idea of managing the supply chain as a holistic entity, using approaches such as supply chain management (SCM), is totally impractical. He considers SCM to be a flawed concept that has been around since 1982, and that industry is still having difficulty with implementing and mastering this area of potential competitiveness. This may well explain, or support, the reason some of the more insular approaches to business improvement still dominate company key objectives, as expressed in documents such as RFQs. This debate will no doubt continue irrespective of whether SCM, or say network management, is the approach for the future. Opportunities for time compression still exist, however, and this will be explored further.

WHAT TIME COMPRESSION IS

The key aspect for the use of 'time' is that it is not necessarily about being faster or the fastest. Quality is paramount to competitiveness, and substi-tuting, say, quality for speed is not the primary objective. A time compression approach focuses on how companies use time to deliver a sustainable fast response to customer needs, through business processes that are organized around a strategic time-based focus. The concept is about strengthening the holistic supply chain structure to achieve time-based objectives, with tactical decisions being made at the correct level to enable the speed of response.

The term 'time compression' was originally introduced by New in 1992, and in its most basic form relates to the reduction of the time consumed by business processes through the elimination of non-value-adding process time. Some processes may be identified as producing very little added value, and this may highlight the need to totally re-engineer them. The majority of business processes, however, do add some value, and should therefore become subject to compression. Both situations can take advantage of a number of possible strategies, detailed below.

One of the reasons the approach is important relates to the levels of time compression that can be achieved across business processes. Within a typical UK manufacturing company, for example, at least 95 per cent of the process time is accounted as non-value adding. This well-established statistic was supported in the United Kingdom by the TCP (University of Warwick's Time Compression Programme) in 1995 and in the United States by Barker in 1994. Consultants in 2002 confirm that these sorts of value-added statistic still hold true, making the approach powerful as well as relevant in today's business environment.

If this statistic is viewed in the context of a typical supply chain, as little as 0.01 per cent of time can add value. However, as New demonstrated, all of these percentages require qualification on two counts. First, a large proportion of the non-value-adding time is the result of product queuing, so the value-adding percentage is a function of how much is being pushed through the supply chain at a particular point in time. Even if a particular supply chain is grossly inefficient, but had only one order during a particular period, the actual value-adding time would be high because of minimal queuing. A second consideration is that inventory should add value and is, therefore, usually included in the overall value-adding percentage. Consequently a view has to be taken on how much of the inventory element of the pipeline – usually measured in days or hours of throughput cover – is actually adding value. The amount of value added by inventory is intrinsically linked to the process cycle times, as well as demand throughput levels and predictability.

The statistics do, however, show the enormity of the opportunities for companies and their associated supply chains – and they differ significantly from any perceived opportunity that might be available from, say, a cost-based approach.

Time compression can be achieved using any one or a combination of seven strategies identified by Carter, Melnyk and Handfield (1994), and these can be applied at company level through to a total supply chain. These are summarized below:

- **Simplification**, removing process complexity that has accumulated over time.
- **Integration**, improving information flows and linkages to create information and process visibility.
- **Standardization**, using generic best-practice processes, standardized components and modules and information protocols.
- **Concurrent working**, moving from sequential to parallel working by using, for example, teams and process integration.
- **Variance control**, monitoring processes and detecting problems at an early stage so that corrective action can be taken to avoid quality- and time-related waste.
- **Automation**, applied to improve the effectiveness and efficiency of agents and activities within the supply chain process.
- **Resource planning**, allocating resources across the supply chain process. Bottlenecks can be controlled by resource planning and the use of multi-skilled workforces to provide resource flexibility.

These strategies should ideally be utilized in the sequence they appear above. However, depending on any particular supply chain or company situation, various stages and combinations may be deployed more pragmatically to account for changes that are already, or are about to be put, in place. Through the use of these strategies the achievement of time compression can directly achieve increases in value-added time and help to contribute to objectives associated with the fundamental principles of generic supply chain properties and best practice. The principles cannot be covered in detail without entering into the debate surrounding SCM. However, Table 5.1 gives a brief description of the nature of the principles and how time relates to the attainment of objectives associated with the principle. It can be argued that these principles hold true irrespective of whether a company is operating in the context of SCM or some other holistic approach to process re-engineering.

THE TIME COMPRESSION APPROACH: COMPETITIVE ADVANTAGE

The time compression approach can be applied at two levels. The first is as a holistic approach in the context of, for example, the above principles, and the second is as a competitive market focus. The former could be regarded as an internal time focus of the key supply chain processes that lie on, or close to, the critical path of the business process. The latter element is the supply chain's external time, which is of direct value to the customer. Both are interdependent and therefore have outcomes that are strategically significant.

When business strategy is examined from first principles, reference can be made to Ohmae's (1965) strategic model. He states that competitiveness relates to three basic elements: the customer, the competition, and the company that is under scrutiny. There must be differentiation between the elements of value and cost if competitiveness is to emerge. A time compression approach addresses these two sources of differentiation in a specific way.

The first objective must be the elimination of non-value activity – that is waste – thereby maximizing the value created in the supply chain. The removal of non-value activity in turn gives rise to a cost advantage, hence it forms the basis of cost differentiation. Tersine and Hummingbird (1995) state that 'managing time is the mirror image of managing quality, cost, innovation and productivity. Reducing wasted time automatically improves the other measures of performance in a multiplier fashion.' If, however, companies go for the reverse and apply cost reduction initiatives without reference to the time-based implications, additional costs may be incurred elsewhere in the supply chain.

An example relating to the inventory positioning principle can be used to demonstrate this point. At the outset of a cost reduction initiative it could be

Table 5.1 Fundamental principles associated with generic supply chain properties and best practice

	Nature of the principle	Useful attributes of a time compression approach
The principle of end-user focus	Long-term supply chain profitability is dependent on the end (ultimate) user being satisfied and acting as the focus for all development and process engineering	Time compression requires that the end-user is identified as the principal anchor point, and thus highlights the time-based relationship between the end-user and the supply chain
The principle of horizontal boundary definition	Different end-user needs are more competitively satisfied by logistically engineered channels (horizontally defined routes or workflows) within the supply chain	Time defines the principal characteristics of the logistically distinct channels and service needs. The time compression approach provides a good diagnostic and basis for redesign.
The principle of vertical boundary definition	Boundaries of ownership and control (dividing the chain vertically) should be positioned to suit the needs of the end-user according to best practice and make–buy theory.	The consumption of non-value time highlights where ownership and general boundary issues exist and require adjustment
The principle of inventory positioning	The positioning and levels of inventory are best determined in a total supply chain context to suit end-user needs in line with stock and postponement theory	Time and cost provide a good deterministic framework, with cycle time as a fundamental driver of stock positioning levels and service. 'Value-added stock' is a time-based diagnostic.
The principle of control over demand dynamics	Understanding and control over demand dynamics is best achieved by having a holistic supply chain perspective. The principal basis of control is through information integration and the use of best practice relationship management.	Time measures the problem and time compression tackles the root causes of demand dynamics
The principle of cooperation and coordination	The attainment of the above principles requires cooperation and coordination between supply chain participants. For this to work effectively each SC participant must have self-defined and motivating objectives based on trust and common business process aspirations.	Time provides a common and trustworthy metric across the supply chain that highlights the opportunities and issues.

proved that upgrading a warehousing management system (WMS) will deliver cost advantages. It may, for example, help to reduce product storage and retrieval times, and drive cost reductions associated with resource utilization. However, a time-based examination of the holistic business process may lead to considerations about whether the particular segment of the supply chain in question should operate on a 'just-in-time' or a 'make to order' basis. This total supply chain perspective may remove or displace the stock point, and hence the requirement for a WMS at this point. In addition, if process times are compressed in other parts of the supply chain, the economic structure of the supply system may change the appropriate locations for inventory stock points, and the short-term cost savings associated with the proposed warehouse system could be negated by a new inventory regime. If the new WMS is still established, its associated payback demands may impose an inappropriate constraint preventing future supply chain optimization. This will have ramifications in terms of cost as well as service levels, flexibility and agility.

THE TIME COMPRESSION APPROACH: COST ADVANTAGE

Cost reduction will generally occur as a direct result of the removal or compression of non-value-added time. This time compression can result in a number of cost savings associated with the removal of fixed and variable overheads (such as rent and management), direct costs (such as labour and materials), and working capital. Other cost savings will depend on the nature of the compression, perhaps minimizing risk in the decision process by making relevant information available earlier in the process. The reduction – or even removal – of a rework activity can result from process change, such as compression of information queues. These improvements can also have ramifications downstream and upstream in the chain, by reducing or removing expediting activities that make up for previous inadequacies.

The cost implications of compressing time are extensive and complex but rarely absent. This is why the prescribed approach is to focus on time that directly affects the service a supply chain can offer, without the complications of having to identify every cost trade-off. The cost-based focus has been encouraged in the past by the use of performance measures linking profit margins with cost. With the 'time compression' approach there may be a requirement to determine cost values associated with the processes, to assist with evaluation and project prioritization. Generally, the time-based implications of any proposal are easy to comprehend and quantify, because the length of time consumed by the process is typically a proportional representation of the costs (New, 1992). Surprisingly, this fact has not prevented the constant preoccupation on cost-based rather than time-based critical success factors.

THE TIME COMPRESSION APPROACH: QUALITY ADVANTAGE

The achievement of time compression requires a quality-based approach. This can be viewed from two perspectives of quality. First, time compression demands that product quality is to a specification that matches customer needs, and more specifically end-user needs. Anything less will obviously have strategic market implications, such as a loss of customers and goodwill. This will consume unnecessary time in the sales, marketing and manufacturing process, which will have to rectify or replace the product or customers. An investigation of these timewasting activities can, therefore, highlight possible root causes of problems that may be founded in quality issues. Time, therefore, provides the focus for quality improvement.

The above complements the second dimension of quality, where it is important not just for the customer but also for the company. This is the total quality management (TQM) approach, which also focuses on waste elimination. One key issue with TQM programmes is that they have been known to lose impetus because of a lack of focus. Mallinger (1993) identifies the need for a holistic approach to provide a focus for TQM to operate effectively. A time compression approach provides this, because it uses a simple measure that is visible to the total supply chain and not just a small isolated segment. It can thus link and integrate all of the elements of a TQM approach using the key metric of 'time'.

THE TIME COMPRESSION APPROACH: TECHNOLOGY ADVANTAGE

Technology should not be applied purely for reasons associated with mimicking what the competition has. Its application must take account of the individual circumstances of the business and its customer needs, and then ensure a competitive differentiation. A focus on the time-based impact of the application of technology will help steer a company to this goal. Examples of technologies that can achieve time compression are numerous, and some of the more notable developments (Barker and Helms, 1992) include CNC (computer numerically controlled) machines, robotics, CIM (computers in manufacturing) and logistics-related examples such as the WMS application mentioned earlier. All of these reduce time for individual activities, but the time-based impact must be considered holistically in order to check that the technology is appropriate for the supply chain.

A key perspective is that many automated systems cannot cope with high levels of demand variation, largely because the technology's batching rules may drive high inventories and lead times. A time compression approach provides the focus for the application of technology when the seven strategies identified by Carter *et al* (1994) are addressed in a carefully considered sequence. This usually considers the low or non-technology strategy solution before jumping to state of the art automated solutions, such as computerized material handling and control, or the various forms of ERP. This approach will ensure that the application of technology is strategically significant, as well as that it delivers tactical productivity gains.

THE TIME COMPRESSION APPROACH: CUSTOMER FOCUS

Different customer and ultimate end-user needs are satisfied by channels that are capable of delivering different types of service. Different people or market sectors have different needs, and the most appropriate way to deliver this service is through channels that are specifically designed to have distinct logistic capabilities. The alternative is to push everything through the same channel, but the result will be that some customers are overserved while others are underserved. This will have an adverse effect on costs, customer goodwill and ultimately sustainable profitability. This is all linked with the principle of horizontal boundary definition, and is important in channel construction because of the significant impact it can have on the customer.

One of the key impacts of the need for different logistics channels is the recognition of the need for different types of customer solution. Figure 5.1

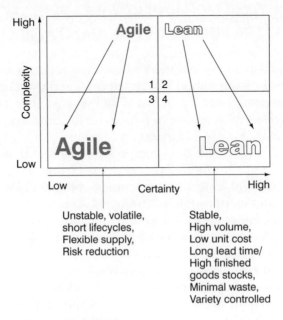

Figure 5.1 Generic product strategies

shows the four generic product categories, with a horizontal axis for levels of demand certainty for a product type, and a vertical axis for levels of product complexity. Different customer types will fit into one of the quadrants according to the type of product that is being demanded.

The chart shows that products that have a volatile demand pattern and short life cycles will require flexible supply operations to minimize risk. The approach required in this situation is called 'agile'. Conversely products that are simpler in structure and have more stable and predictable demand are usually in competitive supply situations demanding lower unit costs through tighter management control. The approach required in this situation is called 'lean'.

There are, therefore, two supply concepts: one where an organizational process must be agile so it can flex and change to meet volatile demand, and one where it is lean so that costs are managed very tightly, and usually high volume throughput helps to generate low unit costs. Different products, product stages of completion and associated levels within the supply chain may require a lean or agile approach. Often there is the need to manage a mix of both approaches, as might be the case in quadrants 1 and 2. The objectives of the time compression approach will differ significantly in either situation, and the priorities between value-adding options will be influenced by the nature of who the immediate customer is, coupled with any end-user objectives. For example, large production stocks may be kept in a commodity production environment (quadrant 4), compared with a company producing fashion products (quadrant 3) where the need for spare capacity is crucial for total flexibility. The make-up of value-added time in the commodity environment will be in the production process rather than the value the stock adds, as opposed to the fashion product environment which has the reverse. The same time compression strategies and supply chain principles are applicable in all quadrant scenarios. The process design outcomes are, however, different because of the nature of the product and the customer-service-related requirements.

BENEFITS OF TIME COMPRESSION

There are two categories of time compression benefit. The first is internal time, which has indirect impact on the customer as it relates to the internal consumption of time within a company. The second is external time, which relates to all aspects of time that have direct impact upon the customer, such as lead time from a stock or decoupling point. The net effect of internal time improvements has ramifications on external time-based benefits through cost and service interrelationships.

Internal time benefits in most manufacturing facilities, such as cycle time reductions, give work-in-progress reductions and productivity increases.

Stalk and Hout (1990) claim empirically that for every halving of cycle times and doubling of work in process turns, productivity increases by 20 to 70 per cent. A halving of manufacturing lead time using the same number of people reduces costs by 50 per cent. These changes are reflected in the return on assets, where increases of 80 per cent are possible. Then 45 per cent less cash is required to grow the company. To substantiate these claims, the Swedish consultancy company Indevo (1991) estimated that a 50 per cent reduction of manufacturing lead times had the following impact:

- Manufacturing cost – 8.5 per cent;
- Productivity +10 per cent;
- Fixed assets –15 per cent;
- Work in process – 47 per cent;
- Profitability +9.5 per cent.

Generally, the longer the elapsed time in the supply chain, the greater the commercial risk associated with under- or over-forecasting demand. This results in the use of speculation stock for future customer needs. If, for example, a fashion-associated product has to be ordered from the Far East nine months in advance, then the risk of forecasting error is high. Consequently, the costs associated with potential markdowns are high where significantly large stocks of inventory are held, and in the converse situation where minimal or understocking occurs, the opportunity cost of lost sales and goodwill is substantial.

The key point for time compression is that if lead times (cycle times) are compressed, not only is cycle stock (pipeline inventory) reduced, but the period over which forecasting has to be performed reduces – and the shorter the period, the better the forecast accuracy. The better the forecast accuracy, the less demand variance will exist, and the less buffer or safety stock is required. Less overall demand for inventory means that less has to be produced, and supply processes can respond more promptly. Again, therefore, lead times compress and a virtuous time compression cycle comes into existence.

The internal benefits provide scope to assist the external benefits of a time compression approach. The first thing to consider is the consequence of compressing customer lead times and the opportunity to increase prices. Stalk and Hout infer that customers of time-based suppliers are willing to pay more for their products for both subjective and economic reasons:

- The customer needs less stock (cycle and buffer stock).
- The customer makes a decision to purchase nearer the time of need, therefore reducing risk.
- There is a reduction in cancelled/changed orders, with less time available and less need to change.
- There is an increase in the velocity of cash flow.

The factors influencing risk have an implication on market share. If a company is faster and more reliable than the competition, its market share can increase. A time-compressed supplier can use its flexible delivery system to supply increased variety to the customer in the form of increased style and/or technological sophistication. If this is delivered with a response advantage, the time-compressed supplier will attract the most profitable customers. Conversely, competitors will be forced to service the customers that are prepared to wait and, as a consequence, are prepared to pay less for the product. Generally, time-compressed suppliers appear to grow at three to four times the rate of their competitors, and three times faster than overall demand, with twice the level of profitability. When the slower competitor companies do decide to become time-based they must do so from the disadvantaged position of having to incur the costs of regaining market share without securing the full benefits.

Experience from TCP has shown that the general price and market share advantage must be regarded relative to the context of the local market and the product being supplied. For example in the United Kingdom during the mid-1990s, time compression enabled significant optimization of business processes at H&R Johnson, giving a positive impact on market share. However, the key strategic benefit was to retain market share against cheap foreign imports, and avoid significant cost from reorganization of the company's UK and overseas production bases.

Demand acquisition approaches such customer relationship management (CRM) help predict, define and place new customer demands on supplying companies within short time spans. The need to respond to this level of rapidly communicated customer transparency will become the next competitive frontier. Companies that do not adjust their business processes fast enough will quickly lose ground to the competition. Agility coupled with lean cost-effectiveness will be key, with a focus on the use of time compression as an enabler of process delivery and reinvention.

EXAMPLES OF THE APPLICATION OF TIME COMPRESSION

Many companies in the United States, Japan and in Europe use a time compression approach, either as an open policy or as something philosophically buried within the strategic mix (Stalk and Webber, 1993). Table 5.2 illustrates the nature of, and results from, a number of TCP projects.

The following case study illustrates the attainment of a number of the supply chain principles in a global context through the application of a combination of time compression strategies. These are highlighted in the text, with the principles addressed being emboldened and the strategies denoted in italics.

Table 5.2 Results of sample TCP projects

Company	Scope of the project	Compression achieved	Strategic significance of the improvement
H&R Johnson	Customer lead times	2 weeks to 2 days	To counter competitive import products and retain a strategic segment of the market
Rover	Cars produced to order	6 months to 20 days	To enhance profitability and retain market niche by reducing costs and offering the customer product variety within shorter lead times
Rover	Supplier scheduling	3 months to 10 days	To develop supply chain flexibility in order to support the make-to-order initiative
Massey Ferguson	Process time	Reduced by 20%	To reduce cost of inventory by compressing cycle times via a manufacturing cell
British Airways	Warehouse link removed	2 days compression	To maximize aircraft flying hours, reduce inventory costs and increase asset utilization by moving into a contract market
Fairey Hydraulics	Component arrears	50% reduction	Retain market share and reduce inventory costs
GKN Hardy Spicer	Inbound logistics	Reduced by 85%	Reduce raw material and operating costs to maintain competitiveness
CV Knitwear	Time to develop product	Reduced by 50%	To meet a customer's time-based requirement for an increased number of ranges each year. Customer retained.

British Airways undertook a complete review of its inbound supply of aircraft spares originating from manufacturers in the United States. For a number of years BA had operated a consignment consolidation operation at JFK Airport. US suppliers dispatched spares via a variety of transport modes (including the US post, trucking, air and railroad) to JFK for consolidation and onward transatlantic shipment via weekly BA world cargo services. This supply structure was only cost-effective in certain aspects, such as good utilization of BA's cargo services on the transatlantic link.

From a holistic supply chain perspective, this system involved extended lead times that were highly variable because of a lack of visibility and control over consignments in transit to JFK. This in turn led to BA holding substantial cycle and buffer stocks (**inventory positioning**) at its maintenance bases in the UK. From an **end-user** perspective, aircraft flying hours were being maximized because a reliable flow of parts for servicing was available. But this was achieved from high levels of inventory that gave impetus to some interesting time compression initiatives.

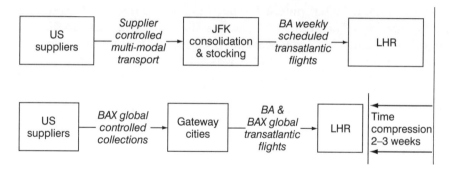

Figure 5.2   Time compression at BA

The first stage of restructuring the supply chain focused on gaining *better control over variance* of supplier dispatches and transit lead times. BA nominated a number of Gateway Airports and a freight agent to collect and consolidate the consignments. This allowed a higher degree of control over the timing and progress of the supplier outbound dispatches. The inbound supply chain to BA was compressed by three weeks, and substantial inventory reductions were realized by compressing transit and airport queue times coupled with reducing lead time variability.

The second stage of the change programme focused on issues of **horizontal channel** structuring and **process ownership issues** (**vertical structuring**). It should be understood that BA's strategic objective is to service the needs of its core market, air passengers. The capability of the airline operation was tuned to this particular **end-user,** and accordingly the logistics of the **horizontal supply channel**, from aircraft purchasing to the delivery of the passenger service, was focused on this requirement in terms of specification, scheduling, resourcing and so forth. In contrast the air cargo business rode on the back (or literally the underside) of the passenger air traffic. As far as BA spares supply was concerned, as an internal customer, the logistical channel specification for spares differed from the specification for passengers. The three key specification requirements were capacity, lead time and frequency of service.

BA saw the need to utilize a new supply channel that fulfilled the logistical service requirement of spares, because on some occasions freight was delayed by the priority given to passengers on certain flights. BA could have considered constructing its own specialized channel for the movement of freight, but (**vertical boundaries**) process ownership discussions relating to make or buy considerations led it to outsource. BAX Global was asked to perform this task, as there was an established relationship between the two companies (**coordination and cooperation linkages**), and it had a global transportation network linked to logistical capabilities such as information and supplier management (see Figure 5.2).

Using the Bax Global network, lead times have been compressed by a further four days. This compression was achieved through the application of integrated systems and team working (*integration strategy*) providing global visibility of where a consignment was within the supply channel. This reduced delays and enabled proactive management. Integration is dependent on the use of standardized communications and procedures (*standardized strategy*) throughout the global network. BAX Global was able to provide this through its global communications network and the use of adaptable communication protocols.

The use of multiple gateways as opposed to one single hub at JFK converted elements of the supply chain from a series to a parallel process (*parallelism strategy*). Consignments arriving at gateways regionally could be dispatched simultaneously for transatlantic shipment, rather than spend extra lead time in transit to JFK and then stand in a non-value-added queue awaiting consolidation for the next available weekly flight. Bax Global provided the resourcing to meet the service standards demanded by BA, which were optimally balanced in terms of taking advantage of synergies that exist in the outsourced network (*resource allocation strategy*). Finally BA were able to take advantage of an *information automation strategy* that Bax Global already had in place through its network of EDI communications and data collection technologies.

CONCLUSION

Time, as a measure, has been established as being strategically significant for contemporary business. The scale of time compression that is possible in most businesses is very significant, and therefore provides a wide scope of commercial benefits. These include increased market share and price, together with productivity increases and reduced levels of commercial risk. Seven strategies to achieve time compression have been described: systems simplification, systems integration, standardization, concurrent working, variance control, automation and the removal of excess resources.

Time compression has been established as a mechanism for addressing most of the aspects of business strategy. It embraces the key supply chain related issues and possible SCM objectives. The approach supports a new source of competitiveness for time-sensitive markets, and as a focusing criterion, it enables one company or supply chain to be compared with another in terms of the internal and external benefits of time. This can provide the impetus for change and an improvement plan. Even the end-user, or the internal supply chain customer not operating in a time-sensitive market, would find it difficult to argue that no benefit could be acquired from the strategic elements that relate to time. Indeed in the future it is likely that all of the strategic elements of a time compression approach will be of great competitive advantage as markets mature.

Looking towards the future, companies must blend leanness with agility in order to be able to respond to at least two possible key challenges. The first is the linking of customer relationship management to the management of the supply chain. This functional and systems integration opportunity will provide the insight and the means to anticipate and plan the fulfilment of customer needs. The second is to manage the supply chain in a dynamic commercial environment that is making network management rather than supply chain management a challenging reality. The simplicity of the time compression approach, and its transparency across company and functional boundaries provide a good platform for meeting these challenges.

REFERENCES

Barker, B and Helms, M M (1992), Production and operations restructuring: using time based strategies, *Industrial Management and Data Systems*, **92** (6)

Barker, R C (1994) The design of lean manufacturing systems using time-based analysis, *International Journal of Operations and Production Management*, **14**

Carter, R, Melnyk, P L and Handfield, S A (1994) *Identifying Sources of Cycle Time Reduction*, Quorum, Texas

Cooper, J (1994) *European Survey*, Cranfield University, (unpublished)

Indevo/PIMS Research (1991) *Identification and Quantification of Potentials from Reduced Lead-Times for the 'Lean Enterprise' Concept*, PIMS, Cologne

Lamming, R (2002) Lecture to Thames Valley Supply Chain Network Group

Mallinger, M (1993) Ambush along the TQM trail, *Journal of Organisational Change Management*, **6** (4)

New, C N (1992) *The Use of Throughput Efficiency as a Key Performance Measure for the New Manufacturing Era*, BPICS Conference, Cranfield School of Management

Ohmae, K (1965) *The Mind of the Strategist*, Penguin, Harmondsworth

Reich, R B (1991) *The Work of Nations,* Simon and Schuster, New York

Stalk, G and Hout, T M (1990) *Competing Against Time*, Free Press, New York

Stalk, G and Webber, A M (1993) Japan's dark side of time, *Harvard Business Review* (Jul–Aug)

TCP (1995) *Profit from Time Compression*, delegate pack, Time Compression Programme Conference, Birmingham International Convention Centre

Tersine, R J and Hummingbird, E A (1995) Lead-time reduction: the search for competitive advantage, *International Journal of Operations and Production Management*, **15** (2), pp 36–53

Womack, J, Jones, D and Roos, D (1990) *The Machine that Changed the World*, Harper Perennial, New York

6

Formulating a logistics strategy

Nathalie Fabbe-Costes and Jacques Colin
Université de la Méditerranée, Aix-Marseille

WHY FORMULATE LOGISTICS STRATEGIES?

Commercial and industrial organizations can be thought of as systems composed of operational processes, structured and regulated by a set of functions that can become strategic; they are currently the object of intense environmental pressures. Never have these forces been so diverse: they are disrupting previous equilibriums and call for rapid and coherent responses, as shown in Figure 6.1.

The multiplicity of corporate responses implies coordination and integration in an approach with a clearly defined strategic character. Indeed, only through the use of strategy, this 'art of using information obtained in operating, integrating it, quickly formulating plans of action and having the ability to gather a maximum of certainties in order to confront the uncertain' (Morin, 1990), will companies be able to overcome the extreme environmental instability that appears to be characterizing the new millennium. Strategy will enable companies to formulate and achieve their objectives, allowing them to seize and take advantage of opportunities as they arise, while at the same time remaining in tune with their environment.

One of the priorities that is considered essential today is an understanding of logistics and supply chain management (SCM), and most priority plans of action now have an asserted logistics character. Logistics – defined as the technology of control of the physical flow of materials and goods and related information that a firm sends, transfers and receives – appears as an organizational approach that

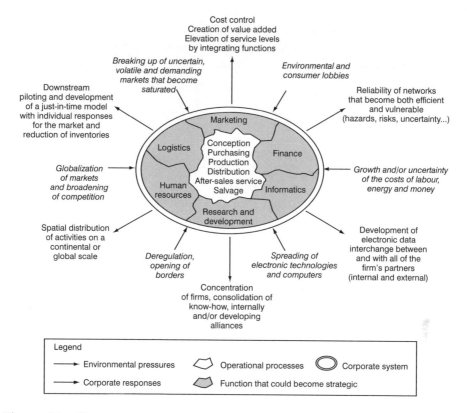

Figure 6.1 Corporate responses to environmental pressures

can conserve and improve the flexibility and reactivity of the firm *vis-à-vis* its environment. Logistics also leads companies to think about the whole supply chains in which they are involved, and to try to improve both their own performance and the performance of the global process. Firms now try to develop a collaborative approach within supply chain management, defined as 'a network of firms interacting to deliver product or service to the end consumer, linking flows from raw material supply to final delivery' (Ellram, 1991).

To satisfy its ideal objectives of continuity (preventing stock-out) and fluidity (limiting overcapacity), logistics has progressively left behind its original operational role, which was a combination of transport, handling and warehousing operations. The concept of a logistics chain, which is today called a 'supply chain', enables firms to control flow from downstream to upstream and to optimize, in terms of cost and level of service, the whole physical movement pulled by demand that launches the operational processes mentioned in Figures 6.1 and 6.2. The field of logistics has, therefore, been considerably broadening, as illustrated in Figure 6.2, and logistics has become one of the most significant driving forces for organizational change.

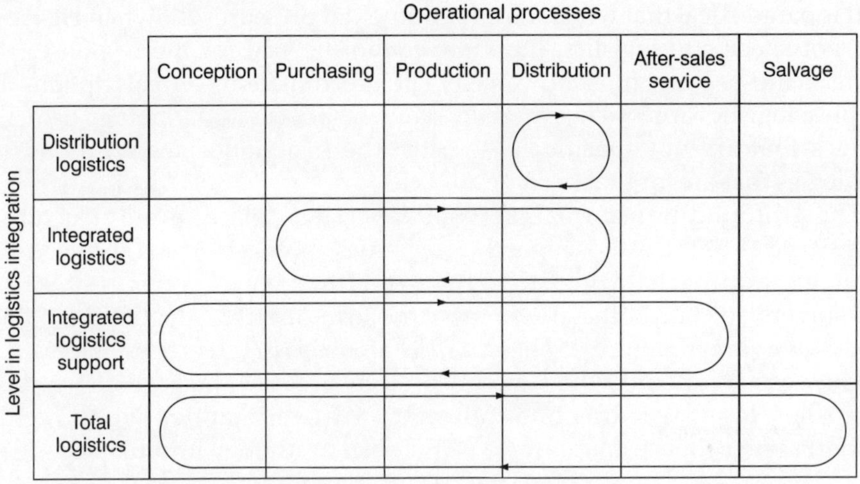

Operational processes

	Conception	Purchasing	Production	Distribution	After-sales service	Salvage
Distribution logistics						
Integrated logistics						
Integrated logistics support						
Total logistics						

Level in logistics integration

Figure 6.2　Evolution of the field of action of logistics

The process-oriented perspective of logistics management, which cuts across the traditional vertical functions of the organization, has been a powerful stimulator for change. This movement participated in a global trend called process-based management (Davenport and Short, 1990; Hammer, 1990) that was in line with other ideas such as lean management (Womack, Jones and Roos, 1990) and time-based competition (Stalk and Hout, 1990). In line with the re-engineering perspective, firms considered in the middle of the 1990s that most processes had to be completely redesigned, thinking differently about the design/manufacturing/distribution/after-sales service/recycling process, with a complete redefinition of partners' role as well as a reconfiguration of information systems. For many companies, in many sectors, the logistics process became a key process, and logistics a strategic capability (Stalk, Evans and Shulman, 1992). Logistics was not only a tool for the global strategy of a company, but also the source of innovative logistics strategies.

Logistics has now become a very far-reaching 'total' approach, which is both transversal and very ambitious, and where skills are applied at the interfaces between the various operational processes (see Figure 6.2). Its main role is to synchronize overall physical flow, and it is indeed in permanent interaction with all of the classic functions of a firm, constituting an active interface between the firm and its environment. In fact, the aim of logistics and supply chain management is to optimize the three flows involved in supply chains: 'the flow of goods from sources to end-consumers, the flow of funds to satisfy the market needs at minimum costs, the flow of information to respond to customer requirements efficiently and effectively' (European Commission, 1999:10).

It is paradoxical that while the environmental pressures shown in Figure 6.1 are not specific to logistics, the same cannot be said for the responses that firms in most sectors must now make. Their formulation conceals options that imply a logistics approach, especially when responses are combined. For challenges that are not specifically logistic, the firm conceives solutions and strategies that are, or that become, logistic.

The profound transformations that have taken place in the structure of firms, as well as the extension of their activities, have confirmed the need for a strategic approach to logistics. Its aim is to give a better response to consumers, to control the areas where the firm operates, the timing of these operations, and finally, the inherent risks involved in the firm's choices.

How can we identify the strategic projects in which logistics could play a key role? To answer this question in a 'creative' manner, we thought it important to propose an innovative approach to strategy formulation.

A CONCEPTUAL APPROACH TO FORMULATING LOGISTICS STRATEGY

From logistics strategy to strategic logistics

The classic approach to formulating a logistics strategy consists in beginning with the firm's overall strategy and then defining the logistics strategy that will enable the firm to reach its objectives. Logistics is thus conceived as a functional support system and a tool for global strategy; logistics strategy should appear as a subset of the overall strategy. The control of the flow of materials and goods all along the supply chain today constitutes a key factor for success in numerous domains, which justifies this downward approach.

Logistics, like other functions such as marketing and informatics, also opens new strategic lines of action. To formulate these new lines, it is imperative to reverse the classic approach, to think strategic logistics rather than logistics strategy.

Strategic logistics consists of imagining and developing strategic actions that would be impossible without strong logistics competence. From being seen first a key factor for success, logistics is becoming a fully competitive advantage, and is even a means to change the rules of the strategic game for an industry, or to adopt new-game strategies (as suggested by Buaron, 1981). This viewpoint makes it necessary to think about logistics at the very moment when the overall strategy is being elaborated, and to foresee how, in certain cases, it can be the very foundation of the strategic action.

The two interrelated perspectives between logistics and strategy shown in Figure 6.3 lead to very different formulations, and to company projects that are also very different. It should be noted that they do not exclude each other,

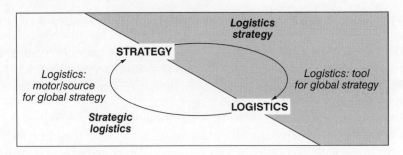

Figure 6.3   From logistics strategy to strategic logistics

but correspond to distinct finalities. The principal differences are summarized in Table 6.1.

The determining factor for 'reversing' the perspectives would seem to be the maturity of the perception of logistics as a cross-functional and deliberately open-ended management domain in the firm, and as a proactive interface with external partners of the supply chain through a cross-organizational approach. Thus, the interactive loop between strategy and logistics is generally initiated by a request from strategy to logistics, historically centred on the control (reduction) of logistics costs.

The experience, know-how and systems developed in logistics action then retro-act on the strategy, becoming the vector of its (re)formulation, enabling the firm to differentiate itself by logistics services, or even diversify in logistics activities. This also increases the flexibility and agility of companies that are able to reconstruct their network at any time when necessary within an SCM (supply chain management) process.

Finally, strategic logistics formulations emerge from this repeated traversing of the interactive strategy/logistics loop, which becomes a 'progress spiral' (Martinet, 1983) for the firm. The purpose of running through this loop is to have a logistics organization that is adapted to the firm's objectives, and to be able to identify, exploit, or even better, create opportunities for the firm. This loop also permits a learning process in both strategic and logistics domains. In particular, it reinforces the development of strategic logistics competencies that are necessary for strategic logistics.

Table 6.1   Main differences between logistics strategy and strategic logistics

	Logistics strategy	Strategic logistics
Perception of logistics stakes	Strategy support	Strategy foundation
Effects on organization	Improvement, evolution	Change, transmutation

Logistics competence: a strategic resource

Logistics depends on three interrelated dimensions of competence: action, expertise and knowledge (Fabbe-Costes, 1997). Figure 6.4 illustrates the inter-relationship between the three dimensions of competence. An upward arrow signifies a demand from a lower dimension, while a downward arrow represents the effect of higher-level knowledge on expertise and, in turn, operating procedures and processes.

Action relates to the way in which logistics processes are actually performed. Expertise relates to all the resources directly associated with the action, including methods, procedures, organizational routines, technologies and engineering. They strongly influence the quality, efficiency, durability and reliability of the logistics process, and are a major source of competitive advantage.

Knowledge represents the highest level of abstraction in logistics management. It is high-level information that must be collected and assimilated in the course of formulating strategy. It also incorporates the experience of senior managers and the general management culture of the business. Knowledge is a key factor for survival, evolution and adaptation; it compels us to invest in high-level management skills and in research and development, and to try to convert everything that is experienced and perceived by people in the company and in the logistics network into knowledge. Intrinsic to the development of logistics competence is information

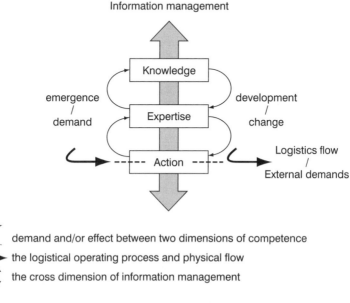

Figure 6.4 Interrelationship between the three dimensions of competence

management. The need for effective collection, communication and processing of information exists on each level. The information collected, created and memorized at each tier enriches the strategic decision making and can motivate new strategic formulations.

Towards logistics strategy formulation

The strategic formulation of logistics can be expressed by three 'classic' concepts of strategy: the profession, the mission and the objectives. In concrete terms, to formulate a logistics strategy, one defines:

- the ranges of movement that it 'produces', and how it produces them (technologies, know-how, organization);
- to whom they are directed (internal or external clients) and the needs that they satisfy;
- the kind of performance it aimed at and the targeted level of that performance.

Consequently, this formulation can identify several 'sectors of logistics activity' or 'logistics business units' that are more or less synergistic. Among them, some can be considered as supports for the firm's overall strategy (logistics strategy perspective), while other sectors can be vectors of its strategy (strategic logistics perspective).

Formulation is then oriented to the choice of organizational solution to adopt in order to reach defined objectives. It should be noted that as a function of coordination for all stages of movement and for the management of both internal and external interfaces, logistics can only be efficient if internally it is linked with the other functions – rather than replacing them – and if externally it coordinates with the other companies of the supply chain. The options chosen in the domain of logistics must, in particular, be congruent with those in the domains of marketing, finance, information systems, manufacturing and human resources. Ideally, logistics strategy should be combined with the other strategies, and strategic logistics should use the levers that other functional domains represent.

At present, information system management is certainly the domain that has the strongest synergy with logistics. The coincidence of the emergence of strategic logistics and strategic informatics is certainly not accidental. It can be explained by the overlapping of physical and informational circulation (the piloting and monitoring concept), to which we could associate financial circulation. It could also be explained by the structure and development of logistics and information communication systems, as well as by the dynamic character of the management processes that they support. In addition, the control and traceability of physical and informational flow develops, and is the support for, a firm's flexibility and adaptability, which are now indispensable for its durability and growth. Information and communication systems supported by 'new technologies' become a cornerstone of logistics management, and each firm looks for a better integration of information systems (Fabbe-Costes, 2002). Most companies try to develop interorganizational information systems (IOS) 'supporting cooperative, intraorganizational and interorganizational, functional teams' (Konsynski, 1993) to win the ongoing time-based competition.

The formulation of logistics strategy also deals with the 'make or buy' decision. The decision to subcontract or, on the contrary, to (re)integrate logistics activities is in any event contingent on several factors. First, it depends on the situation of the logistics supply industry at the time when the issue arises. It also depends on the shipper's perception of the relative risks and benefits of the two options. Moreover, this dilemma usually only arises when a shipper is conducting a strategic review of its logistical system. Discussions with European shippers have revealed that some logistics operations are more likely to be kept in-house or reintegrated than others (Fabbe-Costes and Colin, 1995). Shippers only envisage keeping in-house or reintegrating operations:

- that directly concern customer services (the more an operation affects the shipper's customer, the more it is seen to be sensitive), confirming that logistics has become a strategic marketing element for many manufacturing and retailing companies;
- that require the handling of information thought to be 'strategic' (usually pertaining to customers and/or cost structure);
- considered to be 'critical' in the shipper's logistics process (ie in terms of their service and/or logistics costs), or, more precisely, operations in which security is more important than flexibility;
- that do not require a large amount of new investment, particularly those for which physical or information systems have already been set up within the company;
- that offer a rapid rate of return on investment in logistics assets;
- that require highly specific investment and which logistics service providers, especially those providing mainly shared-user services, find difficult to run profitably;
- that do not require staff with a different culture than that already prevalent in the company;
- that require highly specific skills, not available from a logistics supplier.

The strategic or non-strategic character of a logistics organization provides information on the originality and confidentiality required for the necessary know-how, the expected reliability of the processes, and the significance of the planned organization. In the case of delegated operations or organizations, it brings about the definition of the means required to ensure control. It therefore creates networks of complementary skills and ensures their consistency.

It is not our intention, at this point, to go into existing organizations in detail. However, we do wish to illustrate, through examples of logistics projects, how firms have taken the strategic dimension of logistics into account.

ILLUSTRATED TYPOLOGY OF POSSIBLE LOGISTICS STRATEGIES

To specify and illustrate the conceptual approach to the strategic formulation of logistics, we have selected several case studies of distributors, manufacturers and genuine 'logistics firms', also called logistics service providers or third-party logistics operators. They represent a variety of strategies and are dealt with by category. Our typology, presented in Table 6.2, contains six 'classic' generic strategic axes, and considers strategic formulations by adopting both perspectives described in Figure 6.3. The generic axes are in line with those proposed by Ansoff (1965), Porter (1985) and some others. Wiseman (1985) has discussed these points with respect to formulating an informatics strategy formulation.

Table 6.2 Typology of logistic strategies and strategic logistics

Generic axes	Logistics strategy	Strategic logistics
Cost domination	Reduce logistics costs	Reduce overall costs with logistics
Differentiation	Quality of logistics service	Logistics factor of differentiation
Innovation	Logistics support for innovation	Logistics as a source/ motor for innovation
Alliance	Logistics as a means of alliance	Logistics as a source/motor for alliance
Profession expansion	Logistics as a support for integration	Logistics as a new product
Mission expansion	Logistics as a support for extension	Logistics in order to win new clients
Diversification	Use of logistics synergies	Diversifying through or in logistics

Certain axes correspond to actions conceived (at least initially) without changing the domain of activity (cost domination and differentiation), or imagined in order to move to new domains of activity (expansion and diversification), with alliance and innovation, a priori, allowing for both.

Cost domination

Logistics strategy: reduce costs that are specific to logistics

Becton-Dickinson, a multinational firm in the medical sector, has centralized its stock in a single European site in order to reduce its inventory level and at the same time the financial costs of immobilized capital.

To limit the costs of stock possession, **Bull** distributed its stock of spare parts in a hierarchic network with local, national and European warehouses.

Carrefour, a French hypermarket chain, gave up systematically supplying its outlet network directly from suppliers' warehouses. To reduce the costs of the supply chain, deliveries to retailing stores are made by cross-docking from facilities operated by logistics suppliers. Carrefour also decided to rid its 215 French hypermarkets of clothes, garments and shoes inventories, replacing them by a single stock. This stock is located in a 220,000 square metre warehouse operated by a logistics provider. Each outlet's inventory has decreased from some weeks or months of sales to few days: each outlet has daily deliveries (one outlet = one truck) from the warehouse. Thus the range of products in each hypermarket is directly linked to 'local' weather and fashion trends.

Strategic logistics: through logistics, reduce overall costs

Auchan, a French hypermarket chain, has a network of warehouses, permitting it to considerably reduce purchasing costs through the company's ability to stock massive quantities that it imports or buys on promotion from its suppliers.

Casino, a huge French retailer, does not now process any inventories of ultra-fresh products. On D-day at noon, the stores send their orders to the central informatics system. After consolidation, the orders are transmitted at 2 pm to the provider Yoplait. Then Yoplait delivers on D-day + 1 at 5 am to Casino's local warehouses, which are in fact cross-docking locations: they sort the goods for delivery to the stores at 4 pm on D-day + 1.

Carrefour has also developed such a continuous replenishment programme with some of its suppliers. With Lever, one of those suppliers, Carrefour's inventories decreased from 27 days in October 1997 to 7 days in December 1997.

In the automobile industry, logistics approaches to external flow control, by reducing the number of suppliers, have succeeded in diminishing supply costs. **Renault** now has about 150 'optima' suppliers who are registered (with stricter certification than ISO norms) to deliver just-in-time. Qualitative and quantitative controls on delivery are to be totally eliminated.

Differentiation

Logistics strategy: improve the quality of the logistics service

By rationalizing their logistics, **Becton-Dickinson, Bull, Xerox** and, more recently, **Hewlett Packard** were able to improve their performance in terms of quality of service, availability of references, complete deliveries, guaranteed delivery times and their ability to customize products.

Philips-Eclairage has a highly automated central warehouse in the Paris area that is controlled by computerized logistics, making it possible to deliver to its clients every day. Thus wholesalers no longer need to hold more stock than is needed in between deliveries: they choose to be preferentially supplied by Philips.

Radiall, a supplier of cables and connectors for many industries (telecommunications, train, spatial, informatics, etc), had a problem with some strategic customers: the service was not efficient enough for them. To 'survive' in a very competitive industry, Radiall decided to differentiate its logistics process to give an appropriate response to its strategic customers. Now Radiall runs two logistics processes, and offers a high-standard quality service to its strategic clients.

Strategic logistics: permit an increased differentiation

PSA and **Renault**, like many car makers, have developed a just-in-time logistics that permits them to feed very flexible production lines that are capable of assembling vehicles that conform exactly to client specifications, with synchronized and single deliveries. The Renault Clio, for instance, can be delivered with the following options: air conditioning, power steering, 80 different motors, 20 different gearboxes, five different bodies: a total of 32,000 theoretical combinations, without taking into account the range of paintwork and other options. In 2001 PSA sold 3.1 million cars, representing 2.1 million different 'references', a reference being a model of a certain car that is assembled in a factory according to the options required by the end-customer.

Since November 1994, the integrator **Federal Express** has been offering its customers a tracking/tracing service. Shippers can know the location of their parcels upon request to the Web site Cosmos (http://www.fedex.com) with the parcel's bar code. Between the beginning and the middle of 1997, the number of requests increased tremendously, reaching 10,000 per day in 1998.

Because **Hewlett Packard** has strong logistics competencies, it could survive and develop in the competitive European PC industry. It completely restructured its logistics processes, and can provide customers with a multi-channel distribution system with different levels of logistics service and product customization. It succeeds in operating with low stocks a multiple business model network (called 'channel assembly', 'top value', 'direct express').

Innovation (not only technological but also organizational innovation)

Logistics strategy: logistics as a support for innovation, logistics innovation

La Redoute, a French mail-order firm, promises its customers a two-day delivery service, which has enlarged its market. This commercial innovation, which has since been copied by competitors, depends on a very strong integration of physical and information flows, and on the automation of the sorting centre created for the company by the French postal service.

To exchange logistics information with its suppliers (suppliers' shipment notification, etc), the European automobile sector has set up an electronic data interchange (EDI) (Galia/Odette) network, which is a genuine support for the just-in-time model of production planning. Thanks to EDI, the different actors of the automotive industry (car manufacturers, suppliers, logistics providers) share information related to the whole design–planning–production and delivery process, and can dynamically monitor the supply chain.

To recapture a share of the refrigerated goods market, the **SNCF** (French National Railways) operates an overnight service between the south of France and Paris with refrigerated wagons. These trains are very fast (160 kph). They are loaded in the early evening and arrive at the Rungis wholesale market outside Paris at dawn.

Providing any American customer with a highly customized trousers in 48 hours was the innovation foreseen by **Levi's USA**. To reach its objective, it based this new service on an Internet ordering Web site where customers can design their own product, linked in to a flexible and computerized cutting and assembly service that produces every unit upon request, and alliance with an express parcel operator. The design of the overall supply chain, including the management of stocks (for fabrics and accessories), and the close link between physical and information flows, with new technologies, were necessary to succeed.

Strategic logistics: logistics as a source or motor for innovation

The **IBM** factory in Montpellier, which manufactured the large ES/9000 systems, had linked some of its suppliers to an EDI network. A workstation could therefore make a direct request to a supplier, who then had 48 hours to deliver (15 per cent of factory orders were sent by this system). IBM was able to reduce the duration of production cycles by 70 per cent (better reactivity), reduce costs, and take full advantage of the technological innovations proposed by its suppliers, without being penalized by the obligation to use parts that were still in stock but already obsolete. By the same token, IBM could produce tailor-made products for its customers.

Most assembly manufacturers (eg in the electronic equipment industries) use their logistics competencies, joined to powerful inter-organizational information systems, to develop a postponement approach (to differentiate products as late as possible in the supply chain) and to minimize stocks with VMI. Being pulled by demand, they are more likely to imagine product innovations able to satisfy customers.

As a main organizational and logistics innovation, ECR (efficient or effective consumer response) is now being jointly developed by the industrial and retailer partners of the same supply chain. It enables the two partners to save as much as 5 per cent of the value of the goods. The systematic sharing of the logistics information concerning the accurate daily turnover of the retailer contributes to reducing the average inventories of each partner's warehouses. It appears much more profitable than a confrontation that produces many inventories (speculative and bought-in-advance inventories). This new way of piloting flow contributes to driving the two partners to enhance their co-operation, far beyond the field of logistics.

Alliance

Logistics strategy: logistics as a means of alliance

By negotiating a 'logistics charter' with its suppliers, the **PSA** automobile group seeks to stabilize and perpetuate its client–supplier relationships. This logistics charter identifies the rights and duties of suppliers in terms of delivery requirements transmitted by PSA factories. Members of this network become very interdependent, to the point that in certain cases the car maker transfers its skills to the suppliers (conception of new parts, quality control at the source etc). Some suppliers are no longer 'part suppliers' but have become 'function suppliers' (for example, tightness supplier as opposed to rubber joint supplier).

Logistics is a powerful factor of integration of the **Renault** and **Nissan** organizations (the alliance was signed in 1999). Many logistics synergies (related to supply, cross-manufacturing and international transport, as well as to best practice exchanges) reinforce the alliance between the two companies.

Strategic logistics: logistics as a source/motor for alliance

By developing its own powerful centralized logistics system, dedicated to the stores operated by 'independent' members, the French distribution group **Intermarché** has placed them in a position of total dependence upon the group.

In order to set up in France, **UPS** (United Parcel Service) chose to buy Prost, a French parcel service that has developed very innovative technical solutions for both transport and parcel tracking.

A branch of the **GEODIS Group** designs and operates advanced warehouses, and specializes in the synchronized delivery of parts to factories on a just-in-time basis. It is associated with transport partners (inside and outside the GEODIS Group), in order to respond to all invitations to tender made by automobile and aeronautical manufacturers.

Because **Danone** chose to keep in-house its regional warehouses for ultra-fresh products and to develop expertise in fresh daily deliveries with EDI, it is able to offer a highly integrated service to potential industrial partners (excluding direct competitors) who want to enlarge their range of products by adding ultra-fresh ones. Danone can produce and/or deliver products for its partners (such as **Amora** for fresh sauces, or **Coca-Cola** for Minute Maid Premium), who concentrate on design, marketing and sales, but control product flow thanks to information.

Expansion by profession

Logistics strategy: logistics as a support for integration

Integrators, former messenger services (urgent letters), have become express delivery services by integrating various activities: air transport, sorting, pre- and post-routing, all of which is coordinated and followed up by a very powerful communication and information system.

Andre, a French shoe distributor (a chain of both urban shops and specialized supermarkets), strengthened by its logistics organization, has taken over some ready-to-wear clothing chains (Kookai, Caroll, Creeks).

Strategic logistics: logistics as a new product

The integrators (**FedEx, DHL,** etc) are developing a service in the management of prepositioned spare parts and/or high-value items, close to their continental hubs. Thus they are able to deliver their customers' goods at a continental level very quickly: orders filled late in the evening can be delivered early the next morning.

For **Otis, DEC, Dassault, Eurocopter** and others, after-sales logistics has now become a product that is a source of revenue, and sometimes of profits superior to those made when the products were originally sold.

Expansion by mission

Logistics strategy: logistics as a support for extension

SKF, AVENTIS, IBM and other firms can only ensure their international-ization by entrusting European subsidiaries with specialized factories, and by including them in a complex logistics network composed of central and national warehouses that are in constant contact.

In the same manner, it has taken a powerful logistics system to enable **Renault** to coordinate its two complementary factories in Douai (France) and Valladolid (Spain).

To succeed in its global strategy and to favour the international distribution of the many products of its group, **Danone** built an international information system, with EDI links between commercial subsidiaries spread all around the world and logistics units of the industrial subsidiaries that provide the required products when and where necessary.

Strategic logistics: logistics in order to win new clients/customers

Continent, a French hypermarket chain which now belongs to the Carrefour Group, supplies its new Greek stores in Salonika and Athens with the same logistics tool it uses for its stores in the south of France.

The organization of the **Philips-Eclairage** central warehouse in France enables it to serve such European neighbours as Luxemburg, Italy and Spain.

Informatics printer manufacturers, who profit more from selling consumables than the machines themselves, are encouraged to collect the empty ink cartridges to avoid competition from companies that specialize in refilling them. It seems they are quickly developing strong alliances with third-party logistics outfits specialized in gathering scrap and salvaging end-life items.

Thanks to its logistics differentiation, **Radiall** can develop rapidly in the car industry it has defined as a new 'strategic' client.

Diversification

Logistics strategy: the use of logistics synergies

Numerous road haulage firms, in all European countries, have become specialized logistics suppliers for special traffic or goods that present homogeneous logistics characteristics: **TFE** (Transport Frigorifiques Européens) for fresh products; **Salvesen** for frozen products; **Ducros** (France) and **UPS** (Germany) for deliveries in dense urban zones; **HAYS, ND-Logistics** and **Excel** (United Kingdom) for supplying large distribution chains.

Automobile makers, with their great capacity (commercial and logistic) to mobilize the resources (industrial and technological) of their suppliers, are becoming vehicle designers (imagining more attractive combinations of components for the client) and assemblers (by just-in-time converging of everything necessary to assemble the vehicle ordered by each customer).

Strategic logistics: diversifying through or in logistics

By exploiting its automated warehouse, **Philips-Eclairage** diversified into the creation of a parcel service that allowed it to deliver to all its clients, large and small, everywhere in France and every day, to the point where it now sells more logistics services than electrical equipment. The company has started to deliver articles made by other manufacturers, provided that they are not in direct competition with its own products.

We can consider that **Danone**, with its delivery service for fresh products in France, is in the same situation.

Telemarket, a subsidiary of the Monoprix–Galeries Lafayette distribution group, offers a home delivery service by appointment to its customers who order by phone, Minitel (the French videotex system) or over its Internet Web shop. These customers are obviously different from those who shop in the Monoprix stores in city centres.

STRATEGIC ACTION ITINERARIES IN LOGISTICS

The above examples provide evidence that, on the one hand, firms do not centre their strategy on logistics alone (informatics and marketing, in particular, are always implicitly if not explicitly associated), while on the other hand, they do not strictly aim for a single result (differentiation, for example). The generic strategies mentioned and separately illustrated (for convenience) in the previous section are not only dependent, but are also more generally combined. Hence, three strategic action 'itineraries' can be detected:

- The firm aims at a privileged axis and obtains other advantages from 'spin-offs'. The firm subsequently discovers that other strategies are possible thanks to the first strategic move. The resulting itinerary is an emergent one, which was not foreseen.
- The firm deliberately aims at several axes that may be spread out in time but are conceived as being interdependent. The resulting itinerary is a deliberate one that was designed from the first strategic move.
- Once the firm has aimed at one or several strategic axes and has built a new logistics system, it discovers that it can 'rebound', and from that point on build a new strategy that aims at new axes. In this case, the firm designs its strategic itinerary in process (*in itinere*) (Avenier, 1997), combining emergent and deliberate moves. This kind of itinerary demands a special attention to the learning processes and a strategic mobility of the whole company as well as of its partners.

For each of these itineraries, which can, of course, be linked by firms, we present a figure setting out the various options, followed by several examples. In order to simplify the presentation, we have used the abbreviations lS (logistics Strategy) and sL (strategic Logistics) to identify the perspective adopted by the firm.

The possible spin-offs from a strategic move (see Figure 6.5)

Andre, by expanding through professions (lS) – which were in large part founded on logistics and commercial abilities – will probably endeavour to find logistics synergies in its distribution networks in order to reinforce its cost domination (lS).

Tracking and tracing services – a logistics innovation (lS), developed by a growing number of express delivery services – at first constituted a differentiation approach (sL) from competitors (attempting to obtain a modern image,

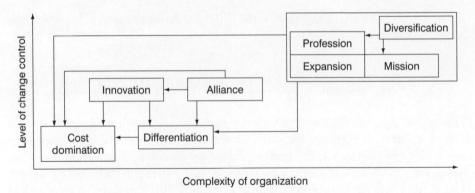

Figure 6.5   Possible spin-offs from a strategic move

without great value in terms of exploitation). By making transfers more reliable (increased control of risks), such technologies make it possible to reduce the level of the consignee's inventory and therefore its costs (sL), while at the same time reducing production cycles (as in the case of IBM). The most dynamic express delivery services now integrate such technologies into their commercial approach, and thus rebound by expanding their mission (sL).

It should be noted that spin-offs are always in the direction of decreasing organizational complexity and towards a lower level of change. Because spin-offs are not foreseen, they are not 'automatic' and, in any case, are of less intensity than when strategic moves are deliberately played in a combined manner. To succeed in such an opportunistic approach, firms need to develop their vigilance and reactivity to catch any opportunity induced from the first strategic move.

Combination of articulated strategic moves (see Figure 6.6)

In distribution, the intention of a firm to equip itself with its own and/or subcontracted logistics corresponds to a combination of deliberate logistics moves: reduction of direct logistics costs (lS) (Carrefour) and overall supply costs (sL) (Auchan and Intermarché); the will to differentiate (Auchan, with its broad range of food products, approximately twice that of Carrefour); the desire to make alliances (sL) (Intermarché) or to permit geographic expansion (sL) (Continent), or even in certain circumstances to open to diversification (sL) (Telemarket). Monoprix-Telemarket is an example of a firm that has more or less implemented all these strategic dimensions, and others will follow the same path.

The development of continuous replenishment programmes shared by manufacturers and retailers (Casino and Yoplait, Carrefour and Lever, etc) and the development of ECR are also combinations of cost domination (sL),

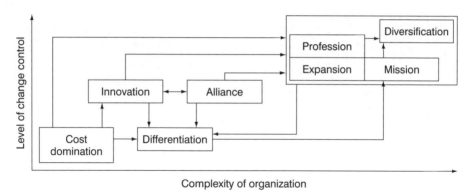

Figure 6.6   Possible combination of articulated strategic moves

innovation (sL), in particular in the domain of information management, and vertical alliance (sL).

Integrators, with their knowledge of complementarities and alliances (sL) (UPS), have sought to integrate mobilized means (lS). Certain firms, such as DHL and TNT, offer their networks to dispatch parts between industrial sites working with the just-in-time system. This corresponds to a strategy of diversification (sL) from their original trade.

For companies such as Xerox and Hewlett Packard, differentiation (lS) is always combined with a powerful cost reduction objective (lS) that was generally the first step of the combined itinerary.

The HP logistics strategy for PCs (sL) is efficient because HP accepted the 'channel assembly' business model to transfer part of the assembly activity to selected resellers, to respect the available-to-promise objective (lS).

Levi's' express customized service was a combination of innovation (lS) in both the offer and the process, differentiation (sL) through the service, and expansion by mission (sL).

This level of strategic maturity is not yet very widespread, which explains the most frequent situation where the firm rebounds by making in-process discoveries of new means of action, taking in account what it has learnt during the strategic process.

Rebounding with new strategic moves (see Figure 6.7)

With a major investment of several hundred million francs (lS) in an automated distribution warehouse, Philips-Eclairage initially sought to differentiate itself from its competitors (lS). With its acquired experience, it then took over the distribution of materials complementary to or different from its range and made by other manufacturers. Can it be said that this diversification (sL) has transformed Philips-Eclairage into a logistics distribution firm?

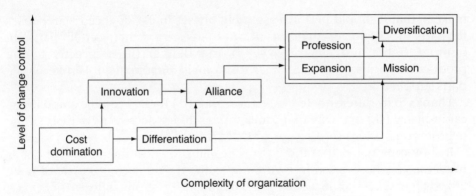

Figure 6.7 Rebounding with new strategic moves

Where are the margins: through the sale of products or the sale of logistics services? Note that a second rebound has led the firm to geographic expansion (sL) by delivering to customers in regions beyond France.

When Danone decided to keep its distribution logistics in-house, it was to differentiate from competitors (lS) through a first-class service provided to retailers. These means and expertise stimulated interest from other 'first-class' manufacturers that wanted to enlarge their range of products but did not have the expertise in fresh products. Logistics became the vector of horizontal alliances for Danone (sL).

The automobile industry (PSA, Renault, etc) has operated a very complex combination of logistics approaches of overall cost reduction through logistics (sL), differentiation (sL), and innovation in logistics EDI (lS), which operates through alliances with logistics suppliers and parts suppliers (sL) and expansion by internationalization (lS). On the strategic level, starting with logistics synergies (lS), a diversification phase can lead the firm to make a radical change in paradigm. With their strong logistics skills, the car makers are becoming conceivers and assemblers, able to offer either very differentiated ranges of cars (such as the Renault Clio), or, on the contrary, very standardized vehicles (such as the Renault Twingo). When this very original car was launched, it was only available in 32 combinations (options: air conditioning, sunroof, eight body/seat colours); and the time from conception to industrialization of the Renault Twingo was only 33 months, for an investment of only 3.7 billion francs. In our opinion, this constitutes a strategic logistics (sL) diversification that essentially depends both on the perfect control of logistics processes and on communication and information systems.

The logistics supplier GEODIS developed know-how for advanced warehouses and just-in-time synchronized industrial deliveries by following first an innovation approach (lS) and then alliances founded on logistics (sL). It is now rebounding on diversification (sL) by proposing to its customers (car makers) that it should perform assembly phases in its advanced warehouses for parts that it already manages. It can therefore assemble certain parts (eg bumper, lights and electric system) and deliver them directly to the production lines as required. Since it is a logistics supplier, it can become a parts supplier.

Thanks to its differentiated logistics service (lS) Radiall could expand in the car industry (sL) in a way that can compensate for decreasing activity of the telecommunications sector.

It should be noted that the possibilities illustrated in Figure 6.7 are not as numerous as those given in Figure 6.6, as the moves are not intended to be linked together. It should also be noted that there is a strong difference between this kind of itinerary and the first one illustrated by Figure 6.5. Here, firms capitalize on the experience acquired when 'acting' their first move, and reformulate their strategy exploiting the new competence. This explains why the first kind of itinerary (Figure 6.5) goes from 'complex' strategies to 'simple' ones, and the third one (Figure 6.7) gives the opportunity for increasing complexity.

CONCLUSIONS

In the end, the formulation of logistics strategies is almost always extremely complex. First, considering the relationship between logistics and strategy, it is the result of the interaction between two types of approach: reactive (logistics strategy, lS) and active (strategic logistics, sL). Second, it strongly overlaps strategies formulated by other vital functions in the firm. Third, it is expressed by simple or multiple strategic moves. The way firms build strategic itineraries is another factor explaining the variety of logistics strategies: firms can either combine deliberately strategic moves, or change a process to suggest new actions, or finally take advantage of spin-offs that were unexpected. There can therefore be no a priori rules for the formulation of logistics strategies.

The analysis grids proposed in this chapter show this complexity, and seem to us to be good tools for the formulation of strategies, supported by or founded on logistics, that can develop on several levels. From this point of view, can it not be said that logistics now constitutes a privileged area in strategic management? At least, logistics according to us offers new ways of thinking about strategy; because it motivates and supports organizational changes, it also offers new frames for piloting managerial action in a strategic perspective. That is why logistics is now an important strategic issue.

SUMMARY

- Firms formulate their strategies in response to intense environmental pressures.

- Logistics is an essential element of that strategy.
- The field of logistics has become progressively broader and is now very far-reaching.
- A trend from the perspective of logistics strategy to that of strategic logistics is apparent, representing a source of competitive advantages and/or new strategies.
- A variety of 'classic' generic strategic axes and formulations can be identified.
- Formulation of logistics strategies must also take into account the way of linking strategic moves, the so-called itineraries.

REFERENCES

Ansoff, I (1965) *Corporate Strategy*, McGraw-Hill, New York

Avenier, M J (ed) (1997) *La stratégie 'chemin faisant'*, Economica, Paris.

Buaron, R (1981) New-game strategies, *McKinsey Quarterly* (Spring), pp 24–40

Davenport, T and Short, J (1990) The new industrial engineering: information technology and business process redesign, *Sloan Management Review*, **31** (4) (Summer), pp 11–27

Ellram, L M (1991) Supply chain management: the industrial organisation perspective, *International Journal of Physical Distribution and Logistics Management*,**21** (1), pp13–22

European Commission (1999) *Transport and Logistics in Europe*, European Commission and PricewaterhouseCoopers, Belgium

Fabbe-Costes, N (1997) Information management in the logistics service industry: a strategic response to the reintegration of logistical activities, *Transport Logistics*, **1** (2), pp 115–27

Fabbe-Costes, N (2002) Le pilotage des supply chains: un défi pour les systèmes d'information et de communication logistiques, *Gestion 2000* (Jan–Fév), pp 75–92

Fabbe-Costes, N and Colin, J (1995) Strategies developed by logistics suppliers facing the temptation for shippers to reintegrate logistics operations, *7th World Conference on Transport Research, 16–21 July 1995*, Sydney, Australia

Hammer, M (1990) Reengineering work: don't automate, obliterate, *Harvard Business Review*, **68** (4) (Jul–Aug), pp 104–12

Konsynski, B R (1993) Strategic control in the extended enterprise, *IBM Systems Journal*, **32** (1), pp 111–42

Martinet, A C (1983) *Stratégie*, Vuibert Gestion, Paris

Mathe, H, Colin, J and Tixier, D (1983) *La Logistique*, Dunod, Paris (in press)

Morin, E (1990) *Science avec Conscience*, 2nd edn, Le Seuil-Points, Paris

Porter, M (1985) *Competitive Advantage*, Free Press/Macmillan, New York

Stalk, G and Hout, T (1990) *Competing Against Time: How time-based competition is reshaping global markets*, Free Press, New York

Stalk, G, Evans, P and Shulman, L (1992) Competing on capabilities: the new rules of corporate strategy, *Harvard Business Review* (Mar–Apr), pp 57–69
Wiseman, C (1985) *Strategy and Computers*, Dow Jones-Irwin, New York
Womack, J, Jones, D and Roos, D (1990) *The Machine that Changed the World*, Harper Perennial, New York

FURTHER READING

Ansoff, I (1979) *Strategic Management*, Macmillan, London
Aurifeille, J M, Colin, J, Fabbe-Costes, N, Jaffeux, C and Paché, G (1997) *Management logistique: une approche transversale*, éditions Management société, Paris
Bechtel, C and Jayaram, J (1997) Supply chain management: a strategic perspective, *International Journal of Logistics Management*, **8** (1), pp 15–34
Chandler, A D (1962) *Strategy and Structure*, MIT Press, Cambridge, MA
Colin, J and Paché, G (2001) Period changes and inventory management: the three ages of retail logistics, *Supply Chain Forum*,2 (2), pp 58–67
Cooper, M C, Lambert, D M and Pagh, J D (1997) Supply chain management: more than a new name for logistics, *International Journal of Logistics Management*, **8** (1), pp 1–13
Croom, S, Romano, P and Giannakis, M (2000) Supply chain management: an analytical framework for critical literature review', *European Journal of Purchasing and Supply Chain Management*, **6** (1), pp 67–83
Fabbe-Costes, N, Colin, J and Paché, G (2000) *Faire de la recherche en logistique et distribution?*, Vuibert, Coll FNEGE, Paris
Larson, P D and Dale, S R (1998), Supply chain management: definition, growth and approaches, *Journal of Marketing Theory and Practice*, **6** (4), pp 1–5
Prahalad, C K and Hamel, G (eds) (1994) Strategy: search for new paradigms, *Strategic Management Journal*, **15** (Special Issue, Summer)

7

Thinking strategically about supply chain relationships management: the issue of incentives

Glyn Watson, Andrew Cox, Chris Lonsdale and Joe Sanderson
University of Birmingham

The study of supply chain management is the study of incentives. Supply chain managers and their vendors are competitors as well as collaborators. The mutual gains from trade bring the parties together in the first place. Additional benefits accruing from closer collaboration can keep them working together thereafter. However, the value generated from the exchange process must be distributed, and this is what makes buyers and sellers competitors as well as collaborators. Consequently, the function of supply chain managers is to ensure that the interaction between the buying and the selling organization generates as much added value as possible, but that the added value passes to their organization, rather than being retained within the organization of the vendor. In order to achieve this, the supply manager must be skilled at crafting incentive structures that will modify the behaviour of the vendor in ways that are consistent with the interests of the buying organization. It is for this reason that the study of supply chain management is the study of incentives.

This chapter is divided into three sections. Section one deals with the incentive issue itself by establishing its central importance to supply managers. Section two deals with outsourcing. Under certain circumstances it will be impossible for the supply manager to incentivize the vendor. Having such activities outside the boundary of the organization, therefore, not only threatens to inflate the costs of the buyer but may also undermine the firm's revenue streams. Knowing where to draw the boundary of the firm is integral to the development of supply chain competence. Once the boundary has been drawn the supplier has to be managed effectively. Supplier management is the subject of the third and final section. Here it is suggested that effective supplier management has as much to do with the management of demand as it does with the management of supply. However, in relation to the management of supply the firm must consider questions of both governance and contractual management.

INCENTIVIZATION AND THE PROCESS OF EXCHANGE

All exchange involves elements of both cooperation and competition. Provided the parties have voluntarily agreed to the deal, the very act of signing a contract is a cooperative activity. The vendor (or seller) is getting something that he/she wants – cash – while the buyer is getting something he/she wants – the products and services supplied. However, the cooperative aspects of an exchange can (and frequently do) go beyond this. Buyers and sellers can actively work together to streamline the contracting process and/or adapt/develop the vendor's products and services so that they more closely match the requirements of the buyer. The creation of such value-adding relationships has today become a staple of supply chain management.

Buyers and sellers are also in competition, however. While both sides gain from a trade (else why trade in the first instance), it is not necessary for both sides to gain equally for a trade to take place. For the buyer, the aim is to get value for money from a deal. If he/she is a rational agent this means maximum value for money. Every time he/she is able to negotiate the price down a notch, the value for money that is obtained increases. Of course, for the vendor, passing value to its customers means smaller profits. Economists refer to the contested ground that exists between the two parties to a trade as the surplus value. Surplus value is the difference between the value that the customer places on the vendor's products (the customer's utility function), and the supplier's costs of production. The portion of the contested ground that passes to the customer is said to be the consumer surplus, while the part retained by the vendor is the producer surplus (see Figure 7.1).

Even when buyers and sellers increase the cooperative element of an exchange by actively working together to add value to the relationship, the

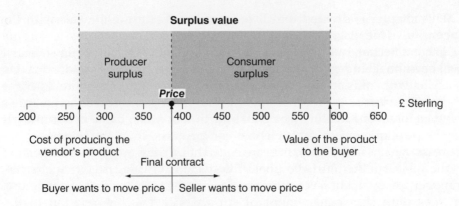

Figure 7.1 The allocation of value in an exchange

competitive element to it remains; in other words, cooperative relationships can be adversarial or non-adversarial. This is because the fruits of the cooperation (in the form of either lower production costs for the vendor, or a higher valuation of the vendor's products on the part of the customer) have to be divided up (see Figure 7.2). If, for example, the effect of collaboration is to reduce the supplier's costs by £100 a unit, one issue is whether the vendor should pass all of the savings onto the customer or retain some of them in the form of higher profits. Alternatively, if the supplier invests £100 in developing its products and as a result increases the value to the customer by £200, should

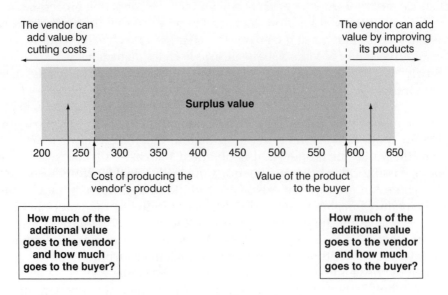

Figure 7.2 The generation of added value and exchange

the vendor raise its prices by £100 to cover just the cost of the investment, or by the full £200?

What determines who wins out in this competitive process is the incentive structure that underpins the exchange relationship. Take for example the vendor that finds itself in a highly competitive market where its many customers are free to choose where they buy their goods and services. Such a context forces the vendor into a Dutch auction in which it is forced constantly to drop its prices to buy its customer's business. In such a situation, the surplus value is bound to pass to the consumer. Compare that to a situation in which a particular customer has invested heavily in the vendor's technologies, even building the value proposition that it offers its own customers around the technologies of a particular supplier. This happened in the PC market, where PC manufacturers fell over themselves to advertise the fact that their machines had an 'Intel inside'. In the end, it became impossible for PC manufacturers to compete unless they were able to make this boast. Unfortunately, this had the effect of handing enormous leverage over to Intel, and as a result the surplus value passed from the consumer to the producer.

Consequently, much of supply management is reduced to a game between poachers and gamekeepers, in which the vendor assumes the role of the poacher (trying to 'steal' its customers' scarce financial resources), while the procurement manager assumes the role of the gamekeeper, in trying to stop them. What follows is a cat and mouse game in which, through a combination of guile and the development of distinctive capabilities, the vendor attempts to close markets, while the procurement manager responds in kind with a range of counter-strategies designed to stop its vendors by keeping its supply markets contested. To the victor go the spoils. Power (formally defined as the ability of one party adversely to affect the interests of another), and the pursuit of power are at the heart of the exchange process (Lukes, 1974; Cox, Sanderson and Watson, 2000; Cox et al, 2002).

To some it might appear that the competitive elements of an exchange have been overstated. While it is true that some people in life are maximizers (ie they are always looking for the highest possible return from a deal), critics would argue that most people are in fact happy to just satisfice (obtain a deal they can live with). If two people cooperate on a venture, then generally speaking those people are happy to split the proceeds. This may or may not be true; it is hard to say. What is true, however, is that such an approach is sub-optimal and imprudent. That satisficing is sub-optimal should be self-evident. The fact that it is also imprudent needs further elaboration.

The issue of prudence arises in a number of contexts. First, it puts the profitability and even the survival of a firm at risk. The reason that firms come into business in the first instance is to make a return for shareholders. While it is true, as a number of resource-based writers have observed, that markets are often heterogeneous (they are capable of supporting laggards as well as world beaters), it is not true that markets are infinitely forgiving of the weak (Peteraf,

1993). Firms that fall too far behind the competitive frontier are on borrowed time. Firms that forget about the competitive elements of an exchange, however, risk seeing their costs rise and falling behind the competitive frontier.

The second problem with cooperation and trust is that it demonstrates an unwarranted confidence in the capacity/willingness of others to reciprocate. Many firms that acquire leverage are happy to use it. Even those who do not possess a structural advantage may attempt to use guile instead, where they think it will pay off for them. Furthermore, denials that this is not true cannot be taken at face value (Williamson, 1985). The thing about people is that very few of them are honest all of the time. One only has to reflect on one's own experience to see that this is true.

According to business economists, economic agents are not simply self-interested, but pursue this self-interest with guile – not all the time, but sufficiently often that opportunism is a fact of commercial life. What permits the existence of opportunism is two things: one, a lack of honesty (obviously), and two, a lack of transparency between buyers and sellers. Economists distinguish between public and private information (Molhow, 1997). Information is regarded as public if it involves something that is widely known; it is regarded as private when access to it is restricted. When 'restriction' means that one side in an exchange knows something that the other side does not, then an information asymmetry is said to exist. It is information asymmetry that permits dishonesty to pay.

Business opportunism exists in a number of forms, but for buyers the twin guises in which it is most common are adverse selection and moral hazard. Adverse selection is *ex ante* opportunism, or misrepresentation that arises prior to the signing of a contract. Shorthand definitions of the concept might revolve around buying a 'lemon' or being sold a 'turkey'. The scope for adverse selection varies, but it is more common under some circumstances than others.

Commentators often distinguish between search, experience and credence goods. Search goods are products that allow buyers to make systematic comparisons prior to a purchase. They are normally tangible products like chairs, pens or iron ingots. Experience goods, by contrast, are products that can only be evaluated subsequent to purchase. Typically they include services like cinemas or restaurants. However, the category can also include tangible products like cars or records. The final category of goods is the credence goods. Credence goods defy easy evaluation, even after consumption. They include intangible services such as advertising, consultancy or medical services. What makes evaluation so hard usually comes down to a difficulty with attributing blame or success. For example, a piece of professional advice might have been responsible for a commercial disaster. However, the blame might lie with some other concomitant factor. The point is, where pre-contractual evaluation of a product is difficult – either because evaluation is inherently difficult or because the buyer lacks the resources or expertise to undertake it – the buyer is open to the risk of adverse selection. Experience goods and credence goods, by definition, are difficult to evaluate prior to purchase.

If adverse selection involves being suckered before a contract is signed, moral hazard involves being suckered once a party has signed on the dotted line. Some things that are bought involve a simple one-off interaction. The product is purchased and it either works or it doesn't. Following this, buyer and seller go their separate ways. Other exchanges, by contrast, require a prolonged association. Either the contract must be serviced on an ongoing basis (eg a facilities management contract) or the buyer requires repeat purchases (eg a contract to supply car engines). Either way, the vendor attempts to change the terms of the deal after the contract has been signed. It might do this openly by seeking to exploit a loophole in the contract; or it might do it covertly by simply not delivering on a promise.

Regardless of the form that opportunism takes, the potential for it means that firms must always be aware of the competitive nature of any trade. Even if a customer is honest and believes in giving the other guy a fair break, it cannot be sure that the other side is operating according to the same code. Because a trade always involves some private information, we just don't know what we don't know – and what we don't know might turn out to be quite important. One of the essential elements of procurement and supply chain competence, therefore, centres on the capacity of buyers to ensure that their vendors offer a good deal (or at least keep to the terms of the deal that has been agreed).

INCENTIVIZATION AND THE OUTSOURCING DILEMMA

Nowhere are the issues of competition between buyers and sellers more acute than in respect of outsourcing. This is evidenced by the fact that so many outsourced contracts go wrong. One survey found that in only 5 per cent of cases did outsourcing prove to be an unqualified success (details of this survey are reported in Lonsdale and Cox, 1998). More often than not, respondents indicated that it was something of a curate's egg (that is, good in parts). Thirty-nine per cent of respondents in the survey said that their outsourced contracts were simultaneously moderately successful and moderately unsuccessful. Of course, this may have something to do with the way in which the contracts were managed. (The issue of contractual mismanagement will be discussed in the next section.) Such is the scale of disappointment, however, that it suggests something deeper than simply poor contracting is at work.

On the face of it, the decision to outsource should not be particularly problematic. It should involve a simple cost comparison between the expenses associated with undertaking the activity in-house and the expenses associated with contracting it out. For example, the size of the firm's requirement might be insufficient to cover the fixed costs associated with production in an efficient fashion. Under these conditions sourcing externally, from a firm that can amortize its fixed costs more efficiently, might make eminent sense. Alternatively, a particular activity might be suffering from a lack of effective managerial oversight. Managerial time within the firm is a scarce resource, and most of it tends to be devoted to the firm's key activities. Residual activities tend to get overlooked, and production suffers as a result. It is this thinking that in effect underpins much of the core competence writing. If your firm cannot do something well, find another firm that can.

Outsourcing tends to go wrong, however, because it exposes the firm to either a strategic or a contractual risk. Strategic risk arises if the firm outsources its competitive differentiator. Within strategy, there are three types of differentiation: cost leadership, product differentiation and niche production (Porter, 1980). In each case the firm is attempting to achieve the same thing through differentiation: break the relationship between cost, price and profit in order that it might earn an economic rent or sustained producer surplus. In a competitive marketplace, the consumer's ability to pick and choose between alternative vendors drives the firms' prices down towards the marginal cost of production. This is the last thing that a firm wants.

In the case of cost leadership the firm is attempting to earn a rent by developing a uniquely efficient production process that it is difficult for its competitors to imitate through the creation of *ex post* barriers to entry. So long as the firm is able to stave off competitive imitation, it can afford to drop its prices below those of its competitors and still make a higher return. In the case of product differentiation, by contrast, the firm is attempting to develop a superior utility proposition for the customer. The idea here is that when people comparison shop and realize that the firm's products are better than those of its competitors, they will be prepared to pay a premium for the product that offers the higher utility. Again, the firm's ability to sustain its producer surplus and turn it into a rent is contingent upon its capacity to hinder or retard competitive imitation. Finally, niche production also seeks to target customers' utility. This it achieves, however, not by creating relatively superior products but by servicing segments of a marketplace in which nobody else is particularly interested.

Because being able to differentiate competitively is so valuable to the firm (and indeed it is what strategy is all about), firms must be able to protect those resources and capabilities that generate the differentiation in the first place. However, if the firm outsources such a resource or capability, the odds are that it will end up paying the rent to its supplier that it should be earning for itself.

Outsourcing can also expose the firm to significant contractual risk (or moral hazard). Again, this involves the surplus value passing to the vendor, rather than being retained by the consumer. Sustaining the performance of a vendor depends upon a firm's ability to motivate it. Motivation might take the form of a carrot (bonuses for good performance), or a stick (the cancellation of the contract if the performance is poor). But in order for the incentive structure to work it must be credible. This means being able to monitor the supplier to see if it is complying with the terms of the deal; and having the ability to punish the supplier (by invoking penalties or by threatening exit), if it is not. Imagine a myopic and doddery old teacher trying to keep discipline in a playground if his head teacher has told him that even if he catches one of the children misbehaving, he is not allowed to threaten them with punishment. Under such circumstances the children in his charge would run wild. So it is with suppliers.

The tasks that the firm has to perform, therefore, concern being able to spot those transactions for which there is significant scope for opportunism, and to craft safeguards against the risk. When contractual safeguards cannot properly be introduced, it is probably better for the firm to retain the competence within the organization, rather than outsource it.

Moral hazard is always a problem with outsourced contracts because effective monitoring is always an issue. However, sometimes the risks are particularly acute. Contracting that takes place in a highly volatile or uncertain environment is difficult because it raises the issue of renegotiation. Buyers attempt to draft contracts in as complete a fashion as possible, but when an environment is particularly volatile, specifying all the terms of an agreement in advance is likely to prove next to impossible. This in itself need not present a difficulty unless the firm becomes locked in to its outsourced provider. If this happens, the supplier may choose to renegotiate on terms that benefit it, rather than its customer (Williamson, 1985).

Contractual lock-in occurs if the contract requires the buyer to make some form of highly specialized investment in the relationship. The investment might take the form of time. An organization that has spent months negotiating and implementing an outsourced relationship might be reluctant to write off all this hard work, especially if re-sourcing means repeating the effort with no greater chance of success next time around. Alternatively, firms might have made substantial and non-refundable investments in specialized training or equipment (otherwise known as asset-specific investments (Williamson, 1985). Less creditably, though, firms are often reluctant to call time on a poorly performing supplier if the managers who negotiated the contract have invested their reputations in the deal. Calling a halt to the affair means admitting they got it wrong, and nobody likes doing that. Whatever the form of the lock-in, the effect is the same: the firm loses its capacity to impose costs on the vendor and thus its ability to impose discipline.

Of course just because an outsourced contract presents the firm with a risk, it does not follow that the risk cannot be managed and that outsourcing should not take place. One strategy often pursued by firms involves unbundling a contract. This means separating out those elements that pose a risk from those that do not. The highly risky elements are retained in-house and only the less risky elements are outsourced. The supplier may even be asked to post a bond or share the costs of the dedicated investments, as a sign of its good faith (to show that its word of honour and commitment to the relationship are credible).

INCENTIVIZATION AND SUPPLIER MANAGEMENT

Outsourcing requires the firm to understand what it is that allows it to leverage its customers (in the case of strategic outsourcing); and what it is that allows its 'potential' suppliers to exploit it (in the case of both strategic and tactical outsourcing). Effective relationship management is about reversing things by understanding what it is that allows the firm to control and leverage its suppliers. The question is, to what end? This is where we are required to reintroduce the subject of surplus value.

The first decision that the firm must ask itself is whether the relationship should include a value-added element. Many commentators would argue yes, citing the benefits that often flow from extending the cooperative elements of a trade. Lean thinking, for example, highlights the seven supply chain wastes that often plague buyer–supplier relationships.

- overproduction;
- unnecessary inventory;
- waiting;
- motion;
- transportation;
- defects;
- inappropriate processing.

(For a discussion of these see Hines *et al* (2000).) Yet, just because extended cooperation might potentially generate additional value, it does not mean that it will, or that the buyer will be the main beneficiary if it does. Four factors play a part in determining the buyer's calculation about whether cooperation is worthwhile: the upfront investment, the potential pay-off, power and risk. Creating a value-adding relationship requires an investment, even if only in terms of the time and managerial effort that it involves. The first thing that the firm must ensure is that the expected payback matches the upfront investment. No firm is going to spend a lot of time developing its supplier of toilet rolls. The improvement for the buyer is likely to be miniscule compared with the effort.

What complicates the calculation is that both the investment and return may be hard to determine *ex ante*. Take defence contractors. Suppliers of defence equipment work closely with their customers (governments) to ensure that the weapons that they develop are the ones that the customer wants/needs. The industry, however, is notorious for delays in introducing new equipment and cost overruns. In a number of instances the additional cost that the customer ends up committing itself to runs into billions of pounds. When the equipment finally arrives, it may be too late to be useful. It may not even work properly. Consequently, there is an issue of which party takes the risk and which party obtains the reward. This is a question of power. A simple example will illustrate the nature of the calculation that the buyer faces.

Take two firms: a buyer (A) and its supplier (B). B proposes to A that an upfront investment of £50 is capable of yielding cost savings of £200. In other words the additional surplus value that has been created through the cooperation comes to £150. If A exercises leverage over B it will probably think that cooperating is a good idea. As it has the power, it will probably insist that B takes all the upfront risk, agreeing to cover B's costs only if the initiative pays off. This is a no-lose situation for A. If, however, A and B are interdependent, the calculation becomes more complex. B will probably insist that A shares both the investment and the reward. This means that A must invest £25 (half the £50 cost) to get a payback of £100 (half the £200 cost savings). This leaves it with a net gain of £75 (£100 savings less the £25 costs). Once again cooperating makes sense, although the pay-off for the buyer is smaller than in the first example.

What if the costs are fixed but the gains are far from certain, however? Say, for example, there is only a 25 per cent chance of a successful outcome. Under these circumstances the firm would be investing £25 to get a 25 per cent chance of £100 return. The cost–benefit calculation here is finely balanced (£25 cost less £25 return = zero). Change the parameters again (say, increase the upfront investment by £1) and the initiative may cease to make commercial sense. This is why power is so important to all relationships: it affects the pay-off structures of buyers and sellers, and thus the management of the relationship. It decides which side takes most of the risks and which side extracts most of the rewards. Furthermore, the same calculations pertain whether the firm is thinking in a dyadic or a wider supply chain context.

The second set of operational issues confronting the firm relate, therefore, to how it acquires or maintains a power advantage over suppliers. Buyers are aware that vendors segment their customer base. One simple segmentation (which nonetheless is still widely used) involves the vendor categorizing customers on the basis of the size of the customer's business and the difficulties associated with servicing it. The attempt here is to determine the overall profitability of a specific contract to the vendor's business. Obviously, what the vendor is looking for is large contracts that are easy (that is, cheap) to service. What it is not looking for is low-value, costly and therefore nuisance business. This is why the procurement functions within many organizations have created commodity councils aimed at rationalizing specific items of spend, so as to maximize their attractiveness/value/leverage to supply markets in general and to specific vendors in particular. The hope here is that if the buyer can select a supplier that is competent and whose interests dovetail with the buyer's objectives, then the buyer will get a better deal.

However, creating this congruence is easier said than done. Operationally, the key to effective supply management is usually effective demand management, but as often as not a supply manager will experience considerable difficulty in getting the managers in other functions to recognize this point. Functional autonomy and principal–agent problems are facts of life. In theory, organizations should be hierarchies or authority structures with a strong focus on maximizing shareholder value. If it has been determined that rationalizing and consolidating a particular item of spend would save the organization money, then the word should go down from the top that a rationalization needs to take place. In practice, though, each department tends to see the world from its own particular point of view, and set its priorities and fight its corner accordingly.

Thus the sales department of an organization is usually more focused on winning business than on the overall profitability of the business it has won. Frequently it will attempt to meet the customer's specification even if this means significantly adapting the firm's existing supply offering at great cost. There was a reason why Henry Ford said that his customers could have any colour of car they wanted, as long as it was black. Whereas sales departments are often trying to buy business regardless of cost, engineering departments tend to strive for technical excellence and quality. The knock-on effect of this is that there is a tendency among engineers to over-specify to insure themselves against the potential for product failure. The fact that this over-specification dramatically limits the organization's supply options, and the price it must pay its suppliers rises accordingly, is of little consequence to the engineer.

The problems that the supply manager faces are not just related to the misalignment of organizational incentives and the fact that others within the organization are reluctant to see things from his/her view. They also concern the fact that when trying to affect a change, the supply manager often finds himself/herself at the bottom of the pecking order. As long as the organization is making money, it may be reluctant to challenge existing practice, preferring instead to muddle through and accept the organizational slack.

The final set of operational issues facing supply managers concerns the management of the chosen vendor. Supply management involves two issues: relationship management and contracting. Relationship management concerns how the buyer and seller interact on a day-to-day basis. Is the association between the two going to be essentially at arms-length, or is something closer called for? If the firm has opted to pursue a value-adding relationship, presumably close interaction is required. The contracting parties will need to trade information, mutually adapt their processes and so on, so the maximum value-adding potential is achieved.

At the same time relationship management will also involve managing the tensions that exist between the two. Some forms of cooperation, for example, might be deemed neutral in the sense that they add value to the relationship without disturbing the commercial balance within it. Other forms of cooperation, however, are far from neutral. For example, if the buyer calls for the supplier to open its books, then the buyer is acquiring a considerable advantage over its supplier in that it now knows just how much money the supplier is making from the deal. Both buyers and sellers, therefore, tend to want to manage the relationship so that while it adds value it does not tip the balance of power the wrong way. The same goes for performance measurement. Performance measurement may be a way of monitoring how quickly things are improving – or if they are not improving, where and why this is the case. However, performance measurement is also a mechanism of control, and both sides tend to be aware of this.

In contrast to relationship management that tends to contain a value-adding element as well as a controlling element, contracts are primarily about control. They are about specifying in a legally binding way the manner in which buyers and suppliers are to work together – that is, who is responsible for doing what. They are also about specifying (again in a legally binding way) the outputs of the relationship: what the supplier is expected to deliver, what the buyer is expected to pay, and which party own the rights to any exploitable technologies or processes should they emerge from the association.

Contracts take three main forms: tight, flexible and relational (Williamson, 1985). The shift from tight to relational contracting tends to occur as the uncertainty within the relationship increases. Where an element of a deal can be specified with a high degree of confidence, a tight contract will tend to be used. Where, by contrast, a degree of uncertainty surrounds a particular aspect of the deal, but that uncertainty falls within clearly defined limits, the contracting parties may seek to draft a flexible element to the contract. This allows the requirement/reward relationship to be adjusted in a predictable way. Relational contracts tend to be used when the future trading environment is unpredictable and cannot easily be contracted for. Under such circumstances the point of a relational contract is to provide a structured framework within which the terms of a deal can be renegotiated as the future becomes clear. Although a contact may be mainly of one of the three types, it can contain elements of each. Short-term arms-length relationships tend to call for tight contracts but may include a subsidiary element. Longer-term arms-length relationships tend to require the flexible element to increase. Long-term cooperative relationships (whether they are adversarial or non-adversarial) tend to call for all three.

Of course, while contracts aim to serve as instruments of control, whether in fact they succeed in this function depends on the *ex post* power balance. As we saw in our discussions on outsourcing and contractual risk, if the buyer loses its power, then the contract may not be worth the paper that it is written on. As the political philosopher Thomas Hobbes once put it, 'contracts without the sword are but empty breath'.

CONCLUSION

Exchange takes place in the first instance because it is mutually profitable. Closer forms of cooperation occur because they can increase this level of profitability. However, mutually profitable exchange is not the same as equally profitable exchange. Buyers and sellers are competitors as well as collaborators. Consequently it is important for supply chain managers to understand the following things. First, they must understand when it is not sensible to exchange (that is, when exchange imposes unacceptable levels of strategic and contractual risk). Second, they must also understand (when it is sensible to exchange) how to craft the incentive structures that will maximize the return to their organizations. At root, therefore, the study and practice of supply chain management is the study of managerial and contractual incentives.

REFERENCES

Cox, A, Sanderson, J and Watson, G (2000) *Power Regimes*, Earlsgate Press, Boston, UK

Cox, A., Ireland, P, Lonsdale, C, Sanderson, J and Watson, G (2002) *Supply Chains, Markets and Power*, Routledge, London and New York

Hines, P, Lamming, R, Jones, D, Cousins, P and Rich, N (2000) *Value Stream Management*, Pearson, Harlow

Lonsdale, C and Cox, A (1998) *Outsourcing: A business guide to risk management tools and techniques*, Earlsgate Press, Boston, UK

Lukes, S (1974) *Power: A radical view*, Macmillan, London

Molhow, I (1997) *The Economics of Information*, Blackwell, Oxford

Peteraf, M (1993) The cornerstones of competitive advantage: a resource-based view, *Strategic Management Journal*, **14**, pp 179–91

Porter, M (1980) *Competitive Strategy*, Free Press, New York

Williamson, O (1985) *The Economic Institutions of Capitalism*, Free Press, New York

8

Supply/demand chain management: the next frontier for competitiveness

Dag Ericsson
University of Skovde, Sweden

THE STARTING POINT

'Customer ecstasy – at a profit!' A new battle-cry is replacing the old 'Customer satisfaction!' Customer expectations should not only be met – they should be exceeded. This is the way to be competitive in the digital economy. For this to happen, some recent marketing and logistics trends have to converge. Then development within information and communication technology (ICT) and process management allows the concept to be realized.

Customer focus has been discussed as the starting point for competitive efforts in marketing ever since the 1940s. The rhetoric and approaches have differed, but in practice it has been more supply push than demand pull. Creation rather than retention of customers has been the main theme, and customer service has often been handed over to logistics.

The most difficult operational problem for logistics has always been to improve the level of service to the customer and at the same time to reduce costs (Ericsson, 1981). Customer ecstasy implies that not only should the service levels dictated by the customer be met, they should be surpassed. Traditional measurements of service levels are no longer good enough. The value of different offerings has to be discussed, and improvement in the level of service has to be expressed in terms of better value to the customer. Proaction rather than reaction to customers' needs is of the essence.

Proaction is also the main theme of supply/demand chain management (SDCM). This concept focuses on doing business with the customer in a new way (value innovation) and about leveraging change at the customer end to enable process improvement. Process improvement is a necessity if the 'at a profit' part of the battle-cry is to be fulfilled. And it has to evolve together with value innovation across the entire supply/demand chain.

The concept of value innovation (Hoover, 2001) refers to the customer's valuation of the supplier's offering – that is to the 'perceived customer value'. A value innovation is supposed to give the customer a quantum leap in satisfaction. It is not a slight efficiency increase based on continuous improvement (*kaizen*); it is a distinct new offering that makes it possible for the customer and the supply chain to change the way they operate.

Going beyond the customer order to the customer's demand chain reveals new business opportunities based on understanding the customer's business purpose and logic, planning processes, and use of the product or service. The starting point, then, of any supply/demand chain programme should be the clear definition and specification of the precise nature of the value to be delivered, market segment by market segment – or even customer by customer. Value innovation and perceived customer value are the springboards for co-evolution at the interface between supply and demand chains.

PERCEIVED CUSTOMER VALUE

In order to exceed customer expectations, they first have to be defined and described in an operational way. The concept of perceived customer value is one way of doing that. The foundation of the concept is the fact that the boundaries between physical products and accompanying services are blurring – and increasingly so in the digital economy (Davis and Meyer, 1998).

The offer to the customer consists of 'a bundle of utilities': a mix of products and services. At the centre is the tangible product that can be described in engineering terms, the traditional 'conformance to specifications'. The core is surrounded by a set of intangible services such as logistics availability and technical support (as shown in Figure 8.1).

The concept of value is customer-specific and essentially subjective to the customer. It represents the perceived benefits that customers believe they receive from ownership or consumption of a product or service. This value can be defined as the quotient of total quality (TQ) – as perceived by the customer – and total costs (TC) – as perceived by the customer. Hence, Value = TQ/TC.

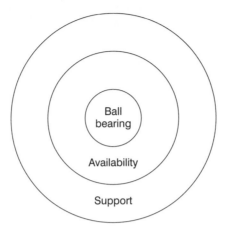

Figure 8.1 The SKF 'offer', based on perceived customer value

In order to make this definition operational it is necessary to define total quality. In several practical situations it has proved useful to define two sets of quality, which refer to the tangibles and intangibles mentioned above. At the centre is a 'hard core' of objective, engineering facts – especially when it comes to physical products. This is the core quality, which is surrounded by several layers of basic and added values, that make up the fringe quality.

The core and fringe approach was used at SAAB-Scania in the mid-1980s as a means of focusing efforts on the total quality concept when the 'One step ahead' programme was launched (see Figure 8.2). It was also used by Volvo of Australia to illustrate and emphasize the 'total experience' of the car.

The total cost concept is also subjective, depending on, for example, the way in which customers value their own time and efforts. IKEA built its approach on the fact that to certain customers the value was higher in buying 'knocked down' products and assembling them than in buying ready-made furniture at a higher price. It all boils down to a subjective valuation of the customer's time and efforts.

Different customers have different requirements and demands. In the same way, different products require different logistics systems. The real challenge for logistics today is to design customized delivery systems. Customized delivery systems refer not only to the physical delivery of products or the presentation of services, but also to the marketing channels employed, the use of the Internet, the flexibility of response, the linking of logistics and information systems, and so on. The design of customized delivery systems is a critical means of engineering stronger linkages between the customer's demand chain and the vendor's supply chain.

For commodities, the solution might be a lean supply chain based on rather accurate forecasts. For innovative products, such as fashion wear, the best

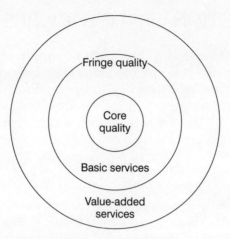

Figure 8.2 Core and fringe quality for SAAB-Scania

match might be a responsive supply chain based on agility and rapid reaction on changing conditions.

The same product, for example a ball bearing, might have different systems requirements based on the use of the product. OEM (original equipment manufacturer) customers have one type of demand on the system, wholesalers another and spare-part users a third. SKF, the Swedish ball bearing company, takes this into consideration and defines perceived customer value for specific segments. Unique 'channels' are then identified to fit end-user requirements, and the efforts are managed by a 'channel captain' (see Figure 8.3).

In order to hit the 'bull's eye', all the activities leading to the hit have to be coordinated, integrated and synchronized. This requires process and systems integration – end to end. The hit has to be achieved at as low cost as possible, for the customer as well as the supplier. The final supplier cannot achieve this on its own. It has to be part of a whole: the integrated supply/demand chain in which the vendor's supply chain is synchronized with the customer's demand chain.

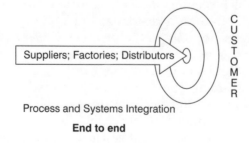

Figure 8.3 The SKF channel concept

THE EVOLUTION OF THE LOGISTICS CONCEPT

Logistics is the backbone and the origin of supply chain thinking. The evolution of the logistics concept, therefore, is an important background to what is happening today. Efficiency in operations and effectiveness in fulfilling customer needs are key phrases in designing total materials flows (supply chains). In the late 1960s the vision was to create 'an even, steady, uninterrupted, and quality assured flow from raw materials supplier to the ultimate user' (Ericsson, 1969a). It is now possible to turn this vision into reality, thanks to developments in IT.

In the United States, several different concepts were developed in the 1960s to refer to materials flow. For example, the concept of materials management focused on the inflow from suppliers (Ammer, 1968), business logistics focused on transportation and internal flows (Ruppenthal and McKinnell, 1968) and physical distribution management on the outflow to customers (Bowersox, LaLonde and Smykay, 1969).

In Sweden a broader and more process-oriented approach – materials administration/logistics (MA) – evolved and was defined as 'planning, development, coordination, integration, control and review of the total materials flow from raw materials supplier to the ultimate user' (Ericsson, 1969a). There is a strong resemblance between this definition and more recent definitions of supply chain management (see eg Christopher, 1998 and Gattorna, 1998).

Initially, the focus of the MA approach was on creating efficiency within the company itself, by tearing down walls and integrating activities within basic materials flow functions such as purchasing, manufacturing and physical distribution. Somewhat later, interfaces with R&D/engineering and marketing were explicitly added (shown in Figure 8.4). The original Swedish

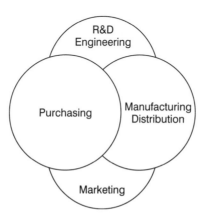

Figure 8.4 Materials administration/logistics: focusing on the interfaces between traditional functions

definition of materials administration emphasizes that the key to success is hidden at the interfaces between traditional logistics activities, marketing, and research and engineering. The interplay with marketing is obvious, at least in theory. The mutual interdependency with research and engineering was highlighted because a major part of the costs occurring in the logistics activities is determined by the way products are designed and engineered.

The MA/logistics concept has undergone a continuous evolution based on external and internal changes, availability of new tools, and skills available in companies. When the first generation of modern logistics was launched in the 1960s, it was cost oriented and focused on reducing total costs in the materials flow. The second generation – in the 1970s – was revenue oriented and focused on increasing revenue by using logistics as a means of competition. The third generation – in the 1980s – was profitability oriented and focused on increasing profitability by reducing cost, increasing revenue and, above all, decreasing capital tied up in inventory. These approaches were all 'children of their time', based on the way of thinking in the industrial society.

In the late 1980s and beginning of the 1990s, the fourth generation – time-based logistics – and the fifth – IT-based logistics – were forerunners of what was to come. They were explicitly process re-engineering and IT focused, and reflected the increasing turbulence and discontinuity of the emerging Information Society.

A NEW PERSPECTIVE

MA/logistics advocates a new perspective of materials flows, emphasizing that the approach has two key concerns. The first concern is the management of rationalization as a conventional, functional responsibility aimed at decreasing cost. The novelty is the focus on total flow costs rather than functional costs. The concept of materials control is used to highlight total cost on the operational level in the materials flow. Efficiency by making the best use of available resources at lower cost is the goal. Transportation costs are balanced against warehousing costs, manufacturing costs against inventory costs; trade-off is the key word.

The second concern is much broader and company-wide in scope, with a goal of developing a cross-functional, coordinated focus on the level of service – in other words, reorienting the entire business to face the market and the customers. Effectiveness by addressing customer needs and demands and measuring goal fulfilment is the goal.

Organizationally this became an issue of how the materials flow should be managed. Traditionally, it was managed as a series of fragmented, functionally based tasks. This quite often led to sub-optimization and duplication of work. The core problem in the implementation of the MA/logistics concept was the lack of coordination across tasks, functions and departments. Vertical organizations – which are hierarchically structured and functionally oriented – often optimize individual functions at the expense of the whole business and the customer. This means that problems may manifest themselves in one part of the organization, even though their root cause remains unattended elsewhere. The result is low levels of corporate performance and even lower levels of service and customer satisfaction. Problems are simply passed from one functionally focused department to the next, in the search for a solution. Unfortunately, performance measurement systems often increase these problems and lead to even further functional emphasis. The introduction of activity-based costing has, however, been very helpful in implementation of the total-cost concept.

Under the new MA/logistics concept, where the flow is seen as a cross-functional process, it is essential that previously dispersed activities should be brought together and managed as a unified system. However, the mere introduction of a new department called 'materials' or 'logistics' caused more problems than it solved. A transient structure was, therefore, often used initially. Key players were drawn together in multi-functional teams or groups that tried to marshal resources to achieve logistics-based objectives by focusing on processes.

The notion of the materials flow highlights the importance of business processes as a sequence of activities whereby value is created and costs incurred. This idea has many implications: for example, pointing out the ways in which level of service and added value could be enhanced at less cost through process re-engineering. The successful management of interrelated processes requires a fundamentally different approach to planning and execution. To maximize customer value at the least cost to the business will frequently require a rearrangement of the sequence in which tasks are performed. In some cases these tasks will be eliminated, combined with other tasks or performed in parallel.

Implementation showed that there is real performance leverage in moving towards a flatter, more horizontal mode of organization, in which cross-functional, end-to-end work flows link internal processes with the needs and capabilities of both suppliers and customers. Early attempts at implementation made it clear that an organizational change has to be accompanied by a transition process in which old habits and ways of working are replaced by new mindsets. Learning has to go hand in hand with unlearning (Ericsson, 1981).

E-LOGISTICS

In the 1970s increasing competition and a slow-growing economy meant that flexibility and coordination within organizations became as important as functional performance. In the 1980s and 1990s fast-changing markets and decreased product lifetimes highlighted not only intra- but also inter-organizational coordination. These new challenges required managers to rethink the way they interacted with their suppliers, other channel members, and customers. In this rethinking, many lessons can be learnt from the development and implementation of the MA/logistics concept. An approach is necessary that organizes the flow of work around company-wide processes that link with suppliers and ultimately with customer needs. This can only be achieved using state of the art information and communication technology (ICT) and advanced process management.

During the first five generations of logistics – up to the mid-1990s – the tools and techniques of ICT were lagging behind the visions of top management. From that point, however, there were more tools available than top management took into consideration (see Figure 8.5). As Christopher Columbus would have put it, 'Man was limited not so much by his tools as by his visions.'

E-logistics – which is a new and in many ways different breed of logistics – has taken this gap between tools and visions as a starting point. The driving force is information rather than materials flows, and one of the goals is to substitute information for inventory. The concept focuses on the leverage effect of ICT and Internet technology on traditional logistics, and most importantly, it makes use of recent progress within process management. E-logistics is an enabler in 'simple' transactions based on e-commerce, but it is also a major key to success in e-business.

The relationship between e-logistics and e-business is a two-way street because e-business technology enables the fulfilment of two major logistics

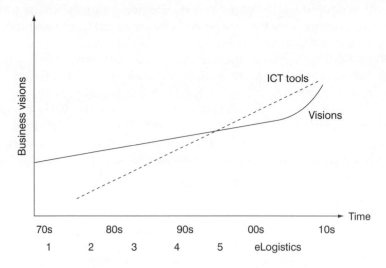

Figure 8.5   The development of visions and tools with reference to logistics generations

goals. First, efficiency can be improved by doing what the company did before, but in a different way and faster, giving process improvement. Second, effectiveness can be improved by doing things the company did not do before, such as offering the customer something more than just a product or service, giving value innovation.

E-logistics focuses on the interfaces between process management, information and communication technology (ICT), and traditional logistics (shown in Figure 8.6). The linkages have to be exploited and the areas have to be aligned more closely. E-logistics is a cornerstone in the creation of agile supply/demand chains. The alignment enables this new development, and it also creates a key to implementation.

The development of logistics, as described above, has provided the experience, the models and the methods for enhancing effectiveness and efficiency in increasingly complex chains and networks. ICT provides the tools and techniques that are necessary to move from materials to information flow oriented approaches, and also from supply chain management to demand chain management. ICT can also help decrease costs by reducing complexity in chain management. Many people are still involved in creating, communicating and executing inaccurate forecasts. This leads to constantly changing plans, turbulence and whiplash effects. Advanced, integrated information systems reduce the need for forecasts, and at the same time offer a better platform for building forecasting and planning systems. They also enable efficient communication of plans and exceptions in the whole chain.

Process management is the key to implementation that focuses on the use of processes to improve relationships and behaviour in order to gain a competitive advantage. ICT in combination with process management – aiming at achieving speed and simplicity by eliminating unnecessary activities and tasks – has a substantial leverage on logistics performance.

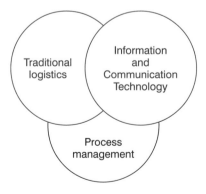

Figure 8.6 E-logistics focusing on the interfaces between traditional logistics, ICT and process management

PROCESS MANAGEMENT

It has been stated elsewhere (Ericsson, 1996) that logistics is the cradle of process orientation in terms of approaches to intra- and inter-organizational relationships and flows (see Figure 8.7). Focus should be more on processes and flows than on functional activities:

> In the future, interest will become concentrated on the various types of flow which exist within the organizations. For example, the materials flow will form the focus for decisions rather than the functionally specialized departmental activities. The flow of other resources, such as men and capital, will be regarded in the same way and the main emphasis thereby altered from vertical departments to flow processes in a horizontal direction. Similarly, the organizations will be defined in terms of information and decision systems with the result that we shall be able to observe the structure of the organization in a different way.
>
> (Ericsson, 1974: 43–44)

Today's process management enables this type of approach to organizational structures. Process management is an interfunctional and interdisciplinary approach. It is aligned with contemporary thinking in different disciplines, so there is general support when it comes to implementing new flow concepts.

The process management part of e-logistics focuses on three core processes: time to market (TTM), time to cash (TTC) and customer creation and retention (CCR). The economics of inter-organizational structure means that the lead

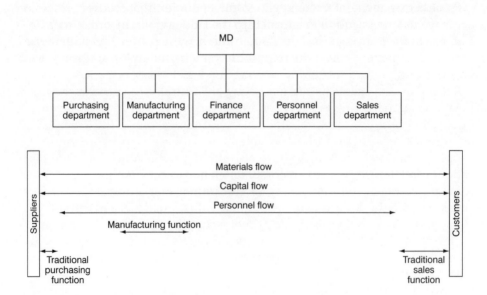

Figure 8.7 Traditional division in company functions related to the flow of resources

times for TTM and TTC are reduced, while effectiveness and efficiency improve CCR. This core process orientation is closely related to the first MA/logistics approach which focused on the interfaces between functions and departments such as R&D and engineering, marketing, purchasing and manufacturing/distribution.

In the digital economy, the distinction between manufacturing and distribution gets more and more blurred, with concepts such as 'merge in transit' and 'postponement of final assembly'. The TTC process is at the heart of traditional logistics, which focuses on the order fulfilment process, from initiation of the order to delivery to the customer. The extension lies in the inclusion of the invoicing and payment activities, which is the reason for the change of term from 'time to customer' to 'time to cash'.

A focus on lead times and synchronization of activities is the main theme in the TTM approach. Just like 'concurrent engineering', it stresses the fact that product development activities cannot be performed in sequence with walls and moats between the functions. Walls have to be torn down and moats bridged in order to perform activities in an integrated and often parallel way. The development of concurrent engineering and the focus on TTM have increased and hastened the development of interfunctional cooperation in product development.

The CCR process consists of two closely related parts: customer creation and customer retention. This reflects the fact that marketing has two main concerns. First, the creation process focuses on transactions and the initiation of customer relationships. This is the traditional marketing concept based on the marketing mix and exchange. Second, the retention process focuses on keeping customers and their transfer up the ladder from customer to partner. The retention part is closely related to the activities after the actual transaction: that is, after sales, spare parts management, follow-up and continuous improvement.

Recent developments within marketing are central to the process approach. Relationship marketing is a process-oriented concept that is closely related to CCR. One-to-one marketing, efficient consumer response (ECR) and CRM techniques are all important enablers of process improvement in the supply/demand chain. But they are also the stepping-stones for value innovation in relationships with customers. Relationship marketing is not a new concept; rather it is a refocusing of traditional marketing with a greater emphasis on the creation of 'customer value', which is perceived as a summation of all the positive effects that a supplier has upon the customer's business. The greater the level of satisfaction with the relationship – not just the product or service – the greater the likelihood that the customer will stay with the company.

In the 1990s the Nordic School of Marketing promoted the view that marketing should be viewed as a business-wide process – a process that has the goal of creating superior customer value (Gummesson, 1987; Grönroos,

1989). Achieving this goal often requires the integration of elements that were previously dispersed across different functions of the business. At the heart of the relationship approach to marketing is the integration – company-wide – of separate functions with the focus on processes. In this way, there is a striking similarity with the development of MA/logistics.

In the 1990s a growing body of literature started to question the relevance of traditional marketing theory, especially when applied to international, industrial and services marketing (Christopher, Payne and Ballantyne, 1991). The traditional paradigm, based on the marketing mix and the concept of exchange, was developed for consumer goods. This short-term, transactional focus is inappropriate for services and industrial marketing where longer-term relationships are critical to success. Furthermore, the traditional approach focuses on product features rather than value and customer expectations. Relationship marketing, on the other hand, is concerned not only with turning a prospect into a customer, but also with turning him or her into a partner. This means that customer retention is at least as important as customer creation, and the interplay between marketing and logistics grows even more important.

SUPPLY CHAIN MANAGEMENT

The development of logistics from intra- to inter-organizational activities and processes, and its focus on supply chain management, have significantly improved effectiveness and efficiency in the value chain. Early efforts at increasing efficiency and effectiveness in value chains focused on creating a lean supply chain, to fit contemporary thinking regarding lean manufacturing, lean organizations and so on. Most academic research and education, and also practical applications, were – and in some cases still are – based on the paradigms of the industrial society, with standardization, continuity, planning, forecasting possibilities, long production runs, mass marketing and mass distribution.

Many companies have implemented the 'lean concepts', and significant advantages are achieved through cross-functional and process-based teams. However, the concept of leanness is based on large volumes, low variability and low variety – which is industrial society thinking. It can be counter-productive in the digital economy, where continuity is replaced by discontinuity, planning by flexibility, mass marketing and distribution by customization. Agility based on high variability, high variety and low volumes is a necessary new element in the competitive strategy (Christopher and Towill, 2000).

A new paradigm that is based on the opposite of the old industrial society thinking is needed. Agility replaces leanness as the main focus. In this context agility refers to an overriding capacity and ability to proact rather than react in terms of organizational structures, information systems, business processes and, above all, mindsets.

The concept of customer focus gets a completely new meaning in this environment. The push-oriented supply chain has to be complemented by the pull-oriented demand chain. The playing field shifts again: the winning game now is synchronizing 'lean supply chains' based on forecasts with 'agile supply/demand chains' based on early information. The shift from continuity to discontinuity means that we have to prepare for the unexpected. As Aristotle once said, 'It is most likely that something unlikely will happen.' The question is 'How do we plan when we can't predict?' and the answer is 'Replace forecasts with early, real-time information directly from the demand chain!'

DEMAND CHAIN MANAGEMENT

Supply chain management in its traditional form integrates purchasing, production and distribution; it addresses how to make the products that customers are supposed to buy. Increased competition has forced early generations of supply chain management to evolve into 'demand-driven supply chains' that highlight customer demand as the starting point for all activities. This evolution shifts the focus from the vendor's supply chain to the customer's demand chain. With increasing 'real' customer focus, marketing needs to be integrated into logistics operations. Demand chain management adds this new dimension by exploring how to build lasting customer relationships and how to deliver value into the customer's operations.

Here, the term 'demand chain' is not used simply as another word for demand-driven supply chains. It is used to denote the concept of a series of activities all the way from the final user to the focal customer – the one in direct contact with the supply chain. Of course, the customer's customer may also be involved in the information flow. Chains of activities communicate demand from markets to suppliers, meaning that activities preceding the actual issuing of an order are also included. The triggering cue for the supply chain is not simply an order, but can be early information about actual production or use. Mapping of the demand chain offers opportunities to differentiate the value offering and adapt to wishes at different levels in the demand chain.

Demand chain management deals not only with how the customer makes the purchase, but also with what drives the purchasing transaction. Marketing provides the necessary understanding of the customer's buying processes – for investment products, for straight rebuys and for planned rebuys. This knowledge of the purpose for which the customer uses the product – the why, what, when, and how of product supply – is essential. The demand chain has to be approached in the same way as the supply chain. It has to be mapped, simplified, integrated and IT-ified. And the links between the supply and demand chains have to be analysed and synchronized.

DEMAND/SUPPLY CHAIN LINKAGES

The supply chain may consist of several levels of cooperating companies, such as first- and second-tier suppliers, manufacturers, distributors and retailers. The border between supply and demand chain varies depending on the type of cooperation at hand. The focal company is one in direct contact with customers, but several core activities might be allocated to different partners in the supply chain. The main internal problems in the supply chain lie at the interfaces between companies, and they are further accentuated by an increasing number of supply chain partners (see Figure 8.8).

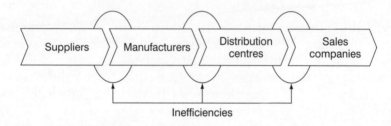

Figure 8.8 Supply chain inefficiencies

Inefficiencies such as long lead times, a low proportion of value-adding time in the processes, duplication of work, duplication of inventories, misunderstandings and errors, sub-optimization and 'cascade effects' are quite often referred to in industry. Improvements in the supply chain can – and must – be made. However, an even greater opportunity for improvement lies at the interface between the supply and demand chains.

A supply chain may include purchasing/sourcing, manufacturing, warehousing and distribution/sales. This means that the contact with the customer can take place on at least four different levels. The first is the traditional transaction-based contact between the customer's purchasing function and the supplier's salespeople, which is followed by a delivery of the order. The next contact may also be based on customized packaging for an order, through direct order production, or by monitoring sourcing (shown in Figure 8.9). In most cases, however, moving the customer order point upstream means increasing lead times. This has to be compensated by gaining time by moving downstream in the demand chain – that is, by getting early information.

A customer's demand chain may start with purchasing, followed by inventory control and scheduling. Transactional marketing aims at developing

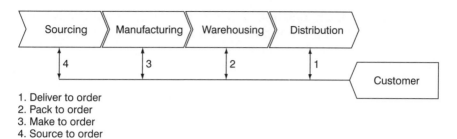

1. Deliver to order
2. Pack to order
3. Make to order
4. Source to order

Figure 8.9   Supply chain: definition of the customer order point

the right offer for the customer's purchasing people: giving an offer to purchase. But it is possible to deepen the relationship by an offer to inventory: by, for example, automatic refill of stock, or taking care of the customer's warehousing through 'vendor managed inventory' (VMI), or going one step further into the customer's own scheduling (see Figure 8.10). In this way time is gained, making it possible to move the supplier's customer order point from 'deliver to order' to 'make to order'. This is a necessary step to achieve profitability. Early information creates the necessary time gain, and opens a window of opportunities for flexibility in planning and execution of supply chain activities.

Supply/demand chain management is an operational combination of supply chain management and marketing, based on mapping the customer's demand and decision chains. The marketer's classic question, 'How do I increase customer value?' is combined and integrated with the logistician's question, 'How do I increase effectiveness and efficiency in the materials flow?', giving the joint question, 'How do we reduce cost by increasing customer value?' The answer to this question needs a deep understanding of the customer's business logic, planning, decision processes and utilization of the product. This, in turn, requires that a relationship be created, maintained and further developed – perhaps with the help of CRM techniques. The

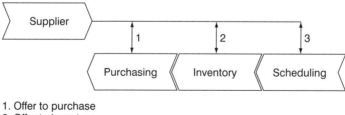

1. Offer to purchase
2. Offer to inventory
3. Offer to schedule

Figure 8.10   Demand chain: definition of the offer penetration point

marketing function, the one-to-one marketing concept and customer relationship management are stepping stones for the improvement of supply/demand chain management. Increasing focus on the customer means that existing theoretical and practical knowledge of purchasing and materials supply behavior can be used with a new and operational angle (see, eg, Ericsson, 1969b; Farmer and Baily, 1971, 1975). The yin of marketing has to be joined with the yang of purchasing and sourcing.

Marketing development has shown that there are no 'average customers'. Mass marketing is replaced by mass customization. The phrase 'mass customization' signifies the philosophy of individualizing the offer – including logistics – while still seeking to achieve cost optimization in the chain. This requires that more flexibility is engineered into the delivery systems. Flexibility in this context refers to the organization's ability to tailor products and services to the precise needs of individual customers or segments to create perceived customer value. Definition of the 'right' delivery system for 'an average customer' is no longer enough. The demand chain for the individual customer has to be analysed and synchronized with the supply chain. This requires a common approach to development and restructuring of processes. Collaboration is the key word!

Focusing on how the business actually delivers customer value will frequently lead to the recognition of the need to re-engineer processes or, in some cases, even to consider outsourcing of certain activities to partners who may be able to enhance the cost-effectiveness of the delivery process. Rethinking will often involve a radical review of conventional wisdom on sourcing, manufacturing and logistics. Take, as an example, delivery of standard products. When supplies and products are bought for maintenance, repair and operations it is not unusual for administration costs to be 150 per cent higher than direct purchasing costs. VMI is often the solution. This may lead to significantly lower costs for the customer, but is very expensive for the supplier even with increased prices. One way of increasing profitability for both parties is to change the approach from 'offer to inventory' to 'offer to schedule', which means integration with the customer's scheduling processes. Early information about the customer's utilization pattern and planned activities allows the supplier to reduce its own inventory without decreasing service. The number of stock points may be reduced, and transportation and purchasing may be performed more efficiently.

E-NETS

The concept of the value chain is a simplification of reality. A company is not part of just one single chain, but is simultaneously part of a huge network of chains and relationships. In some relations it serves as a supplier, in others as a customer, an intermediary or a complementer. Important roles are played by intermediaries (such as third-party logistics companies) or complementers (such as electronic marketplaces). These add products and services that expand the reach and range of a network's total offering. Many-to-many relationships make it important to clarify the role of each of the players in a company's network. However, the roles are not fixed, and cooperation and competition may exist at the same time.

The primary building blocks of the supply/demand network are the focal company and its direct 'exchange partners'. Their shared focus on creating customer value is necessary to determine and define the proper relationships between the partners in the network.

The process and systems integration induced by supply/demand chain management leads to increasingly complex networks of relations between a company and its environment. This development is further hastened by the increased use of outsourcing and also by developments within e-commerce and e-business. There is a move towards more and more complex networks – e-nets – with supply/demand chains and value nets serving as important links. Continuous improvement and rethinking, combined with the rapid inflow of new technology, make it possible to move channel cooperation one step further and benefit from e-nets – forming the next major phase of Internet applications.

The concept of collaboration in e-nets is fundamental for understanding the shift from value chains to value networks, and the accompanying move from supply/demand chains to supply/demand networks. Relationships in complex supply/demand networks are very hard to describe and conceptualize. Metaphors are enlightening in these situations. Johansen and Swigart (1994) used the metaphor of a fishnet to describe the intra-organizational evolution from company hierarchies to network organizations. They concluded that electronic networks are replacing office buildings as the locus of business transactions, and stated that, 'Your network is your business.' This is also true for the new network structures emerging between supply/demand chains. The e-net is similar to a fishnet where every node has a relation to every other – directly or indirectly. When a node in the fishnet is lifted, the rest of the net lattices nicely under it. A temporary hierarchy – a value net – evolves, designed to fulfil a certain need. Layers will appear, consistent with how high the node is lifted and the width of the mesh. The fishnet can form and reform various patterns of connection. The consumer, the competitor, the supplier and so on may at one time be in the apex, at another in the middle. This means that different e-nets can be defined depending on the focus, which might be consumers, competitors, suppliers or whatever (see Figure 8.11).

The fishnet rearranges itself quickly and complex, yet flexible, webs of interconnection appear. ICT, including a combination of telecomms and computing, forms the cords of which the inter-organizational fishnet between companies is woven (Ericsson, 1996).

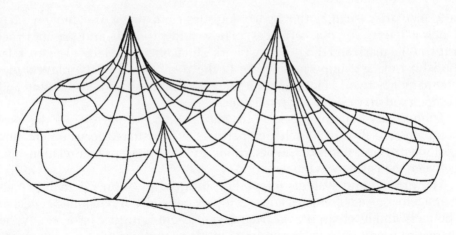

Figure 8.11 Inter-organizational structures are beginning to look like fishnets

Development of fishnet structures may be expensive, but the innovation will lead to new business opportunities. Value innovation is one example of this. ICT can help cable up the fishnet structure to make things happen that were not possible before. This requires a special brand of vision to trigger use of new technology. Technology is the tool of change – but not the main cause.

CONCLUSIONS

The dual objective of value enhancement and cost reduction is the aim of emerging supply/demand chain best practices. Some of these practices increase the effectiveness of the chain, while others improve the efficiency of it. Value for the end-user is enhanced by creating customized bundles of products and services that increase perceived total quality. ICT – and especially database technology – is used to create true images of perceived customer value, to be used as targets for joint efforts. Cost reductions are achieved by lower transaction costs, focused manufacturing, economies of scale through partnering, and reduced transportation, storage and inventory costs.

Supply/demand chain management is rapidly becoming the next major frontier for effective competition. Companies are starting to recognize the need for approaching demand chains strategically, and to develop a portfolio of customers and suppliers. Technological development makes it possible to create distinctive competencies by including the very best partners that add value for the customer. Intermediaries and complementers are, therefore, growing increasingly important – accentuating the evolution of value chains into value nets.

The development of supply and demand chains, interwoven into a complex, continuously changing and evolving network of competitors, suppliers, customers, partners, intermediaries and complementers, is challenging and demanding. Systems architecture and software, processes and relationships, logistics structures, systems and behavior have to be developed rapidly in order to benefit proactively from all the new possibilities.

Forming and improving inter-organizational links is hard. It requires new competencies in trust building, information system linkages, and other communication mechanisms. The technological development opens up new avenues to efficiency and effectiveness through process and systems integration.

However, the major obstacle still remains the need to change mindsets and behaviour of people in different companies and functions in the whole chain. The old MA/logistics statement that 'Result equals systems efficiency times acceptance' still holds.

It is difficult to change behavior within a company, as the early approaches to integrated logistics have shown. It is even more difficult to do it in separate companies. Success will also require unlearning of many existing practices, which takes time. Old habits die hard, and unlearning is at least 10 times more difficult than learning!

REFERENCES

Ammer, D S (1968) *Materials Management*, Richard D Irwin, Homewood, IL

Bowersox, D J, LaLonde, B J and Smykay, E W (1969) *Readings in Physical Distribution Management*, Macmillan, New York

Christopher, M (1998) *Logistics and Supply Chain Management*, Financial Times/ Pitman, London

Christopher, M and Towill, D R (2000) Supply chain migration from lean and functional to agile and customised, *Supply Chain Management*, 5 (4)

Christopher, M, Payne, A and Ballantyne, D (1991) *Relationship Marketing*, Butterworth Heinemann, Oxford

Davis, S and Meyer, C (1998) *Blur*, Perseus Books, Cambridge, MA

Ericsson, D (1969a) *MaterialAdministration/Logistik*, Hermods, Malmo, Sweden

Ericsson, D (1969b) *The Purchasing Function: Goals and methods*, Hermods, Malmo, Sweden

Ericsson, D (1974) *Materials Administration/Logistics*, McGraw-Hill, London

Ericsson, D (1981) *Materials Administration: A top management responsibility*, Liber, New York

Ericsson, D (1996) *Virtual Integration*, Unisource, Norcross, GA

Farmer, D H and Baily, P (1971) *Purchasing Principles and Techniques*, Pitman, London

Farmer, D H and Baily, P (1975) *Corporate Planning and Procurement*, Heinemann, Oxford

Gattorna, J (ed) (1998) *Strategic Supply Chain Alignment*, Gower, London

Grönroos, C (1989) Fundamental research issues in services marketing, in *Designing a Winning Service Strategy*, ed M J Bitner, and L A Crosby, American Marketing Association, Chicago

Gummesson, E (1987) The new marketing – developing long term interactive relationships, *Long Range Planning*, **20**

Hoover, W E (2001) *Managing the Demand/Supply Chain: Value innovation for customer satisfaction*, Wiley, Chichester

Johansen, R and Swigart, R (1994) *Upsizing the Individual in the Downsized Organization*, Addison-Wesley, Harlow

Ruppenthal, K M and McKinnell, H A (1968) *Business Logistics in American Industry*, Graduate School of Business, Stanford, CN

FURTHER READING

Ericsson, D (1990) Business resource management: a framework for strategic management of the materials flow, in *Handbook of Logistics and Distribution Management*, ed J Gattorna, Gower, London

Heikkilä, J (2000) *Developing Demand Chain Management*, Acta Polytechnica Scandinavica, Esbo, Denmark

Raabe, H A (1999) *Strategic Framework for Creating Effective Demand Chain Management*, NTNU, Trondheim, Norway

9

Internet traders can increase profitability by reshaping their supply chains

Robert Duncan
PA Consulting Group

INTERNET TRADING IS SET TO ACCOUNT FOR A QUARTER OF ALL PURCHASES IN THE NEXT FIVE YEARS

The volume of Internet trading grew significantly in the final years of the last century; it continued to grow in the early years of this century and is forecast to grow even further in the next few years. By 2006, Forrester (2001b) forecasts that global online trade, a combination of both business to business (B2B) and business to consumer (B2C) sales, will grow to 18 per cent of all sales. Furthermore (Forrester, 2001a), two-thirds of the massive $12.8 trillion expenditure will be accounted for by business purchases and consumer expenditure in the United States. In the United States, this sum represents 27 per cent of all goods and services purchased in that country. This increase in the United States, it is estimated, will add 1.7 per cent to transport service revenues. It is recognized that the United States leads the way in most e-commerce driven initiatives, and therefore the scale of increases seen in the United States is likely to be seen in other developed countries shortly. With the ever-shrinking world, the less-developed countries will experience the same growth patterns in the not too distant future.

CUSTOMER SATISFACTION SO FAR HAS BEEN LESS THAN SATISFACTORY

Such growth predictions are against a background of dissatisfied customers, press reports that many Internet traders do not fully understand their order fulfilment costs, and transport service providers complaining that their customers tend to be cost rather than service driven. This last situation leads them to suggest that their customers do not fully understand the complexity of home delivery, in the B2C area, and consequently the added value that they provide. This background has been created as a result of an environment in which Internet traders are trying to operate effectively utilizing traditional distribution methods and networks. There has been a tendency to concentrate too much effort on the Web sites and not pay enough attention to the business processes needed to integrate the order-capture function with the business systems and the order-fulfilment activities.

Dissatisfaction in the mind of the customer can be created in a number of ways. Late delivery, damaged goods, poorly handled financial transactions and bad-tempered delivery personnel are just a few. It is generally accepted that because the placing of an order via the Internet is an extremely quick, simple, and in many cases pleasurable experience, the expectation in the mind of the customer is that all aspects of the transaction will be of a similar nature. Customer expectation has been heightened. The ordering process was slick, and customers, not unreasonably, expect the rest of the process to be undertaken with the same efficiency. Under these circumstances it is more likely that the customer will not be fully satisfied unless particular steps are taken to ensure that the level of service provided meets the heightened level of expectations. It is all too easy to undo the excellent work done by the Web site in winning customers and their orders by inadequate business processes and order-fulfilment procedures.

THE INTEGRATION OF THE BUSINESS PROCESSES AND SYSTEMS DID NOT ALWAYS RECEIVE ENOUGH MANAGEMENT ATTENTION

Many organizations, often too late, are now realizing that they should have paid as much attention to their internal business processes, their order-fulfilment resources and systems, and the integration of those processes and systems with those of their suppliers of goods and order-fulfilment services, as they did to their customer-facing Web site. The need is for a seamless end-to-end 'order to cash' process incorporating the Web site, the business' accounting systems and the delivery mechanism. The accounting needs should embrace, as a minimum, accounts payable, accounts receivable, inventory, purchase orders, invoicing and credit control.

The delivery mechanisms in many organizations cannot cope, when Internet trading is added to the traditional market offering, with the requirement for a large number of small orders requiring, to all intents and purposes, instant shipping. They may have historically been shipping relatively large orders to a few intermediate supply chain points on a two to three day lead time basis. The business processes, and perhaps more importantly the business systems, that are required to manage a large number of small orders are different from those required to manage the traditional business. The potential for making mistakes is high when an organization attempts to manage Internet business in the same way as the traditional business. All of the effort and resources that went into winning the business could be wasted as a result of not retaining that business because of the inadequate processes and systems in place to support order fulfilment.

MOVING AWAY FROM TRADITIONAL SUPPLY CHAINS AND DISTRIBUTION NETWORKS ADDS COMPLEXITY BUT PROVIDES AN OPPORTUNITY FOR PROFIT

The situation is made even more complex by the fact that the rise in Internet trading has provided the potential to restructure traditional distribution networks, supply chains and product flows. Much of the thinking to date relates to the traditional ways of moving products from manufacturers to customers. In the B2C area this has reflected traditional mail ordering concepts as typified by those organizations selling products such as books and music CDs. In simple terms, rather than ordering from a catalogue received in the mail and posting their order back to their suppliers, customers are placing their order via the Internet. Their products are delivered to them in much the same way as they were in the traditional mail order manner. The key differences are that the ordering process has been shortened in terms of time, and the manufacturer's order capture and processing costs have been reduced. The major food retailers in the United Kingdom offering home delivery services typically rely on the order that has been received via the Internet being printed in the branch nearest to the customer, picked from the fixtures in that branch and delivered by a branch-based vehicle to the home of the customer.

Internet trading has enabled the introduction of improved supply chains

Recent supply chain trends have reflected changes made possible by use of the Internet as a means of communicating between buyers and sellers. The simple scenario described above, relating to books, no longer requires a network or a supply chain involving the printer/publisher, an intermediate stockholding location and an organization to promote the offering, capture the order and execute the delivery. Potential customers can place their orders using either their own PC at home or a terminal in the branch of a high street book retailer specifically provided for browsing and order capture. The order is then transmitted to the relevant publisher, not an intermediate stock-holding point, for picking, packing and shipping directly to the home of the customer.

Books and CDs, it should be noted, lend themselves ideally to this type of trade, as apart from some minor exceptions they can easily be shipped across borders, and they do not require temperature-controlled shipping conditions. The situation for foodstuffs is very different. A single customer order may be relatively heavy, consist of a number of different-sized cartons and bottles, require a range of temperature regimes, and need to be delivered within a tightly defined time frame. Moves in the industry, as volumes increase, are beginning to result in the emergence of home-delivery picking and delivery depots located away from the prime retail sites. Such facilities enable the use of sophisticated warehouse techniques to be deployed as a result of the auto-matic entry of customers' orders into the warehouse system. The advantages created as a result of customers ordering over the Internet are more effective picking operations in a depot than a branch, improved product availability through monitoring the particular purchasing patterns of Internet shoppers, lower delivery costs as the increased volumes allow sophisticated routing and scheduling techniques to be deployed, and less congestion in the branches.

The monitoring of individuals' consumption patterns and the retailers' Web sites, both prompting and reminding their regular customers of those patterns as they go through the ordering process, could further extend the concept.

Such changes could be introduced into other market sectors

The two examples above reflect modifications of current practices and the adjustment of networks and supply chains as a result of taking advantage of the ability to place orders electronically over the Internet. The concepts could be used by other manufacturers currently not fully embracing the potential of electronically capturing orders and shipping their customers' orders directly to them. Figure 9.1 shows a general distribution network or supply chain for

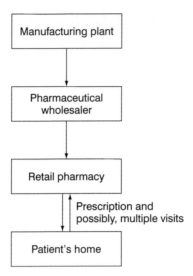

Figure 9.1   A typical pharmaceutical manufacturer's distribution network

the provision of prescription drugs from a manufacturer to its customer, a patient.

The main characteristic is the use of wholesalers and retailers to make the delivery to the patient once a doctor has prescribed the particular drug. In the unfortunate case of hospitalized patients, there is usually another stock-holding point in the hospital, the pharmacy, between the manufacturer and the patient. Large hospitals using large amounts of particular drugs do receive deliveries directly from the manufacturers. They are, however, the exception rather than the rule.

It should be noted that the level of service provided is extremely high, with wholesalers making multiple deliveries per day to retailers to ensure that particular drugs, from the plethora potentially available, are delivered to the patients as soon as possible. However, patients often have to return to the pharmacy for either all or part of their requirements once they have presented their prescription. It is accepted that because of the nature of the products, the flows are highly regulated and some form of control is obviously necessary. However, a more streamlined approach could be envisaged using the Internet as the means of communication. Figure 9.2 illustrates a possible use of the Internet to facilitate the order fulfilment of prescription drugs.

The scenario starts with the doctor prescribing the drugs in an electronic format and sending the prescription via the Internet to the manufacturer once the consultation with the patient has finished. The manufacturer simply picks, packs and ships the products to the patients' homes. The shipping process would utilize the best means available to suit the characteristics of the product. Small and light packets of tablets, for example, could be shipped

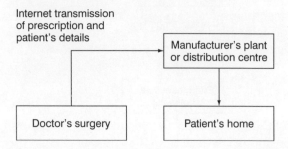

Figure 9.2   A possible pharmaceutical manufacturer's distribution network

using conventional postal services. More sophisticated products requiring careful handling may need to use the specialist express parcels services offered by a number of carriers. A less radical version of the concept could result in wholesalers providing the home delivery service on a regional basis. In each case, the distribution network or supply chain is simplified, and patients do not have to go to a retail outlet, sometimes more than once, to obtain their medication. This is particularly advantageous for elderly and very infirm patients.

The concept can also be applied in the B2B context, learning from those organizations that are already leading the field

The B2B area also provides opportunities to restructure traditional distribution networks and supply chains. For many years, leading-edge supply chain organizations have exchanged information electronically regarding production schedules, raw material and component stock levels, and forecast levels of demand and production capacity. Suppliers and buyers, particularly in the automotive sector, have practised just-in-time techniques relying on electronic communication for some time. They have developed and introduced order-fulfilment techniques, reshaping the structure of the distribution networks and supply chains, enabling minimal inventories to be maintained through line-side delivery and rapid communication.

Other organizations have centralized their storage operations as a result of being able to communicate rapidly and fulfil orders using rapid transport services. The emergence of cost-effective and reliable high-speed transport services has played an important role in achieving the ambitions of those players embarking upon an Internet trading journey. The systems used by such organizations enable their customers to track their own shipments. This is essential in the early stages of using a changed network to give customers, both internal and external to the organization, the confidence that the remote operation will provide the required levels of service. More importantly, they enable the carriers themselves to be proactive on the rare occasion that some corrective action is needed to ensure that the required levels of customer service are achieved.

The impact will not be as large in all industry sectors

The reshaping of the supply chain as a result of Internet trading and the emergence of reliable and cost-effective rapid transport service providers will not impact all industry sectors to the same extent. While communications may improve, a worthwhile end in itself, it is difficult to envisage the network for bulk building supplies – for example, sand, ballast and cement – changing significantly as a result. The biggest impact is likely to be in the order fulfilment of those products that are relatively high in value and easily transported. The B2B environment is more stable than the B2C arena, with a more defined customer base and a better understanding of the demand pattern. The traditional distribution network or supply chain of an industrial company is shown in Figure 9.3. It is characterized by the direct delivery of large orders from factory to customer, and the use of distributors, agents or wholesalers for the delivery of small orders to customers on a geographic basis.

With the ability to capture and process orders more cheaply and quickly via the Internet than by conventional means, manufacturers are beginning to consider reducing the number of intermediaries they use to fulfil customers' orders. Those companies that supply consumables to other companies for use in their manufacturing processes can provide their customers with machine-monitoring devices that will send material usage statistics to them, via the Internet, triggering automatic replenishment orders. Once a history of usage

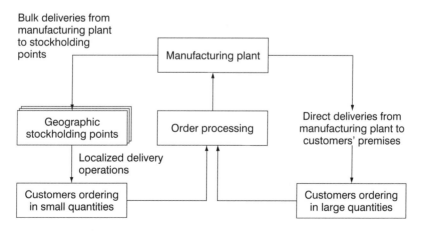

Figure 9.3 A traditional industrial supplier's distribution network

has been established, order fulfilment can be achieved more cost-effectively, as it can be planned better, minimizing peaks in demand for fulfilment resources. The customer does not need to maintain a purchasing function to place purchase orders, and the supplier does not need to incur the costs associated with an order-processing department: a 'win-win' scenario.

There is likely to be an increase in centralized operations

The biggest changes in order-fulfilment infrastructure as a result of Internet trading are likely to be in the area of centralized operations. Establishing a small number of order-fulfilment centres, with the associated software to integrate the Web site ordering process with the organization's business systems, is likely to be more cost-effective than the establishment of a larger number of local operations. Although transport costs are likely to increase as a result, they will be more than offset by lower order processing costs, inventory-related costs and warehouse facility costs. At constant volume, increased margins will be attainable, or lower prices can be charged to increase market share and enhance profitability.

In Europe, organizations that typically operated on a national basis are establishing more regionalized operations. Easily transported products of relatively high value tend to support larger regions than low-value products that require particular transport resources. Companies with spare parts operations tend to centralize those activities, as field engineers and customers can communicate with a central point via the Internet, and inventory control is much simpler with a central stock than several stockholding locations.

As the infrastructures change and the traditional role of intermediaries declines, a new group of Internet traders is emerging, offering purchasing function services. In general terms, they negotiate prices with a range of suppliers in a sector, and offer over the Internet a one-stop service for the products of those suppliers to their customers. Once they have taken an order from a customer it is converted to an order from a supplier. That supplier then fulfils the order in the conventional manner. The benefits of this scenario are that the customers obtain better prices, the suppliers do not have the costs of the customer-facing activities, and the Internet trader makes money by providing an added-value service to both customer and supplier without stocking and handling the products.

Initial performance was not good and the challenge is becoming greater

The growth in Internet trading has not been accompanied by tales of delighted customers and order-fulfilment processes to match the heightened customer expectation that results from being able to order at the click of a mouse.

Early experience suggested that organizations were not particularly good at integrating their Web site order-capturing activities with their internal business systems and those of their order fulfilment service provider. Furthermore, this was before many organizations realized the potential provided by the Internet for streamlining their distribution networks and supply chains. Changing business processes and introducing the necessary systems to trade over the Internet provided a challenge within existing business relationships and infrastructures. The challenge is being made all the more difficult as business relationships, and the physical infrastructure within which those relationships operate, are changing.

HOW INTERNET TRADERS CAN TAKE ADVANTAGE OF THE OPPORTUNITIES AVAILABLE FROM STREAMLINED SUPPLY CHAINS AND DISTRIBUTION NETWORKS

In this ever-changing world not all of the potential Internet-driven supply chain and distribution network changes will be appropriate for all Internet traders. Even within an industry sector, while patterns will emerge, the same solution may not be suitable for all of the players. There are, however, four activities that all Internet traders can complete as a starting point for achieving their objective of optimizing the supply chain and distribution network economies available. They are:

- The establishment of a vision of the future. 'Where are we going and what is it going to be like when we get there?'
- The definition of the partnering arrangements needed for success. 'Who is going to help us get to where we are going, and how are we going to manage them?'
- The reviewing of their business processes and electronic systems. 'Can our processes and systems enable us to achieve our long-term objectives?'
- The undertaking of trade-off calculations. 'What options are open to us and how much will they cost?'

These four activities form the key steps of an overall route to success, as outlined in Figure 9.4.

THE ESTABLISHMENT OF A VISION OF THE FUTURE

It is perhaps a little obvious to state that an organization needs to be able to state the direction in which it intends to go from a business perspective. That vision of the future is not a loose collection of statements amounting to little more than

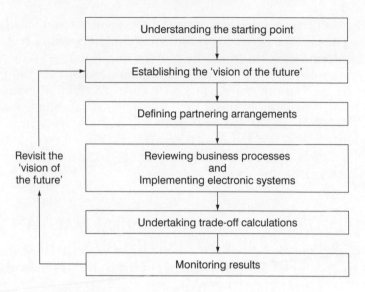

Figure 9.4 A route to success

a wish-list. It should comprise several statements describing in quantifiable terms the nature of the business at some point in the future. That point will vary depending upon the nature of the marketplace in which the organization is operating. In the high-tech sector the foreseeable future may be only a few months, a year at the most. In those traditional industry sectors that do not expect a significant percentage of their business ever to be undertaken over the Internet, the vision of the future may take several years to come to fruition.

The statements should cover the total volume of business, in both value and physical terms, the share that is undertaken over the Internet, the size of customer and supplier bases, the profitability of the Internet business, the costs associated with order fulfilment, and the delivery profile, in order numbers, divided into order size bands of an appropriate scale. Any individual organization will have many other metrics particular to its industry sector and product range. The key issue is that they should be measurable. They will be used to establish key performance indicators (KPIs) for the business. These KPIs will be reported against regularly, and in that way the organization can establish the extent to which it is achieving its vision of the future and reaping the rewards associated with the supply chain and distribution network changes it has established.

The definition of the partnering arrangements needed for success

Organizations wanting to trade over the Internet, with few exceptions, will not have all of the required skills in-house to effectively establish the Web site, integrate it with their business systems and manage the order-fulfilment activities. The need to partner is therefore essential for the vast majority of organizations wanting to establish an effective trade in goods over the Internet. A number of options are available to the potential electronic trader:

- A single one-stop shop able to deliver the Web site, integration with a commerce platform and order fulfilment. The advantages to the new entrant are a single point of contact for its management team and an organization that manages all of the difficult interfaces. Until recently, such organizations have been few and far between. This made selecting partners and a successful outcome something of a lottery. The service providers who developed a formula that works for their original customers are reluctant to change it to meet the needs of new entrants. Such is the pace of change these days that this situation does not provide as large a barrier to progress as it did a few years ago. The investment in IT resources by a number of the major value-adding order-fulfilment contractors is now beginning to manifest itself. The distribution industry, historically a watchword for flexibility, has put in place the skills, resources, hardware and application software to allow it to offer a single end-to-end service.
- Partnerships with a number of specialist service providers to source all of the services required. To achieve this successfully, project management and outsourcing management skills need to be in abundance in the organization. While the individual elements of Web site design, systems integration and order fulfilment may be readily available to the potential Internet trader in the marketplace, the required in-house skills of project and outsourcing management may not.
- An organization that has already done all the hard work, but is not in competition with the market entrant, could be a further solution to the problem of integrating all of the elements and taking advantage of the possibilities of changed routes to market. It is likely that such potential partners will be traditional 'bricks and mortar' traders that have extended their offering to include an electronic commerce element.

Thus there are many ways of developing a partnership to exploit the entrepreneurial flair of the organization. Making the decision will be helped by the development of a vision of the future as a starting point. An organization that expects a huge growth in volume in a short period may favour the use of an added-value service provider, as the influx could overwhelm a traditional business that currently has only a small share of its business handled by the Internet. Organizations that see a relatively slow but steady growth may favour managing the situation themselves or partnering with an organization that has already made the leap to Internet trading. Of course, those organizations that are hoping to move into new markets and/or geographies are likely to favour the added-value service provider route.

REVIEWING BUSINESS PROCESSES AND ELECTRONIC SYSTEMS

An Internet trader should include both electronic software systems and business processes in a review of in-house systems. The simplest questions about electronic software include:

- Can our systems cope with a significant increase in transactional volume?
- Can our systems interface with modern Web sites?
- Can our systems interface with those of our suppliers of both goods and services?
- Can our systems enable us to deliver the required level of customer service?

A few years ago, some of these questions would have sent shivers down the spine of would-be Internet traders. Modern systems typically do not present significant difficulties regarding interfacing, and thankfully extra capacity is no longer the hugely expensive item it was in the past. However, the most critical area for most businesses is not the software systems and supporting hardware networks, but the business processes employed by the organization. Will any of the order processing, credit checking, inventory allocation, manufacturing, warehousing, shipping, invoicing and cash collection processes within the overall order-to-cash process negatively impact the requirements of the Internet business?

If an organization is a true intermediary and expects not to hold stock but to convert a sales order into a purchase order in a back-to-back manner for eventual fulfilment by the supplier, its internal processes will need to able to cope with this business approach. It may be necessary to have a different process for Internet trade from that used for conventional business, in those organizations handling both routes to market. The questions needing to be answered under these circumstances include:

- Who will design the required processes to ensure that all customers' requirements are met?
- What will be the impact of those new processes on existing processes and the consequent risk to our traditional business?
- Will we achieve the predicted levels of economies of scale employing two or more order-to-cash processes?

These questions will be easier to answer if a clear understanding of the business direction has been established. In those circumstances in which the Internet business is seen to grow steadily but will never be a significant part of the business, the duplicated process route may be the easiest way of dealing with matters. Alternatively, if the Internet business is expected to grow rapidly and both the conventional and Internet trades become significant elements of the total business, a single process route would have merit.

Undertaking trade-off calculations

Analyses of the overall network and the options available to achieve the required levels of customer service are essential. To undertake the trade-off calculations associated with changing supply chains and distribution networks, in order to select the best route to market for any individual Internet entrepreneur, a full knowledge of current and potential operating costs is needed. Again, the importance of a vision of the future can readily be appreciated. While having that vision is important, understanding the starting point is also extremely important. Key questions to be answered include:

- What volumes are being dispatched?
- What levels of service are being achieved?
- What costs are being incurred?
- Do we feel that we are obtaining value for money?

The vision of the future will be able to provide answers to the questions regarding future volumes and expected margins. The Internet trader must then define a number of options for delivering the future volumes within the required customer service level constraints. They are likely to be network models with decentralized or centralized direct delivery, or via distributors and stockless or inventory-holding themes. A number of evaluation criteria will be required in addition to those that are strictly cost-related, to establish the most appropriate solution for each particular trader. While industry sectors may demonstrate similar solutions, an individual organization in that sector will be driven by its vision of the future and its culture in achieving that end goal.

THE OPPORTUNITY IS WAITING TO BE EXPLOITED

Internet trading is here to stay, and if recent experience is any guide, volumes are set to grow significantly in the very near future. Suppliers to both the consumer and business markets have a tremendous opportunity given the growth predictions. They are setting out on the journey against a background of heightened customer expectation and a history of failure to meet those expectations. The winners going forward will be those organizations that take the opportunity afforded by the Internet to change the manner in which they capture and fulfil their customers' orders.

To date, in many instances, the traders have implemented an Internet 'front end' to their existing business processes. Consequently, the initial limited volumes have been treated in the same way as their mainstream volumes. Those customers ordering via the Internet have different customer service level needs and expectations from most traditional customers – hence the levels of disappointment expressed by customers placing their orders via the Internet.

The Internet allows for different trading relationships and physical networks to be established. Those traders that develop a vision of the future incorporating the available potential, enter into partnering arrangements to enhance their internal skill base, review their business processes to meet their customers' needs, implement electronic systems to support those new business processes, and undertake the trade-off calculations to identify the most appropriate ways of meeting all of their customers' needs will reap the benefits.

The opportunity, given recent history, is real. The winners will be those that grasp that opportunity of using the Internet as a means of gaining competitive advantage rather than continue to use it as a 'bolt-on' extra to existing traditional operating methods.

REFERENCES

Forrester (2001a) *Forrester Techstrategy Report: ebusiness propels productivity*, Forrester Research (Nov)

Forrester (2001b) *Techstrategy Brief*, Forrester Research (26 Dec)

10

Organization, the supply chain and IT

Philip Schary
Oregon State University

Ashok Chandrashekar
Software Services Group, IBM Corporation

It was only with the shift from client-server to Web-based technologies that a true consolidation of data – a single, extended enterprise systems approach – became possible.

Dale Need (2001: 1)

Supply chains and corporate information systems lead parallel lives. They are symbiotic, as supply chain management needs information and computing power for operations, control and planning; and supply chains provide a major area of application for information technology (IT). In actuality, most firms have multiple supply chains operating independently of each other, with each based on a specific focus: overhead indirect supplies or direct procurement for individual products and markets.

IT not only provides the basis for managing material and product flow, it shapes the future organization of the supply chain. While the path of material and product flow is well defined, corporate information systems are not. Two observers of the current state of IT, Ciborra and Hanseth (2000: 2) note, 'Corporate information systems are puzzles, or better, collages, and so are the design and implementation processes that lead to their construction and operation.' The dominant concept for implementation is strategic alignment, matching the information system to the strategic needs of the firm (Henderson and Venkatraman, 1993). That this does not work in practice is a result of radical changes taking place in both the user environment and the infrastructure (the information system itself). Ciborra (2000) notes that alignment is, at best, a journey and not an event, suggesting the continuing state of flux on both sides.

The Internet is the current transforming agent of the information system. It changes not only computing and communication but the operation of the supply chain itself. While future direction cannot be defined with precision, some general indicators point the way. The open character of the Internet, the ease of connection, and the complementary roles of computing and communication, are transforming both IT and the supply chain. Further, there is a wide variety of supply chain configurations to match strategic requirements (Cavinato, 2002). Of course, when we discuss supply chain design we deal in general terms, recognizing that circumstances may dictate unique problem solutions.

This chapter addresses the ways that changes in information technology influence organization and management of the supply chain. It begins with the traditional supply chain structure, and then describes the parallel paths of supply chains and IT, and shows how IT influences supply chain structure. Then we look at the impact of the Internet-based supply chain on organization. This, however, is not the end of the story. The Internet opens other options in supply chain organization, with new opportunity and new requirements for both management and IT. We close with some observations on the organization of the future.

THE PATH TO THE INTERNET

Both the supply chain and IT owe their development to the concept of business processes. They link functional activities to accomplish a mission of meeting the needs of the ultimate customer. Both have met resistance within the organization.

Figure 10.1 describes four stages of development. The upper panel shows states of supply chain evolution, the lower panel the forms of IT technology that drive it. The four stages have been named traditional, high volume, e-supply and networks. They are broadly named to describe the most important attributes. Underneath is the movement of IT from hard copy and limited computer usage, through large stand-alone computer applications and EDI, to the Internet. Stage four looks to the currently evolving technology of networks.

The traditional supply chain was linear, connecting partner organizations for a sequence of activities to deliver products and services. It was accompanied by a movement to outsource non-critical activities. Communication was oriented

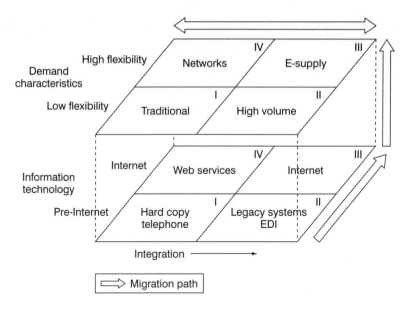

Figure 10.1 Stages of development

towards transactions, with at best only informal joint planning. Integration stopped at the corporate boundary. Even within the organization, battles were hard-fought – and still continue.

As the supply chain matured and processed high volumes of material and customer orders, it was enabled by two developments. The first was increasingly sophisticated computing capabilities associated with stand-alone activities – such as production planning through materials resource planning (MRP) – to give a transaction system for the internal operations of the organization. Crossing functional boundaries gave a major advance in the use of IT for managing the process, but the flow of information stopped at the organization boundaries. Enterprise resource planning (ERP) is today the central core of supply chain management, although installation and connection still present major obstacles (Bowersox, Closs and Hall, 1998).

The second was electronic data interchange (EDI), giving a method for computer-to-computer data communication. This is expensive both for individually configured and dedicated connections between designated partners, and for the necessary training. It has the benefit of offering greater security than the Internet, and has gained widespread – but not universal – acceptance for transactions, with standardized message formats for advance shipping notices, invoices and so on.

The era of e-supply is a radical – and costly – change, which also creates opportunity. It offers access and flexibility on a scale not previously possible, with ease of communication giving more coordinated supply chains. The technical and training requirements for the Internet are lower. It presents opportunities for increased coordination, leading to lower costs and better response to customer requirements. Unfortunately, the transfer costs are high, requiring either new systems or connection to the legacy systems already in place from Stage II. The evidence to date shows reluctance by most firms to adopt more than transaction-based systems (Edwards, Peters and Sharman, 2001). This is unfortunate, as communication is enhanced by the Internet itself, because of its reach and the potential richness of its message capacity. It is further enhanced by the intro-duction of XML (described as a meta-language to allow computer systems in separate organizations to transmit data to each other) supplemented by RosettaNet (vertically oriented software to facilitate ordering processes: see Chudnow (2002)). Together, these both replace and complement EDI, offering flexible communication among differing computer operating systems. All of these developments further the integration of the supply chain.

The future lies in networks. Although they are now familiar in consumer and certain business markets, their potential applications are only beginning to emerge. Networks present a framework for dynamic supply chains, with rapid change in partners to match new market opportunities and supply disruptions. This marks a shift from stable, linear connections to virtual chains linked by temporary connections through the Internet. It also creates new institutions in application service providers, and Web services that shift costs and free supply chains from organizational limits of IT investment. E-supply and networks will exist in parallel: e-supply for closer integration of core supply chains, networks for non-critical and temporary connection.

THE INTERNET IMPLICATIONS

Three organizational themes emerge with e-supply: closer integration with, first, suppliers, second, customers through collaborative software, and third, real-time operation. The focus since the emergence of e-supply has been on procurement and supplier relations. Part of this is driven by the need for cost reduction in the present climate, but also because of the predominant orien-tation of supply chains to support production. Customer relations, however, have aroused interest, particularly because of the need to differentiate offerings by customizing products to match individual customer requirements. The issue comes to a head with the movement towards real-time operations, taking customer orders directly into production schedules, possibly for direct delivery. Real time emphasizes speed of response and control over the entire chain, centralizing management, even over separate organizations.

Software and supplier relations

Supply chain software comes in an almost bewildering profusion, but it can be categorized by orientation into execution and planning (cf Accenture, 2002).

Execution has generated more interest, with its orientation towards transactions, cost reduction and immediate investment payback. Planning in a supply chain context invokes partnership and varying degrees of collaboration. Adoption here has been slower, because of difficulties in organizational data and computer coordination, and the need for a longer-term perspective. An intermediate level has also appeared, with a 'digital cockpit,' providing management with overall surveillance, and with aggregate performance measures used to indicate deviations or identify potential problem areas.

There is an implied quest for uniformity in both the supply chain IT system as a whole, and compatibility between software modules. However, in a global context, a completely uniform information system may not match local management requirements or respond easily to local conditions, but will create a tension stemming from differing objectives. Examples of this include partner characteristics, computer protocols and local shipping schedules. There is also software incompatibility stemming from differences in programming, which is driven as much by competitive differentiation by vendors as technical requirements.

An essential characteristic of management is the need for control. Most control software deals with processes in aggregate. A new category, supply chain event management (SCEM) software is now appearing, which offers a new degree of micro-management (Bartholomew, 2002). SCEM can track individual items through procurement, production, and distribution processes, noting progress or exceptions. It strengthens centralized management relative to individual work groups, because the individual operations now become distinctly visible. SCEM becomes an essential element in real-time operations (Mulani and Lee, 2002: 16), even though it reduces local control and has the potential to overload centralized management with information.

In a supply chain, there are three levels of involvement: arms-length transactions, coordination and collaboration (Bressler and Grantham, 2000). *Transaction-based relationships* imply no further involvement or data sharing beyond the immediate transaction, although there may be informal communication relating to specific problems or future sales. These favour execution systems, and may include the creation or use of electronic catalogues, or auction arrangements such as market exchanges. They also include transaction-related information such as production progress reporting, shipping or availability-to-promise information.

Transaction systems that do not involve human judgement, such as procurement with narrowly defined product and service specifications, lend themselves to automation. Intelligent agents can survey internal or vendor catalogues, or enter the marketplace, search for price, calculate other costs (such as transportation and inventory costs) and make selections without human intervention.

Coordination involves partners in joint production and shipment planning, sharing forecasts and capacity estimates. Coordination stresses visibility throughout the supply chain, although in practice this may be limited to first-tier suppliers or customers (Fawcett and Magnan, 2002). Negotiation is possible for quantities, scheduling, production and shipping priorities requiring interactive communication. Data content is richer, although usually within limits prescribed by the lead firm. While XML relieves some of the problem of inter-organizational data flow, non-technical problems may still remain with data coding and interpretation (such as forecast data involving customer purchase patterns). Programs such as collaborative production management (CPM) and supplier relationship management (SRM) enable joint control over production operations.

The highest level, *collaboration*, places the greatest demands on the information system. Suppliers become active participants, taking responsibility for process development and operations, and in some cases product design and development. The highest process level is synchronization, where supplier, lead firm and distribution all match scheduling and capacity to achieve balanced throughput. Several software programs are now being offered to optimize inventory levels, or to match pricing to capacity for revenue maximization.

Collaborative product commerce (CPC) supports the product development process over the full product life cycle from design through to production (Keenan and Ante, 2002). This has been described as the most crucial part of collaboration. Software such as the widely used Catia, or Virtual Reality Modelling, make possible direct visual collaboration on design, with three-dimensional modelling capabilities (Ward, 2001). Digital design collaboration opens doors to much faster and more efficient collaboration with other members of the supply chain.

The first step in collaboration is to develop trust between partners. Sako (1992), examining British and Japanese supply chain relationships, defines three kinds of trust: contractual trust, competence trust and goodwill trust. Contractual trust deals with the reliance on the other partner to fulfil its specified obligations. The Internet and collaborative software can establish competence trust fairly objectively through the volume and quality of data exchanged and the patterns of use. There are strong reservations, however, about the ability of the Web to detect the subtleties of human encounters and establish goodwill trust. Perhaps it will be possible in the future to utilize video face contact, although the evidence to date is mixed.

Customer relationships

The parallel to a supplier orientation is customer relationship management. This has not received the same attention, although interest appears to be building (Hewitt, 2001). It has taken two forms: one for collaboration with intermediate customers and resellers, and another for mass customization for final customers.

Customer collaboration aroused interest following initial experiments in joint forecasting between manufacturers and retailers, as customer planning and forecasting (CPFR). It has demonstrated its value for retailers where the customer exerts market power, as it ensures stock availability and avoids unnecessary inventory. Forecasting to set production schedules and distribution gives a 'push' inventory system, holding stock close to the market – but with the risk of misestimating demand. Forecasters and operations on both sides can, however, share information and coordinate actions on promotional activities and logistics.

The alternative is build-to-order, which is growing in importance with increasing product variety and shorter product lifecycles. Individual customer orders come directly into the production schedule in lieu of forecasts. In mass customization, a range of options for the product or service is pre-specified, customers select their preferences, the order is executed, and the product is delivered. The execution point, a factory or distribution centre, becomes the balancing point of the system – the farthest point of customer penetration into the system, and the bridge into the supply system (Sharman, 1984). Information requirements differ on either side of this point. Order information beyond this balance point deals with aggregated quantities, although individual orders can be carried back to suppliers if they are supplying customized components (Hoekstra and Romme, 1992).

An alternative for production is to develop postponement strategies, where standard modules are combined in final assembly at the last possible moment. For the supply chain, the significance of mass customization lies in the change from standard to individualized product orders. There are a variety of possible strategies, including product modularity, process modularity, product and procurement standardization, and postponement (Swaminathan, 2001). Ultimately, the approach could lead to different supply chain configurations for each order.

In the information system, component control, processing time, tracking capabilities and flexibility to meet changing requirements become critical factors (Zipkin, 2001). Tracking demand for components can give severe data coding requirements when a wide variety of products are assembled. However, the introduction of SCEM software could accelerate the growth of customization because of its control over individual orders.

Real-time supply chain management

Real time is the culmination of the integrated supply chain, offering rapid response, synchronization with suppliers and customers, and flexibility to manage capacity, product variety and value. It also stresses a high degree of integration with suppliers (Exostar, 2002). Real time turns the Internet into a distributed operating system, connecting computers, applications and databases almost instantaneously. It responds immediately to customer orders, entering them into an advanced scheduling and production program, passing signals to suppliers for components and materials. Renner (2002; also see Ranadive (1999); *Economist* (2002)) suggests that the real-time system requires the 'the three V's': visibility, velocity and value. It requires complete visibility to identify constraints and potential conflicts, as well as data compatibility for clear identification. Data must be consistent for all partners and free of distortion. Velocity requires the ability to identify constraints and optimize the supply chain for an order in real time. Value describes the performance of an integrated system to execute orders through multiple software applications – possibly Web-based but also including off-Web legacy computers and software – organized to respond to and process individual orders. It also suggests a high degree of automation, both in the process itself and by the use of intelligent software to select manufacturing and other processing applications and then to schedule them for production.

Real time offers an opportunity to respond to the market, producing for each order as it enters the system. Dell Computers currently operates in this mode, assembling computers within hours of receiving an individual order. Suppliers send parts as soon as the order arrives and maintain limited stocks themselves. Finished product planning is thus entirely short term, although there must be tentative capacity commitments for production. Component planning horizons are longer because of production lead times.

Several automobile manufacturers, notably General Motors, Toyota and Nissan, are moving towards real-time, build-to-order systems in their North American operations (Bradsher, 2000; Pritchard, 2000; Moozakis, 2002; Simpson, 2000). The precursor is a Japanese system that predates the Internet by several years, and promises delivery in five days (Womack, Jones and Roos, 1990). At present, North American systems promise delivery in weeks. However, more than information flow is involved. Customers order vehicles either through dealers or directly over the Web, and the data flows through CRM into ERP systems where these orders become scheduled for production. But real time also depends on flexible production and managing components from suppliers. Movement towards real time has been cautious, but persistent.

Real time ties several themes together: customer response, collaboration and flexibility. It also indicates a future in which supply chains will focus on individual orders. Partner relationships and their capabilities become more important because of the need for close coordination. It also suggests attention to product design to create modules for sub-assembly that can be passed on for rapid final order assembly and fulfilment.

NETWORKS AND THE NEW PLAYERS

The role of the Internet extends beyond integration. It has created new institutions with previously unavailable possibilities, such as the now-familiar market exchanges and virtual private networks (VPNs). Some players are now defining their roles (such as application service providers and Web service organizations), others are barely on the horizon (such as virtual supply chains). And there are, of course, newer technologies that hold promise, such as wireless and automation.

Market exchanges

These are the most familiar part of the Internet landscape. In procurement, they are reverse auctions, where suppliers bid for business with standardized products, production capacity or services, to be selected by customers usually on the basis of price. Buyers and sellers, however, have differing perspectives. There may be many possible sellers but only a few buyers, depending on the structure of the industry. Then buyers get lower prices, but sellers face harsh conditions. And activities on either side could be under public surveillance, giving away valuable information to competitors.

Price is not the only cost involved in purchasing, which is one of the factors limiting the use of market exchanges. The legitimacy of the parties, delivery conditions, transportation costs, handling and inventory holding costs, and so on all affect the total cost of the transaction. Some do well, such as Exostar (2002), an aerospace exchange, because they fulfil a need for efficient transactions for routine supplies. Others, such as Covisint, an automotive industry marketplace, have introduced additional services such as inventory management for both buyer and seller in order to attract and retain customers.

Kaplan and Sawhney (2000) foresee a variety of roles for market exchanges:

- the current price-oriented model;
- specialist originators guiding buyers and sellers through transactions;
- e-speculators, seeking profits by taking risk positions;
- solution providers with analytical decision support;
- asset swaps, exchanging commodities, future positions and production capacity.

Market exchanges have limitations. They are transaction oriented, their fees can be high, service can deteriorate as the number of buyers increases, there may be limits to the number of requests for quotation or purchase orders from one buyer that can be handled at one time, and so on. If the exchange computer system fails, can the transaction be salvaged? In a complex market exchange, the chances of system supply chain failure increase with the number of servers involved. And how secure is the exchange against intruders? On their Website, Covisint (2002) recognizes that their customers may use it for part of their supply requirements, using other supply chains for the rest.

Market exchanges influence other parts of the supply chain. While some such as Covisint have coordination features, their role in collaboration appears to have limits. Market exchanges invite a dual process: first the product market, followed by a logistics service provider searching for subcontracting carriers and other service providers in another exchange (Lewis, 2001). As spot markets for commodity products from a potentially wide range of vendors from an equally wide range of locations, they require new, flexible logistics services for transport and inventory holding to deal with non-repeating vendor locations and routings (Delfmann, Albers and Gehring, 2002). Exchanges are also responsible for 'disintermediation', substituting auction mechanisms for full service market intermediaries that formerly were part of many business and consumer goods distribution channels.

Private exchanges

Some companies prefer private exchanges (VPNs) with the potential for closer collaboration, reliability and security. Volkswagen recently introduced a VPN where 4,000 pre-certified suppliers enter through an electronic portal into negotiations and auction transactions and collaborate with the corporation (Volkswagen, 2001). Initial experience indicated a 95 per cent reduction in order process times. Further plans would extend it to second tier and lower-level suppliers, placing procurement entirely through the exchange.

Cisco, which owns virtually no manufacturing capacity of its own, has taken the concept of the VPN one step further in a configuration that a trade journal called 'the supply chain for the 21st Century' (Grosvenor and Austin, 2001; Kahla, 2002). Suppliers are certified to enter a portal to participate in the Cisco e-hub. Suppliers can not only bid for business, but negotiate and collaborate among themselves, using the e-hub as a communication centre for non-transactional information. The hub reaches 650 suppliers and participants, and becomes a centre of a supply chain manufacturing community, with visibility to respond to changes in the market. For example, partners can review each other's order books to check on over-inflated component orders, thereby reducing a problem that has plagued Cisco. From a first stage of information exchange, the e-hub was planned for two further stages: optimization and design collaboration.

Public networks are useful for procurement of standardized products for indirect overhead and standard production requirements. Beyond their auction role, they can become catalogues for access by procurement specialists. As part of supply chains, public networks serve a limited role, as they must be supplemented by human contact for negotiation and collaboration. In addition, they reduce the close relationship of collaboration.

The use of automatic routines and intelligent agents can reduce the burden of procurement. These intelligent agents are 'computer programs that include artificial intelligence to provide active assistance to users in computer-based tasks' (Tucker and Jones, 2000). Agents are given parameters of product specification, lead time, cost and any other constraints on the search, and there may also be a pre-programmed negotiation strategy. These systems are ideal for routine transactions where frequency is low and short-lived and criteria are objective. As negotiation begins to involve judgement, human inter-vention may be introduced, and the employment and collaboration of trans-action-based agents become complementary. The result is a duality of chains, one for routine, a second for strategic procurement.

ASPs and Web services

These may be crucial to the ultimate success of supply chain information systems. ASPs (active server pages) hold software applications such as vehicle routing or inventory management for client companies, connecting to users through XML links, and charging user fees for services. Web services go a step further, managing supply chain information as a process. They become process managers, holding and routing data, requesting and integrating software from ASPs (Hagel and Brown, 2001). These integrated services have several advantages:

- managing software compatibility among supply chain members, providing access through a single interface regardless of user computer protocols or operating systems;
- shifting information system management from the user to specialists;
- shifting fixed costs to the Web service provider in exchange for transaction or rental fees as variable costs;
- creating supplier and customer access to select information without entering the corporate information system;
- creating flexibility with ease of access by authorized users.

Early ASP vendors were often unstable and short tenured, leaving clients without service – clearly threatening the performance of the supply chain as a whole. This has changed as Web services converge towards a few dominant players such as IBM, Microsoft and Oracle. Another concern now is security, which is in the hands of a third party and may be threatened if unauthorized users gain entry to data files or disrupt services. Web services centralize infor-mation and control through a single server. At the same time, local decisions require local computer support. The result is to push relevant applications to local users, 'outside the firewall' (Margulius, 2002). Again, their role is still being defined, but the net effect decentralizes decision making.

The dynamic supply chain

The future for many supply chains will be characterized by short product life cycles and expanding product variety. Demands will be temporary, suggesting that supply chains must be increasingly nimble. They must be formed at short notice, with pre-established communication and control, to be dissolved when their task is complete. Competitive advantage will lie with the supply chain management that first recognizes and responds to opportunity. This brings the supply chain in close partnership with marketing, shifting from a supply to a demand orientation.

All Internet-based supply chains are virtual, in the sense that they are connected and coordinated electronically. The term 'virtual supply chain' can also be construed to mean that it is organized for short-tenured flexibility for individual projects, then to disappear, as an agile supply chain. Here 'agility' refers to the capability of an organization to respond to both threats and opportunities (Whitman and Presley, 2001) The chains can focus on products or capacity, depending on their particular role at that time (Chandrashekar and Schary, 1999). They are necessarily customer-oriented because customer needs specify the configuration of the supply chain.

Moshowitz (1994), referring to virtual organizations in general, identifies three enabling factors that also relate to supply chains: simplification, combinatorial freedom and switching. Simplification assigns specific activities to organizational units; combinatorial freedom allows the manager to assign tasks and units as necessary to meet new requirements; switching makes new connections as needs arise. The virtual supply chain requires leadership to organize and manage what is essentially a federal system of governance. Management acts as entrepreneur and broker (Miles and Snow, 1992). Independent organizations are brought together in cooperation, with specific capabilities focused on one objective, to be reorganized for another when another customer requirement appears. The critical management role is providing the 'glue' to hold the virtual chain together (Pihkala, Varamaki and Vesalainen, 1999). One writer (Rahman, 2002) observes five defining characteristics for this.

- a shared vision;
- clusters of activities based on core competencies;
- work performed in teams of core competence groups;
- information processed in real time for rapid decisions;
- decisions delegated from the bottom up.

The idea of temporary connection is not entirely new. Building construction has followed this pattern, but with personal contact. Alcatel built custom digital telecommunication switches 15 years ago, using a pool of firms that would be brought into a project selectively, then released as the individual switch was finished. Supply chains for the garment industry indicate a similar pattern, but often relying on electronic connections. Li and Fung was formerly a Hong Kong trading company, but now manages temporary product-focused garment supply chains in Southeast Asia for small and medium-sized retailers in Europe and North America (Magretta, 1998).

The Internet extends these possibilities, relying on the speed of connection. Then virtual chains would rely on a Web community, consisting of a set of organizations with common interests operating through pre-agreed rule-based systems and tied to a particular industry (Franke, 1999). Active organizational links would be temporary, but embedded in latent relationships. The lead firm would recruit and impose standards on other members, but would also be responsible for maintaining the community. The important element is to maintain a knowledge base among members (Hedlund, 1994; Fahey et al, 2001).

The virtual chain relies on electronic connection for both transactions and planning. It uses automation for transaction processes to a degree that varies depending on their complexity. Coordination will use more verbal and possibly visual communication, requiring greater bandwidth capacity. While the direct communication costs would be low, computer and software infrastructure requirements are high. Virtual chains can operate within a completely proprietary VPN framework with sufficient transaction volume. Another solution is to rely on a third party for process management.

The outsourcing of supply chain software to Web services invites speculation about future forms of the virtual supply chain. The concepts, the supply chain and the virtual organization have an inherent conflict. Effective supply chain management requires centralized control. Virtual organizations have localized decisions. Outsourcing the supply chain to external partners may provide a compromise, but it would take operating decisions away from the original partners. This is already taking place on a major scale, such as Vector SCM (a joint alliance between CNF Corporation, a logistics services provider and General Motors (Cullen, 2001)) or the management services offered by UPS to their clients (UPS, 2002)

Web services are dominated today by large computer-oriented companies, including IBM, Microsoft and Oracle. It is possible to envision Web software services and logistics service providers combining to become complete supply chain management services. Companies such as Li and Fung fulfil this role in the garment industry. As more firms outsource manufacturing, procurement, distribution and logistics, supply chain management service providers will continue to expand into a major industry.

Microsoft exemplifies rapid deployment in setting a supply chain for the Xbox console (Carbone, 2002; Shah and Serant, 2002). With little previous presence in hardware manufacturing, it engaged a manufacturing partner (Flextronics) and suppliers using open communication and integrated systems to share data and collaborate in real time. Within eight months, Microsoft selected 40 major suppliers, negotiated supply contracts, ensured adequate capacity, and integrated procurement with its suppliers, including automated reordering. Its chip supplier, Nvidia, invested heavily in software and servers for the design and coordination with its foundry, while Taiwan Semiconductor Manufacturing Company committed a fabrication plant to Nvidia. Flextronics worked simultaneously with Nvidia, Intel and Microsoft, preparing one plant in Mexico and a second in Hungary (later moved to China). Flextronics had already developed its own local supply networks to support production.

Virtual chains challenge management in many ways. A primary management task is to plan, recruit and maintain a Web community, defined in terms of capability and common vision, with common technical standards for information and communication, communicating a common culture, and providing inter-organizational mechanisms for sharing and managing the product development process to define product modules for partner production. Technical knowledge will retain its importance, particularly in IT, but it must be complemented by the softer skills of inter-organizational management.

THE NEW ORGANIZATION

One observer of IT asked about the future of e-business, looking backwards from 2006, commented that technology was relentless and that change would take place incrementally (Malone, 2001). The gaps are large, both between technology and managerial culture and between technology and organizational systems (Jaegersberg et al, 2001).

The environment of the supply chain is predictable, to a point. It will include competition between supply chains as systems. Demands will continue to determine supply chain configurations. Product cycles will be short, and products and services will emphasize broad variety. All of this will take place within a context of rapidly evolving information technology. The Internet has opened a Pandora's Box of possibilities. How will organizations evolve to meet these challenges?

The prerequisite to management is strategic vision and development of an infrastructure of IT and organizations. The balance of power shifts towards the customer, although management must organize the response to match specific demands. Customers will control the chain, indirectly through product and service preferences, or directly influencing the actual configuration of the system through product and service preferences.

Some chains will remain stable, serving established, mature markets. For them, the major task is to improve efficiency through closer integration, while maintaining sensitivity to prospective change. Outsourcing depends on the sources of competitive advantage and the ability to reduce total system costs. Other chains must demonstrate their agility in responding to rapidly changing demands through flexible operations and possibly their ability to configure as virtual chains.

It is possible to anticipate a taxonomy of supply chains:

1. Transaction-based routine supply operations.
2. Coordinated networks involving separate organizations in limited cooperation.

3. Collaborative networks where partners work closely together.
4. Open network structures.

(This discussion is based on categories described in Johannesen and Solem (2002).) Some organizations will have all of these, using each for a different purpose. Note that in the options 1 and 2 the organizational boundaries are relatively firm. Only in option 3 does the concept of separate organizations diminish, although it does not disappear completely. In option 4, organizations become modular blocks to be assembled for a particular task. The management tasks would logically differ among the four.

Transaction-oriented networks are essentially mechanistic, operated through rule-based procedures. They will become at least partially automated to deal with routine processes that change slowly, while various extensions to the Internet expand the potential scope of automated procedures. It is possible to envision parallel information networks that signal for automatic inventory replenishment, maintenance service and status reporting as in SCEM (see Semilof, 2001; Abell, Martin and Romanow, 2002; Ferguson, 2002). The trend to treat more products as commodities makes procurement routine, with decisions based on specification and price. The expanding use of artificial intelligence encourages automated systems for more areas that were once reserved for human judgement.

There are several management tasks in transaction-based systems:

- surveillance to ensure that the system is performing to expectations;
- monitoring for exceptions, and tracking progress of orders and individual items through the supply chain;
- developing and gaining acceptance for standardized procedures and safeguards across the supply chain;
- planning for system change in anticipation of shifting information technology;
- responding to changes in markets and supply structures.

Coordinated networks involve partners in joint decisions in carefully prescribed areas such as supply synchronization. Central control is maintained over the supply chain as a whole, but allows for local control where specific knowledge takes precedence. The major problems are coordination across different organizational, physical and national environments. Management must define the boundaries between global and local decisions, and ensure information system compatibility in computer protocols, software and data. A study of the buyer–seller relationship indicates that the degree of face-to-face contact declines as the relationship moves towards integration, allowing for more electronic communication (Ellram, 1991). The future of this category can go either towards routine and automation, or towards freer interaction through collaboration.

Collaboration establishes close working relationships, to the point of blurring organizational boundaries. The patterns of collaboration are well documented, and the tasks are less well defined in general terms. It is, as one set of writers describes it, an 'electronic hierarchy' replacing vertical integration by ownership (Monteiro, 2000). It includes building alliances between organizations, sharing risks and rewards, with open sharing of data and ideas. The role of the organization itself may change, depending upon its degree of differentiation and bargaining power, from a reservoir of task-oriented resources to a unique position controlling its associations. From an IT perspective, it will be enabled by collaborative software and broadband communication where images and other media create rich message content. The need for computer system compatibility becomes more important as the sophistication of communication increases.

Open networks are relatively new, although precedents have appeared in pre-Internet form (Chandrashekar and Schary, 2002) How much significance they will have is not yet clear. Ultimately, they are organizations of free-floating partners, organized in communities, in some cases with rotating leadership. Normally the lead firm, the network structure and infrastructure providers (such as Web services and logistics service providers) are stable elements, forming constant islands in a sea of change. Partners in production or distribution will change to meet specific project or customer requirements. The infrastructure of procedures and standards must be pre-established to allow for rapid response and flexibility.

The open network imposes new management requirements. These include, first, direction of a complex system, and second, recruiting and motivating a community of potential partners, when these firms are used not on a continuous basis but as latent partners, called when needed for specific projects and then released. For the organizing firm, selecting partners will require close attention to the market, because the strength of the virtual supply chain will be in their technologies and the quality of managements. They may belong to several communities serving competing interests, raising questions of motivation, security and differences in procedure.

A third requirement is to standardize information systems, including data and communication. These would undoubtedly be uniform across a given industry, but there will be problems in defining industry boundaries. It is possible that some community members would belong to more than one industry group, forcing conformity into a broader arena.

A fourth requirement of developing and maintaining inter-organizational relations is a major constraint. The effectiveness of the supply chain depends on both the information network and the underpinning bonds that support it. Management must establish both trust and a sense of affiliation for community members, which are necessary for motivation, planning and control.

A fifth requirement is to utilize the collective knowledge of the supply chain, with organizations using collective learning as knowledge to gain competitive advantage. This knowledge is both explicit and tacit. Explicit knowledge is tangible; it can be recorded, embedded in software and is potentially available to anyone. Tacit knowledge is embedded in personal relationships, developed over time, and creates ways of working which become hard to emulate, because they are unspoken. The virtual chain by its temporary nature does not build tacit knowledge because partners may not have continuing contact with each other, losing a potential source of competitive advantage.

Some general comments apply to all supply chain configurations. First, there are limits to the role of Internet connections. Beyond simple transactions, there is an apparent need for human contact, not only for verbal communication, but also for non-verbal cues (*Economist*, 2000). Whether this can be completely overcome through video connection is not clear, but at present it indicates a need for proximity and frequent, casual contact. This is the weak element of the virtual chain.

There are also organizational issues for management. One is defining the role of member organizations. When we move from transactions to integration, we select specific functional activities from members, with organizational cultures that can be distinctly different. We may leave the member organization intact, or consider it as a pool of resources to be incorporated into product flow processes. The difference will also mean a difference in information requirements. Much will depend on the relative power of the lead firm to build a cohesive organization.

CONCLUDING REMARKS

This discussion began by tracing the development of information systems that accompany supply chains. We then explored the impact of the Internet on the supply chain, examining its potential in inter-organizational relations and particularly for collaboration. We then moved to new developments in exchanges, Web services and virtual supply chains. Finally we offer some speculative comments about future organization.

In any discussion of future IT applications to the supply chain, the future is highly speculative. Either events that can be projected have already been demonstrated somewhere, or the technology leads in new directions that we cannot anticipate. If IT is part of the infrastructure of the supply chain, it is reflexive, in that it builds on itself. Its development has first, been influenced, through multiple anonymous actors both human and non-human (the IT network); second, progressed on specific paths, influenced by the organizations in which it has been embedded; and third, been connected to other IT and social networks that also determine the direction of growth (Hanseth, 2000). While the technology presents a dynamic frontier, most organizations have been slow to adapt – partly because of culture, partly because of the high costs of switching into new systems. The result is a future that is still for the most part undefined. The advice given to high technology management is that the only viable strategy is to experiment through trial and error (Brown and Eisenhardt, 1998). The future will not be determined by technology alone but by the ability to use it.

REFERENCES

Abell, P, Martin R and Romanow, K (2002) ePC and RFID are for real, *AMR Outlook* (26 Aug) [Online] http://www.amrrresearch.com

Accenture (2002) *Achieving Supply Excellence through Technology 4*, Montgomery Research, San Francisco

Bartholomew, D (2002) Event management: hype or hope? *Industry Week* (May), pp 29–31 [Online] http://web19.epnet.com

Bowersox, D J , Closs, D J and Hall, C T (1998) Beyond ERP: the storm before the calm, *Supply Chain Management* (Winter), pp 28–36

Bradsher, K (2000) The long, long wait for cars, *New York Times* (9 May) [Online] http//www.nytimes.com

Bressler, S E and Grantham, C E (2000) *Communities of Commerce*, McGraw-Hill, New York

Brown, S L and Eisenhardt, K (1998) *Competing on the Edge*, Harvard Business School Press, Boston, MA

Carbone, J (2002) Outsourcing the Xbox, *Purchasing* (15 Aug), p 23

Cavinato, J C (2002) What's your supply chain type? *Supply Chain Management Review* (1 May) [Online] http://www.manufacturing.net/scm

Chandrashekar, A and Schary, P B (1999) Toward the virtual supply chain: the convergence of IT and organization, *International Journal of Logistics Management*, **10** (2), pp 27–40

Chandrashekar, A and Schary, P (2002) The virtual Web-based supply chain, in *Managing Virtual Organizations in the 21st Century*, ed U Franke, SDG Publications, London

Chudnow, C (2002) XML helps untangle the Web, *Computer Technology News* (January), p 44 [Online] http://proquest.umi.com

Ciborra, C U (2000) A critical review of the literature on the management of corporate information infrastructure in drift, in *From Control to Drift*, ed C U Ciborra, Oxford UP, New York

Ciborra, C U and Hanseth, O (2000) Introduction: from control to drift, in *From Control to Drift*, ed C U Ciborra, p 2, Oxford UP, New York

Covisint (2002) *Questions and Answers* [Online] http://www.covisint.com (accessed Sept 2002)

Cullen, T (2001) Vector, *SCM Automotive Logistics* (Aug), pp 20–29

Delfmann, D, Albers, D and Gehring, M (2002) The impact of electronic commerce on logistics service providers, *International Journal of Physical Distribution and Logistics Management*, **32** (3), pp 203–22

Economist (2000) In a wired world, physical presence counts more than ever, *Economist* (22 Aug) [Online] http://www.economist.com

Economist (2002) A survey of the real-time economy, *Economist* (2 Feb)

Ellram, L M (1991) Life-cycle patterns in industrial buy-seller partnerships, *International Journal of Physical Distribution and Logistics Management*, **21** (9), pp 57–70

Exostar (2002) [Online] http://exostar.com (accessed Sep 2002)

Fahey, L, Srivastava, R, Sharon, J S and Smith, D E (2001) Linking e-business and operating processes: the role of knowledge management, *IBM Systems Journal*, **40** (4), pp 889–918

Fawcett, S E and Magnan, G M (2002) The rhetoric and reality of supply chain integration, *International Journal of Physical Distribution and Logistics Management*, **32** (5), pp 339–61

Ferguson, G T (2002) Have your objects call my objects, *Harvard Business Review*, **80** (Jun), pp 138–44

Franke, U (1999) The virtual Web as a new entrepreneurial approach to network organizations, *Entrepreneurship and Regional Development*, **11**, pp 203–29

Grosvenor, F and Austin, T A (2001) Cisco's eHub initiative supply chain, *Management Review* (7 August), p 14 [Online] http://www.manufacturing.net/scm

Hagel, J and Brown, J S (2001) Your next IT strategy, *Harvard Business Review*, **79** (October), pp 105–13

Hanseth, O (2000) The economics of standards in *From Drift to Control*, ed C U Ciborra, Oxford UP, New York

Hedlund, G (1994) A model of knowledge management and the N-form corporation, *Strategic Management Journal*, **15**, pp 73–90

Henderson, J C and Venkatraman, N (1993) Strategic alignment: leveraging information technology for transforming organizations, *IBM Systems Journal*, **32** (1), pp 4–16

Hewitt, F (2001) After supply chains, think demand pipelines, *Supply Chain Management Review* [Online] http://www.manufacturing.net/scm (accessed 12 May 2001)

Hoekstra, S and Romme, J (1992) *Integral Logistic Structures*, McGraw-Hill, London

Jaegersberg, G et al (2001) *Managing Socio-Technical Processes in the Supply Chain*, paper presented at the Cranfield Supply Chain Knowledge Conference, [Online] http://www.supplychainknowledge.com

Johannesen, S and Solem, O (2002) Logistics organizations: ideologies, principles and practice, *International Journal of Logistics Management*, **13** (1), pp 31–42

Kahla, P (2002) Inside Cisco's $2 billion blunder, *Business 2.0* (March), p 3 [Online] http://business2.com

Kaplan, S and Sawhney, M (2000) E-hubs: the new B2B marketplaces, *Harvard Business Review*, **78** (May–Jun), pp 97–103

Keenan, F and Ante, S E (2002) The new teamwork, *Business Week* (18 Feb) [Online] http://proquest.umi/pqdweb

Lewis, I (2001) Logistics and electronic commerce: an interorganizational systems perspective, *Transportation Journal*, **40** (Summer), pp 5–13

Magretta, J (1998) Fast, global and entrepreneurial: supply chain management, Hong Kong style, *Harvard Business Review*, **76** (Sept/Oct), pp 102–14

Malone, T W (2001) The future of e-business, *Sloan Management Review*, **43** (Fall), p 104

Margulius, D L (2002) Apps on the edge, *Infoworld* (27 May) [Online] http://webpublisher.lexisnexis.com

Miles, R E and Snow, C (1992) Causes of failure in network organizations, *California Management Review* (Summer), pp 53–72

Monteiro, E (2000) Actor–network theory and information infrastructure, in *From Drift to Control*, ed C U Ciborra, pp 71–85, Oxford UP, New York

Moozakis, C (2002) Nissan wants to be like Dell, *Internet Week* (7 Jan), p 11

Moshowitz, Abbe (1994) Virtual organization: a vision of management in the information age, *Information Society*, **10**, pp 267–88

Mulani, N P and Lee, H (2002) New models for supply chain excellence, in *Achieving Supply Excellence through Technology 4*, p 16, Accenture/Montgomery Research, San Francisco

Need, D (2001) *e-procurement*, Prentice-Hall, Upper Saddle River, NJ

Pihkala, T, Varamaki, E and Vesalainen, J (1999) Virtual organizations and the SMEs: a review and model development, *Entrepreneurship and Regional Development*, **11**, pp 335–49

Pritchard, T (2000) Ford and Toyota test the sale of cars online in Canada, *New York Times* [Online] http//www.nytimes.com

Rahman, Z (2002) Virtual organisation: a stratagem, *Singapore Management Review*, **24** (2), pp 29–46

Ranadive, V (1999) *The Power of Now*, McGraw-Hill, New York

Renner, K (2002) The future of real time [Online] http://Manufacturingsystems.com

Sako, M (1992) *Quality and Trust: Inter-firm relations in Britain and Japan*, Cambridge University Press, Cambridge, cited in Stuart, F I and McCutcheon, D M (2000) The manager's guide to supply management, *Business Horizons* (March), pp 35–44

Semilof, M (2001) Bar codes in a chip, *Internet Week* (19 Nov), p 1

Shah, J F and Serant, C (2002) Microsoft's Xbox sets supply chain standard, *EBN* (11 Mar), pp 1, 56

Sharman, G (1984) The rediscovery of logistics, *Harvard Business Review*, **62** (Sept–Oct), pp 104–09

Simpson, R L (2000) GM aims to become build-to-order firm but custom online sales are daunting task, *Wall Street Journal* [Online] wysiwyg://23/http://interactive.wsj.com

Swaminathan, J M (2001) Enabling customization using standard operations, *California Management Review*, **43** (3), pp 125–36

Tucker, D and Jones, L (2000) Leveraging the power of the internet for optimal supplier sourcing, *International Journal of Physical Distribution and Logistics Management*, **30** (3/4), pp 255–67

UPS (2002) New UPS supply chain solutions links logistics, freight and financial services [Online] http://pressroom.ups.com (accessed 6 March)

Volkswagen (2001) Volkswagen driving transactions through its VWGroupSupply.com Exchange [Online] http://www.amrresearch.com/preview/ (accessed 3 Dec 2001)

Ward, S (2001) The dreams of digital designers, *Business Week Industrial Technology Section* (9 July), pp 28a–30a

Whitman, L and Presley, A (2001) *The Agile, Extended Enterprise*, paper presented at the Cranfield Supply Chain Knowledge Conference, 2001 [Online] http://www.supplychainknowledge.com

Womack, J P, Jones, D T and Roos, D (1990) *The Machine that Changed the World*, HarperBooks, New York

Zipkin, P (2001) The limits of mass customization, *Sloan Management Review*, 42 (Spring), pp 81–87

11

Performance measurement and management in the supply chain

Alan Braithwaite
LCP Consulting

INTRODUCTION

If you can not measure it, you can not improve it.
Lord Kelvin (1824–1907), physicist and mathematician

The measurement of business performance is deeply grounded in the accounting disciplines of recording profit. As a means to enhance profits, management now measures and reports on a wide range of business performance from customer perception to strategy consistency and adherence. At the operational level of customer service attainment and economic performance, the supply chain is the kernel of the business. Indeed, the potential from supply chain thinking and practice is founded in realigning operations through the chain to reduce total cost, and maximize service and return on assets. So measurement is a core discipline, and capability to provide a framework for defining realignment and reporting progress to its attainment.

But the supply chain is also a complex system with many interfaces and dynamic interactions. Defining the measures at each point in the chain that are appropriate and consistent with the overall desired results is a significant challenge. The desired outcomes in terms of service, stock, assets and costs cannot be managed directly; while there is a general expectation in most companies that sales growth will drive profits, the connections to stock, service and cost are less direct.

Performance management in the supply chain is therefore about setting balanced goals between and within functions, that will lead to the desired results with balance and without conflict. Ideally, these goals, expressed as service level agreements, are then embedded in the fabric of the management measurement and reporting of the functions of the firm, its customers, suppliers and service providers. Each function is responsible for delivering its part of the chain to the performance objectives; and when things do not work as planned, the requirement is for failures to be identified and recovery actions mounted. Learning organizations will take the lessons of actual performance and the experience of failure and recovery to adjust the goals across the chain as a 'steward' of the supply chain. This stewardship role is a key responsibility for supply chain and logistics managers, since they often do not have functional responsibility for all the chain, though they are judged and rewarded on its overall performance.

Defining the metrics for use and establishing the systems by which the data can be captured, analysed and reported is a key skill and should not be under-estimated. The stewardship role is a cornerstone of future corporate success.

Looking to the future of performance measurement in the chain, there are two requirements: understanding and embedding the value and importance of measurement in a strategic framework for supply chain management, and creating a predictive framework of supply chain risk. The strategic crystal for the supply chain and the value index are platforms for development of these key priorities.

KEEPING SCORE – A BASIC MANAGEMENT PRINCIPLE

Revenue is vanity, profit is sanity, and cash is reality.

Anon

The essence of business is to generate profits and cash from satisfying customers through investment in assets and capabilities. Compared with investing deposits in a bank or building society, investors seek a premium return on investment that reflects the additional risk of trading with the assets as compared with the relative safety of the bank.

Modern financial theory has identified that investors can mitigate risk by holding a number of investments in a portfolio, since some investments will go up while others may go down (or out). The idea of share and sector risk has also been analysed and developed into a theory that captures the performance of an investment as a function of both the market as a whole (alpha representing the movement of the market) and the potential of the specific stock (beta representing the risk of the sector relative to the market).

Investors generally cannot run the businesses in which they participate, so they appoint management to do this for them with the aim of increasing returns. They therefore want information on the financial health or otherwise of the business, so that they can make judgements on the management and the prospects of the investment. Banks want the same information in order to assess the viability of making loans, and governments need it so they can exact the tax dues that society demands.

The requirement for compilation of performance in terms of financial health and its disclosure is therefore vital for the stakeholders, and for quoted companies there is an 'industry' of financial analysis that picks over the reported results and statements, and attempts to forecast the prospects. Accounting standards bodies such as the Securities and Exchange Commission in the United States and the Accounting Standards Authority in the United Kingdom regulate the preparation of company information, and the trend has been to require increasing disclosure not just financially but also in respect of subjects such as equal opportunities and environmental compliance achievement.

The importance of trust and integrity in the preparation of financial statements was brought into sharp focus during 2002 with the exposures of corporate catastrophe and financial deceit at Enron and WorldCom. The scale of these cases was unprecedented, but there have always been such cases; Maxwell Communications and Atlantic Computers are UK examples from the last 20 years.

Setting aside these high-profile scandals, there are two major difficulties with financial reporting. The first is that even financial reports prepared with absolute integrity can stretch the notion of 'profit' to meet the aspirations of management and option holders, or to defer taxation liabilities (*inter alia*). The second is that reported performance is essentially historic, and has been likened to driving down a highway steering through the rear-view mirror.

Performance measurement, reporting and management for day-to-day management is therefore needed to come closer to the reality of serving customers and the operational demands of day-to-day decision making. In the context of both business direction and the detail of the supply chain, the task of measuring performance unpacks into many layers of detail; it is a subject in its own right.

THE BALANCED SCORECARD: THE STANDARD FOR GOAL SETTING AND MEASUREMENT

Since neither historical performance nor company budgets can be assured to bear directly on a business's long-term strategic objectives, a considerable effort in the development of models and theories has been dedicated to this problem. Amongst these are the Deming Prize (isixsigma, 2002a), the Malcolm Baldrige Award (isixsigma, 2002b), the EFQM's business excellence model (EFQM, 2002) and the balanced scorecard (Kaplan and Norton, 1996b) In addition, theories such as the learning organization (Senge, 1990) and knowledge management (Snowden, 2000) devote much energy to similar issues.

All these models have strengths and weaknesses depending on the purpose for which they are being used. However, the balanced scorecard offers a contained and comprehensive approach to addressing the strategic direction and control issues; it is the reference for many corporations and it fits especially well with supply chain thinking. With no disrespect to the other contributions, this chapter will treat it as the reference point for performance measurements.

A balanced scorecard provides a picture of a business by combining financial measures with assessments for customer satisfaction, key internal processes, and organizational learning and growth. The conceptual framework is captured in Kaplan and Norton's diagram (Kaplan, 2002) in Figure 11.1.

The balanced scorecard strategy map requires specific measures of the company's goals for customers in terms of time, quality, performance, service and cost as well as relationship, brand and product leadership. The internal perspective provides focus on the core competencies, processes, decisions and actions that have the greatest impact on attaining customer satisfaction. The learning and growth perspective measures continual improvements to people, systems and processes. Sitting above this framework are the financial measures, which are essential for showing whether executives have correctly identified and constructed their measures in the three preceding areas.

Fundamentally a balanced scorecard should have a balance between 'output' measures (financial, customer) and performance drivers (input measures), such as value proposition, internal processes, learning and growth. Every measure selected for a scorecard should be part of a link of cause-and-effect relationships, ending in financial objectives that represent a strategic theme for the business.

Kaplan and Norton (1992) outline four key processes that the balanced scorecard relies on to connect short-term activities to long-term objectives:

1. Translating the vision – managers are required to translate their vision into actual measurements linked directly to the people who will realize the vision.
2. Communicating and linking – the scorecard indicates what the organization is trying to achieve for both shareholders and customers. The high-level strategy map is translated into 'business unit' scorecards and eventually 'personal scorecards' so that individuals understand how their personal goals and performance support the overall strategy.

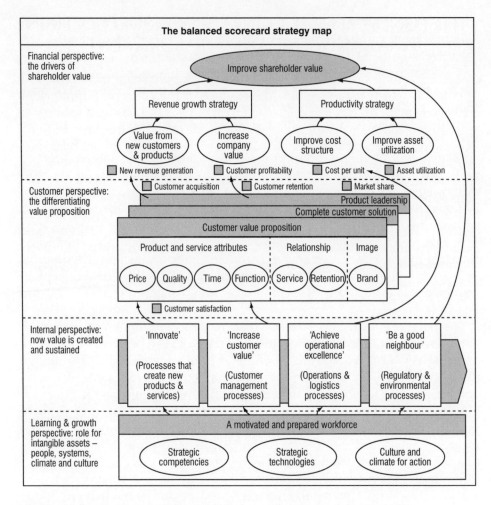

Figure 11.1 Kaplan and Norton's balanced scorecard framework

3. Business planning – once the performance measures for the four perspectives have been agreed, the company identifies the key drivers of the desired outcome, and defines the milestones that mark progress towards achieving their strategic goal.
4. Feedback and learning – this allows for regular performance reviews to enable continuous improvement of the strategy and its execution.

In summary, the scorecard puts strategy and vision, not control, at the centre. The measures are designed to pull people towards the overall vision. This methodology is consistent with the approach of supply chain management, by helping managers overcome traditional functional barriers, and ultimately leads to improved decision making and problem solving.

THE FUNDAMENTAL CONCEPTS OF SUPPLY CHAIN MANAGEMENT AND MEASUREMENT

There are countless definitions of logistics and supply chain management in circulation which try to capture the essence of the concept. Supply chain management (SCM) was first coined as a term in 1982, and was used to imply an inter-organizational perspective as opposed to an intra-organizational perspective. A detailed academic examination of the meaning, usage and distinctions between the terms 'supply chain management' and 'logistics' found that they are broadly interchangeable in their everyday usage, but that there is not a consistent view of what SCM really is or should be (Kaplan and Norton, 1996a).

The authors found that recent writing was suggesting that SCM goes further than the standard definitions, and that it transcends firms, functions and business processes. This makes SCM more than just logistics, and positions it as a complete business integration framework covering all functions and operating over extended networks. In this context, supply chain management is:

> A process orientation to managing business in an integrated way that transcends the boundaries of firms and functions; leading to co-operation, through-chain business process synchronization, effective ranging and new product introduction, as well managing the entire physical logistics agenda.

The network of entities that together comprise the supply chain works through the mechanisms of shared information and closely aligned processes. The vision for these networks is that they are characterized by high levels of communication and transparency, supported by synchronous operations and performance measurement and management.

Experience of applying supply chain management (even partially across a business) is that improved visibility and synchronization leads to some or all of:

- improved customer service experience;
- reduced inventories;
- lower operating costs;
- improved use of fixed assets.

The ultimate benefit can be taken through improvements in a mix of profitability, shareholder value and market share, depending on the strategic priorities of the firm. The implication is that the potential of supply chain management can transform a company in terms of its performance; the leverage through the combination of many small (albeit radical in their conception) improvements in the economic structure of a company can be remarkable.

The big idea that sits behind the supply chain concept is a move from function to process; the principle is that effectiveness of the chain is enhanced dramatically by optimizing across functions and through the whole chain, compared with the accumulation of optimized functions. Striking a balance between functional and total business is a crucial dimension of SCM, though breaking down the barriers between functions to improve supply chain integration is not a substitute for functional excellence. Companies need to secure both dimensions, retaining and improving their competence in all the functions in the supply chain.

A fundamental law of logistics is that the effect of optimizing individual functional performance can prevent the achievement of the most cost- and service-effective end-to-end supply chain. Not only that, it will also most likely insert further undesirable volatility and actually increase cost. The implications of the law of lowest total cost are that traditional functional and general ledger methods of business and operational planning will never lead to 'breakthrough' thinking in supply chain redesign, and indeed are a cause of organizational problems.

The requirement is for the corporation to measure the end-to-end cost to serve, at least internally, but preferably looking inside both its customers' and suppliers' operations, so as to enable a fundamental rebalancing across the business on a holistic basis of what will deliver the required service at the lowest total cost. This idea is illustrated in Figure 11.2.

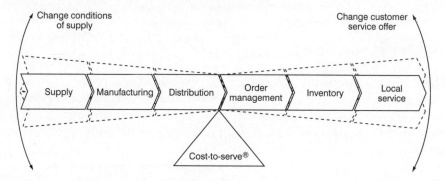

Figure 11.2 Balancing the supply chain

Performance measurement and management are critical components of this rebalancing effort, and a fundamental part of the supply chain and logistics concept. It requires balance and overall goal setting. Supply chain performance measurement and management are the operational microclimate of the balanced scorecard that Kaplan and Norton have given us.

MASTERING THE COMPLEXITY OF SUPPLY CHAIN AND LOGISTICS PERFORMANCE MANAGEMENT

The supply chain and logistics at this microclimate level are complex in their detail. The biggest challenge in setting up measurement and management programmes is mastering that complexity to create an internally consistent framework of goals that reflect the true relationships of cause and effect.

Figure 11.3 shows a framework of cost and performance based on structural determinants and management determinants. These determinants act on the components of cost and effectiveness to create a total supply chain outcome in terms of service, asset utilization and cost.

The idea of structural and management determinants and the distinction between them is important. Structural determinants relate to the 'business we are in' expressed as products and customers. Here the choices for management are limited; if you are in the fertilizer or seeds business you have farmers and merchants as customers and deliver to farms. The characteristics of the product are well defined, and the nature of demand is broadly local and national. In contrast, microchip manufacturers operate on an international scale using airfreight and with billions of dollars invested in plant. The fundamental difference in the products is driven home by the cost per tonne of microchips being as much as $500,000 whereas the cost per tonne for fertilizer is typically less than $300.

Management determinants reflect the areas where management has choices to make within the constraints of the nature of the business. There are big strategy decisions to be made here in relation to sourcing, capacity

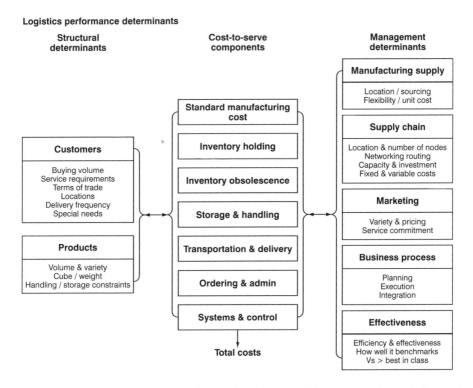

Figure 11.3 The complexity of supply chain and logistics, viewed through determinants

investment and characteristics, marketing positioning and service levels, business process design and operational effectiveness. These choices interact with each other and the structural determinants to drive the end-to-end cost and performance. The figure makes the point that the scale and degree of interaction across the various areas of cost and performance is multivariate and complex. The challenge that emerges for performance measurement and management in the supply chain is to define correctly the relationships and key drivers in the context of the choices that the company has made in its markets. From the definition of these relationships arises the precise specification of the measures to be used and the values to be set as goals for the individual functional managers.

THE PRINCIPLE OF 'INPUT AND OUTPUT MEASURES'

The definition of cause and effect is important. The nature of the complexity illustrated in Figure 11.3 is such that the measures of effect are driven by the structure of the business, and the key choices and designs that management make. The implications of this observation are that the ultimate performance measures on which the stakeholders judge the business are not open to direct action. So as examples of many constructs, we cannot act directly on:

- sales revenue and the economies that go with scale without dealing with the levels of customer satisfaction that are achieved in terms of inventory availability and service turnaround;
- inventory levels in the chain without dealing with processes such as forecasting accuracy and forecasting frequency and horizon, and inventory record accuracy;
- cost to serve by product and customer without having designed the network for sourcing and fulfilment.

These points make the distinction between input and output measures. Of course we need both in order to understand if the actions taken have achieved the desired result. But there is limited value in just measuring the outputs without having first identified the cause and effect relationships and the input measures that are likely to generate the desired change. This is consistent with the thinking of Kaplan and Norton, though their mission is not to address the levels of detail that are necessary for the supply chain and logistics.

Figure 11.4 illustrates a simple example of input and output measures in a case study (it should be noted that the figures are illustrative only). The input measures reflect the major changes that were effected in this company, and the output measures were the consequences of these actions and illustrate the shareholder value that was created. The strategic nature of the input measures is immediately clear, as is the improvement that was attained in this

Measure	Start	Finish
Input measures		
Forecast accuracy	Poor	Improved but less important
Manufacturing change time	8 hours	15 minutes
New product introduction	Months	Weeks
Logistics structure	3 depots	Single national site
Output measures		
Sales		+10%
Customer service	96%	99%
Stock	12 weeks	2 Weeks
Obsolescence	High	Minimal
Distribution costs	14% of turnover	9% of turnover
Manufacturing unit cost		Reduced by 20%

Figure 11.4   Input and output measures in a performance improvement case

manufacturing business. All of these improvements were achieved through a long-term commitment to measurement, stock policy adherence, and stewardship, leading to the rebalancing of the company's supply chain. Cross-functional stewardship is an idea that is developed later in this chapter.

SETTING GOALS ACROSS THE CHAIN THROUGH SERVICE LEVEL AGREEMENTS

In the context of the complex interaction of supply chain variables between functions and the fundamental principle of securing rebalancing for business performance improvement, the question most often asked in relation to performance measurement is, 'How should functional goals be set in the chain to secure the potential?' A further series of sub-questions arise from this major issue:

- How does a function see its role and contribution to improving the whole supply chain?
- What levels of visibility should be given, between functions, of the goals and attainment by others?
- How does a function influence the performance of other members in the chain that can impact its own performance but are out of its direct control?
- Who sets the measures of performance across the chain?

The idea of inter-functional service level agreements (SLAs) is designed to resolve the first three of these questions. SLAs create a framework in which the various functions within a company and between organizations (both customers and suppliers) are measured against meaningful objectives that will generate overall performance improvement.

The first big idea embedded in SLAs is that they are not just sequential between players in the physical chain, but also recognize the obligations of every member of the team to the others, whether or not they are next in line. The second big idea is that SLAs create a team environment; rather like any sport, all players know their place in the side, the contribution they make and the dependencies they have on other positions. So, for example, to use a Rugby Union example, the halfbacks and three-quarters know their respective positions and the moves that they will be making; the output measures are tries scored and the percentage of tackles made on the opposition, while the input measures are adherence to plan and position, quality of individual execution of ball control and tackling, and speed of response to moves by either team. Each member of the back line has commitments to all the others in his line and to the forwards – and not just to the player next to him. Inter-functional SLAs in the supply chain are identical in conception.

Figure 11.5 shows the standard conceptual framework of a sequential chain that, by this definition of SLAs, is incomplete, and also an example matrix (partly populated) of the SLAs that really need to exist. Each box in the SLA framework needs to be populated with input measures, as they reflect the relationship that the two functions have with each other. The matrix is not symmetrical, as the obligations of the functions in the context of the overall goals are not mutual. So for example the relationship between sales and marketing and production planning is that sales and marketing must produce a forecast on time and to the agreed level of accuracy, while production planning's commitment to sales and marketing is to turn that forecast into available product (plus/minus a tolerance) through the creation of timely and economic schedules. Equally, manufacturing will have commitments to the business, including sales and marketing, that relate to adherence to schedule, yield and quality performance; but in return it is entitled to expect acceptable levels of demand volatility and schedule stability from sales and marketing and demand planning.

It is important to note that the SLAs are entirely about input measures such as adherence to schedule, quality, and lead time. It is changes to these measures and improvements in performance that drive value through the company's supply chain.

The creation of this matrix, even in the most rudimentary form, and making it available to the entire business together with published current performance and future targets, answers the first two of the sub-questions. From this platform each function can see where it fits and how it can help to play the game.

The process of setting up the SLA matrix and populating the targets and the performance actually achieved is the way that the functions can start to resolve the tensions relating to the impact they may have on each other. This is a

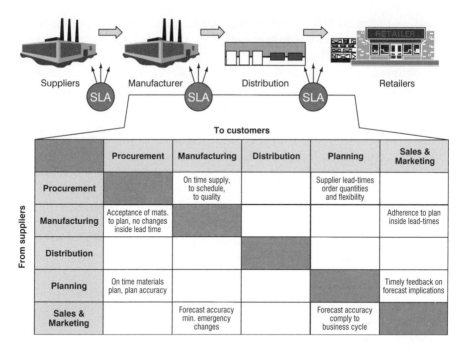

Figure 11.5 The conventional sequential supply chain relationship and the SLA matrix

crucial organizational process, and is a key role of supply chain management – correctly represented at board level. And it is this person (or small team) that sets the matrix, in conjunction with the functional heads, and then monitors attainment and institutes corrective action where necessary. This is the idea of supply chain stewardship. The steward holds the total vision for supply chain improvement for the firm and the individual functional performances that will deliver the result. He or she is in effect the team coach.

The SLA matrix needs to be maintained as a living framework that responds to external forces, actual performance and continuous learning. This is a full-time organizational role. If supply chain management also has direct functional reports, then it will need to isolate the stewardship role within its own organization to ensure that balance and impartiality are achieved.

THE 'DELIVERY, RECOVERY AND STEWARDSHIP' MODEL

Putting the SLA matrix into action is the process and activity of tracking performance against targets and identifying opportunities for improvement, not just looking back at past performance. The focus of performance management should be the future; what do you need to be able to do and how can you do things better?

The 'delivery, recovery and stewardship' (DRS) model is a way of institutionalizing measurement across the business, and is consistent with Kaplan and Norton's balanced scorecard and its requirement for learning. The big ideas in the DRS model are, first, that for cross-chain balancing it is necessary to introduce measures of cost as well as the input measures in the SLA matrix, and second, that recovery is an important activity, with the learning that comes with it. It is critically important that organizations recognize and plan that things will go wrong, but remarkable how seldom this is factored in.

Figure 11.6 is a simple representation of the DRS model, designed to illustrate the cycle of each function, measuring its delivery against its SLA in the matrix and including the cost performance goals. Reports including the identification of failures and the impact of recovery actions are produced at the functional level and then consolidated by the supply chain steward. The stewardship role is to feed back to the functions the impact of overall performance and to propose changes to the SLAs, delivery performance and the means of recovery.

The model is consistent with the so-called Shewhart or PDCA cycle (plan–do–check–act, known in Japan as the Deming cycle) based on the fundamental theory of continuous improvements:

1. Business understanding and strategic directions; *'plan'* the process.
2. Run the operation to try to deliver in line with the plan; *'do'* the operation and record the results.
3. Performance reporting against plan and interpretation of results; *'check'* by analysis and reporting of performance according to key business drivers.

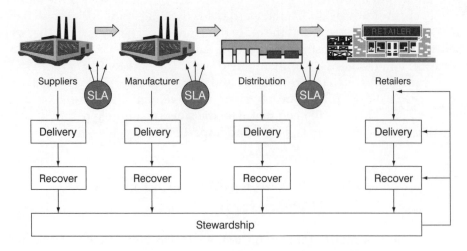

Figure 11.6　The delivery, recovery and stewardship model

4. Tactical and strategic realignment: *'act'* to initiate improvement efforts based on the lessons learnt from experience. These experiences feed into the new plan, since PDCA is a cyclical process.

In summary, the DRS model is a way to capture the supply chain improvement vision for the firm, and to record and manage progress to its attainment. It may seem daunting and potentially complex, and, if this is the case, the key is to start in with the simplest possible framework and build from it as the organization learns. In other words, adopt the same principles of plan–do–check–act to the process of planning and measurement across the chain as are being applied to the chain itself.

The stewardship role as a functionally independent agent in the organization is crucial to the DRS model, and this is a difficult position to define and maintain in the organization. The person who holds the role will require vision, interpersonal skills and tenacity. The role needs the highest level of board sponsorship, and the results of DRS need to be a standard part of the board agenda. It is at this point that supply chain management and corporate strategy meet and can be integrated into the balanced scorecard.

DEFINING THE SPECIFIC METRICS ACROSS THE CHAIN

The input and output measures described earlier are the high-level corporate cause and effect metrics for the supply chain. The measures in the SLAs are, as has been observed, primarily about quality, compliance and time. The stewardship role requires these measures and adds cost measures to the portfolio. In this section, the specifics of the measures that can be applied across the supply chain are unpacked and described. The specification of measures is a subject in its own right, so this description should be treated as an overview rather than a manual.

The supply chain and logistics professional and the corporate steward of the chain will want to develop an overview of the chain; a useful way to think about this is as a 'dashboard' or control panel for the business. This idea is illustrated in Figure 11.7, and many executives find the preparation of such diagrams valuable in identifying the performance issues in the chain and describing them to their colleagues. Measures may need to reflect both changes over time and performance across the product range and of customers and suppliers.

A further important point in relation to this overview is that, while supply chain rebalancing via SLAs will be one of the key drivers for competitive advantage, firms must also recognize that an equal and parallel emphasis should remain on attaining functional excellence. The goals of functional excellence, however, will be tempered at the margin through an understanding that

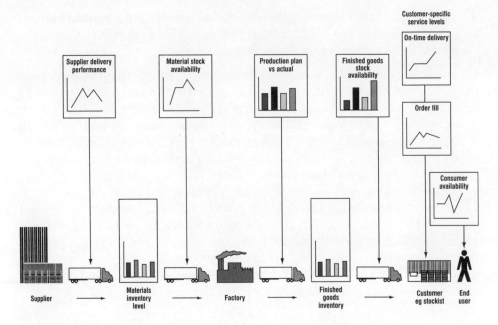

Figure 11.7   Viewing supply chain metrics across the chain

such aims can lead to supply chain sub-optimization; the SLAs are developed over time to eliminate potential conflicts.

Although the measures themselves are generic for most businesses, the precise situation and issues for each firm will vary based on its competitive situation, technology, and product and market characteristics. It is helpful to think of a hierarchy (or levels) of measures across the chain in terms of both input and output measures:

- Level one measures should provide headline measures for the supply chain, such as orders on time in full with no invoice errors (OTIFNIE) and stock cover set in a balanced way that supports the vision for change.
- Level two measures should be used to provide further insight into the results of level one, such as quantity fill per cent, line fill per cent, and invoice accuracy.
- Finally, level three measures should provide diagnostics for use in problem resolution and improvement processes. For example, requests for credit, clear-up rate, number of days out of stock by stock-keeping unit (SKU).

Figure 11.8 provides examples of level one and two performance metrics across a typical retail supply chain.

Figure 11.8 repays detailed study, since it starts to provide insight into the levels of detail that are involved, and it can be used to challenge the organization as to the connections between functions and what are the real drivers. So for

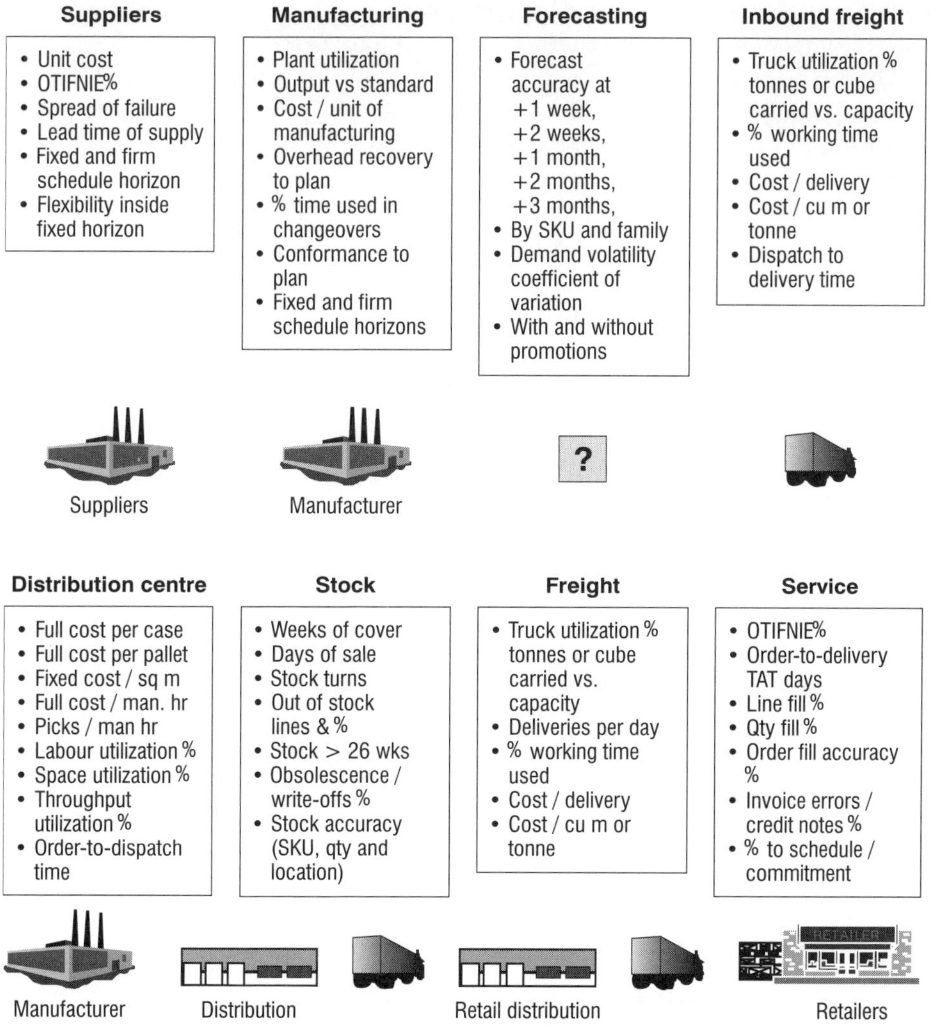

Suppliers	**Manufacturing**	**Forecasting**	**Inbound freight**
• Unit cost • OTIFNIE% • Spread of failure • Lead time of supply • Fixed and firm schedule horizon • Flexibility inside fixed horizon	• Plant utilization • Output vs standard • Cost / unit of manufacturing • Overhead recovery to plan • % time used in changeovers • Conformance to plan • Fixed and firm schedule horizons	• Forecast accuracy at +1 week, +2 weeks, +1 month, +2 months, +3 months, • By SKU and family • Demand volatility coefficient of variation • With and without promotions	• Truck utilization % tonnes or cube carried vs. capacity • % working time used • Cost / delivery • Cost / cu m or tonne • Dispatch to delivery time

Suppliers   Manufacturer   ?

Distribution centre	**Stock**	**Freight**	**Service**
• Full cost per case • Full cost per pallet • Fixed cost / sq m • Full cost / man. hr • Picks / man hr • Labour utilization % • Space utilization % • Throughput utilization % • Order-to-dispatch time	• Weeks of cover • Days of sale • Stock turns • Out of stock lines & % • Stock > 26 wks • Obsolescence / write-offs % • Stock accuracy (SKU, qty and location)	• Truck utilization % tonnes or cube carried vs. capacity • Deliveries per day • % working time used • Cost / delivery • Cost / cu m or tonne	• OTIFNIE% • Order-to-delivery TAT days • Line fill % • Qty fill % • Order fill accuracy % • Invoice errors / credit notes % • % to schedule / commitment

Manufacturer   Distribution   Retail distribution   Retailers

Figure 11.8 Sample level one/two metrics containing both input and output measures

example the figure shows both 'on time in full' (OTIF) and 'order to delivery turnaround time' (TAT). It is immediately obvious that the longer the TAT, the higher should be the OTIF – since there is more time to get it right. But at the same time the longer the TAT, the lower should be the inventory, as the more time manufacturing has to respond to actual demand. TAT is therefore an input measure, and it is also one that management may want to change, as faster service is likely to be more competitive and create increased demand. In the same vein, measures of plant, distribution centre and transportation efficiency will be influenced by customer order turnaround time, forecast accuracy and plant changeover time – all of which are input measures.

This brief introduction to the interaction of measures should be sufficient to demonstrate that Figure 11.8 is not a complete guide; rather it should be used as a prompt for thinking through the measures that are exactly relevant to the company.

Once the appropriate metrics to be used in the performance management framework have been decided on, it is then necessary to ensure that these individual measures are set in a balanced way to provide an overall picture of supply chain performance and support the business in moving to its goals. A sample of a balanced set of objective measures for a fast-moving consumer goods company is included here in Figure 11.9.

The very high service performance with low levels of stock is secured by quite high levels of forecast accuracy, very short manufacturing schedule horizons and exceptional supplier performance. High levels of accuracy are also essential, and the area sacrificed is distribution and freight utilization. Setting these measures consistently, having understood the relationships, is the key to avoiding functional conflicts that can cause sub-optimal performance. Examples of this are:

- Stockholding targets that are set too low will disable customer service attainment and reduce the number of orders received OTIF.
- Freight utilization and cost targets may delay shipments, leading to increased stock and a negative impact on customer service.
- Manufacturing unit cost goals may drive up stocks and downstream distribution costs as a result of long production runs and infrequent line changes.

With performance metrics and the consequent balanced scorecard established, greater focus can be achieved on supply chain issues. This also aids in benchmarking, by identifying current and best practice in companies and their supply chains before using some of the level 3 diagnostic metrics to develop an improvement programme.

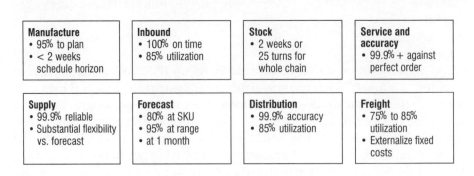

Figure 11.9   A sample logistical balanced scorecard

COLLECTING AND MANAGING DATA

Two of the biggest barriers to a successful performance measurement and management programme are the compilation of data and its analysis and interpretation. Typically this involves hundreds of thousands of transactions, many hundreds of general ledger codes, some thousands of stock-keeping units and many hundreds of customers and suppliers. All these can be linked through a number of plants and distribution centres. Collecting and managing this data is a significant task and an area of expertise in its own right.

Measurement and reporting used to be a labour-intensive and hard-won achievement with limited potential for supplementary diagnosis and interpretation. But recent developments in mass data storage, often referred to as data warehousing, have provided a platform that previously was not available. The changes of the last five years have been revolutionary in terms of low-cost data storage capacity, easy-to-programme queries, and graphical programs to represent the outputs of analysis. The skills and experience to set up these data warehouses are being accumulated, and new software environments are being launched to bring data together from different computing sources to give an end-to-end picture.

There can be no doubt that this is a critical area of capability for the future. The ability to manage supply chains of increasing complexity and at greater levels of detail will only be enabled by these systems and the expertise to derive knowledge and wisdom from them.

FUTURE DIRECTIONS IN PERFORMANCE MEASUREMENT

The major challenges for performance measurement in the supply chain for the future rest in, first, integrating performance management into the fabric of the organization to drive supply chain strategy development and implementation, and second, creating predictive measurement frameworks through which the corporation can identify the levels of risk that are inherent in their supply chains.

Both of these areas are 'work in progress' in terms of the development of a complete understanding and operational frameworks through which they can be applied. They are also each a subject in their own right, worthy of full academic treatment. In that context this section is just a preview of the author's developing thinking.

The word 'integration' is overused in supply chain management, without great clarity as to its meaning and implications. The LCP strategic crystal is an attempt to address this question by describing the elements of an integrated supply chain strategy and showing how they interact to deliver business value in terms of customer satisfaction and economic value added. Figure 11.10 shows the crystal with the key elements of:

- Business processes – the processes of generating planning and execution instructions through the chain that, if correctly designed, will increase customer service and reduce inventories and capital applied. Business process redesign in supply chain management is normally focused on the principles of time compression. Business processes are crucially dependent on systems, organization and KPIs, three other points in the crystal. Business processes are key input measures and a major part of the SLAs.
- Supply chain systems – the computer information systems that are applied must serve the business processes and the organization, support the network and inform the performance measurement environment.
- Supply chain network is the key to the cost performance in the chain, and is enabled by the processes and systems. The organization design must align with the network to enable the lowest cost operation.
- Performance management – through consistent and appropriate key performance indicators is central to an effective supply chain strategy, as we have seen in this chapter. The process of performance management enables the organization, and is dependent on the systems and the processes.
- Organization design – is a most under-represented area of supply chain strategy. An organization that is aligned to the strategy and is served by the systems, processes and KPIs is central to realizing supply chain value. As businesses move from a functional to a process orientation, the boundaries

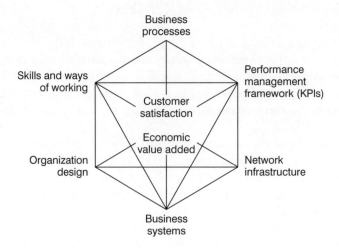

Figure 11.10 The strategic supply chain crystal

of traditional functional power are challenged and tensions are exposed. The SLA approach can reduce the tensions, since functional control is not required under that model. However, the stewardship role is mandatory, and, as discussed earlier, it must be positioned in the organization with both power and independence.

- Skills and behaviours – are the final facet of the crystal, and like organization are under-represented. The skills and behaviours to move to a supply chain ethic, from function to process, are profoundly different from those that have been trained into management over many years. Skills and behaviours are connected strongly to all points in the crystal.

The picture of true supply chain integration to generate business value that emerges from the crystal is a strong one. Performance measurement and management is central to this vision.

The second major challenge in performance management for boards is to recognize the risk that is endemic in their supply chains. Work by Singhal and Hendricks (undated) has shown that supply chain catastrophes are common, and that they destroy shareholder value to the tune of on average 20 per cent. As every CEO knows, the speed with which share prices go down is seldom matched by the speed of their recovery; and of course most CEOs are strongly motivated by their share prices. And with companies' supply chains being run ever more leanly, there is less room for unexpected errors. The requirement exists to evaluate the risk potential in a corporation's supply chain, and this is now a topic of academic research. The LCP Value Index™ is being designed to address this question, and Figure 11.11 shows the conceptual model. The underlying principle is that there are external determinants of risk that relate to the business environment of demand and supply, and there are internal determinants that relate to how the organization is aligned to its external environment.

As an example of how this model works, it should be immediately clear that a company with a volatile market and supplies, on long lead times, with extended planning, scheduling and manufacturing processes and a poor record of performance management, is riding for a fall. In contrast, a company operating in a market where demand is stable and competition well defined can accommodate longer lead times from suppliers and more rigid internal processes.

In the same way as the financial community has defined the probability of bankruptcy through measurements of a company's accounts, the Value Index is intended to be a predictor of supply chain failure. The increasing requirements on public companies to identify and record risks in their published statements, and the intensified interest of governments in risk after 11 September 2001 and various earthquakes, fires and labour actions, means that the measurement of risk in supply chains is a priority for research and development.

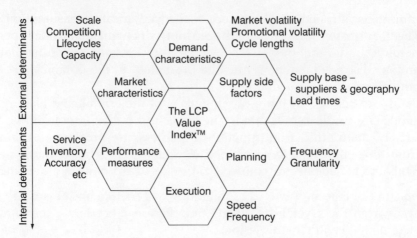

Figure 11.11 The LCP Value Index™: a means to measure endemic risk in supply chains

CONCLUSION

The potential for improvement through the development of performance management metrics across the supply chain is a key differentiator of change capability and organizational agility. Firms that develop supply chain measurement, as a core business competence associated with strategic objectives, will have a strong foundation for defining realignment internally and with both customers and suppliers.

The combined use of supply chain performance metrics, balanced scorecards, and the delivery, recovery and stewardship framework provides the capability to report on improvement, understand the factors that are driven by the change, and identify supply chain management best practice.

In conclusion, there are six key points to hold in focus when developing a supply chain performance management framework:

- No single measure defines supply chain performance: there are many dimensions to measure.
- Measures can be in conflict, accentuating rather than breaking functional silo issues.
- The need is to obtain balance throughout the supply chain and be prepared to change.
- Measuring the overall performance at input and output levels is a key first step to making improvements.
- This requires considerable investment of time and commitment.
- Measurement and its interpretation is a valuable and difficult skill that organizations should develop and nurture.

Organizations that have persevered with supply chain measurement and management have experienced sustained improvements in business performance.

NOTE

The Laws of Logistics® and The LCP Value Index™ are marks registered by Logistics Consulting Partners Ltd. Web site: http://www.lcp-ashlyns.com

REFERENCES

EFQM (2002) *European Quality Awards*, European Foundation of Quality Management [Online] http://www.efqm.org

isixsigma (2002a) *The Deming Prize Check List*, isixsigma LLC [Online] http://www.isixsigma.com

isixsigma (2002b) *Malcolm Baldrige National Quality Award*, isixsigma LLC [Online] http://www.isixsigma.com

Kaplan, R S (2002) *Building Strategy Focused Organisations with the Balanced Scorecard*, presentation, Performance Management Association, Boston, MA (July)

Kaplan, R S and Norton, D P (1992) The balanced scorecard: measures that drive performance, *Harvard Business Review* (Jan–Feb)

Kaplan, R S and Norton, D P (1996a) *Translating Strategy into Action: The balanced scorecard*, Harvard Business School Press, Cambridge, MA

Kaplan, R S and Norton, D P (1996b) Using the balanced scorecard as a strategic management system, *Harvard Business Review* (Jan–Feb)

Senge, P M (1990) *The Fifth Discipline*, Doubleday, New York

Singhal, V R and Hendricks, K (undated) *Report on Supply Chain Glitches and Shareholder Value Destruction*, Dupree College of Management, Georgia Institute of Technology

Snowden, D (2000) *Liberating Knowledge*, Institute of Knowledge Management, Toronto

12

Benchmarking in logistics and supply chain management

Tim Randall
LCP Consulting Limited

INTRODUCTION

> Benchmarking is the continuous process of measuring product, services, and practices against the toughest competitors, or those companies recognized as industry leaders.
>
> David T Kearns, CEO of Xerox Corporation

Benchmarking is an external focus on internal activities, functions, or operations in order to achieve continuous improvement. Starting from an analysis of existing activities and practices within an organization, the objectives are to understand existing processes, or activities, and then to identify an external point of reference, or standard, by which each activity can be measured or judged. A benchmark can be established at any level of the organization, in any functional area. The ultimate goal is to be better than the best – to attain a competitive edge.

Organizations that introduce benchmarking correctly can use it to make a quantum leap in their performance, and develop a culture in which managers and staff constantly search for improvements.

Within logistics and supply chain management, benchmarking can be used for a number of different purposes, from assessing the performance of the entire operation, through prioritizing improvements, to searching for the off-the-shelf improvement strategies in a specific area of a logistics or supply chain activity.

WHAT BENCHMARKING IS

In some senses, benchmarking is imitation and stealing – 'creative swiping', as Tom Peters aptly put it! At its best it is skilful appropriation and adaptation requiring imagination and innovation; at its worst it can be an expensive and time-consuming piece of corporate tourism.

It is a long-term process, requiring senior management commitment, with the emphasis upon continuous improvement and organizational learning. The focus is primarily upon roles, strategic issues, processes and practices, rather than the bottom-line and numerical measures of performance. The mere comparison of operations and costs is not sufficient; considerable attention must be paid to how the activities are organized and performed. This will provide a good understanding of how superior performance has been achieved, rather than just the magnitude of the performance gap.

Benchmarking targets the critical success factors (CSFs) of a specific organization. What needs to be done to ensure long-term success? Where do top management see the potential for competitive advantage? Each organization has a different mission, a unique way of combining its resources, and a cultural system in which this occurs. For example, being close and responsive to the customer may be critical for one company, whereas innovative product development and introduction might be to another. Benchmarking helps to identify those features critical to ongoing success, as well as those parts of the organization that are less important, and from which resources may be diverted.

In benchmarking, a 'role' describes in essence what a person, or function, does for an organization. What responsibilities, services and tasks are offered to a customer or client by the organization? How do these compare with other organizations in terms of process architecture, structure or capability? Are we getting value from our IT investments, or are these resources being wasted? Each of these questions deals with the role the organization plays in collusion with its customers or clients. Roles, in this instance, are bundles of services provided either to the external customer/client, or to an internal customer/client.

Questioning the roles within an organization leads to the question, 'Are we doing the right things?' – in other words, the question of effectiveness – while assessing processes raises concerns about whether things are being done right – in other words, the question of efficiency. Every process within any organization consumes resources. To leverage the most value from processes, an organization must eliminate non-value-adding (NVA) activities in the process itself. Benchmarking supports the targeting of processes, or process elements, that are of most importance to the business, but are perceived to be operating sub-optimally. While every process can be improved, an often-overlooked issue is getting the most value out of every dollar spent on process improvements. Only by continuously benchmarking a process against itself, and with other external sources, can this be truly assessed.

Strategic issues focus on a long-term planning horizon for the development of value for the business, say one to three years into the future. The identification and setting of new goals, projects or ventures is fundamental to the long-term success of any business. The environment within which any organization operates changes rapidly; cost reduction targets that were deemed aggressive months or years ago can quickly become the industry norm. Benchmarking, then, can be used to target strategic issues, gain enough information to prioritize competing projects, and establish an overall programme of events geared towards achieving optimum economic value added.

A BRIEF HISTORY OF BENCHMARKING

The credit for bringing benchmarking into modern business parlance is given to the pioneers at Rank Xerox who, in 1979, first started to use the technique in the West. The most famous pioneer was Robert C Camp, who, in *Benchmarking: The search for industry best practices that land superior performance* (1989), described the Rank Xerox processes and experiences.

The organization's competitive position was deteriorating rapidly with the advent of Japanese products retailing for a price similar to Xerox's production cost. It was clear that setting performance targets based merely upon extrapolations of the past coupled with expected future events was insufficient! Xerox used benchmarking to understand the competitive gap, providing targets for its business plans. Subsequently, benchmarking was performed in all areas of the business, with the focus on understanding customer requirements and employee involvement to assist implementation. The greatest success was achieved when benchmarking was performed against the perceived best performers of each function in a similar or related industry. For example, Xerox benchmarked its order fulfilment and warehousing operations to L L Bean's. This led to the discovery that Xerox and L L Bean had similar packing processes, but that the L L Bean process was three times faster than the Xerox one.

However, benchmarking was being used in some countries long before 1979. In Japan for instance, benchmarking was being developed in several forms, one of which was the practice of *shukko*, or loaning employees to other organizations. This job rotation approach encouraged employees not only to learn about their own organization's internal business processes, but also to go outside and bring new processes back to help their organization move forward.

WHAT IT CAN DO FOR YOU

Benchmarking provides the basis for meeting and exceeding stakeholder expectations. Understanding its potential benefits, though, requires understanding the type of benchmarking to be deployed, and the purposes of conducting such an exercise.

While benchmarking can be performed at any time, it is most often undertaken as a response to an information need associated with a project or issue within the organization. Triggers might include:

- operations, logistics and supply chain improvement efforts;
- management/organizational changes;
- mergers/acquisitions;
- competitive threats;
- cost reduction initiatives.

Benchmarking in any of these situations is a logical step in developing new objectives, setting new performance standards and metrics, and redesigning process and procedures. But, why benchmark? Specifically, benchmarking:

- signals that top management is willing to pursue a course of action that embraces and welcomes change in a proactive, rather than reactive, manner;
- establishes meaningful objectives and goals that reflect an external focus, which fosters quantum leap thinking, and helps organizations to focus and prioritize high-payoff opportunities;
- creates awareness of competitive disadvantage;
- promotes teamwork based upon a clear understanding of competitive needs driven by facts and data, not just intuition.

A company benchmarks because it wants to be the best of the best. To this end, benchmarking should not be considered an optional activity. It is of paramount importance to maintaining an organization's competitive advantage.

Once the 'why?' question has been dealt with, the next logical question is 'With whom do you benchmark?' Benchmarking can focus on internal functions or processes, competitors, industry performance, and 'best in class'.

Internal benchmarking is the analysis of existing processes and practice within various departments or divisions of an organization. The objective is to identify and analyse best performance within the confines of the organization's own boundaries, and drive performance to this level or beyond across the business as a whole. The process will facilitate an understanding of the basic activities that constitute the processes within the organization, and the drivers associated with these. Drivers are the causes of work, the triggers that set in motion a series of activities. In conducting internal benchmarking, management is looking at itself first before thinking about comparisons outside. Significant improvements are often made through internal bench-marking, and these are often the first steps in a benchmarking programme.

While internal benchmarking focuses on specific functions or processes, *competitive benchmarking* looks outwards in order to understand how direct competitors are performing. While knowing strengths and weaknesses of competitors is important to strategic decision making, it has a rather narrow field of view. Competitive benchmarking helps to level the playing field, but it is less likely to provide that innovative, step-out improvement that so many organizations are searching for today.

Industry benchmarking looks beyond the competitive relationship and looks for trends. Yet this too is limited in terms of the production of innovative performance enhancement. Most companies within a specific industry will be playing under the same rule book: the same legislation, constraints and capa-bilities. Analysing industry trends can help to establish baselines, but will seldom lead to quantum leaps in performance.

The final form of benchmarking is called *'best in class'* (BIC) or *'best practice'*. This type of benchmarking looks across many industries in search of inno-vative solutions to problems. The source is irrelevant – the premise is to create a performance target for the organization to aspire to. In this way, quantum leaps in organizational performance can be generated, as the organization makes an effort to achieve these stretch-targets.

SCOPING BENCHMARKING STUDIES

The technique of benchmarking can be focused on specific processes, activ-ities or functions, but this is only part of the answer. An associated issue is the depth to which the analysis is to be performed. Studies can be focused verti-cally upon functions or departments, or horizontally upon specific processes or activities. While early forays into the world of benchmarking might be constrained to functional or departmental performance, the goal has to be a cross-functional view of the value chain needed to meet customer expecta-tions in an efficient and effective manner.

A well-planned, systematic and structured benchmarking programme can provide organizations with a number of important benefits. In essence, the search for industry best practices and the subsequent efforts to maintain competitive superiority effectively provide the basis for superior performance. Almost any study that requires detailed examination of the organization's operations results in a greater understanding of how the business works, its critical success factors (CSFs) and key performance indicators (KPIs). But here again it is important to bear in mind that any form of continuous improvement must be managed strategically. Care must be taken that improvement in one part of the business does not just push issues to another area of the operation – a phenomenon known as the 'waterbed effect'.

Most organizations can learn from the experience of others, even though they may have very different customer requirements and competitive environments. Much can be gained by making comparisons with organizations that have to adopt a fundamentally different approach to the same or a similar task. For example, pharmaceutical manufacturers have had to adopt a highly sophisticated approach to production process documentation, quality assurance and traceability. There are lessons to be learnt from this and many other cases that are of significant value to very different organizations. For example, a manufacturer of complex, highly configurable products might learn how to manage its technical publications process more effectively by comparing its activities with a pharmaceutical manufacturer.

QUANTITATIVE VERSUS QUALITATIVE BENCHMARKING

In most companies traditional measures are based on fiscal and legal requirements. These are then used for planning purposes to facilitate comparison. The problem with these measures is that they are based upon derived information, and as presented have no clear relationship to the organization's operational data. On the other hand, operations develop their own set of KPIs and measures – that may be unrelated to the financial results – to identify levels of customer satisfaction and market needs. This division often leads to conflict in the evaluation of performance, and led to the development of the balanced scorecard concept (Kaplan and Norton, 1996).

Measurements can be either quantitative (numeric) or qualitative (opinions). Quantitative and qualitative benchmarks are not to be viewed as isolated categories, though. Measurements can be spread along a continuum, as illustrated in Figure 12.1.

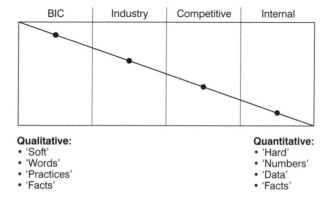

Figure 12.1 The quantitative/qualitative continuum

At one end of the continuum are highly qualitative measurements, for example assessment of customer or employee satisfaction. At the other end of the range are highly quantitative measurements such as cost per unit, or productivity measures. At each point along the continuum information is gleaned, but its nature, implications and relationship to benchmark type change.

There are many tools for approximating qualitative characteristics with numbers, but these techniques will never have precision to back them up. As part of the continuum of measures it is important to recognize that qualitative measures are a mid-point in terms of 'hardness' or reality. Hard measures make the user feel as though they are real. Facts with numbers attached to them take on a life of their own; they appear to possess a certain 'magic', and people tend to believe hard numbers. But, with each gain in precision, relevance or accuracy can be sacrificed. Therefore, in developing benchmark measurements the goal is to set a metric that is as 'hard' as it can get without losing vital insights provided by the 'softer' more intuitive qualitative indices.

A SYSTEMATIC APPROACH

Figure 12.2 illustrates the Rank Xerox benchmarking process. Many organizations have developed their own process, although the main elements should be present consistently. All approaches are fundamentally the same and are based on Deming's plan–do–check–act (PDCA) cycle.

Step 1: Prioritize what to benchmark

The first step focuses on the processes and activities that the organization believes will yield the maximum benefit. In any supply chain there are too many activities and processes to benchmark all of them in one go, therefore improvement effort cannot be spread too thinly, and all areas cannot be addressed simultaneously.

Step 2: Identify comparable companies

Benchmark partner selection can be determined by a benchmarking mechanism, for example through an existing benchmarking network or through an industry trade association. Where this is not done, a number of issues need to be considered:

- Should competitors be approached? If so, how will confidentiality be addressed, and are they likely to have significantly better activities and operations?

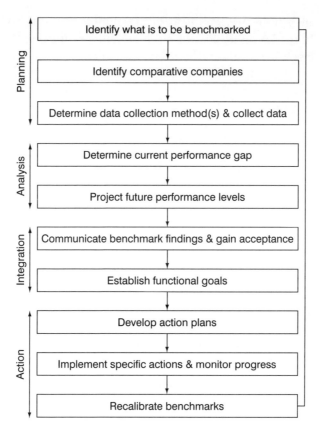

Figure 12.2 The Rank Xerox benchmarking process

- Can best-in-class organizations be identified easily, and what can be offered to them of interest in exchange?
- How many benchmark partners are required?
- Which other organizations have similar requirements or operational processes, but are likely to have developed better processes to deal with them?
- How should the partner organizations' different areas of interest be accommodated within the process?

Step 3: Data and information collection

Once it has been decided what to benchmark, and the organization has identified and gained agreement from partners, the next step is to determine the process for data and information collection. The key here is to achieve a common agreed understanding of the activities, processes, definition, terminology and time periods. Failure to achieve this will result in major problems in both the analysis and comparison activities, which ultimately may lead to rejection of the output by key managers.

All the participants must sign off the common understanding, and a forum needs to be established to discuss and resolve any queries that arise during the process. Deadlines for each stage of the data and information collection need to be set, monitored and adhered to, otherwise it could be a considerably lengthy process.

Step 4: Determine current performance gap

Once the data and information have been collected, the analytical stage needs to convert these inputs into useful outputs. High-level analysis should be used to sense-check the data and information provided. Queries should be addressed to the supplying organization and resolved quickly. Data might be aggregated, and particular attention should be paid to the following:

- data normalization methods;
- root cause analysis;
- best practice characteristic identification;
- identification of relevant process enablers.

When all the data and information have been accepted and analysed, comparisons need to be made and any gaps analysed. The analysis should utilize an agreed framework, focusing on the key areas of interest. These could be points of greatest difference or similarity, and should be presented in a way that will focus the recipients upon the required actions. The output should:

- assess the overall comparison in the areas of interest;
- seek to explain whether there are broader business reasons for some of the differences;
- identify the major performance gaps where the real opportunities for major improvement lie;
- set targets and realistic time-scales;
- outline what is required to close the gaps.

Step 5: Project future performance levels

Analysing the benchmark performance 'gap' can be done as a snapshot or as a trend over a period of time. Either method may be appropriate for the function or process being studied. Indeed, both may be applied simultaneously. When cost, productivity or quality is the metric under study, sometimes it is useful to look at the historical trend as well as the current gap.

Additionally, projecting future performance levels of productivity within your own organization against that of the benchmark partner's – given the current rate of improvement for each – creates projected targets for improvement. This approach helps to create the intent to increase the rate of innovation and improvement within the organization, in order to leapfrog the competition.

A major danger here is that these targets may be either too hard and discourage employees from trying, or too easy and result in a slower rate of improvement than might have been possible. The first danger is by far the most common.

Step 6: Communicate findings and gain acceptance

It is a known fact that people do not like change, especially change that appears to be for 'change sake'. In order to ensure the success of any benchmarking programme it is imperative that a detailed communications plan is created and revised regularly during the course of the initiative.

Even with the support of senior management, there may be resistance to change from lower organizational levels. This resistance to change primarily stems from fear: fear of job losses, loss of status, control, resources and so on. In order to plan for and mitigate against such events, a stakeholder and/or force-field analysis might be used to identify potential areas of resistance and methods of overcoming any such concerns.

Step 7: Establish functional goals

Once outline targets have been drawn up, detailed functional (or cross-functional) goals can be established. The secret in using benchmarking to achieve breakthrough change is to synthesize key actions, taken after consideration of all the information available, to generate innovative approaches. After the enablers of performance within a specific organizational environment have been assessed, careful consideration should be given to the adaptability of these enablers to the organization's circumstances.

Step 8: Develop action plans

The action plans describe each of the key actions at a functional level required to achieve the desired goals. Action plans can be as detailed as required: in some instances they can even identify the core tasks, the desired levels of performance required, and the changes in process, behaviour or systems required to support their achievement.

Step 9: Implement and monitor

All the time and effort expended to this stage is worth very little if the output does not provide clear plans for change, and these are not implemented in real and lasting improvements. Having achieved a successful implementation, the organization must continue to monitor the operational performance, and assess whether there are other organizations that have now developed superior processes or practices.

Step 10: Recalibrate benchmarks

The continuous search for improvement will inevitably result in further development of the processes and practices, and some revisiting of benchmarking efforts.

THE PEOPLE ISSUES IN BENCHMARKING

Benchmarking removes some of the politics and guesswork out of the development of continuous improvement targets within organizations. This is due to the external, politically neutral, nature of the analysis. Some people like to know exactly where they stand and what is expected of them. If measures are used to guide or assess performance these must not be vague or nondescript. Metrics without clarity can lead to individuals incorporating these into a workable framework of their own. The problem is that this framework might not be what management had in mind!

A good example of this type of 'bureaucratic institutionalization' is a materials planner in a business not releasing much needed materials because the appropriate paperwork has not been completed correctly. Deep down the planner knows that releasing the materials is the right thing to do, but saying 'no' within the rules framework is much easier than taking the risk and letting the materials through. Now say that this very same materials planner has been given a mandate to pursue continuous improvement opportunities. What does this individual hear? Speed up or else, you're not doing your job fast enough! No one has voiced a specific complaint or indeed identified specific areas of continuous improvement. In this environment some individuals will truly find ways of improving their performance, others will just rearrange the deckchairs on their misguided ship.

Effective continuous improvement starts with a rigorous analysis of process flows – what work is done where, and why is it done in the way it is done. Report outputs are analysed and the 'why?' question is repeated many times: Why is this report produced? Why does it go to all these people? Why is the information duplicated on this other report going to a different community? The answers to these questions often drive a degree of uncertainty, with respondents asking: 'Is there something wrong?' To which the interviewee may answer: 'No ... but it says here that I have to ask anyway.'

The above scenario happens again and again within organizations following the continuous improvement trail. Continuous improvement is a good thing, right? So let's get out there and improve! But unstructured programmes often yield patchy, sub-optimal performance. Continuous improvement must be managed strategically, with all those involved clearly understanding why a particular course of action is being followed, where the improvement targets have come from, and how and by whom it is expected that the improvements will be implemented.

Benchmarking solves this problem. It develops a set of objective measures within an organizational framework, stabilizes the improvement programme, and provides all parties with a clear understanding of why a particular course, or courses, of action are to be followed. Customer surveys – completed as part of a benchmarking exercise – will point specifically to the areas that need improvement. Clear statements of problems overcome the 'speed up or else' type messages by providing a clear mandate driven by objective statements of performance shortfall. The vague 'continuous improvement is good' message is replaced with specific, actionable statements of improvement, often accompanied by information, gathered during the benchmarking process, that drives creativity and innovative solutions.

Benchmarking, if managed effectively, holds the key to unlocking an individual's defences. It creates a logical, prioritized and – importantly – achievable path to good practice and operational excellence. Unlocking the power vested in individuals and teams in this fashion is the catalyst for organizational creativity and innovation.

THE PITFALLS

As with many management techniques and processes, benchmarking provides organizations with problems as well as benefits. These occur as consequence of:

- the existing organizational culture;
- incorrect application of the techniques;
- the nature of the process.

Benchmarking's application may be limited by the management culture. Some senior executives will publicly state that their business is different and that it is unique. Benchmarking, however, takes a normative approach to management – there are industry best practices that can be generalized between industry sectors and organizations. As with most programmes that require major organizational change, considerable inertia may be experienced from individuals and departments, especially those with the most to lose.

There are inevitable issues around the identification of best practices and the adoption of processes that are not valued by that particular organization's customers. And what is in it for the acknowledged laggards? There is the difficult judgement call to make around the introduction of new practices where a quantum jump is required – the chasm will not be crossed in a series of tiny hops. Indeed, incorrect benchmarking may lead to the wrong conclusions. Benchmarking may lead to a culture of imitation rather than innovation: to adopt rather than adapt, and to achieve parity instead of superiority. This type of approach will never result in competitive advantage.

When the process is approached for the first time, it is worthwhile learning from others who have built up experience of applying benchmarking within their own operations. This is where membership of benchmarking clubs and networks proves invaluable. In general it is important to avoid:

- benchmarking for benchmarking's sake;
- focusing entirely on comparisons of 'hard' performance measures rather than the 'softer' processes and activities that enable the attainment of good practice;
- spending too long on one part of the process at the expense of others;
- expecting that benchmarking will be quick and/or easy;
- expecting to find benchmarking partners comparable in all respects to your own organization;
- asking for information and data without being prepared to share it with others, or, conversely, expecting organizations to share information that is commercially sensitive;
- not agreeing at the outset to abide by a code of conduct to help avoid confidentiality problems.

CRITICAL SUCCESS FACTORS (CSFS) FOR BENCHMARKING

Irrespective of the type and scope of benchmarking, it will be important to ensure that:

- Senior managers support benchmarking and are committed to continuous improvements.
- The objectives are clearly defined at the outset.
- The scope of the work is appropriate in the light of the objectives, resources, and time available, and the experience levels of those involved.
- Sufficient resources are available to complete projects within the required timescale, and that projects are selected based upon a prioritization linked to the achievement of competitive advantage.
- Benchmarking teams have a clear picture of their organization's performance before approaching others for comparisons.

- Stakeholders, particularly staff and their representatives, are kept informed of the reasons for benchmarking and the progress made throughout the course of projects. Where practicable, staff should be involved in undertaking benchmarking to make the most of the opportunities for learning from others.
- The development of recommendations is an inclusive process, and proposed improvements are realistic in the context of local circumstances and other initiatives.

HASN'T BENCHMARKING HAD ITS DAY?

While it is true that benchmarking as a management technique receives considerably less press now than it did five or six years ago, there is still plenty of interest and activity. Clearly any technique that focuses on customers and performance improvement, with the potential for significant advances in efficiency and effectiveness, will continue to provide major benefits, long after the hype in the business press has died away. Benchmarking is used extensively by many organizations to help understand their relative positioning and efficiency of operations. Benchmarking networks, full-time benchmarking managers and consulting assignments are evidence of the continuing interest in this area.

LESSONS LEARNT

Benchmarking raises an organization's consciousness. It provides an external focus on internal activities, and drives an organization to the conclusion that there are always opportunities within every organization to learn something new.

Peter Senge in *The Fifth Discipline* (1990) suggests that the learning organization is more than just copying the processes and practices used by others. To achieve operational excellence an organization needs to experiment in all parts of its business. Everyone – from top management down – has to be willing to roll their sleeves up and get their hands dirty, constantly asking, 'why?' The role of benchmarking in this environment is to provide the creative spur, and to unearth a path that has worked for others in achieving operational excellence.

Benchmarking is about learning from others, as well as learning by doing. It cannot be learnt from a book or a seminar: it has to be practised. And the more practiced you become, the greater the potential for innovation within your business.

As described earlier in this chapter, benchmarking is composed of four distinct phases:

- **Phase 1: Planning.** Identifying what to benchmark, selecting comparative companies, or indeed parts of your own business, and determining how the data collection activities are to be performed.
- **Phase 2: Analysis.** Analysing internal levels of performance and comparing these with the target organization's performance. Also projecting future performance levels and setting targets in order to attain less time-perishable levels of competitive advantage.
- **Phase 3: Integration.** Communicating benchmark findings and helping the organization come to terms with what needs to change in order to achieve new and lasting levels of performance. Developing realistic and achievable functional goals to enable this vision.
- **Phase 4: Action.** Managing change and developing specific action plans in order to make the desired levels of change a reality. Once implemented, the monitoring of progress via a set of clear key performance indicators (KPIs) is of paramount importance, allaying any drift back to old habits. Finally, a recalibration of benchmarks is required in order to lead the business to the next level of operational excellence.

Good benchmarking is about managing continuous improvement strategically, identifying stakeholders and ensuring their interests are being met by any benchmark-based initiative, and managing change. Benchmarking is a tool for enacting change. The critical success factor for any change is the creation of additional value in the eyes of the stakeholders of the business. Benchmarking is all about finding new ways of enacting business processes, and using companies' precious resources to better serve its stakeholders' needs. To achieve this change benchmarking studies have to be specific, comparable, and have a predefined set of performance drivers and KPIs. Without any one of these a benchmarking study cannot hope to be effective.

In putting benchmarking to work in the supply chain it is worth keeping in mind that change will occur once the process has started. By its very nature it will cause participants to look at their world with a new set of eyes. Problems will be uncovered, and new and creative solutions will be developed.

SUPPLY-CHAIN-RELATED CASE STUDIES – BENCHMARKING IN ACTION

Pan-European supply chain structures and responsibilities

As part of the broader organizational change programme, a multinational fast-moving consumer goods (FMCG) manufacturer wanted to investigate different approaches to the management of its supply chain activities across Europe. The company had developed a country-based structure, but recognized that there were significant opportunities to be gained from changing at least some of this structure. The company wanted to look at how businesses in different sectors approached the fundamental management issues that were their key to success. These included:

- division of responsibilities;
- central versus regional management structures;
- support for customer-facing operations;
- information systems;
- implementation and change management.

Given the sensitivity of the areas of interest and the need to assure potential partners of confidentiality, a consultancy was engaged to act as the intermediary and run the process. Initial discussions produced a preliminary document; this was then developed into a questionnaire that could be used in face-to-face interviews. A number of potential partners were identified, approached and subsequently engaged. All participants were taken through the same interview process, to ensure consistency of approach, terminology, interpretation and response. At the conclusion of this process, all data were analysed, comparisons were drawn, and the key findings identified. A summary report was then circulated to all participants, and a presentation given to the FMCG manufacturer's management group.

This process allowed the company's management group to compare and gain insights into how companies with similar challenges had developed different roles, responsibilities and structures. The management group then prepared an evaluation of strategic options, and gained agreement to conduct follow-up, face-to-face benchmarking meetings with the two most interesting benchmarking partners. The output of this second-stage process formed a major part of the proposals to change the supply chain responsibilities and structures to a pan-European organization. The proposal was accepted, and a gradual implementation process provided for progressive centralization of both responsibilities and some activities.

Outsourcing logistics: benchmarking for success

A major Italian sportswear and accessories manufacturer was considering outsourcing its logistics operations to a third-party logistics (3PL) service provider. One of the key concerns held by the management team was the achievement of improved levels of operational performance at lower cost. How was this going to be assessed, how should the 3PL service provider be selected, and how could its performance be measured on an ongoing basis? In order to gain answers to these questions the manufacturer engaged a consultancy to develop an assessment framework. The brief was to design a set of processes to enable the organization to construct and manage a sourcing relationship based on a number of balanced, benchmarkable, metrics.

Initially a model describing the logistics function and its associated activities was developed. This covered activities such as:

- goods receiving inspection;
- warehouse operations;
- dispatch inspection;
- shipping;
- distribution planning and control;
- transportation management;
- support;
- management and administration.

Data were then requested internally covering cost drivers, resources consumed – including FTEs (full-time equivalents), capital equipment, and volumes – and quality and performance metrics. This data, once harvested and validated, enabled the development of a detailed set of performance metrics characterizing the organization's current logistics function performance. These measures were both quantitative and qualitative, covering unit costs, productivity, cycle times, and quality and performance metrics.

The next step was to compare these data with a reference group of data from organizations with a similar set of operational characteristics. This did not mean that the comparators were within the same industry; they just had to provide a reasonable fit in terms of demand uncertainty and organizational/product complexity. The consulting organization engaged to support this initiative already had a significant database of information from previous engagements, and was therefore able to provide reference group data to support this phase of the project.

The analysis that followed identified the areas where the organization's performance was better than that of the reference group mean, and where there were opportunities for improvement. This latter set became improvement challenges for the chosen 3PL service provider. This exercise also provided the base case upon which to assess and select the appropriate 3PL service provider's offerings. It also enabled a framework upon which a set of ongoing, balanced, performance metrics could be developed in order to manage the sourcing relationship over time.

Negotiations with the selected 3PL service provider led to a three-year sourcing contract, with clearly identified performance improvement objectives agreed between both parties at the outset. The manufacturer also had a management framework in place that could be used to assess the competitiveness of the service provider's offerings on an ongoing basis, providing information to ensure full value was achieved from the service provider/service recipient relationship they had created.

CONCLUSIONS

Benchmarking is designed for action, rather than just to answer the question, 'How are we doing?' It is a means to an end, not an end in itself, and is at its most powerful when used as a tool to develop best practices rather than to solve a specific problem.

To benefit from this approach, organizations must first recognize that there are always others who can perform activities and tasks better than they currently do, and that lessons can be learnt from how they do this. Ultimately, the greatest benefits may come from a better understanding of the business and a change in culture to a proactive, creative organization that strives for supply chain excellence and continuous improvement.

When used correctly, benchmarking is a powerful management tool that provides a much-needed external view of the organization's environment, and especially the requirements of its customers. Above all else, the application of benchmarking processes can lead to competitive advantage, through cost-leadership and differentiation based upon excellent customer service.

REFERENCES

Camp, R C (1989) *Benchmarking: The search for industry best practices that land superior performance*, ASQ Quality Press, New York

Kaplan, R S and Norton, D P (1996) *Translating Strategy into Action: The balanced scorecard*, Harvard Business School Press, Cambridge, MA

Senge, P M (1990) *The Fifth Discipline*, Doubleday, New York

13

Outsourcing the logistics function

Alan McKinnon
Heriot-Watt University

INTRODUCTION

Over the past 20 years companies have been concentrating resources on their core competencies and outsourcing what they regard as ancillary functions. As logistics is often considered to be a supporting rather than mainstream function, it has been an obvious candidate for externalization. For many firms, logistics has ceased to be an activity that they directly manage, and become something that they purchase from outside specialists. Others have retained an in-house logistical operation but increasingly supplemented it with contract services. The manner in which these services are purchased can, therefore, have a major influence on the quality and efficiency of a company's logistics operation.

This chapter will review recent trends in the outsourcing of logistical activities, report on the experience of firms that have contracted out their logistics, and outline ways in which users and providers of logistical services can develop more stable and mutually beneficial relationships.

GROWTH OF OUTSOURCING

There has been a long tradition of firms contracting out freight transport operations. In many countries, however, external purchases of freight transport services were constrained by government controls on the capacity of the road haulage industry. These controls generally excluded lorries operated on an 'own account' basis, and thus encouraged firms to internalize their road freight operations. The deregulation of road haulage over the past 30 years in most developed countries has made it much easier and more attractive for firms to contract out the transport function (McKinnon, 1998). The recent growth in contracting out cannot simply be attributed to deregulation, though. In the United Kingdom, for example, road freight traffic remained fairly evenly divided between 'own account' and 'hire and reward' operations for a decade after the liberalization of the road freight market in 1970. Only since 1981 has there been a significant and sustained increase in the proportion of road freight tonnage handled by outside contractors, from 50 per cent to 67 per cent in 2001 (Department for Transport, 2002). The swing away from in-house transport had to await the general change in managerial attitudes to contracting out that occurred in the 1980s and 1990s.

Freight transport statistics present only part of the picture, however, because in addition to giving contractors greater responsibility for transport, firms have been externalizing related activities such as warehousing, materials handling, stock control and order processing. A survey of over 200 European companies in 1998 revealed wide variations in the degree to which individual logistical activities were outsourced (A T Kearney, 1999) (Figure 13.1). It is very common to contract out transport and, to a lesser extent, warehousing, but comparatively rare to outsource order processing. A Delphi survey of a panel of 129 logistics experts carried out around the same time predicted that within Europe, outsourced expenditure on various logistics activities would grow at differential rates between 1999 and 2005 (McKinnon and Forster, 2000) (Figure 13.2). It was forecast that higher value-adding activities, such as information processing, product customization and reverse logistics, would experience the most rapid growth in outsourcing, while the purchase of transport services would only rise by around 13 per cent, though from a much higher base.

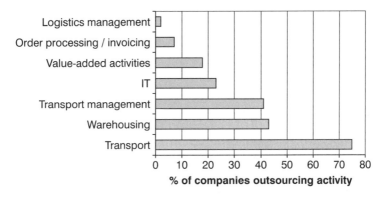

Figure 13.1   Proportion of European companies outsourcing logistical activities

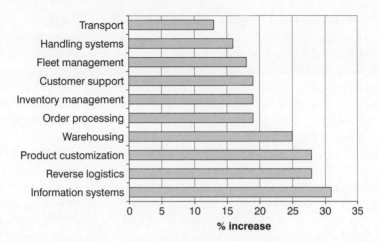

Figure 13.2 Forecast increase in outsourced expenditure on logistics activities: Europe 1999–2005

This broadening of the range of logistical activities outsourced is in keeping with one of the fundamental principles of logistics, which stipulates that the management of transport, stockholding and other related activities should be closely coordinated. The externalization of logistics has, therefore, been a two-dimensional process, with firms increasing both the range of services that they source externally and the volume of traffic entrusted to outside agencies. Companies have also increasingly been demanding an integrated logistical service tailored to their requirements. This places heavy emphasis on the contractor's ability to coordinate and customize logistics services.

Outsourced logistical services are said to be provided on a 'third-party' basis. The first party is the shipper (or consignor), the second party the customer (or consignee), with the third-party logistics (or 3PL) provider responsible for the physical transfer of products between them. In this chapter, we will adopt the broad definition of third-party logistics advanced by Lieb, Millen and Wassenhove (1993), which states that it is 'the use of external companies to perform logistics functions that have traditionally been performed within an organization'. The term 'logistics service provider' (or LSP) is now widely used to describe these companies.

In 1999 around 26 per cent of total logistics expenditure in the European Union was outsourced (Datamonitor, 1999). The total EU market for third-party logistics services was worth around US $38 billion in that year. There were wide international variations between EU member states in the degree of logistical outsourcing (Figure 13.3). In 1999, for example, British firms externalized roughly 39 per cent of their logistics spending, whereas in Italy only 16 per cent was contracted out (Datamonitor, 2000a). It was predicted that by 2003, 30 per cent of logistics expenditure in the EU would be outsourced.

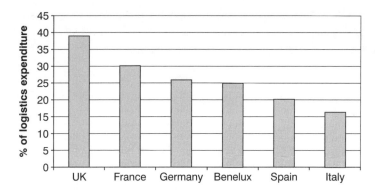

Figure 13.3 Proportion of logistics expenditure outsourced, 1999

Research in the late 1990s suggested that the European market for logistics services was more mature than the American one (Peters *et al*, 1998a). Of a sample of 84 manufacturers in Europe 59 per cent outsourced more than 20 per cent of their logistics budget, whereas only 29 per cent of a comparable sample of 123 manufacturers in North American sample did so. The American third-party logistics market was, nevertheless, forecast to grow more rapidly at around 20–30 per cent per annum, by comparison with a European growth rate of 10–15 per cent.

FACTORS PROMOTING OUTSOURCING

The increasing externalization of logistical services has occurred in response to a range of demand and supply pressures. Razzaque and Sheng (1998), for example, identify 20 'drivers' of logistics outsourcing. Many of the factors promoting outsourcing are fundamental and widespread, though some are associated with particular developments in individual countries.

Demand for logistical services

In a general review of the literature on the outsourcing of services, Maltz (1994) observes that general management papers tend to emphasize the potential cost savings, whereas those written by purchasing and marketing specialists attach equal importance to cost and service benefits. Much of the specialist logistics research has identified the demand for higher service standards as the prime motive for outsourcing. This is the conclusion reached by LaLonde and Maltz (1992) in a study of the outsourcing of warehousing in the United States. More recent surveys, however, suggest that similar importance is attached to cost savings, service improvement and flexibility in the decision to outsource logistics (PE Consulting, 1996; Peters *et al*, 1998b) (Table 13.1).

Table 13.1 Most frequently quoted reasons for outsourcing logistics

PE Consulting	% of firms	Peters, Lieb and Randall	% of firms
Improve service	87	Lower cost	56
Reduce cost	85	Greater flexibility	55
Increase flexibility	79	Improved operational efficiency	53
Avoid investment	61	Ability to focus on core business	51
Non-core activity	59	Improved customer service	49
Obtain specialist		Improved expertise/market	
management	50	knowledge and access to data	29
Improve control	50	Other	8

Sources: PE Consulting (1996), Peters *et al* (1998b).

Another highly-rated factor is the desire to avoid investing in logistical facilities. This was frequently advanced as the main advantage of outsourcing in the 1980s, particularly in the United Kingdom where a change in the system of corporate taxation in 1984 redirected tax incentives away from owning assets towards maximizing their contribution to profit. This encouraged firms to concentrate capital on those core activities that earned the highest rates of return and exploited their main competitive strengths. Approximately 59 per cent of 300 companies surveyed by PE Consulting (1996) did not regard logistical operations as a core activity. The use of outside contractors not only reduces the need for new investment in logistical facilities; it can also release some of the capital already tied up in warehousing and vehicle fleets for more productive use elsewhere in the business.

Outsourcing also gives companies access to specialist expertise in firms whose core skill is logistics management. The management of logistics has, after all, become more demanding as a result of rising customer expectations, the proliferation of regulations on vehicle operation, working conditions and product handling, the rapid rate of technological change, and uncertainties about future economic and environmental trends. Contracting out can also help firms overcome internal labour problems that have traditionally impaired the efficiency of own-account operations. Outsourcing, or the threat of it, has given own-account operators leverage in trade union negotiations and offered a means of escaping restrictive practices and pay scales. Operating parallel in-house and third-party systems has also reduced the risk of the supply system being paralysed by industrial action.

New ways have been found of overcoming the natural resistance to contracting out in firms with extensive and/or long-established own-account operations. Much of this inertia has stemmed from a reluctance to relinquish control over the logistics function (Murtagh, 1991; Croucher, 1998). This has become less of a concern in recent years, partly as a result of growing confidence in the way that contract logistics operations are managed, but also because of advances in information technology (IT). These have made it possible for firms to monitor and control 3PL operations at least as closely as in-house systems. Indeed, 50 per cent of the firms surveyed by PE Consulting (1996) actually advanced the need to improve control of logistics as a reason for outsourcing.

In some countries, particularly the United Kingdom, structural change in the retail supply system has promoted the use of LSPs (Fernie, 1989). Large retailers have greatly increased their control over inbound logistics and contracted out much of its day-to-day management to third-party operators. In 2000, the major British grocery retailers controlled the secondary distribution (from distribution centres to shops) of 96 per cent of their supplies (Marchant, McKinnon and Patel, 2000). On average 50 per cent of their transport and 42 per cent of their warehousing was contracted out. 'Quick response' pressures in the retail supply chain, which have been increasing frequency of delivery and reducing order size, have also forced suppliers to make greater use of shared-user services provided by outside contractors. There is a similar demand for third-party load consolidation services in those industrial sectors, such as automotive and electronics, where just-in-time sourcing is now widespread.

There is also an important international dimension to the externalization of logistical services. Manufacturers tend to rely heavily on LSPs both for international transport and for the distribution of their products within foreign markets. It was estimated in 1990 that across Europe contractors handled around 96 per cent of the international movement of freight by road, as opposed to 58 per cent of road freight movement within countries (*Motor Transport*, 6 Sep 1990). In 2001, 69 per cent of the 589 European logistics centres (ELCs) located in the Netherlands and used by American and Asian manufacturers were managed by third-party logistics companies (Holland International Distribution Council, 2001). Globalization trends are therefore inflating the demand for contract services at both international and national levels.

Supply of logistical services

There have been major improvements in the nature of 3PL services on offer. Standards have undoubtedly risen and operations become more efficient. New types of service have been developed which are more closely tailored to clients' requirements. Logistical services are being much more skilfully and aggressively marketed today than in the past.

Many transport and warehousing firms have evolved into broadly based logistics service providers. In most countries, the general road haulage industry is characterized by low entry costs, high rates of entry and exit, intense competition, heavy reliance on spot hiring, low returns on capital and slim profit margins. By trading up into integrated logistics, the larger carriers have been able to add value to their services, create niche markets with much higher entry costs, and secure longer-term contracts with clients. This has enabled them to improve both their profitability and growth prospects. Table 13.2 shows the range of value-added logistics (VAL) services that some of the larger operators now provide. These firms are becoming increasingly involved in the customization of products, changing the physical character of the goods they handle and thus blurring the traditional distinction between distribution and manufacturing.

Table 13.2   Value added logistics: service portfolio

Transport	Vehicle maintenance
Storage	Palletization
Break-bulk	Packaging/repacking
Load consolidation	Return of packaging/handling equipment
Order picking	Labelling
Order processing	Quality control/product testing
Stock control	Customization
Pick and pack	After sales service
Track and trace	Consultancy advice

THE PROCESS OF EXTERNALIZATION

As explained above, firms can outsource their logistics in various ways. The most dramatic form of outsourcing involves closure of the in-house system and transfer of all responsibility for logistics to an outside contractor. This is too radical an option for many own-account operators, who are unwilling to dispose of existing logistical assets, shed staff and risk disruption of their operations during the transitional period. Some prefer to adopt a more gradual process of outsourcing, phasing the transfer of responsibility geographically, by business sector or product group. It is also possible for firms to ease the transition in other ways.

System takeover

There have been numerous examples of large logistics service providers buying out in-house systems, assuming ownership of vehicles, depots and equipment and taking on much of the previous workforce. Following a takeover of this type, the system may continue to be operated on an exclusive basis for the divesting firm, or the LSP may share the use of the acquired facilities with other clients, thereby improving utilization and spreading overhead costs. Within the EU, it was possible until 1993 for the acquiring firm to alter the terms and conditions of employees absorbed from the own-account operation.

A legal judgement in that year relating to the EU law on the Transfer of Undertakings and Protection of Employment (TUPE) tightly limited the scope for modifying existing employment contracts.

Joint ventures

Some clients prefer to retain part-ownership of distribution facilities and maintain closer involvement in the logistical operation. For them, joint ventures with LSPs offer a more attractive means of injecting outside capital and expertise. A good example of such a joint venture in the United Kingdom is the link-up between the brewer Bass and the 3PL company Exel to create 'Tradeteam'.

System 'spin-off'

Tucker and Zivan (1987) advocate the 'spinning-off' of firms' in-house logistical systems as separate subsidiaries. There have been several examples of own-account operators initially making their distribution department a separate profit centre, allowing it to tender for third-party business, and ultimately selling it off, typically as a management buyout. The parent company thereafter provides the base traffic, but this is increasingly supplemented by third-party traffic.

Management-only contract

Firms wishing to retain ownership of logistical assets can still contract out their management. This has become a popular strategy among large retailers in Britain and other EU countries, many of whom see contracting out more as a way of upgrading the management of their distribution operation than of releasing capital for other uses. As this form of outsourcing is not asset-based it gives the client greater flexibility to renegotiate and, if necessary, terminate contracts at short notice.

RECENT TRENDS IN THE PURCHASE OF LOGISTICAL SERVICES

The recent increase in the level and diversity of firms' external expenditure on logistical services has been accompanied by important changes in the way they purchase them and in the nature of their relationship with LSPs. Seven changes have been of particular significance.

Increase in the proportion of logistical services bought on a contractual basis

The purchase of haulage and warehousing services was traditionally done on a spot-hire, 'transactional' basis. Such services are fairly standardized and generally bought at minimum price. The high degree of fragmentation in the road haulage industry ensures that there are numerous small hauliers available to provide an economical service at short notice.

Buying haulage services in this way, however, has serious shortcomings. The need to deal with large numbers of separate carriers on a daily basis both inflates transaction costs and makes it difficult to ensure high delivery standards. In practice, even within the spot market, firms have been able to alleviate these problems by making regular use of the same set of hauliers. Even in the absence of formal contracts, manufacturers have, for many years, exhibited a high degree of 'source loyalty' to particular carriers (Cunningham and Kettlewood, 1976; LaLonde and Cooper, 1989).

Where firms demand more specialist services tailored to their particular requirements and often involving capital investment on the part of the carrier, they must be prepared to enter into longer-term contracts. In the case of transport operations dedicated to a particular consignor, an LSP would like ideally to secure a contract at least as long as the working life of the vehicles, though, given the competitive conditions in the haulage industry, the typical duration of contracts is usually much shorter. Even where LSPs invest in warehousing facilities for the exclusive use of a particular client, contracts seldom extend beyond five years, though they generally require the client to assume responsibility for the lease if they are not renewed. In situations where the third-party operator merely provides a management service, contracts are usually much shorter, with two to three years being the norm. A substantial proportion of logistics contracts, nevertheless, do not have a fixed time limit and are simply considered to be 'ongoing'. In the United Kingdom, the proportion of companies without formal logistics contracts has been declining. Between 1990 and 1996, it dropped from 37 per cent to under 20 per cent (PE Consulting, 1996). It was estimated in 1996 that the average length of a logistics contract was around 2.8 years in the United Kingdom. Subsequent research has revealed that contract length varies significantly between industrial sectors (Datamonitor, 2000b) (Figure 13.4).

Reduction in the number of contractors used

In both the 'spot' and 'contract' markets, the average number of LSPs used has been declining. Surveys by PE Consulting (1996) in the UK revealed that the proportion of companies using six or more logistics providers declined from 21 per cent to 14 per cent between 1990 and 1996. Concentrating purchases of logistical services in this way enables firms both to reduce transaction costs and to improve the standard of service:

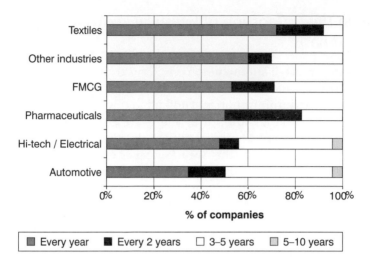

Figure 13.4 Frequency of logistics contract renewal: UK companies (2000)

Transaction costs

In Germany, Sweden and several other European countries a substantial proportion of domestic road haulage services has traditionally been purchased from freight forwarding or 'spedition' companies, who act as middlemen in the freight market. This greatly reduces the number of direct transactions between consignors and hauliers. In Britain, on the other hand, the brokerage services of freight forwarders tend only to be used for international distribution. There has been a tradition in the United Kingdom, as far as domestic transport operations are concerned, of dealing directly with numerous hauliers. This has enabled firms to secure lower freight rates, but at the expense of higher transaction costs. In their pursuit of low haulage prices, many firms underestimate the total cost of buying-in road haulage in this way.

It is, nevertheless, possible for firms to streamline the purchase of haulage services while continuing to exploit the very competitive rates available in the general haulage market. Under a 'freight management' arrangement, some of the larger LSPs, such as Exel, will, on a particular client's behalf, subcontract trunk haulage operations to smaller carriers. Similar 'one-stop shipping' services are provided by many of the 'third-party logistics' firms that have emerged in the United States since the early 1980s (Sheffi, 1990).

Standard of service

The more hauliers a firm employs, the more time it must spend vetting them and monitoring their performance. Concentrating traffic on a smaller number of more reliable hauliers simplifies these tasks. It can also win a greater commitment from these hauliers to maintain or improve the quality of service.

It was estimated in 2000 that only around 20 per cent of UK companies employed a single LSP (Datamonitor, 2000b). An earlier study enquired about the 'critical factors' causing firms to use more than one third-party logistics company (PE Consulting, 1996) (Figure 13.5). Service and cost considerations dominated this decision, though the ability to meet different operational needs, flexibility and geographical coverage were also identified by the majority of respondents as important factors. The majority of companies distributing throughout Europe outsource their logistics to several contractors, usually on a country-by-country basis. This was the strategy adopted by 59 per cent of a sample of 68 of Europe's 500 largest manufacturers surveyed in 1997 (Mercer Management Consulting, 1998).

Many of the firms using more than one LSP are not 'multiple-sourcing' in the conventional sense. When applied to the supply of material goods, the term 'multiple-sourcing' generally means obtaining identical products from different suppliers. Where a firm employs several LSPs, however, they seldom provide parallel services. As noted above, a dominant motive for using several contractors is to subdivide logistics operations geographically. Where more than one LSP is used, it is common for each to be given exclusive responsibility for distribution within a single region. The nature of local storage and delivery operations makes it possible to split a distribution contract geographically among several agencies at little or no extra cost. Purchasing contract distribution on a regional basis can, in fact, yield important benefits by reducing the risk of the entire system being disrupted,

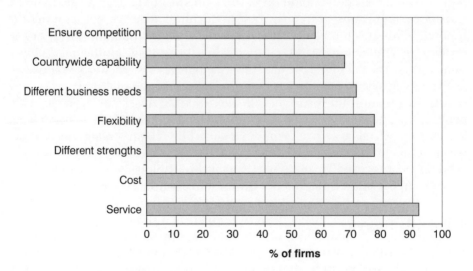

Figure 13.5 Reasons for using more than one logistics service provider

by, for example, industrial disputes or company failure, and permitting inter-firm comparisons of rates and service standards.

More rigorous selection of LSPs

When companies were only outsourcing part of their transport operation, their carrier selection procedures were often fairly crude. This may partly be excused by the facts that the external transport budget then represented a small proportion of total costs, and differences in rates and quality of service, particularly among road hauliers, were perceived to be small. Now that firms are contracting out a broader range of logistics services, total 3PL expenditure has begun to figure more prominently on their balance sheets. This, combined with the increased strategic importance of logistics, the greater emphasis being placed on service quality, the reduction in carrier numbers and the shift to contractual relationships, has made the choice of carrier a much higher-order decision, requiring a more thorough review of the market and more formal selection procedures (Menon, McGinnis and Ackerman, 1998).

Closer involvement of LSPs in the design of logistics systems

In purchasing component parts, many manufacturers are replacing the traditional 'design specification', which describes the required item in detail, with the more open 'performance' specification, which merely outlines the function the part has to perform (Ramsay, 1991). This gives suppliers greater scope to innovate and develop parts that meet the customer's requirements more economically and effectively.

A similar development has occurred in the purchase of logistical services. It is now quite common for firms externalizing their distribution operations to involve LSPs in system design. The decision to externalize is often made at the same time as the decision to restructure the logistics system. Moreover, as one of the major reasons for using LSPs is to exploit their specialist expertise, it is hardly surprising that firms should seek their advice when reconfiguring their logistical systems. As Bask (2001) points out, however, the links between logistics outsourcing and development of supply chain strategy are under-researched.

Participation in system design can be a mixed blessing for LSPs. On the positive side, it gives them the opportunity to set up a system in which they have confidence and which they believe they can operate efficiently. The broad terms of reference also enable them to compete at a strategic as well as operational level for what is then a higher value-adding service. The main disadvantage is the high cost of preparing a tender containing proposals for the strategic redesign of a firm's logistical system. For a major contract, such costs can be in excess of £100,000, and easily deter smaller LSPs from preparing a bid.

Greater emphasis on the development of longer-term partnerships

It can be just as important for a firm to develop close, mutually beneficial relationships with suppliers of logistical services as with suppliers of products. Many such relationships have already been established, and go beyond the formal terms of the logistics contract. Expressions such as 'partnershipping' and 'co-shippership'(!) have been coined to describe the new consignor–carrier links that have been formed.

These relationships are most likely to develop where logistical services are provided on a dedicated basis for the exclusive use of individual clients. As Cooper and Johnstone (1990) point out, 'compartmentalization of the contractor's capacity between clients means that the service needs of any one client will not be compromised by the conflicting needs of other clients, such as may occur when capacity is shared.'

While this usually ensures a high standard of service, it also weakens one of the LSP's traditional roles, that of consolidating many clients' traffic and thus running distribution facilities at a lower unit cost than in-house operators. Many manufacturers and retailers are prepared to incur the higher costs of dedicated services in order to maintain high levels of control and service quality. An increasing number of firms in the UK, however, have been relaxing the requirements of dedicated contracts to give service providers greater freedom to obtain backloads and consolidate loads. There has also been a sharp growth in demand for logistics services provided on a 'shared-user' basis.

Several recent developments have been conducive to the formation of closer partnerships between LSPs and their clients:

- *Adoption of the just-in-time principle.* One of the prerequisites for a successful JIT system is the fast and reliable delivery of supplies. In the absence of buffer stocks, production and distribution operations become much more vulnerable to deviations from the delivery schedule. Ansari and Modarress (1990) found that 53 per cent of a sample of large American corporations implementing JIT purchasing experienced difficulty in getting carriers to provide services of the required standard. This forced them to change the way in which they purchased transport services. In addition to greatly reducing the number of carriers employed and increasing the proportion of work done on a contractual basis, they tried to forge 'closer, longer-term and more interdependent' relationships with transport firms (Crumm and Allen, 1998).
- *Development of computer networking.* Many LSP–client relationships have been reinforced by the establishment of EDI links and more recently Web-based systems. By making the flow of materials through the contractor's system more 'visible' on a day-to-day, or even hour-by-hour, basis,

computer networking increases the client's confidence in the outsourced operation. The integration of the LSP's and client's computer systems also strengthens the operational bond between them and makes it difficult for either party to break off the relationship at short notice. As Ellram and Cooper (1990) point out, 'The integration of information and operating systems creates a relatively unified system that is difficult and costly to replicate should the partnership dissolve.'

- *Increasing specialization of logistical equipment.* Technological developments in the fields of transport and materials handling are making it possible to tailor equipment more closely to individual firms' logistical needs. Such 'client-specific' equipment is an example of what Williamson (1979) calls an 'idiosyncratic asset'. He argues that the inclusion of such assets in a transaction greatly increases the likelihood of a 'relational contract' developing between supplier and customer. This is borne out by experience in the logistics sector (Aertsen, 1993).

- *Change in the degree of interdependence.* It is generally supposed that close, cooperative relationships are more likely to develop where there is a high level of interdependence between customer and supplier. As Rinehart (1989) notes, consignors have traditionally considered themselves to be less dependent on carriers than carriers considered themselves to be dependent on consignors. This reflected consignors' perceptions of the road haulage market as being a 'buyer's market' in which business could easily be transferred between carriers at short notice and minimal cost.

The externalization of a broader range of logistical services to a much smaller number of contractors has increased clients' dependence and made it much more difficult for them to sever their links with an LSP, at least in the short term. Within the 3PL market, contractor–client relationships tend to be unbalanced in the opposite direction from those in the general road haulage market. Companies outsourcing their distribution operations on either a national or regional basis to a single LSP become completely reliant on that firm within the area in question. As a result of the high degree of concentration in the logistics services market, major contractors can have extensive client portfolios. Even quite a large manufacturing or retail client might therefore account for only a small proportion of the LSP's total business. This differs from the situation outlined by Ellram and Cooper (1990) where the shipper is the dominant party and has a tendency to behave opportunistically. Many logistics firms are now large enough to negotiate on equal terms with major corporate clients.

The fact that the pattern of interdependence between client and LSP is often asymmetrical does not appear to be hindering the development of close relationships. Nor is there any evidence to suggest that, in choosing LSPs, firms have a preference for smaller operators over which they can exert greater bargaining power. It should be noted too that, despite the strengthening of contractual and operational ties between clients and third-party operators, only a small minority of firms externalizing logistical services perceive themselves to be 'locked into' a particular contractor's system (PE Consulting, 1996). In non-asset-based, 'management only' contracts, which are now common, for example in the UK retail logistics sector, the degree of client 'lock in' is relatively low.

Online trading of logistics services

Since the mid-1990s, there has been a sharp growth in the number of online exchanges at which logistical services can be traded. It was estimated in 1999 that there were over 300 Internet-based exchanges around the world catering mainly for companies' freight transport requirements. These exchanges give companies a relative cheap and flexible means of exploiting the highly competitive conditions that prevail in the haulage market. It allows them to conduct wide searches for suitable carriers and make transactions at relatively low cost. One of the main European freight exchanges, Freight-Traders, was set up by the Mars group in 1999 and handled 140 million Euro of haulage business in its first year (Mansell, 2001). Numico NV, a baby food manufacturer, estimates that it was able to cut its European road transport costs by 12 per cent by using this online exchange. The nature of the trading platforms, the range of supporting services and the charging schemes vary enormously (Rowlands, 2000). Some exchanges specialize in the movement of goods by particular modes in particular areas. Others have much wider scope both logistically and geographically. The collapse of the dot.com boom, however, has eroded much of the early optimism about the growth in the volume of logistics business transacted online. The share of total logistics expenditure handled by these 'virtual markets' will continue to increase, but at a much slower rate than some companies, most notably eLogistics, were predicting in the late 1990s.

The emergence of 'fourth-party logistics'

In 1996, the consultancy company Accenture coined the term 'fourth-party logistics' provider to describe a 'supply chain integrator that assembles and manages the resources, capabilities and technology of its own organization and those of complementary service providers to deliver a comprehensive supply chain solution' (Bauknight and Bade, 1998). They envisaged this new type of logistics service evolving to provide higher-level strategic support for companies wishing to integrate their supply chains. It was based on the belief that no single 3PL would have the capability to manage all aspects of a company's supply chain (Hastings, 2001). In some cases 4PL involves the formation of a consortium of consultancy, IT, financial and logistics businesses. In others, a 4PL service can be delivered by a conventional 3PL company working in alliance with a software house/consultancy. As Bedeman (2001) points out, however, the coordinating agency 'need not have any specific resources, capabilities or technology itself, so long as it has the ability to analyse the client's requirements and take contractual responsibility for delivering to the client an optimized supply chain solution built from the integrated capabilities and resources of its partners'.

EVOLVING RELATIONSHIP BETWEEN PROVIDERS AND USERS OF LOGISTICAL SERVICES

Despite the major changes in the logistical services market described above, doubts remain about the long-term stability of many LSP–client relationships. Tri-annual surveys by PE Consulting during the 1990s found that around 56–58 per cent of firms change at least some of their logistics contractors over a three-year period (PE Consulting, 1996). Roughly 70 per cent of users regularly claimed that they are seriously considering changing LSPs when the existing contract expired. Curiously, many of these firms also reported that they are 'generally satisfied' with the service they were receiving. It seems, therefore, that many firms believed that, while their existing 3PL service was adequate, other LSPs might be able to improve upon it.

On the basis of a survey of 55 American companies in the automotive and computer industries, Andersson (1997) identified and ranked 10 'key success factors' in the creation of partnerships with LSPs. This established the overriding importance of well-defined requirements, measures, procedures and contracts and the need for 'communications on all levels'. 'Joint effort in the design of the system' was also highly rated. To these factors can be added the adoption of effective appraisal schemes and, in the case of dedicated operations, the use of open-book accounting. These success factors are discussed below.

More precise contract specification

Many of the early distribution contracts were inadequately specified at the outset. This has led to a good deal of misunderstanding and dissatisfaction. Both LSPs and clients have learnt from this experience and are now less likely to repeat earlier mistakes. Attempts have also been made to compile fairly comprehensive checklists of points that firms should bear in mind when drawing up logistics contracts (Farmer and van Amstel, 1991). Some firms, however, have tended to 'over-specify' their contracts, making them too legalistic and relying too heavily on standard templates and clauses (Anon, 1997). Lambert, Emmelhainz and Gardner (1999) argue that the strongest logistics relationships are built on trust rather than tight contractual obligations.

Improved LSP–client communications at all levels

Inadequate communication is frequently cited as the main barrier to the development of close relationships between suppliers and users of logistical services. LSPs often claim that they are not given sufficient information about short- to medium-term changes in the clients' pattern of business and longer-term strategic developments. Their clients, on the other hand, often complain that they are not informed quickly enough about system failures.

Healthy, long-term relationships between shippers and carriers tend to be 'very information-intensive' (Ellram and Cooper, 1990). Information flows freely between the two organizations at different levels in the management hierarchy. This should be combined with vertical communication within each company to ensure that internal perceptions of the relationship are consistent. It is not uncommon, for example, for senior management to rate a relationship much more highly than employees with first-hand experience of its operational shortcomings.

Joint initiatives

Evaluations of logistics service providers by samples of users often indicate general satisfaction with service standards and operational efficiency, but concern that they are not sufficiently innovative and proactive. PE Consulting (1996) observed in the UK that:

> Almost two in three providers are believed to be essentially reactive in their approach. Customers are highly critical of the passivity of their providers. Customers are looking to providers to challenge them, to introduce best practice and to find new ways to add value. Customers believe that too often they are providing the distribution expertise rather than having it provided by their third-party supplier.

LSPs must also, of course, be given the freedom to innovate. Many claim to be denied this freedom by tightly specified contracts and a tendency for clients to manage contractors in a dictatorial manner. A healthy long-term relationship requires a regular injection of new ideas and vision from both sides as well as a joint willingness to innovate.

More open discussions at a strategic level and the sharing of forecasts can help LSPs become more proactive. Given their intimate knowledge both of general developments within the logistics sector and of a particular client's logistics operation, LSPs are ideally placed to provide expert advice on an ongoing basis. Several LSPs have gone so far as to set up 'think tanks' to explore ways of improving the service to individual clients.

They can also exploit more fully their role as intermediaries within the supply chain. This role can extend beyond simply managing freight flows on a routine basis. Beier (1989), for instance, contends that they should 'include problem solving and experience savings among their services'. He concludes that as 'carriers see the logistics flow from a different perspective from either consignor or consignee ... their function should be to act as consultant-middlemen in synchronizing all phases of goods movement between consignor and consignee'.

Refinement of appraisal schemes

Following a five-year review of the relationship between a major US retailer and an international 3PL company, House and Stank (2001) concluded that 'establishing a measurement system that allows easy access and integrated reporting of the status of the enterprise is essential if real progress is to be made in a logistics partnership'. This goes beyond short-term auditing of standard operational indicators such as average transit times, adherence to delivery schedules and stock-out levels. These measures do not provide an adequate basis for assessing the quality of longer term relationships. As Kleinsorge, Schary and Tanner (1991) explain, in appraising this type of relationship, firms must take both a short-term/operational and a long-term/strategic perspective, and supplement 'the 'hard' and more tangible parameters of statistically measured operating dimensions' with 'less tangible measures of satisfaction'.

Adoption of open-book accounting

Although survey evidence (PE Consulting, 1996) suggests that the level of charges is not a major source of contention among users of 3PL services, the choice of pricing scheme can strongly influence the quality and stability of LSP–client relationships, particularly in the case of dedicated services. One of the disadvantages of single-sourcing logistical services is that firms then have difficulty comparing contractors' rates. They therefore need frequent reassurance that they are getting value for money. Increasing numbers of LSPs are offering this assurance by giving their clients detailed cost breakdowns and negotiating their management fee as a separate item. A third of the sample of UK firms surveyed by PE Consulting in 1996 had 'open book' or 'cost plus' contracts, up from a quarter in 1993. Open-book accounting is only appropriate, however, in the case of dedicated operations, where the costs of serving individual clients can easily be isolated. Even under these circumstances, it does not necessarily eliminate conflict between contractor and client. As Newson (1991) explained, conflict can still arise 'if improvements in operating efficiency which lead to substantial savings are claimed by one side as entirely due to its initiative, yet the open book contract states that such benefits shall be shared in preordained proportions'. To operate effectively, therefore, open-book accounting must be accompanied by an arrangement whereby benefits are fairly divided in relation to the costs and risks that each party bears (LaLonde and Cooper, 1989).

CONCLUSION

Since the early 1980s, the management of logistics has been radically reorganized. An important feature of this reorganization has been the outsourcing of many activities previously performed in-house. The resulting growth in the level and variety of external expenditure on logistics has induced important changes in the way that these services are purchased. Fewer carriers are being used; more of the work is being performed on a contractual basis; LSPs are being given greater say in the design of logistical systems; and greater emphasis is being placed on the development of longer-term partnerships. The relationships between logistics service providers and their clients are thus evolving in a similar way to the links between suppliers and customers of material goods. More needs to be done, however, to ensure the longer-term stability of these relationships and to exploit more fully the potential contribution of LSPs to improved supply chain management.

REFERENCES

A T Kearney (1999) *Insight to Impact: Results of the Fourth Quinquennial European Logistics Study*, European Logistics Association, Brussels

Aertsen, F (1993) Contracting out the physical distribution function: a trade-off between asset specificity and performance measurement, *International Journal of Physical Distribution and Logistics Management*, **23** (1)

Andersson, D (1997) *Third Party Logistics: Outsourcing logistics in partnerships*, Linkoping Studies in Management and Economics Dissertations, no 34, Linkoping Institute of Technology, Linkoping

Anon (1997) Terms of endearment, *MT Logistica* (Nov)

Ansari, A and Modarress, B (1990) *Just in Time Purchasing*, Free Press, New York

Bask, A H (2001) Relationship among TPL providers and members of supply chains – a strategic perspective, *Journal of Business and Industrial Marketing*, **16** (6), pp 470–86

Bauknight, D and Bade, D (1998) Fourth party logistics – breakthrough performance in supply chain outsourcing, *Supply Chain Management Review, Global Supplement* (Winter)

Bayliss, B T (1998) Regulation in the road freight transport sector, *Journal of Transport Economics and Policy*, **32** (1), pp 113–31

Bedeman, M (2001) Is 4 more than 3+1, *Logistics Europe*, **9** (1)

Beier, F J (1989) Transportation contracts and the experience effect: a framework for future research, *Journal of Business Logistics*, **10** (2)

Cooper, J C and Johnstone, M (1990) Dedicated contract distribution: an assessment of the UK market place, *International Journal of Physical Distribution and Logistics Management*, **20** (1)

Croucher, P (1998) Insourcing, *Logistics Focus*, **6** (2), pp 3–6

Crumm, M R and Allen, B J (1998) A longitudinal assessment of motor carrier–shipper relationship trends, *Transportation Journal*, **37** (1), pp 5–17

Cunningham, M T and Kettlewood, K (1976) Source loyalty in the freight transport market, *European Journal of Marketing*, **10** (1)

Datamonitor (1999) *European Logistics 1999: Opportunities in a consolidating market*, Datamonitor, London

Datamonitor (2000a) *European Logistics 2000: The blueprint for a developing market*, Datamonitor, London

Datamonitor (2000b) *UK Logistics: Client survey 2000*, Datamonitor, London

Department for Transport (2002) *Transport of Goods by Road in Great Britain*, The Stationery Office, London

Ellram, L and Cooper, M C (1990) Supply chain management, partnerships and the shipper–third party relationship, *International Journal of Logistics Management*, **1** (2)

Farmer, D and van Amstel, P (1991) *Effective Pipeline Management: How to manage integrated logistics*, Gower, Aldershot

Fernie, J (1989) Contract distribution in multiple retailing, *International Journal of Physical Distribution and Materials Management*, **19** (7)

Hastings, P (2001) Party games, *Logistics Europe*, **9** (5), pp 38–42

Holland International Distribution Council (2001) *The Netherlands: Excellence in integrating supply chain capabilities*, HIDC, The Hague

House, R G and Stank, T P (2001) Insights from a logistics partnership, *Supply Chain Management*, **6** (1), pp 16–20

Kleinsorge, I K, Schary, P B and Tanner, R D (1991) The shipper–carrier partnership: a new tool for performance evaluation, *Journal of Business Logistics*, **12** (2)

LaLonde, B J and Cooper, M C (1989) *Partnerships in Providing Customer Service: A third-party perspective*, Council of Logistics Management, Oak Brook, IL

LaLonde, B and Maltz, A B (1992) Some propositions about outsourcing the logistics function, *International Journal of Logistics Management*, **3** (1), pp 1–11

Lambert, D M, Emmelhainz, M A and Gardner, J T (1999) Building successful logistical partnerships, *Journal of Business Logistics*, **20** (1), pp 165–81

Lieb, R C, Millen, R A and Wassenhove, L V (1993) Third party logistics services: a comparison of experienced American and European manufacturers, *International Journal of Physical Distribution and Logistics Management*, **23** (6)

Maltz, A B (1994) The relative importance of cost and quality in the outsourcing of warehousing, *Journal of Business Logistics*, **15** (2), pp 45–61

Mansell, G (2001) The development of online freight markets, *Logistics and Transport Focus*, **3** (7)

Marchant, C, McKinnon, A C and Patel, T (2000) *Retail Logistics 2000*, Institute of Grocery Distribution, Letchmore Heath

McKinnon, A C (1998) The abolition of quantitative controls on road freight transport, *Transport Logistics*, **1** (3)

McKinnon, A C and Forster, M (2000) *European Logistical and Supply Chain Trends 1999–2005: Full report of the Delphi 2005 Survey*, Logistics Research Centre, Heriot-Watt University, Edinburgh

Menon, M K, McGinnis, M A and Ackerman, K B (1998) Selection criteria for providers of third-party logistics services: an exploratory study, *Journal of Business Logistics*, **19** (1), pp 121–37

Mercer Management Consulting (1998) *Third Party Logistics: European providers*, MMC, London

Murtagh, J (1991) Coca-Cola & Schweppes beverages: own-account distribution, *Logistics Today*, **10** (2), pp 21– 23

Newson, P (1991) What happened to goodwill? *Distribution*, **4** (4)

PE Consulting (1996) *The Changing Role of Third-Party Logistics – Can the customer ever be satisfied?* Institute of Logistics, Corby

Peters, M, Cooper, J, Lieb, R C and Randall, H L (1998a) The third party logistics industry in Europe: provider perspectives on the industry's current status and future prospects, *International Journal of Logistics: Research and Applications*, **1** (1), pp 9–26

Peters, M J, Lieb, R C and Randall, H L (1998b) The use of third-party logistics services by European industry, *Transport Logistics*, **1** (3), pp 167–79

Ramsay, J (1991) Purchase specifications and profit performance, *International Journal of Physical Distribution and Logistics Management*, **1** (1)

Razzaque, M A and Sheng, C C (1998) Outsourcing of logistics functions: a literature survey *International Journal of Physical Distribution and Logistics Management*, **28** (2), pp 89–107

Rinehart, L M (1989) Organisational and personal factors influencing the negotiation of motor carrier contracts: a survey of shippers and motor carriers, *Transportation Journal*, **29** (2)

Rowlands, P (ed) (2000) *Online Freight Exchanges: International guide 2001*, Spice Court Publications, London

Sheffi, Y (1990) Third party logistics: present and future prospects, *Journal of Business Logistics*, **11** (2)

Tucker, F G and Zivan, S M (1987) Create integrated logistics third parties: spin them off, in *Proceedings of the 7th International Logistics Congress*, ed J Williams, IFS, Bedford

Williamson, O E (1979) Transaction-cost economics: the governance of contractual relations, *Journal of Law and Economics*, **22**

14

Delivering sustainability through supply chain management

Kirstie McIntyre
URS Corporate Sustainable Solutions

Supply chains span industry groups, cross industry boundaries, have a wide geographical spread and are an excellent vehicle for improving the environmental, social and economic performance of companies and industry sectors over the long term. Supply chain management functions are analysed for their potential impacts on the performance of a company. Practical examples from many industry sectors show the steps that can be taken to improve sustainability for the environment, for society and for the business.

BACKGROUND

Sustainability has traditionally been a concept that is difficult to 'sell' to senior management because it describes a state in the future that has never been experienced, rather than a specific process or methodology of how to get there. Theoretically, the concept makes sense, but translating that into actionable steps has proven to be a significant stumbling block for a number of organizations (Preston, 2001). The concept of sustainability or sustainable development has been around for a while, but is a very recent customer requirement and one that many companies are trying to grapple with.

Sustainability is a difficult concept to grasp in an industrial context. The following definition explains why.

Sustainable development is:

- social progress which recognizes the needs of everyone;
- effective protection of the environment;
- prudent use of natural resources; and
- maintenance of high and stable levels of economic growth and employment.

(DETR, 2000)

When a company considers what the above elements mean, it seems impossible to continue to do business and be sustainable. But sustainability is not just about being altruistic about the environment and workers' rights. It is also about ensuring the long-term viability of a business model and company. Shareholders, customers, suppliers and employees all want to see a future in their businesses. The functions that the supply chain organization manages are an ideal place for a company to begin putting together the actionable steps and investments which will demonstrate positive progress towards sustainable development.

It is suggested that it is the supply chains of the future that will bring true competitive advantage to companies (Christopher, 1993). Supply chain management has risen high on the corporate agenda as companies recognize the potential that it offers for creating sustainable competitive advantage in an ever more turbulent business environment (Christopher and Lambert, 2001). Customers' requirements are becoming ever more stringent, companies aim to be increasingly customer focused, and it is often the supply chain that is able to provide the added value that customers are looking for.

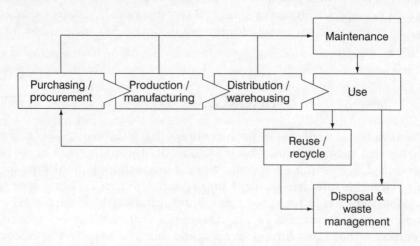

Figure 14.1 Common supply chain functions

As Penman (1994) points out, there have been considerable environmental developments within certain discrete elements of the supply chain, but the danger lies in isolating these achievements. The Sixth Business in the Environment Index of Corporate Environmental Engagement (BiE, 2002) identified that integrating environmental risk into supply chain management poses a real challenge for many companies. Supply chain aspects of sustainable development resulted in the lowest management score, with 17 out of 38 industry sectors scoring below 50 per cent. There is a need to look strategically beyond the immediate environmentally-driven aspects of supply chain management. With customer, stakeholder and investment attention on the quality of management and corporate governance as demonstrated through supply chains and sustainability, this is an ideal time to look at combining the best of both disciplines. This chapter takes each of the major supply chain functions in turn, and looks at them with regard to their ability to improve sustainability in terms of environmental, social and economic impacts.

PURCHASING OR PROCUREMENT

Purchasing is often the first place that companies start to integrate environmental issues into their management processes. This is especially true for service companies – those organizations that do not manufacture physical outputs, but provide a service to their customers from their efforts. Such companies often do not have a large environmental impact themselves, but the products and services that they use to generate their services are frequently the area where there is significant scope for improvement. Environmental performance is certainly now integrated into the procurement function of many large companies, whether for services or raw materials. These large companies affect whole supply chains and cross many industries with their requirements for improved environmental performance.

Some of this is being driven by environmental management systems (ISO 14000 or EMAS) and some is being driven by consumer pressure or even market differentiation. Toyota first laid out its goal of becoming an industry leader in environmental performance in 1992 with its Earth Charter. It is now imposing the same standards on its suppliers in its Green Supplier Guidelines, which are not so much guidelines as mandates. Toyota in North America demands that all suppliers develop and implement an environmental management system that conforms to ISO 14001 by the end of 2003. Suppliers must also obey a ban on 450 chemicals as well as comply with hazardous materials transport rules.

Many of Toyota's suppliers welcome the tough standards, as it brings them to the forefront of environmental performance in their own industries. Toyota has further environmental aspirations with long-term energy reduction, greenhouse gas and zero landfill targets (Zachary, 2001). Such strictures can apply a lot of pressure on suppliers, but Toyota's suppliers appear to have embraced the challenge and feel that they have gained from doing so. Toyota themselves have improved their own environmental performance by leveraging the effort of their suppliers. This seems an increasingly popular way of improving environmental and social performance, particularly by customer-facing organizations such as car manufacturers and retailers.

A growing number of European retail chains are developing their own safety initiatives by banning chemicals in their products. Many retailers are asking suppliers of own-label products to withdraw or phase out chemicals that have been put on priority lists for further research by the European Commission, national governments or environmental monitoring organizations. Fewer organizations have been successful at incorporating social issues into their procurement processes. However, with the recent media attention weathered by Nike and Gap over child labour issues in their supply chain, the clothing retailers have taken a much more proactive approach to supplier assurance. Nike and Gap both have corporate compliance and monitoring teams who use both internal and external resources to audit contract factories for fulfilment of stated aims and objectives. Many British retailers have joined the Ethical Trading Initiative which identifies and promotes good practice in the implementation of codes of labour practice (ETI, 2002). It is reasonable to expect more retail organizations to take these approaches to managing social impacts in their supply chain.

B&Q has been in the forefront of action in this area since the early 1990s when it realized that, as a retailer, the majority of its environmental and social impacts came from its products and suppliers. The company uses both questionnaires and auditors to track environmental and social issues in its supplier base, and has decided that this approach is preferable to requiring environment management system implementation (B&Q, 1995). Recently, B&Q has submitted to suppliers, chemical companies and environmental groups a list of chemicals it wants to ban in its products in order to be able to declare itself toxic free by 2005. Some of the chemicals are among the 15 hazardous substances pinpointed for priority action by the Ospar convention, responsible for protecting the marine environment of the North East Atlantic. Homebase, another UK DIY retailer, is going even further by planning to ban all the chemicals on the Ospar list, even though the governments that set the list have set a deadline of 2020 for ending all emissions. These restrictions, coupled with the current trend for supplier base rationalization, make a compelling case for suppliers at every level to raise sustainability up their corporate agendas.

The pressure to green the procurement function does not only come from companies: governments are also leveraging their purchasing power. The UK government has for some time produced a *Green Government Handbook* which advises central and local departments on environmentally sound goods and services. The EC has recently issued guidelines which clarify the extent to which environmental criteria may be used in the public procurement process and still remain in line with procurement directives which regulate freedom of movement, competition and best value (European Commission, 2001). A *Green Public Procurement Handbook* is being developed. The drivers for this are that the achievement of sustainable development requires that economic growth supports social progress and respects the environment, that social policy underpins economic performance and that environmental policy is cost-effective.

Public purchasing represents 14 per cent of EU GDP. As stated recently, Member States should consider how to make better use of public procurement to favour environmentally friendly products and services. The guidance goes beyond differentiating between products and services, but suggests that there are other possibilities to integrate environmental consider-ations into public purchases, notably when defining the technical specifica-tions, the selection criteria and the award criteria of a contract. This means that public procurement departments may have the ability to change the way that goods are produced or manufactured, or the supplies that service providers use.

Changing methods of public procurement are also being used to drive sustainability into goods and services purchased from the private sector. As the construction sector in the United Kingdom has discovered recently, new procurement methods such as private finance initiatives (PFIs) and prime contracting (an MOD initiative), with their long-term outlook and responsi-bilities (25 years in the case of PFIs), mean that designing, building and main-taining sustainable facilities become key to the successful tendering and managing of contracts.

PRODUCTION OR MANUFACTURING

The primary output of today's production processes is waste. Across all industries, less than 10 per cent of everything that is extracted from the earth (by weight) becomes usable products. The remaining 90 per cent becomes waste from production (Senge, Carstedt and Porter, 2001). Resource efficiency, or doing more with less, is the first place to start in improving sustainability performances. Through their 'waste free factories' programme, Xerox has reduced landfill by over 75 per cent since 1993. Cornwell Parker Furniture's timber minimization programme has saved £250,000 per year and reduced waste by 20 per cent. Cornwell has also overhauled coating procedures, saving a further £180,000 per year and cutting solvent use by 21 tonnes per year. Instead of sending wood waste to landfill, a wood-fired incinerator with energy recovery has been installed. Although this cost £480,000, the reduction in landfill tax and heating fuel gives a payback period of four to five years (Envirowise, 2002). British Airways and its waste management contractor, Grundon, have created a strategic partnership to deal with waste arising from aircraft, engineering facilities and offices. The partnership means that instead of being presented with an opaque final bill for services, BA receives a detailed breakdown of Grundon's waste-handling costs. This has enabled both parties to identify opportunities for cost savings and then share in those savings (ENDS, 2002a).

Many argue that what we need is a different way of looking at products: Firms such as Dow Chemical, Carrier and IKEA believe that higher profits will come from providing better solutions rather than selling more equipment. This creates a potential alignment between what is sound economically and what is sound environmentally. A company's business model no longer requires designed-in obsolescence to push customers into buying new products. Instead, producers have an incentive to design for longevity, efficient servicing, improved functioning and product takeback. Such design allows for maintaining relationships with customers by continually ensuring that products are providing the services that people desire, at the lowest cost to the producer.

The shift from valuing 'stuff' to valuing the service that the 'stuff' provides leads to a radical change in the concept of ownership. In the future, producers may own their products forever, and therefore will have a strong incentive to design products that can be disassembled and remanufactured or recycled, whichever is more economical. Owning products forever would represent a powerful step towards changing companies' attitudes about product discard. When the production function is considered to be a part of the supply chain, there is obviously much which can be done to improve environmental and social performance at this stage. The environmental performance of manufacturing activities has been improving now for many years, much of it driven by energy cost savings.

Social impact assessments are common for large infrastructure projects (roads, pipelines etc) but are not yet a common part of manufacturing activities. However, many companies forget that social impacts include the health and safety of employees and neighbours, community relations and noise and congestion abatement processes. Many of these impacts are already part of environmental management systems. Human resource management processes also play a role in identifying and improving social performance – training, fair pay, equality and diversity activities all contribute to a company's sustainability performance.

The case of Scandic Hotels shows, first, that sustainable strategies and practices can be just as useful in service operations as in manufacturing operations, and second, that such strategies and practices can support a corporate turnaround. In the early 1990s, Scandic Hotels was turned around from collapse using a new value system, embodied in the concept of sustainable development which linked customers and employees. Through employee training programmes, environmental information systems and innovative collaborations with suppliers, Scandic was revived as a profitable corporation (Goodman, 2000; see box below).

Why a sensible environmental decision benefits our finances

Scandic's environmental programme is an important aspect of caring for our environment and being committed to social development. It is also an important means of strengthening our competitiveness and creating long-term success. But there are also other reasons for our commitment:

- We are creating a long-term community of values with our customers by meeting their increased demands for environmental adaptation.
- We are saving energy and other resources through our resource conservation and recyclability considerations.
- We are improving and developing the company's operations by better predicting changes in the market and society.
- The environmental policy is a guide on the road towards becoming a model for the hotel industry. The policy shall primarily help us to become successively better at conserving nature's resources. It is the responsibility of every employee to comply with the environmental policy in their day to day work.

We must:

- follow the principle of recyclability wherever possible in our work, and ensure that our operations are successively integrated into the natural principle of recyclability;
- comply with established laws and norms in the environmental sphere, and preferably be one step ahead;
- develop our products and services so that we utilize natural resources as gently as possible;
- choose raw materials, materials and packaging which are renewable and which do not harm the environment – products which do not meet these requirements shall, if possible, be replaced or removed;
- strive to use environmentally safe and renewable energy sources, and to use technology and distribution systems which have the minimum possible environmental impact;
- reduce waste through safe and responsible methods;
- choose, influence and train our suppliers so that they participate in the fulfilment of our environmental policy;
- evaluate the result of our environmental efforts annually, and conduct environmental audits to ensure our continued development.

Source: Scandic Hotels (2001)

Distribution and warehousing

Cooper, Browne and Peters (1992) maintain that the transport and storage of goods is at the centre of any logistics activity, and that these are where a company should concentrate its efforts to reduce its environmental impacts. These authors claim that 24-hour transport is less environmentally damaging, as fuel consumption is more efficient with less congestion, and that just-in-time raises fuel consumption, as smaller lorries consume more fuel per tonne of goods moved than larger vehicles. This is a very relevant point with the exponential growth of e-commerce and home deliveries. The use of combined transport options such as containers using road and rail links is advocated for environmental improvement. In order to begin the improvement process, the authors suggest a three-stage approach: an environmental audit of the logistics operation, a listing of actions to reduce impacts, and a priority ranking of these actions. The problem with these recommendations is that they are not stakeholder focused, but look only at fuel consumption and economic cost. Improving the efficiency of fuel consumption will indeed reduce environmental impact, but local community issues may become more important when using large lorries in a 24-hour operation.

Supermarkets are only just beginning to take into account the miles travelled by food from its country of origin to our plates. Consumer demand for fresh fruit and vegetables all year round and the falling costs of freight transport have not provided retailers with an economic incentive to reduce the transport associated with their products. However, climate change levies may change this, as transport emissions are counted as part of a company's carbon dioxide burden. Drinks manufacturer H P Bulmer has identified that its second biggest source of carbon dioxide and other air pollutants is transport, with outbound goods accounting for some 85 per cent of its total transport emissions. Bulmers has been testing ways of putting some of its traffic back on the railway (currently 100 per cent is by road). Following trials, a partial switch to rail appears to be reasonably cost-neutral and results in environmental benefits, with carbon dioxide emissions per tonne-kilometre being reduced by about 80 per cent. Through this and other initiatives, Bulmers aims to reduce the environmental impact of its transport operations by 75 per cent in 2004 (ENDS, 2002b).

Transport is often viewed as an activity with a negative environmental impact, yet the transport sector represents 7 per cent of the GDP of Western Europe and employs 7 per cent of the workforce. On the other hand, the cost to society in terms of congestion, pollution and accidents has been estimated to be 5 per cent of the GDP. The energy consumption of the transport sector is one-third of all the energy consumed in the EU, and 85 per cent of that energy is used by road transport. The recent troubles of Railtrack in the UK have done nothing to encourage goods off the road and onto rail. However, the sector is fragmented, very competitive, and disinclined to act in concert to find solutions to these issues (Howie, 1994). Congestion is inflationary, and decreases productivity through delays, stock-outs or overstocking. So there is a dilemma between reducing environmental impact and increasing financial cost. Loading rates or 'loaded miles' and the use of consolidators (organizations that ship many companies' products together to maximize loading efficiencies) can increase the energy efficiency of the distribution function of the supply chain.

Warehouse management is another key social and environmental factor in distribution. The siting of warehousing and distribution centres can be a major issue for local communities because of the noise and congestion effects. The energy consumption or health and safety record in a poorly managed, temperature-controlled warehouse can eclipse all the other efforts that a company may make, yet it is often an overlooked function of the supply chain. Packaging and waste management are also important processes, often based at warehouse locations, which can have far-reaching impacts on the environment. The Packaging Waste Directive (94/62/EC) and national packaging laws now include all types of packaging in aggressive recovery and recycling targets for companies using over 50 tonnes of packaging per annum.

Anheuser-Busch (A-B), the American food processor, is looking at both in- and outbound materials to see how suppliers can improve the company's environmental performance as well as its bottom line. Suppliers have played a major role in A-B's packaging programme, which has resulted in reducing the company's aluminium use, saving US $250 million per year. A-B has also worked with materials-recovery suppliers to increase recycling rates as well as the quality of collected aluminium beverage containers. It is now the world's largest recycler of used aluminium drinks containers, currently recycling 130 per cent of the amounts it ships in the United States. Overall, the company has reduced the amount of solid waste to landfill by 68 per cent since 1991, saving US $19 million. A-B also has a supplier certification programme for packaging suppliers that includes requirements for environmental plans and continuous improvement. A-B follows up with periodic reviews to identify problems and help suppliers correct deficiencies. Such efforts take several years, require collaboration with suppliers, and need to be integrated into existing quality programmes and new business initiatives (*Purchasing*, 2001).

USE AND MAINTENANCE

As many life cycle analyses have proven, it is the 'use' phase of a product or service that often creates the biggest environmental and social impact (McIntyre *et al*, 1998). It is also the 'use' phase that many companies are recognizing as key to customer relationship management. As Volvo discovered years ago, when a company is selling cars, its relationship with the customer ends at the purchase; when it is providing customer satisfaction, it just begins. By interacting with the producer, the consumer can become a co-creator of value, or in some cases a destroyer of value (Senge *et al*, 2001). Xerox found it was not the electricity that its equipment consumed that caused the biggest environmental impact, but the consumption of paper, toner and the visits from the service engineer in his van (McIntyre, 1999). This indicated to Xerox that designing greater reliability into machines and then providing more training to customers would substantially mitigate the environmental impacts of its supply chain. Cooperating with paper and toner suppliers to reduce energy consumption at the production stage would result in greater cost savings and less environmental damage.

BASF's premise is that its products will have commercial advantage if they deliver environmental benefits as well as performing at the same level as the competition. BASF examines all of its major products and processes every three years, and assesses how they can be made more profitable or more environmentally friendly or, where necessary, replaced. The company has now undertaken more than 100 eco-efficiency analyses. For example, plastic fuel tanks for cars are more eco-efficient than metal ones because they are lighter, and during the product lifetime will reduce energy use, and therefore cost to the customer. Collaborations between BASF and its customers to make choices about materials have become increasingly important (Scott, 2001).

As the examples from the above companies show, product stewardship is the key issue in the use phase of products and services. It is a key issue for a number of reasons, not least environmental and social impact, but also as added value to the customer. Corporate governance, ensuring that stated policies are adhered to and maintained, is also being extended by some companies into product stewardship. It is not enough for them that their products 'disappear' onto the next stage in the chain, they are concerned about how their products are being used. Some of this is driven by socially responsible investment organizations (see section on finance below), as suppliers to the weapons industry, for example, would not be included in the portfolio.

It is difficult for industry sectors that provide services as opposed to products to internalize product stewardship, but 'service stewardship' can equally be applied. Understanding the environmental and social impacts that occur through the lifespan of a product or service is the first step to a reduction of those impacts. The hotel industry, for example, has understood that laundering towels is one of its biggest impacts. Many hotels now have a green hotel charter which asks guests to consider whether they need clean towels on a daily basis. Although it is still the customer's choice, the hotel is using its relationship with its customers to mitigate environmental impacts from detergent, water and energy consumption.

DISPOSE OR REUSE AND RECYCLE

Other organizations have focused their environmental efforts on the other end of the supply chain, with recycling issues. Equipment is returned from the customers of companies such as IBM, Nokia, BMW and Xerox (Hopfenbeck, 1993). These companies either recondition the old equipment or reclaim the materials it is made from, reprocessing them for reuse. The logistics discipline is well qualified to deal with cradle to grave issues because of logistics' focus on supply chain management, which emphasizes the control of materials from suppliers, through value added processes and on to the customer.

The interface between logistics and the environment is embedded in the value adding functions a firm performs (Wu and Dunn, 1995). To minimize total environmental impact, it must be evaluated from the total system perspective. The re-engineering of structure and management is an untapped business opportunity. The traditional supply chain has poorly structured operational and financial decision making which has institutionalized poor management of material resources. Reverse logistics management may be the answer to improving the environmental impact of the supply chain by improving material use (Giuntini, 1996).

Pollution prevention and sustainability do not have to be tackled all at once. Stonyfield Farms has been taking sustainability one step at a time for more than 10 years. Like many companies, Stonyfield Farms focused its initial environmental attentions on reducing and recycling waste. The company saves more than US $70,000 annually by reusing and recycling its waste products while preventing thousands of tonnes of landfill. Stonyfield's next focus was on energy conservation. Beyond replacing traditional lighting fixtures with energy efficient fixtures, the company redesigned its yoghurt-making process and installed heat recovery systems to capture waste heat from process water, saving the company thousands of dollars each year. New goals for the company include an audit of the entire supply chain for the company's products, from milk to plastic containers, and a new environmental packaging initiative. 'There is more to be done, but the important thing is to do something. If we had waited until we could do everything at once then we would still be waiting. Companies – even small companies like ours, can make a difference just by taking it one step at a time' (Hershberg, Director of Natural Resources, Stonyfield Farms, in Quinn, 2001).

The construction industry in the United Kingdom consumes around 6 tonnes of material per person per year, and about 10 per cent of national energy consumption is used in the production and transport of construction products and materials. From 250–300 million tonnes of material is quarried in the UK each year for use as aggregates, cement and bricks. According to DETR figures, approximately 13 million tonnes of construction materials is delivered to site and thrown away unused every year. The construction industry produced an estimated 72.5 million tonnes of construction and demolition waste, including clay and subsoil, in 1999, representing some 17.5 per cent of the total waste produced in the UK. Only an estimated 12–15 million tonnes of materials (less than 20 per cent) are recycled per year, as hardcore and landscaping fill. Using these materials more effectively, such as through reclamation and higher-grade recycling, would reduce the use of aggregates, save energy, and reduce pressures on landfill sites, as shown in the case study in the box (Vivian, 2001).

CIRIA Waste reduction project

This project demonstrates the financial and environmental benefits of waste mini-mization for construction by developing and implementing good practice on 10 demonstration projects. MACE, Laing Homes, AMEC Capital, Wren & Bell, Schal, Scottish Executive, Try Construction, the Environment Agency and Carillion have all worked with CIRIA to implement waste minimization plans on their projects. Waste minimization on these sites has resulted in significant cost savings and envi-ronmental benefits. For example:

- recovery of 500,000 roof tiles for reuse in housing development, saving £80,000;
- a major house builder saved £600 waste disposal costs per housing unit built;
- a reduction in over-ordering by use of just-in-time deliveries [however JIT also has other impacts, as discussed earlier];
- minimization of waste at the design stage of an office refurbishment;
- segregation of waste on site, saving 20 per cent on disposal costs; and
- better control of waste by use of rigorous procurement and contractual measures.

Source: CIRIA (2001)

MANAGERIAL AND FINANCIAL SUSTAINABILITY

What about all the support structures around supply chains, such as financial decisions, management systems and governance? Certain preconditions are necessary before an environmentally oriented value chain can be created. These include an environmentally oriented system of corporate management, a culture that allows learning, and a top-down principle with bottom-up support. Development and change aimed at the target audience are more likely to result in the environment (or sustainability) being considered from the beginning of the process (Steger, 1996).

Much of the influence on sustainability comes from outside the firm. Many in the fund management community probably think that sustainable devel-opment has little relevance to their decision-making process, but what about the energy company that is ignoring the rising tide of pollution legislation, or an automotive stock that has not considered the implications of forthcoming vehicle recycling directives? (Belsom, 2001). When the cost of emitting climate change gases is incorporated into the tax regime through the UK Climate Change Levy, then the economics of doing business as an energy company will change. The Society of Motor Manufacturers and Traders estimates that the extra cost for each new UK car after the implementation of the End Of Life Vehicle Directive will be between £115 and £300. These uncertainties reduce the earnings from companies' stock and so their performance on the stock market.

Socially responsible investment aims to influence companies to adopt policies that benefit society at large and the environment. As investors, socially responsible investment funds have a great deal of influence over the way in which a company conducts business (CIS, 2002). A recent EIRiS/NOP survey found that over 75 per cent of UK adults think their pension scheme should operate an ethical policy, if it can do so without reducing the level of financial return (EIRiS/NOP, 1999). Of these, 39 per cent said their pension should operate an ethical policy even when it may reduce the size of their final pension. The growing prominence of ethical issues is also reflected in the spectacular growth in numbers and size of available funds that apply ethical criteria. Research by the Social Investment Forum indicates that in 1999, more than US $2 trillion was invested in ethical funds in the United States, up 82 per cent from 1997 levels (Social Investment Forum, 1999).

Socially responsible investment (SRI) is a growing trend, and there are now a large number of rating organizations that assess and screen companies on a regular basis to provide information to the financial community and private investors. It has been found that there are certain generic issues that all these rating organizations scrutinize: environmental impacts and solutions, sustainability issues, management and external focus. There will continue to be a consolidation of the rating approaches, and companies will need to consider the strategic responses to those approaches (Walker and Farnworth, 2001).

Thus, the reputation or governance of the company (and its supply chain) is also a key issue. One only has to remember the debacle over Brent Spar and how badly Shell appeared, even though it transpired that their solution for the ageing oil platform's disposal was well researched and advised. Shell was unable to recover its corporate reputation, and has since attracted more unwanted attention from NGOs over its operations in Nigeria.

The public and pressure group perception of product and service is also very important, as the next example shows. Suppliers of phosphates and linear alkyl benzene sulfonate (LAS) for laundry detergents in Europe are having mixed success in their fight to gain environmental support for their products. Producers need an improved environmental focus to boost flagging sales. Denmark's environmental authorities are taking such a determined stance over LAS that Procter and Gamble has decided to stop marketing detergents with the surfactant in the country. For the company to be seen as opposing the local authorities is not good for the image of its brands, even though recent research indicates the LAS is more biodegradable than the alternatives (*Chemical Market Reporter*, 2001).

BP looks at the challenge of sustainable development as a business opportunity. 'There are good commercial reasons for being ahead of the pack when it comes to environmental issues', says John Brown, BP's chairman. Business can play a legitimate leadership role as a catalyst for larger changes. Change driven through market innovation is the type of change our society understands best. The challenge today is to develop sustainable business that is compatible with the current economic reality. Dell, Sun Microsystems and Cisco Systems have all identified supply chains as strategic differentiators, using them to forecast and plan future products and services by building trusting relationships through collaboration. As supply chains evolve from linear supplier–customer links to dynamic networking organizations, all members become involved in defining the processes and contributing to the value of the finished product or service. Innovative business models and products must work financially, or it will not matter how good they are ecologically or socially (in Senge *et al*, 2001).

CONCLUSION

This chapter has shown that the pressures are increasing on companies to be more sustainable in terms of the environment, economics and social responsibility. It has also shown that many companies have already started on the long road to sustainable development, some with huge success. Sustainable development is here to stay as a customer requirement, and, as demonstrated, the processes of supply chain management are an ideal place to respond to that requirement. However, meeting customer expectations and market expectations, improving market access and increasing cost savings represent baseline expectations and are important simply to remain competitive as an environmentally responsible company.

Control of the social and environmental aspects of supply chains will lead to better understanding of the supply chain as a whole. This in turn can lead to cost savings and better relationships between partners. Those parts of the supply chain that can respond to 'sustainability' issues will generally be more proactive and able to meet changing customer requirements and market forces. By taking sustainability one step at a time, early in business planning, it is indeed possible to differentiate and innovate to create value. Supply chain management processes are an ideal place to start.

REFERENCES

B&Q (1995) *How Green is My Front Door?* B&Q (Jul)

Belsom, T (2001) Unsustainable investors, *Global Investor*, 142 (May)

BiE (2002) *Sustaining Competitiveness*, 6th Annual Index of Corporate Environmental Engagement (26 Feb) Business in the Environment, London

Chemical Market Reporter (2001) Phosphate and LAS eco profiles under siege in Scandinavia, *Chemical Market Reporter*, 259 (11 June)

Christopher, M (1993) Logistics and competitive strategy, *European Management Journal*, **11** (2) (Jun), pp 258–61

Christopher, M and Lambert, D (2001) *The Challenges of Supply Chain Management*, Cranfield School of Management online conference [Online] www.supplychainknowledge2001.com

CIRIA (2001) [Online] http://www.ciria.org.uk

CIS (2002) *Sustainability Pays*, report by Cooperative Insurance and Forum for the Future, CIS, Manchester

Cooper, J, Browne, M and Peters, M (1992) *European Logistics: Markets, management and strategy*, pp 270–92, Blackwell, London

Department of Environment, Transport and the Regions (2000) *A Better Quality of Life: Strategy for sustainable development for the United Kingdom* (CM4345), The Stationery Office, London

EIRiS/NOP (1999) *Survey of Pension Scheme Members*, EIRiS/NOP Solutions, London

ENDS (2002a) BA's 'shared savings' scheme with waste firm, *ENDS Report*, 324 (Jan)

ENDS (2002b) H P Bulmer: a ferment of sustainability ideas, *ENDS Report*, 324 (Jan)

Envirowise (2002) *Furniture Workbook*, ref GG308, Envirowise, HMSO, London

ETI (2002) Web site of the Ethical Trading Initiative: http://www.ethicaltrade. org

European Commission (2001) *Commission Interpretative Communication on the Community Law Applicable to Public Procurement and the Possibilities for Integrating Environmental Considerations into Public Procurement*, Brussels, 4.7.2001, COM(2001) 274 final

Giuntini, R (1996) An introduction to reverse logistics for environmental management: a new system to support sustainability and profitability, *Total Quality Environmental Management*, (Spring), pp 81–87

Goodman, A (2000) Implementing sustainability in service operations at Scandic Hotels, *Interfaces*, **30** (3) (May/Jun), pp 202–14

Hopfenbeck, W (1993) *The Green Management Revolution: Lessons in excellence*, Prentice-Hall, London

Howie, B (1994) Environmental impacts on logistics, in *An International Review of Logistics Practice and Issues*, ed G Brace, pp 53–55, Logistics Technology International, London

McIntyre, K (1999) *Integrated Supply Chains and the Environment: Establishing performance measurement for strategic decision making application – the case of Xerox Ltd*, Engineering doctoral thesis, University of Surrey (Jan)

McIntyre, K, Smith, H, Henham, A and Pretlove, J (1998) Environmental performance indicators for integrated supply chains: the case of Xerox Ltd, *Supply Chain Management*, **3** (3), pp 149–56

Penman, I (1994) Environmental concern: implications for supply chain management, in *Logistics and Distribution Planning: Strategies for management*, 2nd edn, ed J Cooper, pp 165–72, Kogan Page, London

Preston, L (2001) Sustainability at Hewlett-Packard: from theory to practice, *California Management Review*, **43** (3) (Spring)

Purchasing (2001) Anheuser-Busch 'greens' its supply chain for cost savings, *Purchasing* (17 May)

Quinn, B (2001) Bottom line: minimising waste is good business, *Pollution Engineering*, **33** (6) (Jul)

Scandic Hotels (2001) [Online] http://www.scandic-hotels.com

Scott, A (2001) BASF aligns R&D with sustainable development, *Chemical Week*, **163** (12) (Mar), pp 39–40

Senge, P, Carstedt, G and Porter, P (2001) Innovating our way to the next industrial evolution, *MIT Sloan Management Review*, **42** (2) (Winter), pp 24–38

Social Investment Forum (1999) *Report on Socially Responsible Investing Trends in the United States* [Online] http://www.socialinvest.org

Steger, U (1996) Managerial issues in closing the loop, *Business Strategy and the Environment*, **5** (4) (Dec), pp 252–68

Vivian, S (2001) *Opportunities from Environmental Management*, paper given at the Institution of Highways and Transportation, Cambridge, June

Walker, J and Farnworth, E (2001) *Rating Organisations: What is their impact on corporate sustainable strategy?*, Business Strategy and the Environment conference, Sep, ERP Environment

Wu, H-J and Dunn, S (1995) Environmentally responsible logistics systems, *International Journal of Physical Distribution and Logistics Management*, **25** (2), pp 20–38

Zachary, K (2001) Toyota prods suppliers to be green, *Ward's Auto World*, **37** (7) (Jul)

15

Retail logistics

John Fernie
Heriot-Watt University, Scotland

INTRODUCTION

The principles behind logistics and supply chain management are not new. Managing elements of the supply chain has been encapsulated within organizations for centuries. Decisions such as where to hold stock, in what quantities and how it is distributed have been part of the trade-off analysis that is at the heart of logistics management. It is only in the last 10 to15 years, however, that logistics has achieved prominence in companies' boardrooms, primarily because of the impact that the application of supply chain techniques can have on a company's competitive position and profitability. Retailers have been in the forefront of applying best practice principles to their businesses, with UK grocery retailers being acknowledged as innovators in logistics management. This chapter discusses:

- the evolution of the logistics concept;
- ECR and managing supply chain relationships;
- the application of supply chain concepts in different international markets;
- future trends, most notably the impact of e-commerce upon logistics networks.

THE EVOLUTION OF THE LOGISTICS CONCEPT

The starting point for any discussion on modern logistics management invariably centres around Peter Drucker's seminal article published in *Fortune* magazine in 1962. This piece, entitled 'The economy's dark continent', drew strong analogies with early explorers, in that distribution was one of the last frontiers of business to be 'discovered'. He noted that distribution was viewed as a low-status activity by managers, yet major cost savings could be achieved by managing this function more effectively. It should be noted that Drucker was discussing distribution, not supply chain management. Nevertheless, his ideas stimulated much debate, and most of the early business research emanated from the United States as techniques developed in the context of military logistics began to gain acceptance in the commercial sector.

By the 1970s and 1980s, the supply chain was still viewed as a series of disparate functions. Most textbooks would illustrate logistics management as depicted in Figure 15.1, with materials management dealing with the 'back end' of the supply chain, and physical distribution management focusing upon the flow of product from fast moving consumer goods manufacturers (FMCGs) to their customers (retailers and wholesalers). As a result of this evolution of logistics management, the literature on the subject has developed along two distinct routes, one pertaining to industrial, the other to consumer markets. The materials management literature has its roots in the management strategies of the Japanese and the application of principles of total quality management, just-in-time (JIT) production and supplier associations. More recent terms with the 'Europeanization' of the concepts include 'lean supply' and 'network sourcing', which indicates the strong production/ raw material supplier orientation of this research.

The 'front end' of the supply chain achieved greater prominence from the 1970s, initially as physical distribution management (PDM), but more recently as supply chain/logistics management. Initial work focused upon manufacturers' distribution systems, but as retailers centralized their distribution and began to exert control over the retail supply chain, most research focused upon retailers' logistics strategies. In both industrial and retail logistics research, the emphasis in the 1990s was to view the supply chain as an integrated whole

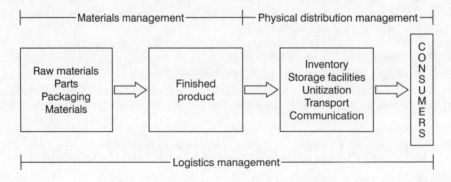

Figure 15.1 Logistics management

rather than a series of disparate parts. What was the point of taking cost out of one part of the supply chain, if it only added costs somewhere else in the chain?

In the context of retail logistics, several UK academics have sought to explain the transformation of logistics practices since the 1970s. McKinnon, in a position paper for the Technology Foresight, Retail and Distribution Panel in 1996, identified six trends which account for this transformation. These are:

- retailers increasing their control over secondary distribution (warehouse to shop. In Britain this process is complete in most sectors);
- restructuring of retailers' logistical systems through the development of 'composite distribution' and centralization of certain commodities into particular supply chain streams;
- adoption of quick response techniques to reduce lead times through the implementation of information technology, especially EDI, EPOS and sales-based ordering (SBO);
- rationalization of primary distribution (factory to warehouse) and attempts to integrate this and secondary distribution into a single 'network system';
- introduction of supply chain management and efficient consumer response;
- increasing return flow of packaging material and handling equipment for recycling/reuse.

More recently Fernie, Pfab and Marchant (2000) have built upon the work of Phil Whiteoak, who charted the evolution of UK grocery distribution from the 1970s to the early 1990s. Fernie identifies four stages:

1. Supplier control (pre-1980).
2. Centralization (1981–89).
3. Just-in-time (1990–95).
4. Relationship (1995 to date).

The first stage, supplier control, is widespread in many countries today and was the dominant method of distribution to stores in the 1960s and 1970s in the United Kingdom. Suppliers manufactured and stored products at the factory or numerous warehouses throughout the country. Direct store deliveries (DSD) were made on an infrequent basis (7 to 10 days), often by third-party contractors who consolidated products from a range of factories. Store managers negotiated with suppliers and kept this stock in 'the backroom'.

Centralization, stage 2, is now becoming a feature of retail logistics in many countries, and was prominent in the United Kingdom in the 1980s. The grocery retailers took the initiative at this time in constructing large, purpose-built regional distribution centres (RDCs) to consolidate products from suppliers for onward delivery to stores. This stage marked the beginning of a shift from supplier to retailer control of the supply chain. There were clear advantages from a retailer perspective:

- reduced inventories;
- lead times reduced from weeks to days at stores;
- 'backroom' areas released for selling space;
- greater product availability;
- bulk discounts from suppliers;
- fewer invoices, lower admin costs;
- better utilization of staff in stores.

Centralization, however, required much capital investment in RDCs, vehicles, material handling equipment and human resources. Centralization of distribution also meant centralization of buying, with store managers losing autonomy as new headquarter functions were created to manage this change. This period also witnessed a boom in the third-party contract market, as retailers considered whether to invest in other parts of the retail business rather than logistics. All of the United Kingdom's 'big four' grocery retailers – Sainsbury, Tesco, Asda and Safeway – contracted out many RDCs to logistics service providers in the mid to late 1980s.

In stage 3, the just-in-time phase, major efficiency improvements were achieved as refinements to the initial networks were implemented. The larger grocery chains focused upon product-specific RDCs, with most temperature-controlled products being channelled through a large number of small warehouses operated by third-party contractors. By the early 1990s, temperature-controlled products were subsumed within a network of composite distribution centres developed by superstore operators. Composites allowed products of all temperature ranges to be distributed through one system of multi-temperature warehouses and vehicles. This allowed retailers to reduce stock in store, as delivery frequency increased. Furthermore, a more streamlined system not only improved efficiency, but reduced waste of short-shelf-life products, giving a better quality offer to the customer.

While efforts were being made to improve secondary distribution networks, initial projects were established to integrate primary with secondary distribution. When Safeway opened its large composite in 1989 at Bellshill in Scotland, it included a resource recovery centre which washed returnable trays and baled cardboard from its stores. It also established a supplier collection programme which was to save the company millions of pounds during the 1990s. Most secondary networks were established to provide stores with high customer service levels; however, vehicle utilization on return trips to the RDC was invariably poor, and it was efforts to reduce this empty running that led to initiatives such as return trips with suppliers' products to the RDC.

Although improvements to the initial networks were being implemented, RDCs continued to carry two weeks or more of stock of non-perishable products. To improve inventory levels and move to a just-in-time system, retailers began to request more frequent deliveries from their suppliers in smaller order quantities. Whiteoak, who represents Mars, and therefore suppliers' interests, wrote in 1993 that these initiatives gave clear benefits to retailers at the expense of increased costs to suppliers. In response to these changes, consolidation centres have been created upstream from RDCs to enable suppliers to improve vehicle utilization from the factory.

The final stage, the relationship stage, is ongoing, but is crucial if further costs are going to be taken out of the supply chain. In the earlier third stage, Whiteoak had noted that the transition from a supplier- to a retail-controlled network had given cost savings to both suppliers and retailers until the just-in-time phase in the early 1990s. By the mid-1990s retailers began to appreciate that there were no 'quick wins' such as that of centralization in the 1980s to improve net margins. If another step change in managing the retail logistics was to occur, it had to be realized through supply chain cooperation.

Efficient consumer response (ECR) initiatives launched throughout the 1990s have done much to promote the spirit of collaboration. Organizations are having to change to accommodate and embrace ECR, and to dispel inherent rivalries that have built up over decades of confrontation. The United Kingdom has been in the vanguard of implementing ECR, with Tesco and Sainsbury claiming to have saved hundreds of millions of pounds in the late 1990s. The key to the relative success of UK companies has been their willingness to share EPOS data with their suppliers through Internet-based information exchanges. Good supply chain management is about managing not only the flow of products but the flow of information.

LOGISTICS AND COMPETITIVE STRATEGY IN RETAILING

Many of the current ideas on supply chain management and competitive advantage have their roots in the work of Michael Porter, the Harvard Business School professor who introduced the concept of the value chain and competitive advantage (Porter, 1988). These ideas have been further developed by academics such as Martin Christopher in the UK (Christopher, 1997). In essence, we have a supply chain model as depicted in Figure 15.2, whereby at each stage of the chain, value is added to the product through

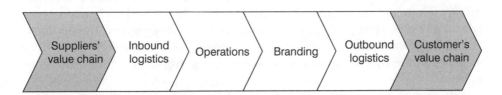

Figure 15.2 The extended value chain

manufacturing, branding, packaging, display at the store and so on. At the same time, at each stage cost is added in terms of production costs, branding costs and overall logistics costs. The trick for companies is to manage this chain to create value for the customer at an acceptable cost. The managing of this so called 'pipeline' has been a key challenge for logistics professionals in the 1990s, especially with the realization that a reduction of time not only reduced costs but gave competitive advantage.

According to Christopher there are three dimensions to time-based competition which must be managed effectively if an organization is going to be responsive to market changes. These are:

- *time to market:* the speed of bringing a business opportunity to market;
- *time to serve:* the speed of meeting a customer's order;
- *time to react:* the speed of adjusting output to volatile responses in demand.

He uses these principles to develop strategies for strategic lead-time management. By understanding the lead times of the integrated web of suppliers necessary to manufacture a product, he argues that a 'pipeline map' can be drawn to represent each stage in the supply chain process from raw materials to customer. In these maps it is useful to differentiate between 'horizontal' and 'vertical' time. Horizontal time is time spent on processes such as manufacture, assembly, in-transit or order processing. Value may not be created but something is going on. Vertical time is the time when nothing is happening, no value is added, but only cost and products/materials are standing as inventory.

It was in fashion markets that the notion of 'time-based competition' had most significance in view of the short time window for changing styles. In addition, the prominent trend in the last 20 years has been to source products offshore, usually in low-cost Pacific Rim nations, which lengthened the physical supply chain pipeline. These factors combined to illustrate the trade-offs which have to be made in supply chain management, and how to develop closer working relationships with supply chain partners. Christopher has used the example of The Limited in the United States to illustrate his accelerating 'time to market'. The company revolutionized the apparel supply chain philosophy in the United States by designing, ordering and receiving products from Southeast Asia to stores in a matter of weeks rather than the months of its competitors. New lines were test marketed in trial stores, orders communicated by EDI to suppliers, who also benefited from CAD/CAM technology in modifying designs. The products, already labelled and priced, were consolidated in Hong Kong, where chartered 747s airfreighted the goods to Columbus, Ohio, for onward dispatch to stores. The higher freight costs were easily compensated for by lower markdowns and higher inventory turns per annum.

Along with The Limited, another catalyst for much of the initiatives in lead-time reduction was work undertaken by Kurt Salmon Associates (KSA) in the

United States in the mid-1980s. KSA were commissioned by US garment suppliers to investigate how they could compete with Far East suppliers. The results were revealing, in that the supply chains were long (one and a quarter years from loom to store), badly coordinated and inefficient (Christopher and Peck, 1998). The concept of quick response was initiated to reduce lead times and improve coordination across the apparel supply chain. In Europe, quick response principles have been applied across the clothing retail sector. Supply base rationalization has been a feature of the 1990s, as companies have dramatically reduced their number of suppliers, and have worked much closer with the remaining suppliers to ensure more responsiveness to the marketplace.

The importance of supply chain integration cannot be understated; however, much depends on the degree of control a company has over the design, manufacture, marketing and distribution of their supply chains. Two of the most successful fashion retailers in Europe – Benetton and Zara – illustrate how an integrated supply chain can enhance the retail offer. Both companies draw heavily on lean production techniques developed in Japan. Their manufacturing operations are flexible, involving a network of subcontractors and, in the case of Benetton, suppliers in close proximity to the factory. Benetton was one of the first retail companies to apply the 'principle of postponement' to its operations, whereby semi-finished garments were dyed at the last possible moment, when colour trends for a season became apparent from EPOS data at their stores. So rather than manufacture stock to sell, Benetton could manufacture stock to demand.

Zara's operation has similarities with The Limited in the United States, in that the company scouts the globe for new fashion trends prior to negotiating with suppliers to produce specific quantities of finished and semi-finished products. Only 40 per cent of garments – those with the broadest appeal – are imported as finished goods from the Far East; the rest are produced in Zara's automated factories in Spain. The result of their supply chain initiatives is that Zara has reduced its lead time gap for more than half of the garments it sells to a level unmatched by any of its European or North American competitors.

Benetton, Zara and The Limited, as the latter's name suggests, have narrow product assortments for specific target markets. This streamlines and simplifies the logistics network. For general fashion merchandisers, rather than specialists, the supply chain is more complex, with thousands of suppliers around the globe. Nevertheless, quick response and efficient consumer response concepts are being applied to these sectors in an effort to minimize markdowns due to out-of-season or unwanted stock in stores.

Retailers have been analysing carefully their supply base and the cost of sourcing/distributing products to their network of stores. The difficulties experienced by Marks and Spencer in recent years led the company to review its entire supply chain. Marks and Spencer's logistics system is centred around the UK, in that even its international distribution centres are supplied from warehouses in the southeast of England. In the case of supplying its Hong Kong stores, it was taking up to 27 days to deliver goods from England by air transport. Although this has been reduced to between 7 and 11 days, it conceals some of the problems further up the supply chain (Jackson, 1998). Good logistics is not solely about reducing product replenishment lead times (time to serve) but also about being able to react to changes in the market. This is a primary distribution problem, and relates to how quickly the pipeline can be turned on or off according to surges or collapses in demand. The Marks and Spencer review has meant that efforts are being made to take inventory out of the whole supply chain system, through buying closer to the particular seasons, and through utilizing air freight for much of its international sourcing.

Although grocery retailers are more oriented to their national or super-regional markets such as the EU than their clothing counterparts, the internationalization of grocery retailers and their customers has led to changing sourcing patterns. Furthermore, the increased competition in grocery markets, with the resultant pressure on profit margins, has acted as a spur to companies to improve supply chain performance.

EFFICIENT CONSUMER RESPONSE (ECR)

ECR arrived on the scene in the early 1990s, when Kurt Salmon Associates produced another supply chain report, *Efficient Consumer Response*, in 1993 in response to another appeal by an US industry sector to evaluate its efficiency in the face of growing competition in its traditional markets. Similar trends were discerned to those from KSA's earlier work in the apparel sector: excessive inventories, long uncoordinated supply chains (104 days from picking line to store purchase) and an estimated potential saving of US $30 billion, 10.8 per cent of sales turnover.

During the last eight years the ECR initiative has stalled in the United States; indeed, inventory levels remain over 100 days in the dry grocery sector. Nevertheless, ECR has taken off in Europe, from the creation of an European Executive Board in 1994 with the support of Europe-wide associations representing different elements of the supply chain: AIM, the European Brands Association; CIES, the Food Business Forum; EAN International, the International Article Numbering Association; and Eurocommerce, the European organization for the retail and wholesale trade.

It was in 1994 that initial European studies were carried out to establish the extent of supply chain inefficiencies and to formulate initiatives to improve supply chain performance (Table 15.1). ECR Europe defines ECR as 'a global movement in the grocery industry focusing on the total supply chain – suppliers, manufacturers, wholesalers and retailers, working close together to fulfil the changing demand of the grocery consumer better, faster and at less cost'.

Table 15.1 Comparisons of scope and savings from supply chain studies

Supply chain study	Scope of study	Estimated savings
Kurt Salmon Associates (1993)	US dry grocery sector	10.8% of sales turnover (2.3% financial, 8.5% cost). Total supply chain US $30 billion, warehouse supplier dry sector US $10 billion. Supply chain cut by 41% from 104 days to 61 days.
Coca-Cola Supply Chain Collaboration (1994)	127 European companies. Focused on cost reduction from end of manufacturer's line. Small proportion of category management	2.3–3.4 percentage points of sales turnover (60% to retailers, 40% to manufacturer)
ECR Europe (1996, ongoing)	15 value chain analysis studies (10 European manufacturers, 5 retailers). 15 product categories. 7 distribution channels	5.7 percentage points of sales turnover (4.8% operating costs, 0.9% inventory cost). Total supply chain saving of US $21 billion. UK savings £2 billion

Source: Fiddis (1997).

One of the early studies carried out by Coopers and Lybrand identified 14 improvement areas where ECR principles could be implemented. These were categorized into three broad areas of product replenishment, category management and enabling technologies (Figure 15.3). Most of these improvement areas had received management action in the past; the problem was how to view the concepts as an integrated set rather than individual action areas.

As the ECR Europe movement began to gather momentum, the emphasis on much of the work conducted by the organization tended to shift from the supply side technologies (product replenishment) to demand-driven initiatives (category management). This is reflected in the early ECR project reports which dealt with efficient replenishment and efficient unit loads. While the supply side is still important, as reflected in projects currently being carried out on transport optimization and unit loads identification and tracking, the majority of recent projects have focused upon consumer value, efficient promotion tactics, efficient product introductions and collaboration in customer-specific marketing.

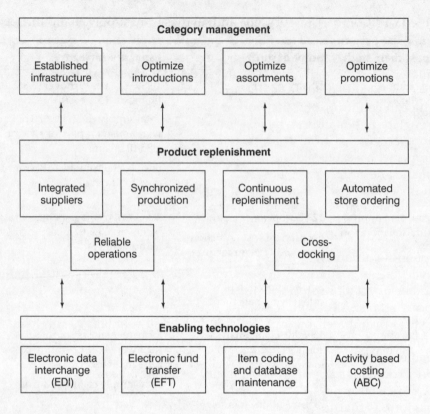

Figure 15.3 ECR improvement concepts

Commensurate with this change in emphasis has been the topics under discussion at the annual ECR Europe conference. At its inception in Geneva in 1996, the concept was being developed, and efficient replenishment initiatives were prominent on the agenda. Four subsequent conferences at Amsterdam in 1997, Hamburg in 1998, Paris in 1999 and Turin in 2000 have tended to emphasize demand-driven initiatives.

It can be argued that the early work focused upon improving efficiencies within the supply chain; the late 1990s was concerned to stress the effectiveness of the supply chain. Thus, the focus now is on how to achieve profitable growth, as there is little point in delivering products efficiently if they are the wrong assortment, displayed in the wrong part of the store! At the 2000 Turin conference, Luc Vandevelde, the co-chairman of ECR Europe, noted that 'Hamburg was all about the consultants presenting good ideas. Now it is being driven by the manufacturers and retailers and they are starting to talk about achievements.' Cynics attending the early conferences argued that the acronym ECR should have stood for every consultant's reward!

The ECR Europe prime objective is to develop best practices and to disseminate these benefits to all members of the food supply chain in Europe. To date it has been highly successful in moving towards this objective. The early conferences were well attended (over 1000 delegates) but the Turin event attracted 3300 people. ECR initiatives are now formally organized in 14 European countries, and the work in these countries is formally recognized through representation on the Executive Board. The Board itself consists of 30 senior executives from leading retailers and branded manufacturers in Europe, who established the policy agenda to initiate new pilot projects and demand and supply strategies.

It is clear, however, that ECR will not be a panacea for all companies. The improvement areas suggested in Figure 15.3 provide a tariff of initiatives from which companies will choose according to their own particular objectives. Each company will have a different starting point and a different agenda depending upon the current nature of supplier–retailer relationships. Nevertheless, a common theme applicable to all retailers is the limited number of relationships which are established with suppliers. The large grocery retailers deal with thousands of suppliers and have only formal partnerships or initiated pilot projects with a small number of suppliers. For example Sainsbury has six-monthly supply chain forums, which bring together senior supply chain staff with 19 of their counterparts (suppliers) who account for a large part of Sainsbury's volume business.

A criticism of ECR Europe conferences, and those held in the United Kingdom, is that these venues are packed with representatives from the largest retailers and their multinational FMCG suppliers. Such concentration, the argument goes, can only lead to restricting consumer choice, high profit margins and higher prices. So much for the consumer in ECR! With Wal-Mart's entry into the European market, this is hardly true, in view of the intense price competition in Germany and the United Kingdom, the initial target markets. ECR can in fact enable companies to compete better in such competitive markets. It is true, however, that smaller companies have been slower to hop on the ECR bandwagon because of the time and resource commitments required to carry out ECR initiatives.

DIFFERENCES IN LOGISTICS 'CULTURE' IN INTERNATIONAL MARKETS

Clearly ECR principles will be adopted by companies according to their own strategy with regard to supplier relationships. Table 15.1 shows that the Kurt Salmon report hoped for an improvement of supply chain time from picking line to consumer from 104 to 61 days. A comparative study of European markets by GEA in 1994 shows that all the major countries hold much less stock within the supply chain. Indeed, the UK figure is now around 25 days.

Variations in Europe are quite marked between and within countries. Mitchell (1997) argues that few of the largest European retailers (mainly German and French companies) have proven to be ECR enthusiasts. Many of those French and German retailers are privately owned or franchise operations, and they tend to be volume- and price-driven in their strategic positioning. By contrast, UK and Dutch firms are essentially publicly quoted, margin-driven retailers who have had a more constructive approach to supplier relations. While it is accepted that there are key differences in European markets, in general there are differences between the United States and Europe with regard to trading conditions. Mitchell (1997: 14) states that:

- The US grocery retail trade is fragmented, not concentrated as in parts of Europe.
- US private label development is primitive compared with many European countries.
- The balance of power in the manufacturer–retailer relationship is very different in the United States compared with Europe.
- The trade structure is different, in that wholesalers play a more important role in the United States.
- Trade practices such as forward buying are more deeply rooted in the United States than Europe.
- Trade promotional deals and the use of coupons in consumer promotions are unique to the United States.
- Legislation, especially anti-trust legislation, can inhibit supply chain collaboration.

While legislation has imposed controls on US retailers in terms of pricing and competition policy, there are significantly fewer controls on location, planning and store choice issues. This has resulted in US retailers being able to operate profitably on much lower sales per square metre ratios than the higher fixed costs associated with the more 'controlled' markets of Europe.

To understand how different country logistics structures have evolved, it is necessary to understand the nature of consumer choice and the range of retail formats, prior to seeking explanations for the nature of logistical support to stores through supplier relations, cost structures and other operational factors.

CONSUMER CHOICE AND RETAIL FORMATS

US tourists coming to Europe are probably puzzled at store opening hours and the restrictions on store choice compared with their own country. Although liberalization of opening hours is beginning to happen across Europe, the tight planning restrictions on store sizes and location have tended to shape format development. Furthermore, cross-national surveys of attributes influencing a consumer's choice of store have shown the strong influence of price in France and Germany compared with the United Kingdom, where price tends to be ranked behind convenience, assortment range, quality and customer service. (It can be argued, however, that if an entrant such as Wal-Mart established in the United Kingdom, and the price spread between it and the UK competition was significant, consumers would revalue these store attributes.) In the United States, price and promotion are also strong drivers of store choice; however, US consumers spend their food dollar in a variety of ways, including eating out, which has always been more common than in Europe. Indeed, the KSA survey on ECR was initiated because of the competition from warehouse clubs and Wal-Mart into the traditional supermarket sector.

A partial explanation for the high inventory levels cited by KSA in their survey is that US consumers buy in bulk. With such an emphasis on price and promotion, consumers shop around and stockpile dry goods in garages and basements. Compared with their European counterparts, who have neither the space nor the format choices, US consumers have their own household 'backroom' warehouse areas.

In Europe the pattern of format development follows a broad north–south division. The southern Mediterranean and eastern European markets continue to have a predominance of small independent stores, and the supply chain is manufacturer-controlled. This is changing, however, as northern European retailers enter these markets. In northern Europe, retailers have developed large store formats but in different ways. For example, it is not surprising that Wal-Mart chose Germany as its entry market for Europe because of its strong discounter culture. This is reflected in its large number of hypermarkets and hard discounters, but the German consumer also shops at local markets. In France, the home of the hypermarket, large-scale formats coexist with superettes and local markets, whereas in the United Kingdom and the Netherlands fewer formats are evident, with superstores and super-markets respectively dominating their markets.

In these northern European countries, different logistics networks have evolved in response to format development. As discussed earlier in the chapter, many of the largest supermarket chains in the United Kingdom, with their portfolios of superstores, have developed composite distribution to improve efficiency throughout the supply chain. Here all product categories – produce, chilled and ambient – are consolidated at a regional distribution centre for onward distribution to stores in composite trailers which also can carry a mix of products. In Holland, Albert Heijn has utilized cool and ambient warehouse complexes to deliver to its smaller supermarkets, whereas the German and French retailers have numerous product category ware-houses supplying their wide range of formats. (With hypermarkets, depending on spread of stores, products may be delivered direct by suppliers.)

MANUFACTURER–RETAILER RELATIONSHIPS

A major feature of retail change in Europe has been the consolidation of retail activity into fewer large corporations in national markets. Many grocery retailers in Europe were small privately owned family companies 30 years ago, and they were dwarfed by their multinational branded suppliers. This is no longer the case. Some may remain privately owned, but along with their PLC counterparts they are now international companies that have grown in economic power to challenge their international branded suppliers. Although the largest companies are predominantly German and French in origin, a high degree of concentration also exists in the Netherlands and the United Kingdom. Indeed, the investigation by the Competition Agency on the operation of multiple retail grocery companies in the United Kingdom illustrates this shift in power from manufacturer to retailer.

An indication of the growth of these European retailers can be seen in the way in which they have been able to dictate where and when suppliers will deliver products to specific sites. Increasingly, the product has been of the distributor label category. This is of particular significance in the United Kingdom where grocery chains have followed the Marks and Spencer strategy of premium value-added brands that compete directly with manufacturers' brands.

The implications of these changes in power relationships between retailers and their suppliers have been that manufacturers have been either abdicating or losing their responsibility for controlling the supply chain. In the United Kingdom, the transition from a supplier-driven system to one of retail control is complete compared with some other parts of Europe. As mentioned earlier, most grocery retailers in the United Kingdom have not only centralized over 90 per cent of their products through regional distribution centres, but have created primary consolidation centres further up the supply chain to minimize inventory held between factory and store. Although this degree of control is less evident in other European markets and in the United States, the spate of merger activity in the late 1990s and the expansion of retail giants (Wal-Mart, Carrefour, Tesco, Ahold) with their 'big box' formats into new geographical markets is leading to internationalization of logistics practice.

Despite these shifts in the power balance, it is generally accepted that to apply ECR principles, the greatest challenge for European retailers is the breaking down of cultural barriers within organizations, to move from a confrontational culture to one of collaboration. Organizations will change from a traditional functional 'internal' structure to that of a multi-functional 'external' structure. The changing organizational forms are shown in Figure 15.4, which depicts the traditional 'bow tie' and the new cross-functional team approach.

To achieve the significant supply chain savings mooted in ECR reports, companies are having to change their attitudes, although because of the

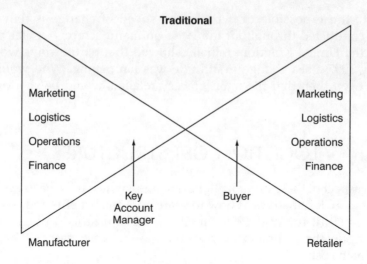

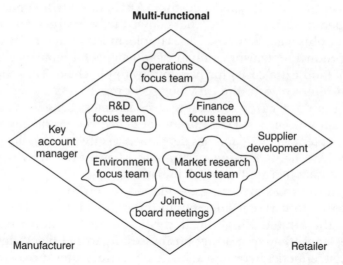

Figure 15.4 Transformation of the interface between manufacturer and retailer

politics and inherent rivalries built up over the decades, it will take years for this cultural revolution to take place. It was significant that Sainsbury was the retailer represented at the ECR session in Paris in 1999 in 'ECR – the human side of change'. Sainsbury was initially cynical about the benefits of ECR, but has made significant progress in the last two or three years, and is aware of the time and resources required to modify working practices. One of the Roland Berger consultants represented at this session commented that the Anglo-Saxon countries were more proactive in implementing cultural change to move to a trusting partnership approach than the French and German companies.

Despite these possible drawbacks the speed of change is remarkable. Surveys conducted throughout the 1990s on manufacturer–retailer relationships in the United Kingdom initially showed that partnerships would not work. By 1997 a sea change in attitude was happening. Who would have thought even then that the main grocery retailers would be sharing EPOS data?

LOGISTICS COST STRUCTURES

A critical aspect of these organizational changes, which have been evolving in response to ECR initiatives, is how to share both the benefits and costs of the initiatives. Until the mid-1990s much of the emphasis on logistics costs focused upon the company or industry channel costs rather than overall supply chain costs.

The advent of activity-based costing (ABC), one of the enabling technologies identified in Figure 15.3, has allowed for a 'process' approach to be taken to supply chain activities. For example, much of the initiatives undertaken on product replenishment had clear benefits for retailers but required extra work (and extra costs) further up the supply chain. Thus, the cultural revolution referred to in the previous section is necessary for retailers to establish 'ground rules' on attributing costs as well as benefits when seeking supply chain efficiencies. ECR Europe launched the Profit Impact of ECR project in September 1997, and has developed a software modelling tool, 'the wizard', which helps trading partners to identify the activities that are impacted upon when applying ECR initiatives.

Although the tools are being developed to improve existing practice, logistics costs do vary considerably in different countries. This was aptly shown in the United Kingdom in 1999 and 2000, when road haulage companies and other supporting businesses organized blockades in major cities and oil refineries in protest at hikes in fuel duty after successive budgets have made fuel costs the highest in Europe. Fuel costs are only part of the cost equation; labour costs in warehousing and transport, property prices and interest rates lead to differences in European markets. With the implementation of the EMU and standardization of interest rates, distortions created by national governments' fiscal policies should be less significant than in the past. For example, high relative interest rates in Britain were often the reason cited for destocking by British retailers and innovations pertaining to JIT distribution. Also, the cheaper land costs in France and Spain have been responsible for more speculative forward buying of stock and for holding more inventory in hypermarkets. This is similar to the United States, where the cost trade-offs in the logistics mix differ because of relatively cheaper fuel and land costs but greater geographical distances to cover.

ROLE OF THE THIRD-PARTY CONTRACTOR

One area of collaboration that is often overlooked is that between retailer and professional logistics contractors. Historically the provision of third-party services to retailers varied markedly from country to country. In the United Kingdom, where centralization of distribution occurred early, a major market was created for third-party providers to manage RDCs. In the rest of Europe, less enthusiasm for 'contracting out' was shown initially, with a tendency for companies to retain warehousing in-house and possibly contract out transport. Financial conventions differ by country, and in Germany, for example, strong balance sheets are viewed positively compared with the United Kingdom; also the opportunity cost of capital (investing in logistics infrastructure compared with retailing assets) may result in retaining rather than outsourcing these functions.

In recent years, however, the role of logistics service providers has been enhanced. This can be attributed to the internationalization of retail and transport businesses and the need for greater coordination of supply chain activities. The supply chain is now more complex than before. Retailers are optimizing traffic loads to minimize empty running, and are backhauling from suppliers and recovering packaging waste from recycling centres. As efficient replenishment initiatives are implemented, consolidation of loads is required within the primary distribution network. Logistics service providers are better placed to manage some of these initiatives than manufacturers or retailers. Furthermore, the internationalization of retail business has stretched existing supply chains, and third-party providers can bring expertise to these new market areas. Some British companies, especially Marks and Spencer, have utilized British logistics companies as they opened stores in new markets: for example the establishment of RDCs in Paris and Madrid with Exel Logistics. Similarly, the world's largest retailer has utilized the expertise of a British logistics company (Tibbet and Britten) to provide logistical support to stores acquired in Canada and Germany. Indeed, the internationalization of Tibbet and Britten from its United Kingdom base was significant in the 1990s, and a major part of its overseas business is now in North America, where major structural changes are occurring in the grocery market.

THE INTERNATIONALIZATION OF LOGISTICS PRACTICE

The gist of our discussion on differences in logistics cultures was to show that implementation of best practice principles has taken place differentially in various geographical markets. Nevertheless, the impetus for international-ization of logistics practice has been achieved through the formal and informal transfer of know-how between companies and countries. ECR Europe conferences, their sponsoring organizations and national trade associations have all promoted best practice principles for application by member companies. Many of the conferences initiated by these organizations have included field visits to state of the art distribution centres to illustrate the operational aspects of elements of ECR. At a more formal level, companies transfer know-how within subsidiaries of their own group, or through formal retail alliances.

To illustrate how logistics expertise is being transferred across international boundaries, we will look at two European case studies, Tesco and Ahold. Both are global players although their history of internationalization is very different. Tesco internationalized late and concentrated primarily in Europe; Ahold has around 60 per cent of its sales in the United States, and is only beginning to refocus its attention on the European market.

Tesco in Ireland and Poland

Tesco's most recent acquisitions in Europe (in Ireland and Poland) offer an insight into how changes in logistics practice can be implemented in different markets. In the wake of its acquisition of Wm Low in Scotland, Tesco plc turned its attention to Ireland in 1997, with the acquisition of 110 supermarkets from Associated British Foods. In the South, Power Supermarkets were part of this acquisition, and at the time Power had plans to consolidate distribution. With the takeover, Tesco inherited a 'push' logistics system:

- only 12 per cent of volume was centralized;
- high stockholding levels at store (2 weeks);
- high stockholding levels at depot (4+ weeks);
- up to 600 deliveries per week per store;
- unknown supply chain costs.

Tesco initiated a three-year plan to transfer Tesco UK know-how to Tesco Ireland. This involved

- consolidation of all product categories, initially through third-party contractors (except one inherited warehouse);
- move to a composite chilled distribution facility by 2000;
- the transfer of best practice ECR principles developed in the United Kingdom to Ireland;
- the upgrading of systems technology to achieve this.

In essence, Tesco Ireland is focusing upon replenishment areas of ECR in the first instance, before tackling the demand side of ECR with regard to product assortments, promotion and new product launches.

What is interesting about Tesco's entry into Ireland is that it has speeded up the process of consolidation throughout Ireland. Superquinn also had a supplier-driven logistics system, and in a matter of two years began to put in place centralized distribution. The Musgrave Group, which operates franchised convenience stores and supermarkets in both Northern and Southern Ireland, had centralized ambient products prior to Tesco's entry. Since 1997, Musgraves has taken the lead in Ireland in implementing a supply chain strategy. Two new chilled distribution centres have been opened, and the company has been active in ECR projects, which has resulted in organizational changes within the company.

Tesco's entry into Poland has posed a very different set of challenges to logistics managers. The acquisition of the Savia supermarket chain in 1995 followed on from a series of acquisitions in Hungary, the Czech Republic and Slovakia a few years earlier. In all these cases, Tesco has adopted a similar strategy: gradually introducing the Tesco brand and opening larger supermarkets and hypermarkets. Whereas the supply chain is supplier-led, this has a different meaning to the push system pre-1997 in Ireland. In Ireland, much of the discussion on Tesco's entry to the market was about the possible fate of Irish suppliers. In Poland, it is not the case in that most goods will be locally sourced; however, there is a need to improve operational relationships with respect to quality, packaging and delivery.

Ahold in Europe

Ahold has benefited from the transference of logistics practice because of its relationships in retail alliances, in addition to synergies developed with its expanding web of subsidiaries. During the 1990s Ahold partnered with Casino of France and Safeway of the United Kingdom in the European Retail Alliance. In 1994, a 'composite' distribution centre was very much a UK phenomenon; now it has been developed by Safeway's European partners. These logistics practices have been applied not only in France and the Netherlands, but in the parent companies' subsidiaries in the United States, Portugal and the Czech Republic.

In the Netherlands, Albert Heijn (Ahold's Dutch subsidiary) has developed a state of the art distribution system based on a modified UK 'composite' model. Because Heijn's stores are much smaller than those of the superstore operators in the United Kingdom, these composite distribution centres consist of three independent units, unlike in the United Kingdom where all products are stored in one facility. The three centres are a fresh centre dealing with the cool chain, a regional distribution centre for ambient and non-food products, and a returns centre for reallocation and recycling of returned products and handling materials.

ECR initiatives, especially those pertaining to efficient replenishment, have been a feature of Albert Heijn's supply chain strategy, with cross-docking and continuous replenishment playing important parts in their relationships with key suppliers such as Coca-Cola and Heineken. On a global basis Ahold attempts to synchronize best logistics practices across its operating subsidiaries. Clearly this is quite a challenge as the company operates in Latin America, Asia Pacific and the United States. Like Sainsbury, Ahold has retained the local store names in the United States post-acquisition, but has initiated best practice principles to achieve supply chain efficiencies.

THE FUTURE

Clearly there has been a transformation of logistics within retailing during the last 25 years. Centralization, new technologies in both materials handling and information handling, ECR and the implementation of best practice principles have resulted in logistics becoming a key management function within retailing. But what of the future? Are we about to experience evolution or revolution of retail logistics? Much depends upon the pace of retail change in the two areas identified in earlier chapters as drivers of change in the future: the extent of the internationalization of retail businesses, and the eventual size of the e-commerce market. These two key strategic factors are interlinked, however, as the Internet brings together consumers seeking products and services in international markets, and retailers join with their suppliers in global exchanges such as World Wide Retail Exchange (WWRE) to reap the benefits of reduced costs by streamlining procurement. Much of what was discussed in the previous section will continue. The large global retailers will force further consolidation of retail markets in North America, Europe and Southeast Asia. Their presence in these markets will necessitate a review of their supply chains to consider how to provide logistics support to new markets as they develop.

The biggest challenge facing retailers is how to respond to the market opportunities offered by e-commerce. Shopping from home is hardly a new experience for consumers. Mail order shopping arose in many markets because of the lack of fixed stores in rural communities, and catalogue and other non-store offerings have developed throughout the 20th century. Compared with the United States, however, where 'specialogues' for upscale consumers became the norm 20 years ago, the bulk of the mail-order business in the United Kingdom is still rooted in traditional catalogues targeted at lower socioeconomic group consumers. (It was the lure of cheap credit that provided a catalyst for growth in this market in the first place.) The traditional players such as GUS and Littlewoods have the logistical infrastructure in place, but until digital television takes off as the medium for e-commerce ordering, Internet consumers are the 'wrong' segment for traditional catalogue shopping.

Success in the e-commerce market will be dependent largely upon getting fulfilment and therefore logistics right. If time-constrained consumers are to be lured to e-commerce shopping, they have to be persuaded that the retail offer is better in terms of quality, value and customer service – that is, getting the product delivered when specified (Christopher's 'time to serve'). Take for example the situation in the United States between Thanksgiving and Christmas, the period when Internet ordering is at its peak. In 1999 40 per cent of online shoppers reported problems, from finding products to late delivery and high shipping costs (*Retail Week*, 21 July 2000). It is not surprising that Amazon.com and other high profile e-retailers have made substantial losses, because of the high marketing costs to grow the brand and thus their customer base, in addition to the investment in a logistics infrastructure. In the United Kingdom, the demise of Boo.com in 2000 and difficulties in 1999 at Jungle.com to meet customer service targets illustrate the difficulties encountered in this market. The creation of a healthy third-party market in the United Kingdom, using the logistics infrastructure of traditional mail-order companies (such as N Brown and GUS), and more recent specialists (such as Zoom), offers a solution to the fulfilment problem.

Much of the recent attention on e-commerce has focused upon the grocery sector, which is coming through the experimental phase with a greater commitment to online retailing. The initial reticence is understandable, in that major supermarket operators invest heavily in property assets, and they did not wish to cannibalize their existing store customers with a competing e-commerce offer. Over time it has been shown that online retailing can complement the store offer, and can indeed lead to switching of customers from one chain to another.

The United Kingdom has lagged behind the United States in the early development of retail logistics e-models. Netgrocer, Webvan, Peapod and traditional grocers such as Safeway and Schucks have established a logistics infrastructure to support their online business. In the United Kingdom much of the early experimentation focused upon the London region, because of the higher density of drops that could be achieved, with specialists such as the traditionalists delivering from stores, or in the case of Waitrose, delivering to the workplace. As the market has developed, picking centres have been developed in the South of England by Asda and Sainsbury (the former to capture sales from the competition because of its low penetration in this market area). By contrast, Tesco has opted for the store fulfilment model, which has enabled it to serve 90 per cent of the UK population through its spread of stores.

Currently, there are two main logistics models for grocery e-commerce: the store-based order picking and the dedicated order picking model, as illustrated in Figures 15.5 and 15.6. The store-based system used by Tesco makes use of existing distribution assets, in that products pass through RDCs to stores, then store staff pick and distribute orders to customers. The advantages of this system are the speed of implementation and the relatively lower initial investment costs. This system offers customers the full range of goods available in the local store; however, 'out of stocks' occur because the online shopper is competing with in-store customers.

Tesco's approach is interesting because it is reminiscent of Asda's delayed entry into centralized distribution in the late 1980s. Asda's decision not to

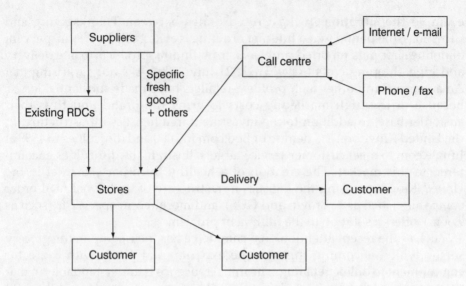

Figure 15.5 Logistics model for store-based picking of e-commerce orders

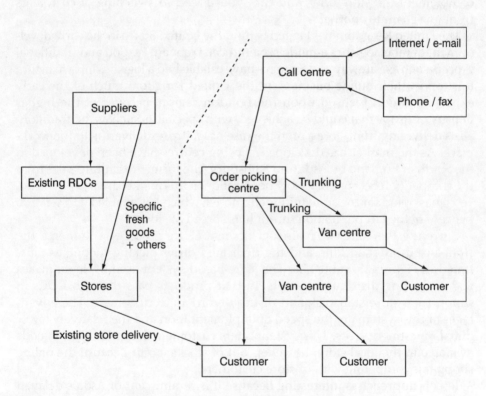

Figure 15.6 Logistics model for the e-fulfilment centre route

centralize in the 1970s like some of its regional competitors meant that it could achieve national penetration quickly (compared to the national leader of the time, Sainsbury, which has only opened an RDC in Scotland in 2000!). Ten years later, Tesco is delivering 'direct' from stores rather than centralizing e-commerce because it gives greater market penetration.

The dedicated order picking model (Figure 15.6) utilizes e-fulfilment centres to pick and deliver orders to customers. These picking centres are augmenting existing networks, and provide a dual distribution strategy for the companies adopting this approach. The advantage of this system is that 'in stock' levels should be high, in that orders are solely for e-commerce customers. Also, as demand grows, overheads are reduced, as the cost of the investment is spread over customers covering a wide geographical catchment area. Because of the distances to be covered, it would be unrealistic for a 12-metre articulated lorry to delivery to customers' homes. This is why 'van centres' may be used, whereby a small tier of small depots are used to transfer goods into local delivery vans (Figure 15.6).

'There is a consensus that the cost per delivery needs to be controlled if the e-commerce revolution is to be a success' (Foresight, 2001: 19). The report by the DTI's Foresight Retail Logistics Task Force claims that the current delivery charge to the customer of £5 nowhere meets the actual costs of supplying that customer. They quote that it costs approximately £13 to pick a single order. But who is the average customer? It would be exceedingly difficult to undertake an ABC analysis on Internet logistics systems. Clearly a customer who orders entirely ambient products in a £50 order will be much cheaper to serve than one who orders chilled, frozen and ambient products for the same amount.

In a special e-commerce issue of *Retail Week* on 28 April 2000, Alastair Charatan of PA Consulting reported the results of the company's costing model to compare the costs of the two e-logistics models. He concluded that:

> Detailed cost modelling confirms that distribution centre based fulfilment is the longer-term solution for supermarkets to adopt. In addition to higher costs, there are other drawbacks to the store-based approach. Store-based fulfilment does not relieve store congestion, so if home grocery shopping grows fast, stores could become increasingly crowded with the risk that customers in the store will be put off.

In reality a mixture of these logistics models will be utilized by supermarket operators, as their logistics networks evolve to meet the challenge of e-commerce. RDCs, recycling centres, store warehouse sites, all have potential for development, especially as existing assets would be deployed to complement any new investment into e-fulfilment centres.

Much of the discussion in this section has been about medium- to long-term trends, when much remains to be done to improve efficiency of the current retail logistics networks. Fernie *et al* (2000) undertook a survey for the Institute of Grocery Distribution (IGD) in 1999 to assess medium-term trends in retail logistics in the United Kingdom. The survey, which represented grocery retailers, manufacturers and logistics service providers, included questions on the factors that would impact upon the cost, service and structure of the supply chain, and where inventory would be held in the medium term. As can be seen from Table 15.2, the key factors affecting cost and service were:

- road traffic congestion;
- transport taxation/24-hour trading;
- home shopping/home delivery;
- recycling initiatives.

The key differences between groups were that logistics service providers viewed taxation levels as most important, while manufacturers rated 24-hour trading, and retailers, recycling initiatives. Although home shopping is ranked highly, and more so than in previous surveys, these food supply chain respondents considered fiscal and environmental-related factors to have the biggest impact upon their business. This has been borne out by events in the United Kingdom and other parts of Europe in 2000, when logistics service providers were actively involved in lobbying governments over the cost of fuel and the rate of fuel duty.

Table 15.2 Medium-term forces for change on cost, service and structure, within the grocery supply chain, average scores

Change category	Total survey	Retailers	LSP	Manufacturers	F	Sig
Road traffic congestion	4.2	4.3	4.2	4.0	2.53	1%
Transport taxation levels (eg fuel, road fund licence, road pricing)	4.1	4.1	4.5	3.9	4.61	5%
24-hour trading	3.8	3.4	3.6	4.1	5.71	1%
Home shopping/ordering (via Internet or catalogue)	3.7	3.9	4.1	3.5	2.06	NS
Home delivery (from store)	3.7	3.8	4.1	3.5	2.39	NS
Use of returnable transit packaging	3.5	3.7	3.7	3.4	1.19	NS
Recycling initiatives	3.5	3.9	3.7	3.2	6.68	1%
Working time directive	3.5	3.4	3.6	3.5	0.25	NS
Greater foreign retail penetration into the UK	3.4	2.9	3.7	3.6	5.12	1%
Access to urban areas	3.4	3.5	3.4	3.3	0.14	NS
Use of multi-modal services (eg road and rail)	3.0	3.4	3.0	2.8	3.14	5%

Key: 1 = less importance to 5 = much more importance

Table 15.3 shows where inventory is expected to be held in the supply chain in the near future. This shows a continuation of current trends, with reductions in store and RDC stock levels, and greater consolidation of primary loads at suppliers' DCs or consolidation centres. While reductions in inventory levels are currently attributed to reduced lead times and increased delivery frequencies, it is anticipated that further inventory reductions will be the result of more sharing of sales and promotional forecasts, and greater collaboration between supplier/customer project teams.

Table 15.3 Forecasts of inventory levels at different holding points in three years' time, average score

Inventory holding point	Total survey	Retailers	LSP	Manufacturers	F	Sig
Store	84	82	82	85	0.53	NS
Retailers' RDC	78	81	78	76	0.73	NS
Manufacturers' DCs/consolidation centre	105	109	113	100	2.83	NS
Manufacturing plant	98	99	103	96	0.91	NS
Raw material suppliers	100	101	106	98	0.88	NS

Key: 1 = large reduction to 5 = large increase

With a 'business as usual' scenario emanating from this survey, and indications that an increase in small van traffic because of online shopping will lead to greater congestion in residential areas, greater road traffic congestion is inevitable. Already it has been predicted that traffic congestion in the motorway network will be 20 per cent worse in 2007 than 1997. As the British government is keen to tackle both congestion and the reduction of noxious emissions, there is much pressure on the logistics sector to reduce transport trips throughout the supply chain. At Heriot-Watt University, a series of surveys have been undertaken on vehicle utilization and energy efficiency in the food supply chain. These surveys have had strong industry collaboration, through the development of key performance indicators (KPIs) to measure the efficiency of current transport operations. The results have shown that:

- Vehicle utilization can be improved by either redesigning the vehicles or improving the 'stackability' of material-handling equipment.
- The heavy lorry debate has little relevance to the food sector, because only 7 per cent of loads are weight constrained. Vehicle utilization is a volume not a weight issue.

- Vehicles only spend 35 per cent of their time on the road, yet much of this running time occurs in the morning when the network is busiest and fuel efficiency poorest because of congestion.
- 25 per cent of all trips were subject to a significant delay worth recording, but most delays were the result of problems at collection or delivery and internal company problems rather than traffic congestion.
- Rationalization of returns handling equipment is needed to free capacity for backhauls.

In an environment of escalating fuel costs, retailers can ill afford to inflate transport costs further by adding to existing road congestion. The research cited above does illustrate how supply chain initiatives can alleviate some of this congestion and improve energy efficiency in the UK logistics network.

REFERENCES

Christopher, M (1997) *Marketing Logistics*, Butterworth-Heinemann, Oxford

Christopher, M and Peck, H (1998) Fashion logistics, in *Logistics and Retail Management*, ed J Fernie and L Sparks, Kogan Page, London

Drucker, P (1962) The economy's dark continent, *Fortune* (Apr), pp 265–70

Fernie, J, Pfab, F and Marchant, C (2000) *Retail Logistics in the UK: planning for the medium term*, Proceedings of ACRA/AMS Conference, Columbus, Nov

Fiddis, C (1997) *Manufacturer–Retailer Relationships in the Food and Drink Industry*, FT Retailer and Consumer Publishing, Pearson Professional, London

Foresight (2001) @ Your Home: New markets for customer services and delivery, Foresight Retail and Logistics Task Force, DTI, London

GEA Consultia (1994) *Supplier–Retailer Collaboration in Supply Chain Management*, Coca-Cola Retailing Research Group Europe, London

Jackson, P (1998) Taking coals to Newcastle: the movement of clothing to Hong Kong and the Far East, in *Logistics and Retail Management*, ed J Fernie and L Sparks, Kogan Page, London

Kurt Salmon (1993) *Efficient Consumer Response: Enhancing consumer value in the supply chain*, Kurt Salmon, Washington, DC

McKinnon, A C (1998) *Vehicle Utilization and Energy Efficiency in the Food Supply Chain*, Heriot-Watt University, Edinburgh

McLaughlin, E W, Perosio, D J and Park, J L (1997) *Retail Logistics and Merchandising: Requirements in the year 2000*, Cornell University, Ithaca, New York

Mitchell, A (1997) *Efficient Consumer Response: A new paradigm for the European FMCG sector*, FT Retail and Consumer Publishing, Pearson Professional, London

Porter, M E (1988) *Competitive Advantage*, Free Press, New York

Whiteoak, P (1993) The realities of quick response in the grocery sector: a supply viewpoint, *International Journal of Retail and Distribution Management*, **21** (8), pp 3–10

16

Managing the financial supply chain: scope, services and problems

Lars Stemmler
BLG Consult GmbH

SUMMARY

Traditional supply chain management focuses on the optimization of material and information flows. However, as every supply chain is basically a cash-to-cash cycle, the financial element should be included in an enlarged scope of supply chain management. Supply chain finance encompass services prior to and after the physical materials flow. Banks and third-party logistics providers alike are already tapping into this market. Any successful market penetration relies on the ability of the service provider to ensure a secure handling of the information, as customer data and order data, as well as financial information, are pooled at the provider.

INTRODUCTION

Traditionally, supply chain management (SCM) is associated with designing and optimizing material and information flows through and between organizations. Savings can be achieved through an integrated management of both the physical flow of materials and the flow of information along the chain. However, an integrated approach to SCM must include the management of financial flows along the supply chain.

The tasks of optimizing supply chains tend to be limited to tangible cost elements such as transport and warehousing. The costs to finance products moving through the supply chain tend to be forgotten. These costs include not only inventory financing costs but also those costs associated with taking credit risks upon sale, supporting trade credit and taking out insurance. Logistics-driven finance costs also include process-related costs incurred through suboptimally designed processes for invoicing, monitoring receivables and payments. Furthermore, the cash flows and the revenue stream generated by successful order fulfilment have to be looked at closely. The generation of a reliable and predictable cash flow out of order fulfilment is a prerequisite of the ability of any commercial organization to survive – that is, not to become insolvent. This is not an isolated task of the treasury department. On the contrary, it is the scope of SCM to integrate three flows: material, information and financial.

After the role of finance in a supply chain has been defined, the drivers that influence finance-related logistics costs have to be identified. The chapter also tries to answer the question why supply chain finance does not yet play a prominent role within SCM. Based on this theoretical framework, practical solutions adopted in the logistics industry are explored, answering the question of how to integrate financial flows into logistics. Then this market review will be put back into the theoretical context developed beforehand.

ENLARGING THE SCOPE OF SUPPLY CHAIN MANAGEMENT TOWARDS FINANCE

In recent years SCM has evolved into a management concept aimed at designing, optimizing and controlling processes along the supply chain (Baumgarten, Kasiske and Zadek, 2002: 35). Problems occur when determining the scope of the processes to be included in SCM. Whereas Cooper, Lambert and Pagh (1997: 1) focus on a holistic view and include all value-driving processes in SCM, there are plenty of definitions that limit the definition of SCM to materials and information flows (eg Harrington, 1995: 30; Handfield and Nichols, 1999: 2). The latter definition has been developed out of early approaches to SCM that view it as purely logistics-driven. In many companies this view still prevails, as we shall see later in the chapter. By definition, an integrated management concept cannot exclude financial processes from the scope of SCM.

Cash is the lifeblood of every business (Pike and Neale, 1999: 7). Cash translates into liquidity: that is, the ability of the company to meet its payment obligations in full at any time. As profits may be distorted by accounting practices, cash flows are a more reliable indicator. The balance of incoming and outgoing payments of a company in any given period of time determines its liquidity (see Figure 16.1).

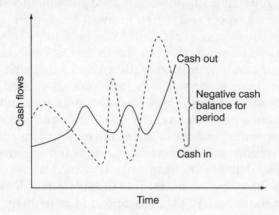

Figure 16.1 The cash gap threatens liquidity

The length of any supply chain is determined by its cash-to-cash cycle. As investors are interested in a decent return on their invested capital, any supply chain is basically finance-related. Cash is turned into goods, and these in turn are sold to generate more cash. This implies the integration of finance flows beside information and material. Lee and Ng (1997: 191) recognize this requirement in their definition: 'There are at least three kinds of flow in a supply chain: materials, information, and finance.'

From an SCM perspective the cash inflows after successful delivery and invoicing of the goods are of particular interest. The generation of revenue in

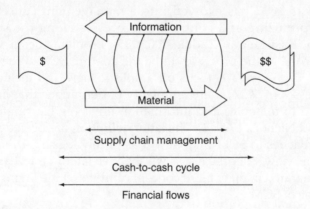

Figure 16.2 The integrated supply chain encompasses material, information and financial flows

cash terms is directly related to successful SCM activities. The customer orders, gets the ordered goods, and pays: this is the complete supply chain for a distribution operation! Hence, SCM has to include the management of financial flows (see Figure 16.2), and this particular task can be termed supply chain finance (SCF).

DRIVERS OF FINANCE-RELATED LOGISTICS COSTS

There is no doubt that a successful business depends on accurate and timely delivery of goods or services to its customers. SCM aims at minimizing mass and time in the pipeline. Needless to say, an efficiently managed supply chain requires the measurement of the costs associated with the physical movement of goods and the related information flows.

When financial flows are integrated into the scope of SCM, there are three cost drivers for finance-related logistics costs. Finance-related logistics costs (FRLC) are costs that can be associated with financial processes and activities but that are driven by logistics. These drivers are time, risk and processes (see Stemmler, 2002: 118).

As far as the influence of time on FRLC is concerned, we can, first, identify finance-related logistics processes before and after the physical movement of goods. Invoicing, for example, is mainly done after the successful delivery of goods. Second, inventory costs are related to time by the length of the pipeline. From a finance point of view, the related cost drivers are the agreed payment terms – for example, 10 days net – with finance costs pushed up by lengthy payment periods. Very often payment terms of 'net 30' – where an invoice has to be settled within 30 days from the invoice date without deductions – become 'net 60' or even worse. These terms are often accepted in order to keep an important customer. The longer the payment terms, the more interest is paid to fund the transaction. These unproductive assets tie up scarce financial resources. This is where the second driver comes in – risk.

Inventory finance involves a high degree of risk. For example, risk is reflected in insurance premiums for work in progress. Furthermore, risk-adjusted interest rates charged by banks for short-term inventory finance have to be taken into account. The risk of not receiving the agreed payment (that is, generating a positive cash flow from order fulfilment) can be summarized as the risk of customer default, and this translates into the risk portion of the interest rate. According to an analysis of Credit Swiss First Boston (CSFB), companies were able to cut inventory carrying costs from 5.4 per cent of GDP in 1990 to approximately 4 per cent in 2000 (Palmieri and Africk, 2001). Whereas it can be claimed that reduced inventory levels contributed to this cost-cutting, a great proportion of the benefits were driven by a reduction in interest rates having had a positive impact on the costs to finance the inventory (Palmieri and Africk, 2001).

The processes involved in SCF are – besides inventory finance – invoicing, managing receivables and monitoring payments from customers. These processes incur some costs. For example, in airfreight the invoice-related process costs associated with an airway bill amount to about US $0.39 for a particular company (*Deutsche Logistik Zeitung*, 16 Apr 2002: 7). Speed and accuracy of invoicing heavily affect the cash flow and the accounts receivables management. A short order cycle time requires the fast issuance of the invoice. An inaccurate invoice can deter a customer from paying, which results in an extended payment lead time, and in turn in unstable and unreliable cash flows (Christopher, 1991: 18).

CONTROLLING YOUR FINANCE COSTS IN THE SUPPLY CHAIN

The control of FRLC is the key for a successful integration of supply chain finance into SCM. We will discuss the opportunities for a reduction of FRLC along the supply chain before, during and after the material flow.

Cost reduction potential before the physical material flow

Let us start with those processes that trigger the individual supply chain from a customer's point of view – the order (see Table 16.1). Processes before the physical flow of material lay the foundation to manage time and risk in the supply chain. A customer scoring and rating procedure may determine appropriate payment conditions, for example prepaid or cash on delivery. This helps the company to establish a balanced risk-related customer portfolio. Services before the physical material flow can also include credit card validation. Then with agreed payment terms, inventory finance can be optimized, as cash flow dates become far more certain and predictable.

Table 16.1 Cost drivers in supply chain finance

	Tasks in SCF: the physical materials flow		
Cost drivers	Before	During	After
Time		Inventory finance	Payment conditions
Risk	Risk management, scoring, validations	Inventory finance insurance	Payment conditions
Processes			Invoicing, payment infrastructure, accounts receivables management, factoring

Cost reduction potential during the physical material flow

The costs to finance inventory can be reduced by increased information sharing. Finance costs are mainly determined by the interest rate to finance inventory and receivables that is charged by the company's financiers. The interest rate reflects the cost to fund, plus a risk premium the financier considers necessary to cover the credit risk, and associated costs such as auditing and inspection expenses. The costs to audit and inspect inventory are influenced by the availability of accurate information about levels and locations of the material. Obviously, financiers and logisticians require the same set of information.

Increased information sharing

Information on inventory levels and status can thus be shared between logistics providers and financiers. From a financing point of view, reliable information of inventory status delivered on a real-time basis reduces the risk associated with financing inventory. A lower risk exposure will be reflected in the costs of credit the company has to shoulder. Hence, the integration of financiers into the information flows along the supply chain is credit-enhancing.

Insurance services are the icing on the cake of financial services within supply chain finance. Information required and collected by third- or even fourth-party logistics providers (3PLs/4PLs) to manage the materials flow can be used to facilitate managing the risk exposure when taking out insurance. This applies in particular to information about the status of the inventory to be insured.

Enhancing coordination

In addition to the potential reductions in the costs of credit through optimized information sharing, improved coordination between supply chain participants who provide finance can result in a lower margin, and hence lower costs. Typically, each participant in the supply chain arranges for its finance independently. Lines of credit to finance product in the pipeline are established by suppliers, manufacturers and retailers separately. This practice results not only in costly duplication of processes, but also in higher individual costs to finance, as each participant negotiates for its own account. Improved coordination in terms of joint negotiating or eliminating duplication provides the opportunity to build a powerful cost-saving tool.

Case study: inventory finance

The following example (taken from Palmieri and Africk, 2001) illustrates cost-cutting opportunities based on optimized inventory finance within the supply chain. It considers the inbound logistics of a major computer assembler. A logistics provider, which is contracted to supply the assembly line, picks up the material from the vendors and delivers it just in time (see Figure 16.3).

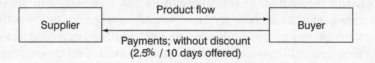

Figure 16.3 Cash and product flows prior to optimization

Let us assume that at any given time US $250 million in inventory value is outstanding, that is, has not yet been paid by the assembler. In financing terms this represents the average net investment to be financed. According to the trade terms, the assembler can make use of a 2.5 per cent prompt payment incentive offered by the vendors, which the assembler has chosen to ignore. What solution has been developed? A structure has been developed to address the arbitrage opportunities hidden in this supply chain (see Figure 16.4).

The 3PL remains responsible for the inbound material and the associated information flow. A special purpose company (SPC) is set up to make and receive payments between the assembler and the supplier. Payments to the supplier are made less the 2.5 per cent trade discount. At this stage it is necessary to mention that the SPC owns the inventory; it does not appear on the balance sheet of the assembler. This set-up boosts the assembler's return on investment (ROI) by reducing its exposure to current assets. The assembler in return reimburses the SPC under its normal payment practice. The SPC finances the average net investment by gaining competitive funding based on the credit rating of the computer assembler. According to the bank that initiated this scheme, a free cash flow of US $3.3 million is generated annually. After deducting the costs to fund, service risk, underwrite and insure (which

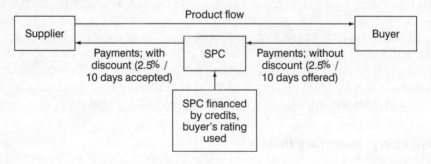

Figure 16.4 Cash and product flows after incorporation of a single purpose company (SPC)

is also provided), the remaining cash is distributed equally between the assembler, the bank and the logistics provider.

This example clearly illustrates the basic mechanics of SCF: the logistics provider shares its information management capabilities with financial service providers to arbitrage out excess charges between trading partners for financing and insurance. Taking the inbound logistics as an example, arbitration comes in the form of accelerated payments. The payment situation and the level of capital costs of the supplier determine the economics of accelerated payments. It is important to note that the assembler's liabilities do not increase, as payments are made by a party unrelated to the assembler, in our case the SPC. The prompt payment discount of 2.5 per cent is used to cover the transaction costs. Of greater importance, however, is how the credit rating of the transaction partners compares. In order to be able to use cheaper funding than the supplier can obtain, and so to make the scheme commercially viable, the funding source must have a higher rating than the supplier.

The solution that has been developed in our example is partly based on well-known financial instruments. This might not sound very innovative, but the most important aim of SCF is to show how to use logistics information that is already available in order to integrate financial flows into the 'traditional' supply chain.

Cost reduction potential after the physical material flow

The cost reduction potential after the physical material flow addresses process-related costs in SCF, such as costs incurred from invoice-related processes. Furthermore, payments have to be monitored.

In terms of process-driven costs, electronic billing (e-billing) might be the answer. E-billing delivers invoices electronically, facilitates the dispute resolution process, and allows a speedy settlement of invoices online (Citibank, 2001). E-billing is a prime example of how financial services can be integrated seamlessly into the logistical information flow, as invoice data are based on order and delivery information provided by the transport provider. E-billing reduces the need to check invoices manually, and the ability to establish the related IT-based procedures can cut process costs. Banks also provide online settlement and clearing infrastructure for transactions generated, for example by exchanges and e-marketplaces. Foreign exchange trading and settlement capabilities can be embedded into this infrastructure.

Accounts receivables management goes beyond providing a rather simple payment transaction infrastructure. It is not only about trading receivables at a discount on their carrying value, but also – more generally speaking – about enabling customers to meet their financial obligations. This requires a deeper understanding of the relevant markets that only a specialist SCF provider can offer. Providing billing services, payment infrastructure and accounts receivables management in the broadest sense means managing the complete range of financial transactions and the related cash flows along a supply chain (Driese, 2000). Here, substantial value can be added by offering integrated supply chain (financial) management.

CREATING VALUE THROUGH SUPPLY CHAIN FINANCE

The 'basic' forms of SCF, such as e-billing and electronic payments, can give reduced process and transaction costs. Furthermore, substantial cost reduction potential is generated through reduced risk premiums and enhanced creditworthiness that, in effect, translates into lower interest expenses. To apply the supply chain finance structure described above to our inbound logistics problem, the supplier receives an immediate payment for the delivered goods subject to the terms and conditions of the sale. Issuing a receipt and the related funding requirement can be avoided. As the source of funding is geared to the rating of the assembler, larger credit exposures can be taken. In other words, financing for general corporate purposes can be joined together more easily, as the credit decision taken by the banks is based not only on the company's financial standing, but also on the relationship with its customers. What can be learnt is that, in general, the value driver can be categorized as shown in Table 16.2.

Table 16.2 Value drivers in supply chain finance

Product value	**The higher the product value the higher the savings; the product volume is of minor importance here.**
Inventory turns	Faster turn products, ie higher cash flows, also create cost improvement opportunities.
Trade terms	Tapping yet unrealized cost saving opportunities by taking trade discounts.
Payment cycle	Elongated payment terms are responsible for unnecessary interest expenses arising from the need to finance the receivables.
Cost of capital	Key enabler to make use of arbitrage opportunities exploiting the difference in costs of capital between the seller and the buyer.

Source: Palmieri and Africk (2001).

INTEGRATING FINANCE INTO SUPPLY CHAIN MANAGEMENT

The requirement to integrate SCF into a company's supply chain management must be seen against outsourcing tendencies across many industries. Companies focus on their core competencies such as production and marketing, and outsource logistics functions to third parties. Providers not only offer purely logistics-related services such as transport, warehousing and distribution, but also value-added services related to the product (packaging, final assembly etc) and the finance function in the supply chain.

Supply chain finance: more than supply chain management

The key characteristic of SCF is the integration of financial flows into the physical supply chain. It is not a new (financial) product, it can be characterized as an essential part of the management concept commonly known as supply chain management. Supply chain management encompasses all those 'activities (that are) associated with the flow and transformation of goods from a raw materials stage, through to the end user, as well as the associated information flows. Supply chain management is the integration of these activities through improved supply chain relationships, to achieve a sustainable competitive advantage' (Handfield and Nichols, 1999: 2).

This rather traditional definition, focusing on transport, warehousing and the related IT-processes, clearly demonstrates the limited scope of established SCM methodology. In order to accommodate the additional view on financial flows along the pipeline, the scope of supply chain management has to be widened. Suitable approaches are already at hand: 'The idea is to apply a total system approach to managing the entire flow of information, materials, and services from raw-materials suppliers through factories and warehouses to the end customer. The focus is on those core activities that a business must operate each day to meet demand' (Chase, Aquilano and Jacobs, 1998: 466). Within this context supply chain management must try to reduce uncertainty and risks, thereby reducing inventory levels and cycle times while improving processes, and ultimately end-customer service levels.

Of interest here is the phrase 'services', which includes financial services. From a company's point of view, however, discussing definitions is only of scientific value (see for instance Weber, Dehler and Wertz (2000) on the difference between logistics and SCM). But it illustrates necessary changes to the way that supply chain management has to be approached. What matters are cost savings, regardless of the name of the game. With Cooper and Ellram (1993: 13), 'SCM is viewed as lying between fully-vertically integrated systems and those where each channel member operates completely independently.' They see each player in the channel as affecting – either directly or indirectly – every other member of the channel, as well as the overall channel performance. This reinforces the moves towards integration and coordination of processes and activities across the entire channel and not just between a few channel pairs. The basic idea behind SCF – closer integration and information exchange between the logistics and the finance functions – is similar in nature. It is based on the same key enablers – namely building trust, establishing partnerships and sharing of information. SCF is a necessary additional element within supply chain management. Hence, it is not 'more' than supply chain management, but a core element of it.

Being aware of supply chain finance

From a theoretical point of view, savings potentials have been identified within the scope of SCF. However, the limitations seen in definitions of SCM might cause us to conclude that financial flows are of limited importance to logistics, and do not imply that they need to be considered for integration into SCM. What is the actual level of integration of finance-related logistics tasks into SCM? Two surveys indicate that companies really do associate SCM with materials and information flows only. Recent research carried out by Göpfert and Neher (2001) suggests that only a fraction of companies regard the management of financial flows as an integral part of supply chain management. The majority of companies surveyed view SCM as incorporating only traditional tasks, such as transport and warehousing. While only 8 per cent of the companies see logistics as a transportation-only business, 57 per cent claim to pursue an all-embracing approach that includes cross-functional planning. However, such planning inevitably focused on materials and information management (Göpfert and Neher, 2001: 50).

Another empirical study by Corsten, Lenz and Klose (2002: 48) ranks logistics services in accordance with their perceived mean importance from the point of view of 3PLs. For this study 200 international logistics providers were surveyed between April and May 2000. There is no doubt that traditional transportation and warehousing activities rank ahead of everything else. However, under the 'top 10' logistics services falls inventory management, ranking seventh, while trade financing and letters of credit ranked forty-third, inventory financing (a separate category) ranked forty-fifth and receivables management ranked forty-sixth.

We have to raise the question why is this the case? We have to assume that companies always look for opportunities to add value when outsourcing services. A possible answer might be that SCF offers low added value, as functions and processes are already well established in other organizational functions, such as 'treasury'. Furthermore, as finance-related data are sensitive there might be a lack of trust when outsourcing SCF functions to third parties.

An integration of SCF into supply chain management requires the management of sales data, customer data and order-related data, thus giving a complete picture of the company's operations and customer base. Any third party has to prove that internal data protection mechanisms are not only in place but are working smoothly (with Chinese walls).

In terms of streamlining payment processes, information to be transferred, for example via e-billing, and infrastructure needs to comply with uniform standards in order to be manageable. In shipping this is given by EDIFACT, which is a common standard to exchange shipment data. Furthermore, legal requirements need to be reviewed about, for example, the requirement to issue printed invoices.

THE MARKET FOR SCF SERVICES

If outsourcing is to become a viable option, banks and 3PLs are competitors, but with different strengths and weaknesses. Both see SCF services as a suitable expansion of their service portfolio in accordance with strategies of differentiation. While banks market their primary experience in the financial sector, logistics providers focus on their information management capabilities.

The banks' traditional strength is in providing a reliable and established payment infrastructure. Furthermore, they provide related financial services to supplement their basic payment services, and hedge certain risks involved (derivatives trading, foreign exchange transactions, etc). Banks are famous for their secrecy, which, in finance, is a major competitive advantage.

3PLs offer one-stop-shop services to their customer as they can make the most of the synergies that come from the integration of material, information and financial flows. 3PLs are used to handling large quantities of customer- and cargo-related information, including tracing and tracking of orders. On this basis, it seems ideal for SCF to merge both strengths to make the most out of both organizations' competitive advantages.

CONCLUSION

Managing financial flows related to logistics is a major task within supply chain management. However, the task of supply chain finance lacks the attention of both academia and industry. The scope of supply chain management is to integrate three flows, from sourcing to the customer: material, information and financial. To limit supply chain management to logistics and information management forgoes many opportunities to tap yet unrealized cost saving potentials. Supply chain finance is not a new product. It is about coordinating existing processes in logistics and financing. Supply chain finance-related tasks can be identified to be carried out before, during and after the physical material flow.

Finance-related logistics costs are in particular driven by time, risk and processes. The length of the pipeline, the reliability of the cash flow out of regular business activities, and process-related costs when invoicing, influence finance-related logistics costs. What is needed is the integration of sales, customer and order data in a drive to add value to a supply chain management operation through supply chain finance. A prime focus is on information sharing between logistics providers and financiers, particularly with a view to inventory status information.

From a financing perspective, accurate and timely information reduces the risk exposure, and hence the costs to finance the product in the supply chain. Another key issue is accounts receivables management, which provides arbitrage opportunities. Banks and logistics providers alike offer a range of packages of varying degrees of scope and complexity. In one sentence, integrated processes, information sharing and innovative financial structures form the basis for successful supply chain finance.

REFERENCES

Baumgarten, H, Kasiske, F and Zadek, H (2002) Logistik-Dienstleister – Quo vadis? – Stellenwert der Fourth Logistics Provider (4 PL) (Logistics providers – where are they heading to?), *Logistik Management*, **4** (1), pp 27–40

Chase, R B, Aquilano, N J and Jacobs, F R (1998) *Production and Operations Management Manufacturing and Services*, 8th edn, Irwin/McGraw-Hill, Boston

Christopher, M (1991) *The Strategy of Distribution Management*, Butterworth Heinemann, Oxford

Citibank (2001) *Financial Services Solutions for Supply Chain Integration* [Online] http://www.ascet.com/documents.asp?grID_133&d_ID=529# (accessed 23 May 2001)

Cooper, M C and Ellram, L M (1993) Characteristics of supply chain management and the implications for purchasing and logistics strategy, *International Journal of Logistics Management*, **4** (2), pp 13–24

Cooper, M, Lambert, D M and Pagh, J D (1997) Supply chain management: more than a new name for logistics?, *International Journal of Logistics Management*, **8** (1), pp 1–14

Corsten, D, Lenz, M and Klose, M (2002) Logistics services providers and information-based logistics services: an explanatory study, *Logistik Management*, **4** (1), pp 45–50

Driese, W F (2000) Wie begleiten Banken die Expansion in der Logistik? (How do banks support the growth in logistics?), *Handelsblatt Beilage Logistik* (18 Oct)

Göpfert, I and Neher, A (2001) Verbesserungspotenziale (Potential for improvement), *Logistik Heute*, **23** (5), pp 49–51

Handfield, R B and Nichols, E L (1999) *Introduction to Supply Chain Management*, Prentice Hall, Englewood Cliffs NJ

Harrington, L (1995) Logistics, agent for chance: shaping the integrated supply chain, *Journal of Transportation and Distribution*, **36** (1), pp 30–34

Lee, H L and Ng, S M (1997) Introduction to the special issue on global supply chain management, *Production and Operations Management*, **5** (3), pp 191–92

Palmieri, R P and Africk, J (2001) Combining logistics with financing for enhanced profitability, in *Achieving Supply Chain Excellence Through*

Technology [Online] http://www.ascet.com/ascet/wp/wpPalmieri.html (accessed 6 Mar 2001)

Pike, R and Neale, B (1999) *Corporate Finance and Investment*, 3rd edn, Prentice Hall, London

Seuring, S (2001) *Supply Chain Costing – Kostenmanagement in der Wertschöpfungskette mit Target Costing und Prozesskostenrechnung* (*Supply Chain Costing with Target Costing and Activity Based Costing*), Verlag Franz Vahlen, Munich

Stemmler, L (2002) Supply Chain Finance Eine notwendige Erweiterung der Lieferkettensteuerung (Supply chain finance: broadening the scope of SCM), in *Wissenschaftssymposium Logistik der BVL 2002 – Dokumentation*, ed Bundesvereinigung Logistik eV, pp 113–24, Huss Verlag, Munich

Weber, J, Dehler, M and Wertz, B (2000) Supply Chain Management und Logistik (Supply chain management and logistics), *Wirtschaftswissenschaftliches Studium*, **29** (5), pp 264–69

17

Training in logistics

David Granville
Logistics Training International

Most organizations aspire to be better than their competitors. This means working effectively to keep current operations running smoothly, while at the same time working to create future operations. Achieving this necessitates learning.

Few people would deny that there have been substantial changes in the business environment over the last few years. Indeed very few will not have experienced the aftermath of re-engineering, downsizing or delayering. Most will have experienced apprehension at having to master new information handling and communication skills, or at having to return to formal learning simply to stand still in their job. Sadly, most of these developments happened with little or no thought to people. Even fewer will have been seen as a learning experience. Failure to think about people usually means the change is less successful than desired. These actions beg the question, 'Are people really important?'

It may seem a surprising question to ask: after all, the answer is surely obvious. No matter how sophisticated we become, people create the ideas, people plan the changes, and people provide the action necessary to make things work.

Organizations spend considerable energy thinking about why they exist and the direction in which they wish to go. They follow it by thinking about what needs to be done in order to progress towards their goal. Senior managers spend time presenting the ideas, either personally or on professionally designed videos. Yet all this effort will be wasted unless it is supplemented by thought about how people need to change and how people must interact in relationships. While it may be possible to buy skills, you cannot buy relationships.

It is the 'how' of change that will give you your edge. It is about people's habits, behaviours, attitudes and skills. It is about why things get done in the way they do. It is invisible to competitors, which makes it a sustainable advantage. Slowly there is a growing realization that people may be important, and that it may be sensible to begin to consider how we can assist them to perform to the peak of their potential. Business performance is about people performance. People are important!

Accepting that people are important means that significant attention needs to be given to learning, since:

You cannot change without learning

And you cannot learn without changing.

ABOUT LEARNING

The key question to begin therefore is how do people learn? Coming into any new task or situation, all individuals have a mental map of how to respond. This map will be based upon their existing skills and knowledge, their experience, their attitude and beliefs, and their standards of work. People use this mental map as the basis for approaching the task. As they undertake the task in this way they will receive feedback in various forms indicating whether the approach is a successful one or not. If they recognize that this feedback is telling them it is unsuitable, they are in fact beginning to challenge their mental map. This is the first key stage in learning.

Once they have accepted the feedback, the second key stage is being willing to change. It is possible that even though they recognize that they are challenging their mental map, they may decide that they are unwilling to change. If they are willing to change, they have a motivation to learn. Without this motivation they will simply stagnate. If they have a motivation to learn, the next step is to help them build a vision of a new mental map, and then to construct an action plan of how it can be achieved.

Using an implementation plan can help people to change their beliefs and approach, which should then result in their changing their actions and behaviour. At this stage they have learnt. The final stage then involves reinforcing and sustaining this change to ensure the complete development and absorption of the new mental map. The result is personal growth for the individual and improved business performance for the company.

So how do we start? Just before we explore an approach, it is important to stand back from the melee of business change and examine some clear business and development trends that will create the environment for logistics activity in the next decade.

BUSINESS TRENDS

Globalization

There are very few large organizations that do not have an international aspect to their supply chains, but the global issue goes much deeper. Improved information and communication mean that new product and service ideas receive international exposure much more quickly. This means national operators are exposed to international competitors more quickly, and customers become much more demanding, knowing they can get what they want from somewhere else in the world.

Organization structure

As supply chains span different companies, new organization structures will emerge. Few organizations do everything for themselves, and there is an increasing reliance on outsourcing partners. The ability to maximize such relationships will be a source of superior competitive competence. In many instances it will require new organization structures with less reliance upon the traditional hierarchical models.

Technology

The use of technology will grow in every facet of business. While the power to cost ratio continues to fall it is inevitable that more and more application areas will emerge. Two major technology changes are having a significant impact on logistics activity. The first concerns the installation and implementation of ERP systems, which enable information to be shared more easily. In particular this makes it possible to combine internal functional activities, which encourages a more process-driven approach to conducting business. The second change is the application of e-business, which enables organizations to work more closely on a collaborative basis with other supply chain partners, such as customers and suppliers. These technology enablers are having a profound impact on the way we conduct business, and as a consequence on the skills of our people.

Business performance

There will be a growing realization that business performance is linked to people. As technology replaces the mundane repetitive jobs, more and more people will gravitate towards jobs that will add more value and hence have the capability to be competitively important. Their performance will then be thrust to the forefront of business discussions.

Change

The rate of business change will accelerate as knowledge develops. The pace of change will not slow. All these trends have the potential to create new learning opportunities that, if grasped, will in turn multiply the number of further openings. The speed of change will be influenced by the capability of people to absorb new ideas.

Relationships

The way in which relationships are managed will directly affect an organization's competitive competence. There will be an increasing emphasis on the development of internal and external relationships, moving from confrontation to collaboration. In the same way as attention to teamwork grew in the 1990s, improving the supply chain relationship will be a focus in the future.

Competitive advantage

Competitive advantage will increasingly involve using information, knowledge and people. The traditional sources of advantage such as product and price are becoming very visible, very quickly, and their ability to deliver sustainable advantage is limited. Knowledge, information and the way we manage and organize people are invisible, posing greater challenges to competitors who seek to copy.

DEVELOPMENT TRENDS

Skill requirements

Skill requirements will continue to increase in response to rapid technological change. Already significant skill shortages are beginning to emerge.

Diversity

The workforce will become significantly more educated and more diverse. More students are being encouraged to pursue higher levels of education, though whether the financial aspects will enable this trend to continue must be open to question. With the global influence, many organizations are becoming more diverse in their profile of employees, with increasing representation from different religions and cultures. Development practices must reflect this diversity.

Restructuring

Corporate restructuring will continue to reshape the business environment and development practices. A few years ago development activities had to wait while restructuring took place. Now, since restructuring is almost a permanent feature of corporate life, development must be an integral part of the process.

Format of training departments

Corporate training departments will change dramatically in size and composition. While they may have been the last focal point for the downsizers, they have not been immune. In the last few years we have seen a dramatic reduction in their size. This has resulted in more training being outsourced. The role of those who are left has changed from doing to managing, and to being seen as an integral part of the change process. Many do not have the skills required, and unless they spend time on their own development they will find the transition a difficult one to make.

Learning technology

Advances in technology will revolutionize the way training is delivered. Why not? There is a rich prize here: the hidden training costs that are made up of employee travel and salary costs while attending training. If training can be delivered just in time, just when it is needed, huge savings could be available.

Training departments will find new ways to deliver services. They must. If they are smaller, yet the demand for their services is greater, then new delivery methods must be found. As in other areas of business, technology is having an impact on learning through the introduction of e-learning facilities. However, probably the most significant trend that is now emerging is how we piece together all the different facets of the learning process to create a blended solution.

Performance improvement

Training professionals will focus more on interventions in performance improvement. The emphasis on people performance will require short-term actions requiring immediate attention. It will require knowledge of the area in which the performance is deficient.

Responsibility for learning

Greater emphasis will be placed on individuals becoming responsible for their own learning. This is a fall-out from the previous trend. If the training department is focusing on the short term, someone else must consider long-term needs. This task is likely to transfer to the individual, and possession of the appropriate skills could become the passport to employability. In some parts of the world this could be a real problem, since many have forgotten how to learn !

High-performance work systems

Integrated high-performance work systems will proliferate. Again, the emphasis is on performance, and in crucial areas all aspects of the system need integrating. This will mean that training needs to become an integral part of the system, not something that is seen as isolated from work. For high performance to be achieved, people who have skills and motivation must operate in an environment that maximizes the opportunity to use those skills.

Learning organizations

Companies will transform into learning organizations. Different people have different definitions of a learning organization, but to learn you must experience failure. The huge pace of change is not going to allow the time to assimilate the full impact of change issues before action is required. The best way of learning is by doing, and there will be plenty of opportunity. Many organizations find failure hard to tolerate, and many people are terrified of the fall-out from such an experience. Proper frameworks and processes are needed to support such experimentation.

People performance

Organizational emphasis on people performance will accelerate, and perhaps we shall see meaningful actions to support the CEO's often-hollow statement, 'Our people are our most important resource.'

RESPONDING TO A CHANGING ENVIRONMENT

Recognizing the trends in the business environment is a necessary first step in providing a strategic response to the people issues. Careful examination will highlight a clear theme of performance that provides a starting point. When we consider the factors that impinge on performance, two groups can be identified: those that are focused on individuals, and those that are focused on the organization.

Table 17.1 Performance factors

Individual factors	Organizational factors
Knowledge	Information
Skills	Consequences
Motivation	Involvement
Ability	

As Table 17.1 shows, the individual factors are knowledge, skills, motivation and ability. Most trainers will feel comfortable with knowledge and skills, since this is their traditional domain. Obviously people must have the knowledge and skills needed to do a job. In addition, they need to be motivated, which necessitates that they be committed. The type of commitment is important. Commitment displayed simply in response to external pressure is not as powerful as commitment generated inside an individual. Doing things because you feel a sense of ownership and personal benefit is likely to result in more purposeful action than doing things because you have been told to. A large part of commitment stems from the confidence an individual has to use knowledge or skills. Developing confidence requires practice, emphasizing the learning by doing paradigm.

Simply equipping individuals with knowledge and skills will not result in improved performance. It is necessary to consider the environment in which the skills will be practised. The organizational factors in Table 17.1 show that information, consequences and involvement need to be thought about. Information includes values and strategies, goals and accomplishments as well as key performance measures. People need to have regular information to know what is required and to provide feedback on progress.

Consequences focus on reinforcement and reward. As progress is made, reinforcement is needed to ensure the improvement is maintained. The simplest reinforcement is praise. It is critical that reward systems recompense the behaviour that is required. Frequently reward systems act as a major constraint on people performing in the desired way.

Finally, involvement is the active part of engaging everyone in the performance process. It needs to be non-voluntary to ensure all take part, and it must be management directed to ensure the appropriate areas are focused upon. Since performance is influenced by both individual and organizational factors, any people development initiatives should consider both of these aspects.

THE LOGISTICS ENVIRONMENT

Special mention is needed of some aspects of the environment that are unique to logistics operations. Logistics spans a wide field of business activity, and at the core of logistics thinking is trade-off analysis. The ability to get people to see the wider picture and to overcome the functional myopia that is dominant in many organizations is a particular challenge to people development. Development will need to be provided to equip people with specific skill sets to manage functional activity in a way that does not compromise supply chain optimization.

The length of supply chains can also mean that the time lag of decisions is considerable. For example, after a decision by an inventory manager it may be several months before the outcome can be evaluated. Many people have difficulty in linking the decision with the outcome over such a long period. By using computerized learning technology this time lag can be compressed, allowing decisions to be made in an atmosphere of experimentation.

Many logistics operations now operate 24 hours a day, seven days a week, which again presents difficulties in planning development activity. As supply chains stretch across the world, the target audience for development becomes more diverse and geographically dispersed. Getting people from different cultures to work together effectively represents a real challenge.

PERFORMANCE DEVELOPMENT MODEL

If training is to deliver a business benefit by improving performance, then it must contribute to the achievement of an organization's goals. It should be expected that training:

- targets the right audience;
- is effective enough to increase employee productivity;
- closes organizational skill gaps;
- shows a return on investment.

The model in Figure 17.1 provides a framework for developing an approach that will secure all of the above requirements.

The first step involves determining the business needs. It is likely that these will be linked to either deficiencies in current performance levels or the introduction of new ideas or technologies. It is important to specify clearly and unambiguously exactly what the business needs are. Where more than one need is identified it will be necessary to prioritize them, and to determine any links between different needs. The goals of the training process will be linked directly to these needs.

Next the performance needs must be identified. This involves:

- determining exactly what you want people to be able to do;
- specifying how well you want them to be able to do it;
- deciding what you want people to stop doing;
- identifying what you want people to be able to do differently.

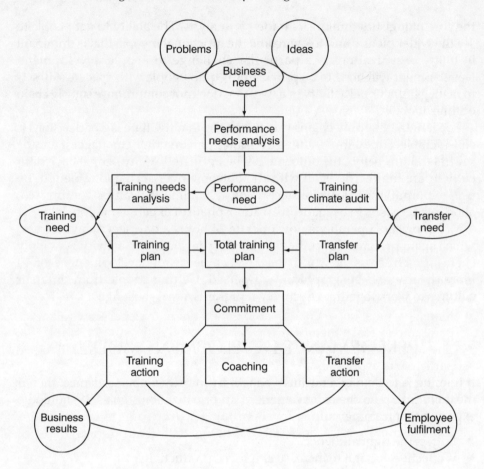

Figure 17.1 Performance model

The way in which this is done will depend on the nature of the need. In the case of deficient performance, some diagnostic technique is needed to enable the problem to be defined correctly and the cause identified. Where the need arises from new initiatives, a technique must be used that enables the new performance levels to be defined.

At this point the model splits into two parallel activities. Individuals within the target audience can be compared against the performance needs. This can be achieved using a variety of approaches, from observation to interviews or questionnaires. Increasingly use can be made of computerized methods, which are quicker since the subsequent analysis can be performed automatically.

Clearly once the 'performance gap' has been identified, the training needed to bridge the gap can be specified. The design of the training plan must take into account the training needs, and utilize an appropriate delivery method.

While training courses can tackle common needs, it may not be possible for them to cover individuals' specific needs. In such a case other action must be planned.

Alongside the design of the training plan, the parallel work must be to specify a transfer plan. This is the plan that seeks to eliminate or minimize the presence of the barriers to transfer. These barriers are the actual or perceived factors that inhibit the success of training and development efforts, and act as impediments to the transfer of learning.

Successful learning experiences need a partnership approach between the trainer, the trainee and the manager. To maximize the possibility of successful transfer, the following must be achieved:

- Participants and their managers must know what the training will contribute.
- Participants and managers must help to define the direction of the training.
- Participants must want to be trained.
- Managers must want to send their people to the training.
- Managers must know enough about the training to discuss it with participants and to coach them afterwards.
- The appropriate support tools and technologies must be available at participants' work sites.
- Senior level managers must visibly demonstrate their support for the training and its desired outcomes.
- The organization's culture must encourage participants to use what they learn in training. If it does not, the things that get in the way must be identified.

Importantly it will be noted that most of these requirements can be met only by designing specific actions prior to training and following training. In other words, successful training is not just about delivering good training courses. The factors that must be covered are:

- *Measure me*: the measurements which will be used to monitor the desired performance.
- *Give me*: the work conditions necessary to make the job agreeable.
- *Let me*: have the amount of discretion permitted in the conduct of the job.
- *Assist me*: by investing in ensuring the job is doable.
- *Respect me*: using the right treatment on the job on a day-to-day basis.
- *Convince me*: by giving me confidence that senior managers understand how important the training is.

The 'measure me's' are very important. Often people state that what gets measured gets done, and what gets rewarded gets done repeatedly. However, frequently words are not converted into meaningful action. A training climate audit can help with devising an effective transfer plan.

The training climate audit specifically addresses the transfer management process. Frequently the existing situation resembles the one shown in Figure 17.2.

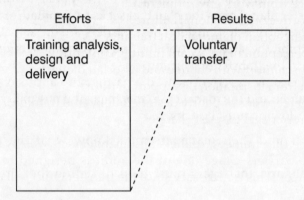

Figure 17.2 Frequent training climate

The purpose of transfer management is to design specific effort that stimulates additional transfer, as shown in Figure 17.3.

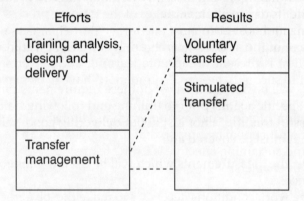

Figure 17.3 Ideal training climate

Being prescriptive about transfer effort is dangerous, simply because the dynamics of different sites, even within the same company, can be incredibly different. The purpose of the audit is to:

- identify the presence of any barriers to the transfer process;
- identify any efforts that are used to overcome the barriers;
- test the foundation on which training is to be conducted.

In their book, *Transfer of Training*, Mary Broad and John Newstrom (1992) identified the significant barriers which hinder transfer as:

- lack of reinforcement on the job;
- interference from work environment;
- non-supportive organizational culture;
- trainees' perception of impractical training;
- trainees' perception of irrelevant training content;
- trainees' discomfort with change and associated effect;
- separation from inspiration or support of tutor;
- trainees' perceptions of poorly designed/delivered training;
- pressure from peers to resist changes.

You will notice that trainees, trainers and managers as well as the company influence the barriers. Stage one of the audit is designed to identify the restraining forces. This is necessary since the transfer effort will need to:

- remove them;
- diminish their magnitude;
- convert them to positive focus.

Stage two involves identifying any efforts that are in place, consciously or unconsciously, which are helping the transfer. Clearly the transfer effort will seek to increase their magnitude, and/or add new focus. The transfer plan must develop different ideas to help trainers, trainees and managers develop positive transfer forces in all three stages of the training process: pre-training, during training and post-training.

In Stage three of the audit, enquiries are broadened to ascertain whether a good foundation is present to facilitate learning and performance. For any transfer effort to succeed, these five foundations have to be in place:

- strong, committed, visible leadership;
- basic skills for thinking such as numeracy and literacy;
- overcoming functional myopia so that the big picture can be seen;
- building and sustaining effective learning teams;
- managers as enablers.

We look for inhibitors and accelerators in building these foundations. Typically these include:

- measurements/rewards;
- policies and procedures;
- systems and support;
- organizational design;
- management practice;
- alignment.

The process used for the audit is like any other, in that it involves asking a cross-section of the people involved in the activity lots of questions. A mixture of site visits, interviews and questionnaires should be used.

Both the training and transfer plans come together to make up the total training plan. Progressing one without the other will only result in wasted effort. Obviously before action is taken it is necessary and sensible to get commitment to the plan. Commitment is important if action is to result.

To conclude the development process, action needs to be engaged. The actions will involve work in providing the appropriate training and in overcoming the transfer barriers. Importantly the transfer plan will include follow-up activity which can be developed by using coaching. It is investment in consistent and constant real-time coaching that helps people to move from core tasks to the extras that give the invisible edge.

If the model is followed, then the outcomes will provide the desired business benefits to the organization, while giving participants satisfaction and fulfilment.

LEARNING FOUNDATIONS

Within the audit process five elements of a learning foundation were mentioned. These warrant further discussion.

Leadership

Without strong, committed, visible leadership, no change is going to happen. Most people are willing to change old habits and work methods if they know that leadership is serious and committed to making change happen. Evidence that leadership is committed to change is as follows:

- There is a well-defined, easily understood vision for the entire company.
- There is total agreement on the vision across all levels, functions and divisions.
- All leaders are committed to changes needed to make the vision a reality.
- Management has developed thorough plans to implement the change, and has committed sufficient resources to ensure success.
- The change effort spans all parts of the company with no group exempt.

Basic skills of thinking

All employees at every level must have the basic skill set if they are to contribute to their full potential. The basic skills should include:

- communication skills to enable clear, open communications, including reading, writing, listening and speaking skills;
- maths skills to enable work-related documents such as spreadsheets to be read and interpreted;

- self-management skills so that employees can plan their own lives and careers;
- business skills so that employees can understand the company's overall business and how their individual work contributes to company success;
- function-specific skills – most jobs will require additional function-specific skills.

Evidence that thinking skills exist are as follows:

- The sets of business skills needed for all jobs has been identified.
- The company has assessed the basic skill levels of all employees to determine training needs.
- The company sponsors needed remedial basic skill instruction for all employees.
- All employees are encouraged to exceed the basic skill level, and opportunities are provided for development.
- Investment is made in basic business, team, communication and self-management skills training.

Supply chain thinking

Even in logistics and supply chain companies, functional myopia can exist. Evidence that it does not is as follows:

- Company business processes have been charted and analysed.
- Employees understand the company's basic value chain and how their work fits into the chain.
- Cross-functional teamwork is common practice.
- Employees are measured not only by functional goals but by how much they contribute to overall success.
- Administration policies and procedures encourage a wide view of the company's business.

Learning teams

Teamwork, within and across functional and organizational boundaries, has become a key element of most companies' efforts. The only reason that a team should ever be formed is so team members can learn either from each other or together, in order to meet individual or organizational goals. Evidence that this foundation exists is as follows:

- Teamwork is viewed as a common way of working rather than as an exception to normal work practices.
- Measurement and reward systems recognize the value of teamwork and not just of individual achievement.

- Comprehensive plans for team development, including formal training and ongoing coaching, are in place.
- Empowered, self-managed teams are eliminating the need for some managers.
- Teamwork has resulted in significant business results.

Managers as enablers

Traditionally management has tended to control employees, whereas there is a trend for a new style where managers enable their staff to get their work done. Possible evidence to look for is as follows:

- Management jobs have been redefined, making managers responsible for the development of their staff.
- Training and development programmes exist to help managers learn new skills such as coaching.
- Managers view their roles as teacher, team builder and coach positively.

The presence of these foundation elements is critical if real and powerful learning is to take place in the organization.

IF YOU THINK TRAINING IS EXPENSIVE, TRY IGNORANCE

Training is frequently perceived as being expensive, a nice thing to do when money is available. Come recession and cutbacks, the training budget will be one of the first to suffer. Like any other business activity, training can be expensive if it is badly planned, badly organized, badly conducted and badly controlled. Get these right, however, and training can yield astonishing benefits.

It is important to identify all of the costs associated with training. These are:

- training costs;
- ignorance costs;
- lost opportunity costs.

Training costs

These costs can be broken down into five areas:

- *Analysis costs:* associated with the initial problem identification, needs analysis and development of objectives. They will include salaries, materials and consulting fees.

- *Development costs:* directly related to the programme development. These costs are usually substantial, but could be spread over several runnings of the programme if the assignment allows.
- *Delivery costs:* include all the costs associated with delivery of the programme, including materials, accommodation, salaries and expenses of participants, instructor fees and equipment rental.
- *Evaluation costs:* include the evaluation material and the time to administer the evaluation, analyse the results and report the findings.
- *Transfer costs:* include all the costs of providing the transfer work to ensure that there is a conducive training climate.

Ignorance costs

These costs can be broken down into two categories. The first is costs of failure, which covers the costs of correcting mistakes both internally to the business and externally with customers. Examples include:

- cost of shipping wrong product;
- cost of retrieval;
- cost of returning to stock;
- cost of loss, damage or shrinkage;
- cost of premium transport to replace;
- cost of administration and overheads;
- cost of lost sales;
- cost of lost goodwill;
- domino effect costs;
- cost of accidents;
- cost of theft;
- cost of recruitment.

The second category is costs of exceeding requirements. These are incurred for providing services for which no known requirement exists. Examples include excess stocks, extra transport cost from quicker delivery, excess cost from inappropriate distribution network, and excess cost of under-utilization and performance of resources.

Lost opportunity costs

Costs of lost opportunities are reflected in the profit impact of the lost revenues resulting from cancellation of orders or lost business, as a consequence of the actions of the logistics department. Typically, these occur from not delivering in time or from not having stock available. The relationship between these costs is shown in Figure 17.4.

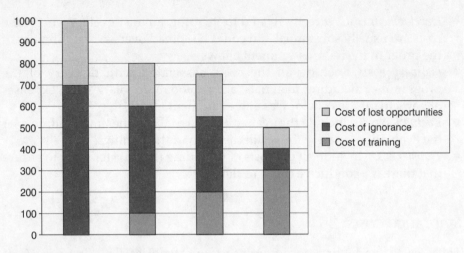

Figure 17.4 Costs of training

Before training commences there is likely to be considerable waste in the form of ignorance and lost opportunity costs (column 1). As training gets under way, training costs obviously increase, but slowly the costs of ignorance will decrease (column 2). As the training initiative nears its conclusion, the costs of lost opportunity will start to decrease (column 3). At the end training costs, which will largely consist of transfer activity at this stage, will be the greater cost (column 4), but the overall cost will have reduced considerably. This is conclusive proof that training can be free!

CONCLUSION

The logistics environment is rapidly changing. People will continue to be important, the skills required will change, and training has a role to play. If it is performance-related, the results obtained can represent a significant return on investment.

Training can be expensive. The benefits can, however, significantly outweigh the cost, and the cost of ignorance can be enormous. The success of training depends on management commitment.

In closing I recall a conversation between a doctor and his patient. After a lengthy explanation, the doctor told the patient that rest was the answer to his illness. 'The best thing for you to do', said the doctor solemnly, 'is to give up drinking and smoking, get up early in the morning and go to bed early at night.' The tired businessman considered this advice for a moment, then shook his head slowly. 'No, doctor, I don't deserve the best', he said. 'What's second best?' In failing to recognize the importance of developing people, second best is ignorance.

REFERENCE

Broad, M and Newstrom, J (1992) *Transfer of Training*, Addison-Wesley, Reading, MA

18

City logistics: the continuing search for sustainable solutions

Tony Whiteing
University of Huddersfield

Michael Browne and Julian Allen
University of Westminster

INTRODUCTION: THE URBAN LOGISTICS DILEMMA

Between the mid-1970s and mid-1990s, researchers and policymakers paid relatively little attention to the increasingly severe logistics problems facing urban areas. More recently this has changed, and there is growing interest in the logistics of collection and delivery services in town and city centres in particular. Numerous projects in Europe and elsewhere have attempted to pinpoint the key urban logistics problems and identify potential solutions. Despite such efforts, relatively little progress has been made towards resolving the basic urban logistics dilemma, which is that the future success of city centres depends on their effectiveness in different, often conflicting dimensions.

On the one hand, city centres must be attractive places to work, to shop and to spend leisure time. In these respects they face increasingly severe competition, notably from out-of-town retail parks. If retailers and other employers and income generators are to retain confidence in city centres, efficient logistics systems must be provided so that commercial premises can be serviced in a cost-effective manner. On the other hand, urban planners are very conscious of the need to maintain or improve the quality of city centre environments, to attract shoppers, tourists and workers, and perhaps to persuade people to live there. There is a popular perception that commercial vehicles – and especially larger lorries – are highly detrimental to the urban environment, contributing significantly to the problems of congestion, pollution, safety and noise. It is not surprising therefore that conflict can arise between commercial interests and the environmental lobby as far as urban logistics is concerned.

THE EC AND UK CONTEXTS

The late 1980s and early 1990s saw very little urban logistics research in the United Kingdom, possibly because of the disappointing outcomes of earlier work, which identified high costs of proposed solutions such as urban freight trans-shipment centres (Whiteing and Edwards, 1996). By the early 1990s, however, research on a European scale was under way. The 'COST321' urban freight research programme deliberated for a number of years. A report produced by its working group in conjunction with TNO Delft identified a wide range of policy measures with potential to reduce urban freight problems (Tanja *et al*, 1995). In the European arena, the mantle has now been assumed by the 'Best Urban Freight Solutions' (BESTUFS) programme. This is a thematic network funded under the European Communities (EC) Fifth Framework programme. Its aim is to establish and maintain an open European network of freight transport experts, user groups and associations, interested cities, various ongoing research projects and the relevant EC direc-torates, in order to identify and disseminate best practice with respect to the movement of freight in urban areas (BESTUFS, 2002).

In the United Kingdom, the government has now affirmed its commitment to bringing about more sustainable urban distribution operations. The general approach was set out in the 1998 Transport White Paper (DETR, 1998) and the *Sustainable Distribution* daughter document (DETR, 1999). This approach acknowledges the need to balance economic and environmental considerations when establishing freight transport policies. Local authorities must set out freight strategies in their local transport plans (LTP). Moreover, they are expected to work together with freight transport companies and their customers, to encourage these organizations to distribute goods in a way that will reduce distribution costs for the companies concerned and bring about environmental benefits for those living and working in urban areas. This has led to considerable interest in freight quality partnerships (FQPs), which will be discussed later in this chapter.

A RANGE OF POTENTIAL URBAN FREIGHT SOLUTIONS

The aim of this chapter is to evaluate some of the urban logistics measures most commonly believed to offer significant environmental benefits, namely:

- the development of urban freight trans-shipment centres, possibly multi-modal;
- the promotion of consolidated freight movements in urban areas, possibly involving cooperation between different retailers and/or different transport operators;
- promoting the use of appropriately sized vehicles for urban logistics work;
- the use of alternative vehicle fuels and quieter vehicles;
- information systems and telematic applications with scope to improve logistics efficiency in urban areas;
- time-of-day or vehicle size restrictions;
- urban collection and delivery at night.

It must be made clear at the outset that these measures should not be treated entirely in isolation. There may be significant synergies between them, such that worthwhile benefits may require some combination of two or more measures. This theme will be developed in the discussion that follows. In fact one can go further than this. Most of the measures listed above are concerned (at least in part) with increasing the amount of load consolidation achieved in urban logistics work. The key distinction is that proposals for trans-shipment centres typically involve a significant element of compulsory consolidation for delivery or collection in city centres (or at least penalties for not consolidating in the approved manner). This is in contrast to other measures on the list, which are more concerned with voluntary consolidation schemes, in circumstances where consignors, operators and recipients can be persuaded as to the potential benefits of such consolidation. The essential policy choice thus boils down to enforced consolidation or the encouragement of consolidation.

URBAN FREIGHT TRANS-SHIPMENT CENTRES

Trans-shipment centres are frequently suggested as a solution to the environmental problems caused by lorry traffic in urban areas. Freight destined for urban areas would be unloaded at a depot on the periphery and trans-shipped into small vans for final consolidated delivery. These vans would also undertake to collect consignments from city centre premises. Proposals may envisage compulsory use of such facilities, with all other lorries banned from a designated area, or they may be more voluntary in nature. In the latter case, various incentives may be employed to promote their use. In addition, operators choosing not to use the facilities may face severe time-of-day or vehicle size restrictions imposed by local authorities within the urban area (Ogden, 1992).

In the 1970s a study of a trans-shipment centre proposed for Swindon suggested that it would not be commercially viable, and it became generally accepted that such facilities would require an urban population of at least

150,000 to approach viability (Whiteing and Edwards, 1996). Despite these reservations, proposals were developed in the 1990s to establish trans-shipment systems in a number of Dutch towns and cities, following consultancy studies of their potential use and cost-effectiveness. Experimental schemes were proposed in four cities. The first such experiment eventually got under way in Maastricht in the early 1990s, but the volumes going through the depot were low. Progress on schemes for other cities was hampered by problems in agreeing the precise nature of these schemes. Who should own the facilities – the public sector or private enterprise? Should their use be voluntary or compulsory? What sort of licensing system should be put in place for operators involved in the collection and delivery work in the area concerned? What restrictions should be placed on vehicle size, type and hours of operation for operators remaining outside the scheme? Many operators seek exemption from such schemes, usually on the grounds that the goods they carry are highly perishable, may contaminate other goods, or require high levels of security.

Despite these problems there is still interest in trans-shipment centres as a potential solution. Several UK local authorities have investigated their feasibility in recent years, though none has progressed beyond the initial investigation stage. In France, a scheme got under way in 2001 in the historic town of La Rochelle, where narrow cobbled streets in the town centre are not suitable for large vehicles (BESTUFS, 2002). The most significant problems facing such schemes appear to be the relatively high costs of the trans-shipment operation and the loss of control suffered by the shippers of the goods.

One significant advantage of trans-shipment centres is that they can be used in conjunction with other measures to generate wider benefits. Sites adjacent to railway lines and waterways may be chosen to maximize the scope for intermodal operations, for example. Trans-shipment strategies can also be linked to relatively severe time-of-day or lorry weight restrictions in city centres, as explained above. Perhaps their most important advantage is that because the fleet of vehicles based at the centre is dedicated to urban collection and delivery work, such vehicles can be specified most appropriately for the town or city concerned. Attention can be paid to the most suitable vehicle size, and more environmentally friendly vehicles, perhaps with quieter engines or powered by gas or electricity, can be used. Assessment of electric powered small delivery vehicles is in fact one of the objectives of the La Rochelle scheme outlined above.

PROMOTING CONSOLIDATED FREIGHT MOVEMENTS IN URBAN AREAS

If significant numbers of commercial vehicles in urban areas are less than fully laden, then there are obvious environmental advantages in promoting greater load consolidation. Trans-shipment centres on the model discussed above are only one of several ways to promote such consolidation, however.

An obvious way to achieve consolidation would be to deliver larger loads to shops, but less frequently. Unfortunately this runs counter to the trend towards inventory reduction and just-in-time logistics, and would require a major change in outlook on the part of retailers. Significant increases in fuel prices or other elements of vehicle operating costs, or the imposition of road pricing in city centres, may lead eventually to a review of delivery frequencies.

Many retail chains in the United Kingdom, and especially food and clothing retailers, demonstrate a strong preference for dedicated distribution services, which are often contracted out to major logistics operators. In such circumstances, those contractors will frequently achieve full loads for their clients' retail outlets. If individual outlets do not warrant full loads, consolidation options must be investigated. In larger city centres, major retailers may have several shops, and consolidated deliveries then become feasible. In smaller towns, where the retailer probably has just one outlet, effective consolidation is much harder to achieve. One way forward may be for retail chains sharing the same ultimate ownership to develop common distribution systems. This practice is not widespread at the present time, however.

Many city centre premises require both collection and delivery services, and it is common for parcels and 'groupage' operators to call at the same premises twice in one day, typically to deliver packages and parcels in the morning and to collect in late afternoon. In principle such operators could achieve time-of-day consolidation, though this would require a significant change in working practices on the part of city centre businesses.

On mainland Europe, a wide variety of distribution systems can be found, but as a general rule shared-user distribution networks and supplier deliveries remain more common than dedicated distribution on the UK model. One development in Germany during the 1990s was the emergence of cooperation between companies involved in urban freight work. In a number of cities, companies signed agreements to divide work and revenue on a formula basis in order to avoid duplication and inefficiency (Bendel, 1996). A depot might be established specifically to handle collections and deliveries for the area concerned, perhaps with financial assistance from local government. Such schemes became known as 'city logistics'. They provide an interesting example of private sector cooperation to improve the efficiency and reduce the environmental problems associated with urban freight movements.

Research by Kohler and Straub (1997) into a 'city logistics' scheme in Kassel found that typical vehicle fill of the operators involved was raised from 40 per cent to 80 per cent (by volume) and from 25 per cent to 60 per cent (by weight) as a result of the programme of cooperation. An element of caution is necessary, however. In the Kassel example, environmental benefits were partly offset by an increase in the total costs of operation. Other examples, such as in Nuremberg (BESTUFS, 2002), have collapsed, either when a key partner has withdrawn from the scheme or when public funding has come to an end.

The German 'city logistics' model may well have potential application elsewhere, though it is not compatible with the prevailing UK model of dedicated retail distribution. Hence in the United Kingdom its successful adoption would depend on some change of attitude on the part of larger retailers, and also by the major logistics companies, to develop a willingness to cooperate where advantageous rather than simply to regard competition as the norm. The 'Joint Retail Logistics' partnership between Exel Logistics and Tibbett and Britten on behalf of Marks and Spencer in the United Kingdom may be a precursor of such cooperation.

BIGGER VEHICLES OR SMALLER VEHICLES FOR URBAN LOGISTICS WORK

Little progress has been made in establishing the optimum vehicle size for urban logistics operations, and this remains a research priority. The debate has centred on a simplistic picture of large vehicles versus much smaller vehicles. Environmental lobbyists frequently call for the use of much smaller vehicles in urban areas, and the common view of trans-shipment centres is that collection and delivery vehicles based at such sites should be relatively small. In the La Rochelle example quoted earlier, small (car-derivative) vans are used, dictated by the restricted access to the town centre.

Research undertaken at the University of Huddersfield however, suggests, that this approach may be over-generalized and too simplistic. The vehicle size issue is of course closely related to the issue of load consolidation discussed above. There are three separate constraints limiting the amount of consolidation that can be achieved on a collection and delivery round. The first two – weight and volume – relate to vehicle capacity. Hence larger vehicles allow more consolidation, and fewer commercial vehicles on city streets in total. The third constraint relates to the realistic amount of work that the driver can achieve in the time available. This may be quite limited, for example if there are significant amounts of handling, order picking or barrow work, or if time must be spent on paperwork or obtaining signatures for proof of delivery. Parcels and groupage operators may well suffer from such effects, and if their vehicles have significant spare space for much of the time, there may well be a case for the use of smaller vans. IT solutions such as electronic proof of delivery may mean that more calls per vehicle per day can be scheduled, allowing better capacity utilization of larger vehicles.

The economics of vehicle operation clearly point to the cost advantages of larger vehicles – assuming of course that they can be fully utilized. Tables of commercial vehicle operating costs show very significant economies of scale with respect to vehicle size, so that operators able to practise consolidation will find it cost-effective to use larger vehicles. The larger 17 tonne rigid vehicles are highly cost-effective compared with smaller vehicles, and so are the 'urban articulated' lorries used by many brewers, for example.

There are other factors in support of the case for relatively large vehicles in city centres. Much of the retail trade experiences significant seasonal variation, so that tailoring vehicle size to the average workload may not be appropriate. It can also be argued that the environmental pressure in favour of smaller vehicles is extrapolated from a relatively small number of high-profile examples of European cities (such as La Rochelle) that suffer badly from the impact of heavy lorries. Examples include cities with narrow streets hemmed in by fragile historic structures, and streets with weak underground cellars where weight restrictions are necessary. Such cases obviously call for special treatment, but there are probably relatively few towns and cities in this category, and few examples in the United Kingdom. It would be dangerous to generalize a case for the widespread adoption of smaller vehicles on this criterion alone.

One obstacle to the use of appropriately sized vehicles in urban areas is that few operators can justify dedicating vehicles to such work at present, because they undertake a variety of work across large areas. As a result, fleet mix is often a compromise across a range of requirements. Hence the link with transshipment centre solutions: such centres would require fleets dedicated to urban collection and delivery work which could be specified to suit local conditions.

VEHICLE TECHNOLOGY: ALTERNATIVE VEHICLE FUELS AND QUIETER VEHICLES

There seems little doubt that the use of environmentally friendly vehicles will increase, particularly if tax inducements for alternative fuels and for cleaner and quieter engines are stepped up, and if alternative fuels are made more readily available.

At present, technologies for alternative fuels and quieter operation are relatively new, and vehicles incorporating such technologies are comparatively rare. As a result, they are more expensive to buy. In the United Kingdom, the highly competitive nature of the transport and logistics industry may be holding back the introduction of such vehicles, given their high prices at present. Operators need to be reassured that lower fuel prices as a result of tax concessions will be maintained into the future, to allow payback on their capital outlay. Operators might be also be persuaded more easily to change fuels if there was more guidance available on which of the various alternative technologies (electric, gas, fuel cell, biomass, etc) are likely to become generally adopted in the future.

A UK example well publicized a few years ago is the use of natural gas powered vehicles by BOC Distribution Services (now part of Gist) on their dedicated contract to supply Marks and Spencer outlets in central London (*Distribution*, 1997).

There appears to have been more interest in environmentally friendly urban freight vehicles on mainland Europe than in the United Kingdom. Some Scandinavian and German cities have experimented with low noise and low emission vehicles, for example in Heidelberg. ELCIDIS, an EC THERMIE project, has established demonstration sites in three large European cities (Rotterdam, Stockholm and Milan) as well as three smaller cities (Erlangen and Stavanger in addition to the case of La Rochelle mentioned earlier) for the trialling of electric-powered distribution vehicles. Interest in the United Kingdom is likely to increase, however. Air quality is routinely monitored in UK cities, and in London, where air quality is the worst in the United Kingdom, the feasibility of a low emission zone is under investigation. While such a zone would not be implemented until 2005 at the earliest, such proposals will encourage operators to seek out and evaluate low emissions technologies.

Following on from the arguments set out in previous sections, it is more likely that operators will specify environmentally friendly vehicles if such vehicles can be dedicated to urban work.

INFORMATION SYSTEMS AND TRANSPORT TELEMATICS: URBAN LOGISTICS APPLICATIONS

There is massive scope to improve the efficiency of logistics operations through the greater use of information technology. Transport modelling work reported in Taniguchi *et al* (2001) has demonstrated that effective use of dynamic vehicle routing and scheduling systems can produce significant benefits in terms of both economy and the environment. In-cab information systems and mobile data systems allow operators to save time and money by advising drivers on how to avoid congestion. Electronic proof-of-delivery systems, as used increasingly by express parcels companies, can reduce the time parked outside customers' premises.

Information technology may also facilitate voluntary consolidation schemes. Operators willing to cooperate on the German 'city logistics' model could use real-time information systems to track consignments destined for the city centre, identify operators with spare capacity to handle such consignments, and route them accordingly. Electronic tagging and scanning of consignments facilitates traceability throughout the supply chain, which may allay shippers' fears over the loss of control at trans-shipment centres.

TIME-OF-DAY OR VEHICLE SIZE RESTRICTIONS IN URBAN AREAS

The number of vehicles delivering to city centre retail premises and the total number of retail deliveries per day are relatively low, certainly as a proportion of the total volume of private and public passenger traffic in most cities. As a result urban freight movements will not contribute significantly to city centre congestion if they are properly managed.

Many UK cities appear to have more restrictive time bans than their European counterparts. Very restrictive delivery time windows can lead to serious bunching of delivery vehicles immediately before and after restricted periods, possibly with queuing for access to premises, which can cause traffic congestion. Moreover, they may reduce the scope for load consolidation. They also reduce the likelihood that suitable vehicles will be dedicated to city centre work. There may therefore be a case for easing restrictions in some cases, allowing delivery over longer periods, but avoiding times of peak shopping activity and with the enforcement of low speed limits. Urban planners should ensure that adjacent city centre streets have the same access times. There are also advantages in coordinating restrictions in neighbouring towns, particularly in metropolitan areas, to assist operators in planning their delivery rounds across the area as a whole.

Analysis of vehicle size considerations set out in earlier sections suggests that relatively severe gross weight limits should also be avoided, except where local circumstances strongly dictate to the contrary. This will help achieve the benefits of greater load consolidation, and reduce the total number of commercial vehicle movements in the city centre.

To assist traffic flow at those times when deliveries are permitted, coordination of urban freight policy with other policies is important. Pedestrianization and traffic-calming schemes need careful design, for example. Severe restrictions on access, or obtrusive street architecture, will cause vehicles to obstruct each other while parked at premises. Narrow traffic lanes segregated from pedestrian areas by bollards also hinder delivery operations and lead to tailbacks during deliveries. It is also important to enforce existing parking regulations, to keep delivery bays free of parked cars, and to prevent disruption to deliveries through illegal car parking generally. These are typical issues raised by FQPs, as discussed later.

URBAN COLLECTION AND DELIVERY AT NIGHT

There has been very little research into the advantages and disadvantages of night-time operation, especially in urban environments. Cooper and Tweddle (1994) identify fleet size economies and a range of vehicle operating cost savings through night operation. Although their research was concerned primarily with trunking operations, they highlight significantly higher average speeds in central London during the night. They also raise various problems facing companies wishing to make deliveries at night. The first problem is that in an era of driver shortages it is increasingly difficult to find drivers willing to work at night. Labour costs are typically higher for night work, offsetting some of the cost savings. The second problem is that special arrangements must be made to accept goods at the destination. To these can be added a third disadvantage, in that some cities are trying to promote the city centre as a place to live. Noise from night-time deliveries may then become an issue. This assumes even greater relevance if delivery rounds cover suburban premises as well as the city centre. Quieter vehicles offer a partial solution, but handling equipment such as roll cages can also contribute to noise levels.

In some cities, environmental issues have led to the imposition of night-time lorry bans. Since 1985 London has been subject to a night-time (and weekend) lorry ban. Lorries above 18 tonnes gross weight are banned from non-trunk roads. Exemption permits are only available in the case of a demonstrated need to use restricted streets at controlled times.

Despite the various issues discussed above, night-time deliveries may well increase in significance in the future.

FREIGHT QUALITY PARTNERSHIPS IN THE UNITED KINGDOM

The 'freight quality partnership' (FQP) approach was launched by the Freight Transport Association (FTA) in 1996 and was tested in four UK urban areas: Aberdeen, Birmingham, Chester and Southampton (FTA, 1997). The approach brings together industry, local government and representatives of local and environmental interest groups to pursue the following agenda:

- To identify problems perceived by each interest group relating to the movement and delivery of goods in their city.
- To identify measures within the group's competence to resolve or alleviate such problems.
- To identify best practice measures and principles for action by local government and industry to promote environmentally sensitive, economic and efficient delivery of goods in towns and cities.

The UK government has been promoting FQPs since 1999 (DETR, 1999), and regards progress in establishing FQPs as a characteristic of a good LTP. One of the main advantages of FQPs is that they can facilitate improved dialogue about urban freight transport issues between local authorities, freight transport companies, retailers, manufacturers and other businesses, local residents and other interested parties. This can lead on to more efficient operations which cause less harm to the environment.

Approximately 50 UK local authorities have referred to the development of FQPs or similar schemes under a different name in their LTPs. It is apparent, however, that there are significant differences in how local authorities choose to define FQPs, and that some are merely at an embryonic stage. Among the 15 to 20 local authorities that have already put in place formal agreements and arrangements for FQPs are Surrey, where an FQP has been established in Guildford, and Kent, with an FQP in Canterbury. Problems identified by the Guildford FQP include poor road signage causing inefficient vehicle routing, and difficulties in lorry parking at the kerbside because of car parking infringements. These appear to be not atypical of issues raised by FQPs to date.

FQPs should help to ensure that freight transport receives the level of attention it deserves and that progress is made towards finding a suitable balance between economic and environmental pressures in UK urban areas. However, there are several unresolved issues concerning FQPs. It is hard to engage the involvement of more than a fraction of the number of all relevant companies. It is also unclear how compatibility can be ensured between policy making at the local, regional and national levels. It is important to ensure that FQPs cover a meaningful area – with metropolitan urban areas possibly being problematic in this respect. At the end of the day there is only a limited amount of public funding available for policy measures, initiatives and enforcement, and hence the need to maintain a realistic outlook as to what might be achievable.

CONCLUSIONS: THE PREFERENCE FOR ENCOURAGEMENT RATHER THAN ENFORCEMENT

In the course of this chapter it has become clear that there are no standard, easily applicable solutions to the problems of freight in urban areas, but the key is to identify policies that ensure safe vehicle operation in urban areas, promote economic vitality, and lead to environmental improvement. If operators specified their fleets carefully with their urban operations in mind, some of the inherent conflicts between cost-effectiveness of vehicle operation and protection of the urban environment could be reduced significantly.

A number of conclusions follow from the analysis set out in the sections above. The first is that strategies designed to increase load consolidation and/or less frequent retail deliveries could reduce the number of commercial vehicle rounds quite considerably. To achieve increased levels of consolidation, it may be necessary to allow the use of relatively large rigid lorries, or urban articulated vehicles, in town centre streets, and to avoid the use of very restrictive time bans on delivery operations. Such policy changes, if implemented successfully, would reduce the total number of commercial vehicle rounds, with relatively few countervailing effects, either on the efficiency of the operators or on the urban environment.

Another important conclusion is that the case for publicly organized trans-shipment facilities appears to be weak, and would only be justified in special local circumstances. They represent an extra link in the logistics chain, and as such are almost certain to add costs without adding value. Hence the sceptical view of such facilities in the logistics industry.

The case for cooperative ventures between private sector logistics operators, perhaps on the German 'city logistics' model, appears only a little more promising, as such initiatives do not appear to sustain themselves into the long term. Such cooperation seems unlikely to develop in the current competitive climate in the United Kingdom, which promotes dedicated retail logistics solutions.

The overall conclusion is therefore that more progress is likely to be made by encouraging private sector schemes to improve load consolidation than by enforcing public trans-shipment schemes. In the United Kingdom, the FQP approach appears to be achieving some success, at least in raising the level of dialogue between all the parties involved and in identifying the key issues and problems in each area under investigation. Whether the FQP approach can move well beyond the discussion stage towards achieving sustained progress in the implementation of economic and environmentally sustainable urban freight solutions remains to be seen.

REFERENCES

Bendel, H J (1996) City Logistics, *Logistics Europe*, (Feb) pp 16, 20, 23

BESTUFS (2002) BESTUFS Newsletter 8, (Jun–Jul), BESTUFS Administration Centre, Rijswijk

Cooper, J and Tweddle, G (1994) Distribution round the clock, in *Logistics and Distribution Planning*, 2nd edn, ed J Cooper, Kogan Page, London

DETR (1998) *A New Deal for Transport: Better for everyone*, Department of Environment, Transport and the Regions, London

DETR (1999) *Sustainable Distribution: A strategy*, Department of Environment, Transport and the Regions, London

Distribution (1997) M&S goes for gas, *Distribution*, **10** (5) (Oct), p 2

Freight Transport Association (1997) *Delivering the Goods: Best practice in urban distribution*, FTA, Tunbridge Wells

Kohler, U and Straub, S (1997) City-logistics concept for Kassel, in *Proceedings of 25th PTRC European Transport Forum: Seminar B – Freight*, pp 97–103, PTRC Education and Research Services, London

Ogden, K W (1992) *Urban Goods Movement: A guide to policy and planning*, Ashgate, Aldershot

Phillips, J (various dates) Cost tables, published quarterly in *Motor Transport* magazine

Tanja, P, Claus, M, Dunnewold, W and Vanderschuren, A (1995) *Urban Goods Transport: State of the art, description of measures and first assessment of selected measures*, Report produced by TNO Delft for EC Directorate General for Transport

Taniguchi E, Thompson R G, Yamada T and Van Duin, R (2001) *City Logistics: Network modelling and intelligent transport systems*, Pergamon/Elsevier Science, Kidlington, Oxford

Whiteing, A E and Edwards, S J F (1996) *Urban Freight Trans-Shipment Facilities: A European comparative study*, Paper presented at 28th Universities Transport Study Group Annual Conference, University of Huddersfield (Jan 1996)

FURTHER READING

Browne, M and Allen, J (1997) Strategies to reduce the use of energy by road freight transport in cities, in *Proceedings of 25th PTRC European Transport Forum: Seminar B – Freight*, pp 79–96, PTRC Education and Research Services, London

Department of the Environment (1994) *Vital and Viable Town Centres: Meeting the challenge*, DoE Planning Research Programme Report, HMSO, London

Distribution Business (1997) Peripheral transhipment centres loom larger as logisticians consider options for sustainable freight, *Distribution Business*, 6, p 7

Dunning, J (1997) Lorries in towns: could transhipment schemes really deliver the goods? *Local Transport Today*, 219 (28 Aug), pp 10–11

Whiteing, A E and Edwards, S J F (1997a) Goods deliveries in city centres: have we got the policy balance right? in *Proceedings of 25th PTRC European Transport Forum: Seminar B – Freight*, pp 67–76, PTRC Education and Research Services London

Whiteing, A E and Edwards, S J F (1997b) Towards a reappraisal of urban freight policies, in *Logistics Research Network 1997 Conference Proceedings*, Institute of Logistics, Corby

19

Global enterprise logistics: one tradition ends and another begins

Derek Gittoes and Larry Simcox
G-Log

INTRODUCTION

Traditions are often things we do until we know better. For instance, enterprises have traditionally evaluated the acquisition of business application software primarily as a function of return on investment (ROI). Certain assumptions were required for this model to provide a meaningful yardstick, and chief among those assumptions was the premise that the new system provided a more efficient means of addressing a current set of processes and activities. Moreover, and almost without exception, these replacement decisions focused exclusively on improving the efficiency of internal enterprise processes.

But the world has changed, and along with it, so have the fundamental notions upon which enterprises base their marketplace advantage. Now new business models – courtesy of the e-commerce revolution – are displacing traditional methods of transacting business. As a result, strategies that base competitive advantage solely on current intra-enterprise process excellence are at the very least under threat, with a likely fate of being relegated to the proverbial woodshed. Looking beyond traditions, one sees the intriguing concept of transforming internal processes, functions, and cost centres into competitive weapons or even profit centres. As an enterprise looks outwards into its value chain – defined as the trading partner ecosystem encompassing suppliers, partners and customers – is there an opportunity to leverage internal excellence into inter-enterprise competitive advantage?

Nowhere else in business are these issues of more relevance than in the world of logistics. E-commerce and global enterprise logistics (GEL) solutions are destroying traditional ways, and logistics is now emerging as an area that can deliver tremendous benefits. This chapter not only explores the impact of GEL systems from a traditional ROI perspective, but more importantly, we investigate the return on value (ROV) from these solutions. Rather than focusing purely on return as a function of cost, we consider the ROV from its impact on revenue, customer satisfaction and long-term competitive advantage.

To demonstrate the ROI and ROV dimensions of GEL, we analyse three case studies based on hypothetical corporations with logistics challenges and problems that are all too real. We discuss how you can analyse your business to uncover opportunities for value from a GEL solution. To get started, let's first discuss GEL in more detail.

GLOBAL ENTERPRISE LOGISTICS

Global enterprise logistics redefines the traditional model of supply chain management. GEL encompasses all material movements across the value chain, from raw materials to finished goods. And now, thanks in large part to the advent of the Internet as a flexible and robust medium of collaboration and process execution, GEL strategies may be conceived and executed for immediate and sustainable competitive advantage. The complete GEL footprint includes:

- indirect (non-manufacturing) materials procurement;
- direct materials procurement;
- global inbound (cross-border);
- domestic inbound;
- intra-enterprise (example: production site to warehouse);
- finished goods;
- domestic outbound;
- global outbound (cross-border).

GEL solutions enable an enormous reduction in safety stocks for global companies.

Enterprises implementing GEL solutions today have recognized that the traditional view of logistics management as a cost centre is too limiting, and in fact places them in a disadvantageous position in relation to the competition. Also, limiting their logistics strategy to domestic outbound (customer-centric) finished goods movements is short-sighted. The real value, and hence sustainable competitive advantage, will be found in attacking the entire value chain from supplier to customer holistically.

As Figure 19.1 shows, logistics can have a far wider reaching and profound impact when viewed from ROV and inter-enterprise perspectives. GEL solutions are of the utmost importance as companies face and overcome the global logistics issues that are now confronting them.

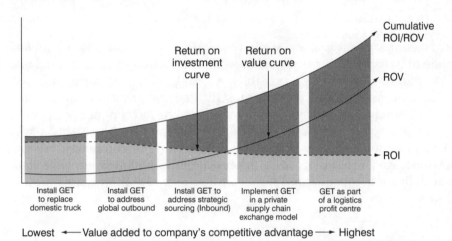

Figure 19.1 ROI and ROV from global enterprise transportation (GET)

GLOBAL LOGISTICS: CURRENT ISSUES

There are three major business forces at work that are driving the need to change the way logistics processes operate today: e-commerce, globalization and customer expectations.

- *E-commerce:* a primary factor propelling the forces of increased globalization and increased customer expectations. The Internet and related technologies are dramatically changing the ways in which companies transact all aspects of business with their suppliers and customers.
- *Globalization:* corporations continue to internationalize their production, supplier and customer bases to exploit opportunities for revenue growth and cost reduction.
- *Customer expectations:* the Internet drives everyone's expectation of a satisfactory customer service experience. Consumer and corporate buyers demand more choices, accurate and faster fulfilment, and greater value from reliable suppliers.

These market forces are placing new demands on a corporation's logistics capabilities, and those companies without the ability to adapt to this changing environment will be left behind. Corporations with lacklustre and dated logistics processes will not be able to capitalize on the revenue and profit opportunities offered via e-commerce and globalization. Success requires a GEL solution. The rewards generated from GEL are many, including the following.

Reduce costs

Logistics operations that are segmented – domestic versus international, by mode of transportation, or by business division – should be combined into a GEL platform whenever possible. A single GEL platform eliminates redundant systems and procedures. GEL reduces transportation costs by pooling purchasing power, consolidating freight movements, selecting the right rate, mode, route and service provider, and by decreasing partner communication expenses. This type of process and technology change is obviously easier said than done. Success requires a phased implementation that delivers a consolidated GEL solution at a rate the organization can absorb.

Take control

Corporations can take control of logistics processes, even when they are managed by external service providers. The key to control and more effective decision making is information visibility. Information visibility stems from collaboration and streamlined communications with external logistics partners. Control translates into reduced variability and improved customer service reliability. Studies show that the variability in transportation lead times in a supply chain have a tremendous impact on inventory pipeline and safety stock costs – even more so than variability in customer demand.

New business models

Logistics can be a 'money maker'. Effective logistics capabilities, people, systems and procedures, are very valuable assets. An increasing number of corporations are transforming their logistics departments from cost centres to profit centres by selling their services to other companies. Another opportunity lies in e-commerce marketplaces. Dominant participants in specific industry supply chains are establishing private marketplaces to improve the operations of the entire supply chain. These marketplaces can be stand-alone businesses that provide value-added services, such as logistics, to the marketplace participants.

Increase revenues and profits

E-commerce initiatives and globalization represent a vast opportunity for revenue growth via marketplace expansion on a domestic and international basis. Most corporations do not have the logistics processes in place to effectively and efficiently scale to meet this demand. Logistics is a key determinant of overall customer satisfaction and profitability growth. Unsatisfactory fulfilment experiences provide motivation for customers to take their business and your profits elsewhere.

The time to act is now. Change will not come easy or overnight. Forward-looking companies who recognize the opportunities enabled by world-class global logistics capabilities have already started down paths of process and technology change that will enable them to gain or maintain market-leading positions in the years to come. In the following sections we turn our attention to three very different companies, each with its own set of challenges and problems. In spite of their differences, these organizations share a common opportunity to cultivate tremendous ROI and ROV from their GEL solutions.

CASE STUDIES

Global enterprise logistics solutions generate substantial ROI and ROV across a diverse set of industries: high-tech, manufacturing, automotive, consumer packaged goods, retail and chemical, to name just a few. To demonstrate the potential of GEL solutions, we examine three representative companies:

- a packaging and container manufacturer;
- a high-tech semiconductor manufacturer;
- an industrial equipment manufacturer.

Case 1: a packaging and container manufacturer (PCM Corp)

Industry: packaging and containers
Revenue: US $2 billion

Overview of operations

Consider PCM Corp, a manufacturer of packaging and container products with multiple business divisions, each producing a highly differentiated set of products for a broad base of customers.

Geographically, PCM Corp operates several production facilities throughout North America. Customers are located primarily in North America, with the remainder in Europe. Suppliers are located in North America and Asia.

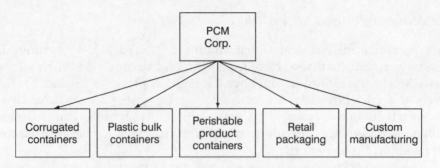

Figure 19.2   Business divisions of PCM Corp

PCM has an internal logistics unit, which manages all of the outbound distribution for all business divisions. In addition, the logistics unit manages some inbound raw materials for the different business divisions, and it has recently started to provide outsourced logistics services to other manufacturers with similar supply chains.

The distribution network is composed of several internally operated warehouses for storage of finished goods, along with a mix of internally and externally operated cross-docks and pools for consolidation, merge in-transit, light assembly, inspection and packaging services. The cost of transport is US $90 million a year.

Opportunities for improvement

The primary problem with PCM's current logistics is the vast amount of manual and labour-intensive intervention required throughout the logistics life cycle. As a result, these ineffective processes are error prone and cannot get any efficiencies of scale by increasing shipping volumes. Part of the problem lies with the company's technology, where the legacy transportation management system is centred around domestic trucks, and lacks the functionality required to manage efficiently the complexities of the company's overall logistics operations. Moreover, in-transit inventory visibility is almost non-existent, which translates into to having most service exception processes starting when the customer calls in with a late delivery – in other words, when it is too late to fix the problem.

A summary of current logistics problems includes the following:

- Manual processes.
- Independent planning across business divisions.
- Cannot get high-volume shipping.
- Legacy technology and logistics systems.
- No in-transit inventory visibility.
- Customers are in the United States and Europe, while suppliers are located in North America and in Asia.

A GEL solution to these problems would deliver many hard and soft benefits to PCM Corp (shown in Figure 19.3). Let us examine a few of these.

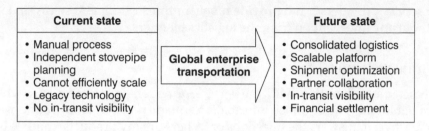

Current state		Future state
• Manual process • Independent stovepipe planning • Cannot efficiently scale • Legacy technology • No in-transit visibility	**Global enterprise transportation**	• Consolidated logistics • Scalable platform • Shipment optimization • Partner collaboration • In-transit visibility • Financial settlement

Figure 19.3 Opportunities for improvement at PCM Corp

Consolidated logistics processes

The various logistic processes should be consolidated onto a single technology platform that enables them to be managed via one system. For example, international and domestic logistics, inbound and outbound, and the various modes should be managed within one logistics system. Consolidating the disparate logistics processes reduces administration and information technology (IT) overhead, while enabling opportunities for transportation costs savings through crossover consolidation and volume-leveraged rate negotiations. Savings through automation more than compensate for any increases in headcount required to manage more logistics transactions.

Scalable platform

Growing the logistics unit's external customer business in a profitable manner is impossible with the current processes. A modern technology platform would facilitate growth in customers, orders and users without loss in performance, thereby keeping the cost of adding incremental business to a minimum.

Shipment optimization

Optimizing the shipments on a dynamic basis in real time would enable the logistics unit to maximize the benefits from the distribution network. For example, orders could be dynamically routed through a cross-dock or distribution pool for consolidation opportunities. Currently this type of complex planning scenario is accomplished through the vigilance and experience of the planners, which results in missed cost savings.

Service provider collaboration

Today, a lot of time and effort is spent communicating with service providers by phone and fax. This paper-based, labour-intensive process could be completely eliminated with a 'self-serve' tendering process where carriers would have instant visibility to their shipments over the Internet. Likewise, the service providers could provide timely in-transit shipment status updates without any intervention from the logistics planners.

In-transit visibility

Enhanced collaboration with the service providers is the means by which invaluable real-time in-transit information is made possible. From a customer's perspective, it answers the questions of 'Where are my products?' and 'When are they going to arrive?' without the need for a PCM customer service representative (CSR) to make a lot of phone calls. From the planner's perspective, in-transit information is the lifeblood of a logistics 'early warning system' that can detect and recover from potential service failure situations. This type of visibility would eliminate the current embarrassment of having a customer call in about a late delivery, and the logistics planner not knowing what happened.

Financial settlement

The current process for paying service providers and billing customers is a mixed outsourced and manual solution. This process could be replaced completely by a freight payment and customer billing management system that would be much more efficient and accurate, which would eliminate costly errors and speed up cash flow.

A summary of the ROI/ROV results include the following (see also Figure 19.4):

- lower inbound and outbound costs;
- increased labour efficiencies;
- in-transit inventory visibility;
- establish outsourced services business unit;
- provided partner collaboration.

Case 2: a high-tech semiconductor manufacturer (HTSM Inc)

Industry: high-tech semiconductors
Revenue: US $2 billion

Overview of operations

For our second case study we will look at HTSM Inc, a semiconductor manufacturer. This analysis will focus on GEL and its impact on order fulfilment cycle time, on-time delivery performance, and inventory management.

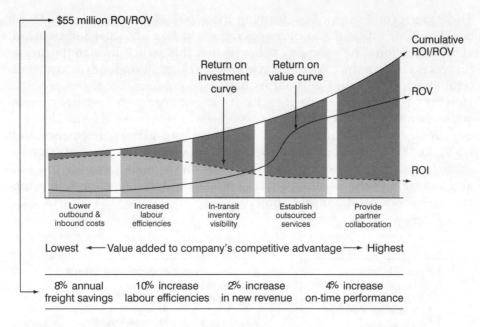

Figure 19.4 ROI/ROV impact on PCM Corp

HTSM has production facilities located in Asia, sourced from multiple fabrication vendors also located throughout Asia. The current manufacturing process is to make to stock, and consists of assembly, testing and packaging. The distribution network is composed of internally operated distribution facilities located in Asia, which deliver products to customers around the world. The company is currently utilizing a 'push' manufacturing process, and is in the process of implementing a 'pull' manufacturing process.

Opportunities for improvement

The primary problems with HTSM's current logistics processes are how to deal with short product lifecycles, high product value, long order fulfilment cycle times and inaccurate demand synchronization. Customers in this industry demand a 10-day order fulfilment cycle time. HTSM's results prior to implementing a GEL solution included a 56-day average order fulfilment cycle time, 90 per cent on-time performance, and US $1,500,000 investment in finished goods inventory. A summary of current problems at HTSM includes:

- loss of business;
- short product lifecycle;
- high product value;
- long order lead time (industry expects 10-day order delivery cycle time);
- excessive inventory obsolescence.

There are several ways of overcoming these (see Figure 19.5). First, HTSM could reinforce its make-to-order operations to take advantage of demand synchronization. The company believed that this switch in manufacturing processes would reduce its order cycle time and keep its on-time performance level above 90 per cent without its having to change its logistics process. However, HTSM soon realized that if it did not change its logistics process while changing the manufacturing processes, its results would include a 10-day average order fulfilment cycle time, 50 per cent on-time performance, and US $1,500,000 investment in finished goods inventory. Such unsatisfactory reliability is typical for companies that focus on the manufacturing process, and lose sight of the resulting logistics process and its impact on fulfilment, customer service and transportation cost.

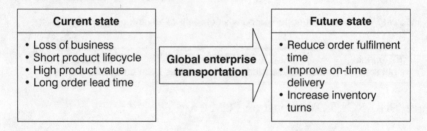

Figure 19.5 Opportunities for improvement at HTSM Inc

A second step for HTSM was to decide how it could leverage its manufacturing improvements by linking them with its logistics processes. The company needed to determine at order entry when the customer needed the product. Since HTSM did not have capital to invest in new distribution centres that were located closer to its customers, the company decided to utilize local third-party distributors. Its fear in outsourcing was that it would lose control and visibility of its pipeline inventory. If this happened, HTSM would not know when or how to ship its products to its customers.

HTSM required a solution that could set 'available to promise' expectations at the point of order entry. Certain customers could expect delivery directly from the manufacturing plant, which could take up to one week. This option typically allows customers to purchase products at a lower cost based on flexible delivery. Alternatively, for customers needing delivery within a 24-hour window, the product would be allocated from a local distributor. HTSM was now able to deliver to the customer's expectations, while at the same time reducing the order fulfilment cycle time, improving on-time delivery performance, and dramatically reducing finished goods inventory levels.

The benefits achieved by linking a make-to-order process with a GEL solution include the following (see also Figure 19.6):

● four-day average order fulfilment time (93 per cent reduction);

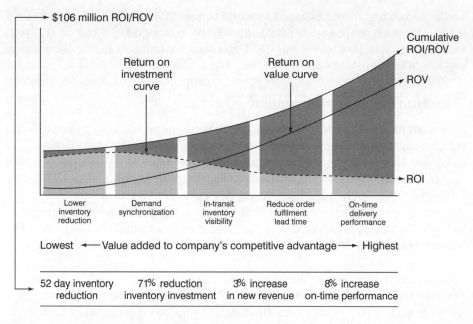

Figure 19.6 ROI/ROV impact on HTSM Inc

- 97 per cent on-time delivery performance (8 per cent improvement);
- US $440,000 inventory investment (71 per cent reduction).

Case 3: an industrial equipment manufacturer (IEM Inc)

Industry: industrial equipment
Revenue: US $11 billion

Overview of operations

IEM Inc is a global manufacturer and distributor of industrial equipment – engines, pumps, compressors and components – serving such diverse markets as agriculture, aerospace, mining, forestry and construction. Over 15 independent business divisions comprise IEM Inc, and as a whole the company generates annual revenues of US $11 billion, with US $220 million in annual freight expenditures.

IEM operates globally, with manufacturing facilities in the United States, Canada, Mexico, Argentina, the United Kingdom, France, Poland, South Africa, Indonesia, Singapore and Australia. Thousands of suppliers and customers span the globe. IEM acts as both an original equipment manufacturer (OEM) and a supplier to other OEMs. Across its divisions, IEM utilizes all modes of transportation – air, truck, rail and ocean – with shipment sizes varying from less than a pound to several tonnes. The inbound and outbound logistics functions have traditionally been managed by the individual business divisions. Over time, IEM has sought to consolidate its various logistics functions.

Opportunities for improvement

As part of its global procurement effort, IEM has been working to consolidate purchasing and logistics functions across its business divisions. To date, the company has been successful in placing 25 per cent of its inbound supply logistics functions under the auspices of its corporate logistics unit (CLU). The CLU manages such functions as carrier contract negotiations, shipment planning, and coordinating activities with carriers, third-party logistics providers and freight forwarders. The goal is to accommodate 100 per cent of inbound logistics within the CLU, and eventually all of the outbound logistics as well.

Moreover, the manufacturer seeks to establish a private marketplace for its tier-one and tier-two suppliers. The marketplace's purpose is to increase the performance of the supply chain through improved information sharing, collaboration and shared services. For example, a tier-two supplier could access shipment optimization functions from the marketplace, and utilize carriers with rates negotiated on behalf of IEM Inc.

A summary of current problems in IEM includes the following:

- limited order lead times;
- lack of integration with ERP systems;
- manual and independent processes;
- poor inbound and outbound supply chain visibility;
- no shipment optimization.

To overcome these, the CLU needs a GEL platform that will enable it to achieve its goals (see Figure 19.7). The current logistics processes and technologies are not up to the task. Let us explore some of the current obstacles and improvement opportunities from a world-class GEL solution.

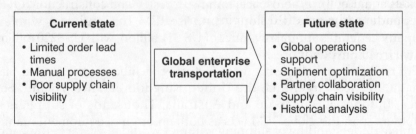

Figure 19.7 Opportunities for improvement at IEM Inc

Global operations support

To achieve its global logistics management goals, the CLU needs a system that can support a network of users around the world. To that end, the system needs to support multiple weights, measures, currencies and languages. A single system would replace the multiple systems now in place, thereby reducing IT maintenance overhead.

Shipment optimization

The current transportation system cannot optimize orders that require multi-leg multi-mode solutions. Nor can the system manage all of the manufacturers' contracts and rates across its vast network of service providers. Potentially large cost savings stem from improved routing, consolidation, equipment and carrier selection. Examples are consolidating air or ocean shipments from multiple suppliers to multiple production sites into full container loads, and avoiding expensive expedited services when cheaper alternatives exist that provide the necessary level of service.

Partner collaboration

Integration is a major obstacle. In today's world, the majority of communications with the transportation service providers are manual. For example, shipment status updates to support the track-and-trace system are largely accomplished through periodic phone calls to the carriers. Much of the time and expense associated with these manual processes could be eliminated via electronic and Internet links with the service providers. CLU staff would only need to intervene when an expected shipment update was not provided by the carrier in the expected time-frame.

Supply chain visibility

Currently, the CLU has limited visibility into the sales and manufacturing processes of the business units that it supports. Integration with these systems would provide greater lead times for shipment and resource planning, and improved data quality for ship-by and deliver-by dates. Improved lead times and data quality would have a substantial impact in reducing transportation costs, particularly expedited shipping costs.

Historical analysis

The CLU currently utilizes a number of information systems to manage its operations. As a result, there is no robust centralized repository of historical information to support strategic decision making. For example, a more complete understanding of shipping volumes would make for better contract rate negotiations and distribution network decisions.

Using these approaches, IEM improved performance (see Figure 19.8) with:

- consolidated purchasing and logistics;
- increased labour efficiencies and lower IT expenses;
- establishing a private marketplace;
- improved partner collaboration.

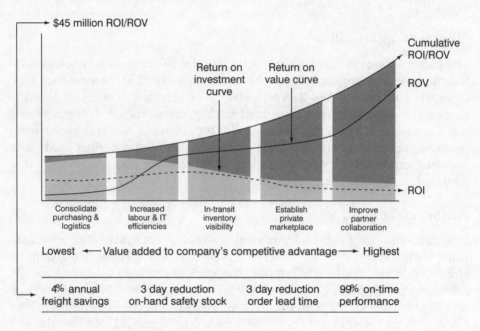

Figure 19.8 ROI/ROV impact on IEM Inc

UNCOVERING VALUE WITHIN YOUR LOGISTICS ORGANIZATION

Let us now turn our attention to how GEL solutions can be of value to a business. Traditionally in the world of logistics, transportation management system (TMS) projects have been based on an ROI business case. Moreover, the scope of TMS business cases has usually been limited to domestic outbound cost reduction. New business opportunities are shifting these projects from a standard ROI perspective to a focus that also emphasizes ROV.

Transportation management systems

There are several reasons why we want to look at ROV in addition to ROI. First, TMS evolved at a time when many companies' efforts were focused on improving internal enterprise systems. Second, transportation has long been viewed as a non-value-added necessity and not a strategic business process – this has now changed dramatically. Furthermore, TMS solutions were oriented towards a single mode of transportation (mostly domestic trucking); they performed a single optimization on a batch of orders, tendered those orders out to carriers and then 'forgot' about them. The value proposition was to achieve a small percentage savings in total transportation costs by consolidating smaller shipments into larger shipments. We are now in the era of the global economy of competing supply chains, where the objectives are completely different.

Improved business processes produce conflicting objectives

Business objectives today are centred on total supply chain performance, and driven by the implementation of new just-in-time (JIT) and assemble-to-order (ATO) business processes. These new processes have led to business objectives that include reduced inventory, shortened order/delivery cycle time, and improved customer service. Safety stock is fast becoming a thing of the past, while at the same time companies are striving to deliver faster and improve customer satisfaction. Older TMS platforms were not able to deliver the breakthroughs in customer service that were needed with these new business processes, thus there has been no dramatic decrease in safety stock. The new business objectives have led to the realization that the real opportunity in logistics is not found in simply lowering transportation costs, or enabling visibility into order status, but rather in being able to extend supply chain planning, execution and optimization across time and inventory in motion.

The automation of existing and creation of new business processes enable dramatic ROV in the following areas:

- enhancements in time and motion efficiencies;
- inventory in motion, which is the ability to react proactively to changes in demand during order execution;
- taking control of global supply/sourcing initiatives to include directing freight forwarders;
- savings associated with improved optimization capabilities using multi-leg, multi-mode, multi-geography freight movement beyond traditional domestic outbound consolidations.

Time and motion

In order to uncover the return on value associated with time and motion it is necessary to be able to determine quantifiably the time it takes to perform logistics transactions. The easiest way to determine the amount of time spent routing, rating and tendering a shipment is to look at the number of hours it takes to completely process x number of shipments. We will call this performance metric the hour per shipment ratio. Once the number of shipments that are performed in an hour has been determined, it is possible to determine the number of full-time employees needed to process all the existing freight volume.

An automated GEL solution will enable profitable freight volume growth without the necessity of adding employees in a directly proportional manner. The more automated the logistics process becomes, the more efficiently the business can grow. Cost-effective scalability is of vital importance in an era of increasing global growth via expansion and acquisition.

Inventory in motion

Managing bidirectional inventory propagation – the two-way flow of inbound and outbound inventory in motion – is of vital importance for overall supply chain performance. GEL solutions enable enterprises to view their inbound and outbound inventory pipelines to determine the optimal location to source or fulfil an order. New business processes are forcing logistics professionals to take a hard look at reducing order and delivery cycle times, without increasing safety stock or negatively impacting customer service levels. Numerous studies have been written on the impact that accurate delivery cycle times, both inbound and outbound, have on reducing safety stock which otherwise would have been carried due to delivery uncertainty. These studies have found that an increase in delivery cycle time certainty of one day would reduce the need of safety stock by at least one day. Over time, this will equate to an enormous reduction in on-hand safety stock for global companies. Efficient logistics networks for such operations as merge in transit, cross-docking, and multi-stop/multi-pick-up all lead to reduced delivery cycle time uncertainty.

In order to determine the return on value of a one-day reduction in safety stock it is necessary first to look at delivery cycle times. The uncertainty of inbound delivery cycle times from suppliers or manufacturing locations should be compared with the on-hand safety stock. The amount of safety stock held on hand is a direct result of not having faith in delivery cycle times. Customers can do the same for the outbound process. Any additional increase in delivery certainty leads to an equal reduction in safety stock.

Taking control

This value analysis section focuses on the ability to take control of logistics information so it can be provided collaboratively with trading partners: customers, suppliers, carriers and so on. The ROV stems from increased customer service by offering self-serve logistics information to those customers that need it. GEL solutions provide instant proactive alerts to all parties in the supply chain. GEL platforms ensure that only meaningful alerts are generated, by first determining if a given event has a material effect on a downstream process. No one wants to be the bearer of bad news if the problem can be corrected without impacting downstream business processes.

The key to control and more effective decision making is information visibility.

Taking control also extends to tackling inbound supplier and sourcing operations. There are many costs and opportunities associated with inbound transportation processes. When an inbound logistics process is examined, it will probably prove to consist of myriad individuals and organizations: freight forwarders, consolidators, carriers and brokers, all using multiple modes of transportation across multiple country boundaries. Many forward-thinking corporations see the value of taking control of their inbound processes. One opportunity exists with freight forwarders. If they are allowed to control the consolidation process they may bill for each bill of lading that is generated. They then consolidate shipments based on their own cost and service requirements. If an enterprise is able to consolidate its shipments for its freight forwarder it will only be billed for the one shipment. This type of savings could easily add up to hundreds of thousands of dollars.

Improved optimization capabilities

Shipment optimization is an analytic process that takes as input information business rules and objectives, and translates these into recommendations that enable the organization to make better logistics decisions. Optimization decisions take many forms:

- How to route orders from origin to destination.
- Which modes to use.
- Equipment loading configurations.
- Which service providers.
- Consolidation opportunities.
- Hold versus expedite.
- Where and when to sacrifice cost for service and vice versa.

GEL optimization engines provide robust solutions to these questions by planning shipments across business divisions, countries, routes and modes simultaneously to deliver the best service consistently at the lowest possible cost. Shipment optimization can deliver savings in a number of ways. Consider the following examples:

- *Outbound pool distribution.* Instead of less-than-truckload (LTL) shipments being sent direct from origin to destination, an intermediate point is used to consolidate shipments in a full truckload (TL) prior to local delivery. For example, 20 by 2,000 lb LTL shipments into New Jersey, Delaware, and Pennsylvania can be consolidated into a single 40,000 TL shipment to Philadelphia followed by 20 'local' LTL shipments. The cost savings by doing this can be 10–50 per cent.

- *Inbound container consolidation.* Consider a situation where buyers in independent departments are sourcing from suppliers in Asia. Separately, the shipments are not enough to fill an entire ocean container, but when combined, they enable the company to book an entire container at a discounted rate.

- *Expedited transportation.* A distributor's default method for servicing expedited shipments has been to utilize airfreight services. Significant cost savings could be realized by optimizing over multiple modes by opportunistically employing truck-based services, especially when shipping over the weekends.

CONCLUSION

Traditions die hard – but they die just the same. As a result of the business forces of e-commerce, globalization and customer expectations, logistics is being transformed from an activity with a pure cost minimization focus, to one where value maximization wins the day. To reflect the new ground rules, systems are now evaluated with a return on value (ROV) model that encompasses revenue growth and customer satisfaction, displacing the traditional approaches that focus only on short-term cost reductions. As businesses look to sustain and grow competitive advantage into the future via inter-enterprise logistics process excellence, global enterprise logistics (GEL) solutions have been propelled to the forefront.

As our analysis has demonstrated, regardless of industry, GEL solutions deliver ROV for an organization by leveraging existing capabilities and enabling new ones.

20

The changing supply of logistics services in the UK

Colin Bamford
University of Huddersfield

INTRODUCTION

In the relatively short time since the publication of the first edition of this book in 1988, the organization and nature of the market for logistics services have undergone substantial change. In that first edition, the late James Cooper (1988) started the text with the positive statement that 'the UK distribution industry is in a state of rapid change, a condition that seems likely to continue for some time to come'. How true this prediction has been; moreover, the extent of change has in many respects been remarkable, due to the internal and external dynamics of the market. For example:

- The overall market has continued to grow, broadly in line with the ups and downs of the annual changes in Gross Domestic Product (GDP).
- The value and share of the third-party logistics (3PL) sector has consistently grown within the market, with fourth-party logistics (4PL, the assembly and integration of 3PL capabilities) coming to fruition.
- Structural changes in ownership have intensified, with logistics now matching the oligopolistic market structure of most of its customers.
- The globalization of supply chains and the emergence of real rather than theoretical pan-European networks have produced new market opportunities for the UK's major players and niche market operators.

- The UK market has remained highly competitive, between domestic providers and the growing number of non-UK operators that have penetrated this market.

In short, the scale of change has produced an outcome whereby the logistics market in 2002 has very few of the underpinning characteristics of that first analysed by Cooper in 1988.

UK MARKET TRENDS

Table 20.1 shows that the overall market, in terms of goods moved, experienced steady growth to 1998, followed by overall stability thereafter. To some extent this is in line with the state of the economy; the stable market since 1998 is most likely because of ongoing deindustrialization and efficiency improvements in the ways in which vehicles are used. Significantly, that in the hands of 'mainly public haulage' operators, which includes 3PL contractors, now accounts for over three-quarters of the total market. Some of this growth has been at the expense of the 'mainly own account' sector, which has been more static at a time of modest yet real overall market growth. The success of specialist contractors, identified by Cooper in 1988, has been a key factor in this market growth. Companies such as Exel, the Tibbett and Britten Group, Christian Salvesen and Hays Logistics UK are now not just powerful logistics operators, they are major players in the EU economy.

Table 20.1 Freight transport by road: goods moved in vehicles over 3.5 tonnes, 1991–2001 (billion tonne-kilometres)

Year	Mainly public haulage	Mainly own account	Total	% public haulage
1991	85.8	38.8	124.6	68.9
1992	86.4	34.9	121.3	71.2
1993	93.2	35.4	128.6	72.5
1994	100.8	37.2	138	73.0
1995	106.5	32.7	139.2	76.5
1996	109.1	37.7	146.8	74.3
1997	112.2	37.4	149.6	75.0
1998	114.3	37.6	151.9	75.2
1999	110.9	38.3	149.2	74.3
2000	113	37.5	150.5	75.1
2001	114.7	34.7	149.4	76.8

Source: adapted from DoT (2002)

The basic arguments in favour of businesses using a 3PL contractor are well documented and have stood the test of time (see eg Buck, 1988; Institute of Logistics, 1994). Publications from the former Institute of Logistics have increased awareness of how to get value for money from such contracts from a buyer's perspective (Institute of Logistics, 2000). As 3PL operators, companies are able to offer a full supply chain management service to their clients. This involves not only the traditional services of transport and warehouse management but also the assembly and management of stock and the full integration of IT systems support. Most of the major players are strong in the retail sector. The market, though, is becoming increasingly segmented: automotive parts, home deliveries and food services are important growth areas, for example. The biggest companies are involved in primary as well as secondary distribution, and temperature-controlled as well as ambient distribution. A sign of maturity in the market is that niche operators are well established in drinks, dairy products, fuel oil, pallet and express parcels distribution.

The annual round of contracts being awarded remains extensive. Whether service levels are being met has always been a crucial factor in determining the outcome of the renegotiation of an existing contract when this is up for renewal. In an increasingly competitive market, this has become more critical along with other so-called 'hard' issues such as cost, systems and shared user support. Industrial opinion remains divided over whether these issues or 'soft' ones like cultural fit, management quality and strength of partnership are more important in determining just who does what and for whom.

Certain parts of the UK market appear saturated in terms of the potential for future growth for 3PL operators. The retail and FMGC areas especially seem to have relatively modest further real growth potential compared with (say) chemicals, electronics, brewing, pharmaceuticals and former public sector services such as health care and postal services.

Finally in this section, reference must be made to the growing importance of the 4PL, or fourth-party logistics provider. The role of the 4PL is that 'it is outside the organization and has the task of assembling and integrating capabilities from other third parties to achieve logistical efficiency' (Bumstead and Cannons, 2002). At a time of economic downturn, as evidenced since 2000, the value of the 4PL has become even greater, as businesses seek to take costs from their supply chains.

The key function of any 4PL is as an architect or integrator, and through this it makes sure that its client is provided with the vision that is necessary for continuous innovation and improvement in supply chain performance. This hierarchical role, involving total supply chain management provision, clearly requires there to be a sincere partnership between client and provider. This strategic role is arguably best provided by a specialist consultancy.

The term 4PL, when first used, was never intended to be a cover for the work of the lead contractor or the third-party operator managing a particular site. Even so, some of the large 3PLs now see themselves as 4PLs, usually through ensuring that much of the supply chain management function for a client manifests itself in appropriate contract work for themselves, with some token work for other businesses.

MARKET STRUCTURE: A RECENT OLIGOPOLY

An oligopoly is the term used by economists to describe a market structure that contains only a few competing firms (Chrystal and Lipsey, 1997: 247–76). Consequently, the level of industrial concentration is high when measured by the market share of say the top five companies. Activities such as brewing, grocery retailing, vehicle production, certain types of food processing and pharmaceuticals are examples of markets that have been oligopolistic for a good number of years. Logistics has very rapidly and very recently joined them.

An alternative form of oligopoly is one where in addition to a few large firms, there are a large number of small firms making up the rest of the market. This type of market structure, it could be argued, is also evidenced in logistics, where small niche market firms can still compete with those that are fighting it out for the multi-million pound contracts that become available.

In theory, oligopolies have other characteristics such as:

- strong inter-firm rivalry that prevents any business considering its demand curve to be its own;
- interdependence in the decision-making process; for example, if one firm cuts its prices the others are obliged to follow;
- branded products, with a strong brand image that is perceived by customers;
- collusion between companies, usually with the objective of squeezing a rival out of the market;
- a market leader is usually in evidence.

Table 20.2 shows the current market leaders, ranked on the basis of their turnover in 2001. Accurate data on the extent of their contract operations is not available. For some, such as Wincanton, virtually all of the turnover shown will have been derived from 3PL activities. For others, such as Ryder, that have other transport-related interests, the information could be misleading, since the number of vehicles also takes into account their vehicle hire activities.

As Table 20.2 indicates, Exel is the clear market leader; it has been renamed following the merger of Exel Logistics and MSAS Global Logistics in 2000. Exel has an estimated turnover three times greater than its nearest rival, the Tibbett and Britten Group. This former state-owned business has maintained its lead position since privatization 20 years ago. A major restructuring

Table 20.2 Specialist 3PLs: the market leaders in 2001

Company	Overall turnover (£'m)	Employees	No of vehicles in UK	Warehouse capacity ('000ft²)
Exel	4,500	60,000	11,000 (TT)	n.a
Tibbett and Britten Group	1,406	32,200	11,000 (TT)	4850
P&O Trans European	1,045	8,600	9,000 (TT)	950
Hays Logistics UK	893	15,300	750	395
Christian Salvesen	835	15,200	4400 (TT)	n.a
Wincanton	746	16,600	3900	8500
TDG	530	8,600	1600	1000
TNT Logistics UK	500	6,500	2500	700
Securicor Omega Logistics	339	12,400	800	1500
DFDS Logistics	283	1,850	300	550
Ryder	235	4,500	13,000	770
Gist	231	3,100	530	25 units

Note: TT refers to tractor units and trailers

Sources: *Motor Transport* (2002), *Distribution* (2002), various company Web sites.

occurred in the late 1990s, with parts of the NFC operation being sold off to allow the company to concentrate on its 3PL activities. This is the company by which others are benchmarked and comparative performance is measured. The presence of this powerful business is entirely consistent with the oligopolistic market structure.

The 'rising star' over the 1990s has undoubtedly been the Tibbett and Britten Group. Total turnover from its worldwide operations is now £1.4 billion, compared with just £150 million in 1990. Its growth has been both organic and through the acquisition of businesses such as Lowfield, Silcox and Tolman, which were in segments where Tibbett and Britten were relatively weak. Its purchase of Applied Distribution in 1997 has given the company a strong foothold in intermodal operations through its ownership of the Daventry International and Doncaster rail freight terminals. In recent years the company has also expanded worldwide, and it now has a presence in North America, South East Asia and Central Europe.

TDG, second to the NFC plc for much of the 1980s, may have slipped in the hierarchy but has recently had a major restructuring to reposition itself as a specialist in the FMCG, retail and chemical sectors. To achieve this it has sold off its contract hire, plant hire and other businesses, as these did not fit within its revised corporate strategy.

Wincanton, unlike its main business rivals in the top 10, has made it very clear to customers that it will continue to focus its activities on the domestic market. From its original base of milk and dairy products, the company has experienced substantial market growth in recent years through providing 3PL services in grocery product, chilled and fuel distribution.

By way of contrast, Christian Salvesen has also taken a strategic decision to concentrate resources on its supply chain management activities, but across the rest of the EU. It distributes a wide range of consumer and manufactured goods through dedicated and multi-user distribution networks.

The firms not shown in Table 20.2 had turnovers of £200 million or below in 2001, with most being well below £50 million per annum. Although substantial companies in their own right, many have found it necessary to specialize in particular niche markets in order to compete with the largest players.

An outcome of the oligopolistic market structure is that the largest contracts on offer, from retailers especially, will be awarded to one of the market leaders. In 2001, for example:

- B&Q awarded a new contract to Tibbett and Britten for the storage and distribution of its products to 80 stores in southeast England.
- Comet signed a major new contract with Wincanton for the storage and distribution of white and brown goods.
- Sainsbury gave new contracts to Exel, Wincanton, Ryder, and Tibbett and Britten.
- Tesco awarded massive new contracts to Christian Salvesen, Tibbett and Britten, and Wincanton.

Realistically, major operators such as the above and others shown in Table 20.2 are best placed to have the financial resources as well as the expertise to be able to fund multi-million pound contracts.

A final, though very limited, piece of evidence of oligopolistic structure is the way in which firms form alliances or partnerships to win a major contract. The Exel/Tibbett and Britten bid to win a lucrative Marks and Spencer contract in summer 1999 is a good example of how businesses may be expected to behave in the future in what will undoubtedly be an increasingly fiercely competitive marketplace for 3PL services.

'EUROPE SANS FRONTIERS': NEW MARKET OPPORTUNITIES AND THREATS

On the evidence of the last section, one might legitimately conclude that UK logistics contractors have a very strong hold over the domestic market and that they have little to fear from operators in the rest of the EU. This conclusion might well be substantiated from the work of Cooper, Browne and Peters (1994: 126) and the Institute of Grocery Distribution (2000). The former undertook research to determine comparative logistics efficiencies in major European countries and the United States. Their results showed that the

Netherlands (with a score of 2.7) was the most efficient logistics provider in Europe, with the United Kingdom in second place (with a score of 1.8). Spain, France and Germany lagged behind. The IGD went further by concluding that for retailing, the UK contract distribution sector was now widely recognized as the most developed and efficient in the EU.

The acceleration in pace of economic integration in Europe has given UK 3PL operators little cause for complacency, though. The UK market has been penetrated by new suppliers from the rest of the EU; at the same time, UK firms have themselves found new business opportunities in the market, as will be shown later. All in all, it has brought a new dimension to what was already a fiercely competitive market.

It is beyond the scope of this chapter to go into the processes of economic integration in detail (for details see Bamford, 2000: 194–221). Very briefly, the two most significant factors have been, first, the completion of the Single European Market (SEM) from 1 January 1993. This has removed many non-tariff barriers to free trade, which had remained with the European Community (EC). As the Cecchini Report (1988) clearly stated, their removal gave a tremendous boost (between 2.5 per cent and 6.5 per cent) to GDP within the EC, and enhanced the global competitiveness of EC firms relative to their rivals in the United States, Japan and the rest of Southeast Asia.

The second factor is the realization of Economic and Monetary Union (EMU) from 1 January 2002 by 12 of the 15 EU member states. Central to EMU has been the introduction of a single currency, the euro, which has reduced business transaction costs and brought price transparency. The removal of exchange rate risk and the stabilization of interest rates are additional factors that affect business well-being. Although eligible to join, the United Kingdom has opted for the time being to 'wait and see', a decision which has had little support from many areas of industry, no doubt very mindful of the fact that EMU eliminates many obstacles to cross-border direct investment in the EU.

The logistics function, the free flow of goods especially, is central to the concept of the SEM. Prior to 1986, very little progress had been made towards the realization of a Common Transport Policy, despite its explicit inclusion in the articles of the Treaty of Rome (see Gwilliam, 1994). In the negotiations to achieve an SEM, liberalization and harmonization were key objectives.

The basis of liberalization is the removal of unduly restrictive regulations, which had limited entry into markets for freight transport and distribution operators. In other words, there should be a truly single market for all EU-based companies. A major stumbling block to its realization has been the issue of cabotage, the picking up and setting down of goods in one country by a vehicle registered in another member state. Significantly, from 1 July 1998, full cabotage has finally come into being, allowing any holder of an EU authorization to operate road freight services without any quantitative restriction (see Croners, 1997 for full details).

Harmonization has been less successful. This involves the removal of distortions to competition between transport and distribution companies in different EU Member States. In popular terms, it can be seen as establishing a 'level playing field' through states having the same rates of taxation on fuel and vehicles, the same weight limits and a common operator licensing system. With full harmonization, logistics firms across the EU would be competing with each other on a fair basis. So far, particularly from the stand-point of factors directly affecting operating costs, harmonization is a long way from being achieved.

Notwithstanding, the realization of the SEM has unquestionably brought new market opportunities for international freight transport and distribution movements across Member States. Customers now have a wider choice of provider to satisfy their needs. No longer are clients in one Member State restricted to using a domestic operator. It is also easier to set up new 'green-field' logistics sites within the EU. Significantly also, there are genuine business opportunities for an operator in one Member State to purchase a company based in another. Market conditions are now very favourable for the effective realization of an international market for logistics services in the EU.

Peters and Jackel (1998) have carried out an extensive study of the European third-party logistics market. Drawing upon market research by Market Line Inc in 1996, they show that of all EU markets, the United Kingdom is the most highly developed. Contract logistics has a 34 per cent share compared with an average penetration of 24 per cent throughout the EU as a whole. Germany has the largest overall potential market; it has a relatively low current contract penetration of 23 per cent. The countries of southern Europe and Austria have the lowest per cent contract shares, largely because they have a weaker manufacturing base than their north European counterparts. The overall market is very extensive, and set to grow in the future by as much as 10 per cent per annum. The obvious conclusion to be drawn from this is that UK operators should be well placed to transfer their expertise to other EU markets, yet equally, the established market in the United Kingdom provides relevant opportunities for third-party operators from other Member States.

The impending geographical enlargement of the EU, to include countries such as Poland, the Czech Republic, Slovakia, Hungary and Estonia, has also presented market opportunities for EU operators, including many UK businesses. The risks and uncertainties of committing resources in these markets are much greater than in dealing with the core EU market. Some operators have followed their established clients such as retailers and manufacturers, yet in other cases they have sought to gain a foothold into a potentially huge market through private purchases and partnerships.

UK LOGISTICS COMPANIES IN THE REST OF EUROPE

The years prior to the realization of the SEM provided UK 3PL companies with the opportunity to make an early entry into the European market, either through direct acquisition or through setting up new operations. On the surface, it seemed very appropriate for them to gain experience of other European markets prior to 1993 so that they could be in a strong position to make the most of the SEM when the time came.

Some major UK operators (eg Exel Logistics and TDG) did this with mixed results. Others (eg Tibbett and Britten, and Wincanton) quite deliberately held back and used the time to develop their own positions in the domestic market. In the late 1980s and early 1990s, some unsuitable companies were put up for sale, and purchasers were often willing to pay premium prices to gain a market foothold. A big question mark was whether customers in one particular Member State would be willing to purchase logistics services from a company based elsewhere.

By 1998, as Peters and Jackel stated, 'there are clear signs that concentration is occurring in Europe's logistics industry... geographical scope and service offered by providers is being extended' (Peters and Jackel, 2002). Table 20.3 shows in broad terms how the major UK operators have penetrated the market in the rest of the EU and, increasingly, the global market.

Table 20.3 Stated network opportunities

	Pan-European	Global
Exel	✓	✓
Tibbett and Britten Group	✓	✗
P&O Trans European	✓	✓
Hays Logistics UK	✓	✗
Christian Salvesen	✓	✓
Wincanton	✗	✗
TDG	✓	✗
TNT Logistics UK	✓	✓
Securicor Omega Logistics	✓	✗
DFDS Logistics	✓	✓
Ryder	✓	✓
GIST	✓	✓

Source: *Distribution* (2002)

Over the last decade, some of the largest UK 3PL operators have made substantial market penetration into the rest of the EU (see Table 20.4). As certain sectors of their UK market approach saturation (including retailing), there are clear opportunities for a skill transfer in order to generate further business.

Although the risks are considerably less than they were, even the largest and most experienced firms have made mistakes (Meczes, 2002: 24). A common mistake that was made, in retrospect, was that UK operators felt that they could do in the rest of the EU what they do in the United Kingdom. The problem with this approach is that supply chains operate in a different way and 3PL operators have different roles in the other EU Member States. Cultural variations in management style and worker relations have also posed problems for some companies. Penetrating the French and German markets in particular has posed many problems for UK companies. Based on their early experience, companies are now in a much stronger position to make the most of new market opportunities.

Of those companies shown in Table 20.2, Exel, P&O Trans European, Tibbett and Britten, Gist and Hays have also moved into Eastern Europe, either by acquiring companies or via partners. As in the EU, there are potential clients in the many Western European retail companies and manufacturers who have bought into this market and who are looking for effective logistics solutions to help them establish themselves in a new, emerging and potentially lucrative market.

Table 20.4 UK logistics providers in other European markets

Christian Salvesen	Now a leading European provider in France, Germany, the Netherlands, Belgium, Italy, Spain and Portugal. Recognized strengths in IT systems and overall supply chain management.
Exel	Merger in 2000 with MSAS has created a world-class provider of supply chain management solutions for manufacturing and retail clients. Virtually full European market penetration.
P&O Trans European	As its name indicates, the company has considerable presence in the EU, Hungary, Poland and the Czech Republic. It provides an extensive range of operational and supply chain management services.
Tibbett and Britten Group	Remarkable growth record in recent years. Now clearly established in the EU and in Central and Eastern Europe, Hungary especially. Provides full range of international supply chain management services.
TDG	An early entrant into other European markets, now well established in the MCG and bulk chemicals sectors.

OTHER EUROPEAN LOGISTICS OPERATORS IN THE UNITED KINGDOM

Logistics operators in most of the rest of Europe tend to be smaller than their UK counterparts. Peters and Jackel (1998), in their analysis of the top 29 pan-European contract logistics companies, include nine UK operators in their corporate listing. France has five companies and Germany four in this analysis. The German operators especially all have European turnover broadly comparable with Exel (Logistics) and Tibbett and Britten, the UK's two major players.

From a reciprocal standpoint the transition towards and reality of the SEM has provided the demand-side stimulus that other European logistics operators needed to establish themselves in the UK market, although a few had a very limited presence before 1986. Table 20.5 shows the main companies now operating in the UK.

Table 20.5   Other European logistics operators in the United Kingdom, 2001

Company	Parent/ owner origin	UK turnover (£m)	Estimated % growth since 1998
CAT – UK Services	France	70	46
Culina Logistics	Germany	36	n/a
DFDS Logistics	Denmark	283	19
Frans Maas (UK)	Netherlands	112	12
Gefco UK	France	93	33
Hellmann Worldwide Logistics	Germany	62	n/a
Hoyer UK	Germany	98	n/a
Kuehne & Nagel	Switzerland	175	n/a
Nippon Express (UK)	Japan	118	n/a
Norbert Dentressangle UK	France	45	n/a
UCI Logistics	Japan	65	

Sources: *Distribution* (2002), company Web sites

Various points of perspective can be made, particularly when comparing Table 20.5 with Table 20.2. These are:

- Apart from DFDS Logistics, Frans Maas, and Kuehne & Nagel, all of which have long-established operations in the UK, the UK turnover of the companies shown in Table 20.5 is relatively modest. Broadly speaking, in these terms, they compare in size with the next tier of UK operators too small to be included in Table 20.2.
- French and German-owned operators are the most numerous; CAT-UK and Gefco specialize in the distribution of vehicles and automotive parts for their respective customers.

- Many of the companies listed in Table 20.5 provide a variety of services, although most are seeking to establish themselves in the lucrative 3PL market.

The development of the 3PL market in many other EU countries continues to lag behind the United Kingdom. This has presented a major obstacle to many companies seeking to establish themselves in the UK market. It must also be recognized that UK customers are understandably reluctant to use a contractor whose performance credentials are not widely known in the domestic market.

The effects of the removal of cabotage restrictions cannot be understated, particularly when set alongside the controversial issue of comparative fuel prices between the United Kingdom and its near neighbours, France and Belgium. 'Flagging out' has received much attention in the trade press, as indeed has the seemingly unfair practice of German hauliers employing cheap labour from outside the EU. All in all, it can be argued with justification that the other EU 3PL operators have an immediate cost advantage to help their entry into the UK market. An alternative scenario is that an efficient and innovative UK 3PL sector is able to provide the expertise and systems that are needed to give UK companies in the rest of the EU a distinct competitive advantage. They would not have had this if they had continued to manage their supply chains in a pre-1999 way.

CONCLUSIONS

Demand-side influences through the realization of the SEM and EMU have created a market environment that is very conducive towards the continuing development of third party logistics services in the United Kingdom. At the same time, the UK domestic market seems set to continue to grow in the future, and there remain considerable opportunities for new business development.

Supply-side structures are now clearly in place to meet these challenges. UK businesses have made substantial progress towards establishing themselves in the rest of the EU. In turn other European operators now have a share of the UK market. The process of corporate acquisitions and partnerships, across national boundaries, will continue in the future as companies seek to add value to the supply chains of their clients.

REFERENCES

Bamford, C G (ed) (2000) *Economics*, Cambridge University Press, Cambridge

Buck D (1988) Changing to contract distribution, in *The UK Distribution Industry: Logistics and distribution planning*, ed J Cooper, pp 180–91, Kogan Page, London

Bumstead, J and Cannons, K (2002) From 4PL to managed supply chain operations, *Logistics and Transport Focus,* **4** (4) (May)

Cecchini P (1988) *The European Challenge 1992,* Wildewood House

Chrystal, K A and Lipsey, R G (1997) *Economics for Business and Management,* Oxford University Press, Oxford

Cooper J (ed) (1988) *The UK Distribution Industry: Logistics and distribution planning,* Kogan Page, London

Cooper J, Browne, M and Peters, M (1994) *European Logistics,* 2nd edn, Blackwell, Oxford

Croners (1997) *Road Transport Operations* (May), Croners, Kingston upon Thames

Distribution (2002) Business reports, *Distribution,* **15** (2) (Apr)

DoT (2002) *Transport Statistics Great Britain 2002,* The Stationery Office, London

Gwilliam, K M (1994) *The Economics of the European Community,* ed A El-Agra, Philip Allen

Institute of Grocery Distribution (2000) *Retail Distribution,* IGC, Letchmore Heath, Watford, Herts

Institute of Logistics (1994) *Making the Right Choice: A guide to distribution solutions,* IOL, Corby, Northants

Meczes R (2002) Taking over Europe: a growth opportunity? *Distribution,* **15** (3) (Jun)

Motor Transport (2002) Top 100 companies, *Motor Transport* (11 Jul) [Online] http://www.reedbusiness.co.uk

Peters, M and Jackel, O (1998) The day of the mega-carrier, *Logistics Europe,* **20** (June), p 24

Walters P J (1994) *In or Out: The contract distribution dilemma,* Distribution Dynamics

21

Global strategy

David Hatherall
Hatherall Associates

INTRODUCTION

Many organizations – both large and small – are examining every area of their business as they adapt to the rapidly changing environment. Some of the most dramatic changes are to the supply chain. Keeping a flow of goods moving through the supply chain, at the lowest cost, with the highest quality and in a highly complex and changing environment, requires management of the highest calibre. Organizations need to develop strategies and people who can cope with such periods of rapid change, and who are willing to adapt to new conditions.

Let us start by defining a supply chain. In my view, it is all the activities of an organization that ensure customers receive what they want. These activities are primarily purchasing, production, planning, physical distribution, transport, materials management, sales, forecasting and order processing. Some of these, particularly production and sales, are often viewed as disciplines in their own right – but an integrated logistics system needs good understanding and effective communication between each part. With the rapid changes taking place in the field of logistics, it seems that organizations are finally looking at their overall supply chain rather than at its individual components – and are also giving purchasing the attention it deserves.

REQUIREMENTS FOR INTEGRATION

My experience in the chemical and pharmaceutical industries leads me to believe that we must be flexible, adaptable and multiskilled to meet the future needs of our business – particularly as we are competing in an increasingly global market. There is intense competition in the marketplace for technical products and services, and it is essential to establish strategic alliances with selected suppliers. The aim is to develop a network of communications locally, regionally, nationally and internationally, to ensure that we maximize our buying power and benefit both our own business and that of our suppliers. Developing this network has implications for business structure – and what seems like an alliance or partnership can quickly develop into a merger or take-over.

But the aim is to look at the network that defines the whole supply chain, and take advantage of synergies. Then we can develop the correct structure for the organization – with some functions being centralized and others decentralized; some units offering services to our own organizations and others restructured to provide services to other businesses. Central to these issues is the need for businesses to recognize the need for change. International competition is intense, and operations move at an ever-faster pace. What used to take months now takes weeks; what used to take weeks now takes days, and what took days now takes hours. We have to consider the implications of such rapid changes on employees, who must be flexible and able to adapt. They must have the training and resources to develop the skills needed to adapt to businesses' changing requirements. This is particularly important when working internationally, when they may suddenly have to face the issues of different cultures, organizational structures, European monetary union, currency fluctuations, market changes and changing legislation for transport and packaging. They must clearly recognize that what happens in one part of the world has an impact on all other countries. This needs different approaches and methods in different regions. Operational blindfolds must be removed and mutual understanding encouraged.

Wherever we work, we must use all available management tools to make sure that our organizations are effective. These tools include basic analyses like ABC, value added, price performance, portfolio and gap, as well as more sophisticated approaches. We should be consistent and use best practices and skills across the whole supply chain. Perhaps the best starting point to look for change is to review our current activities to see how we can meet future demands. This review will look at contingency planning, business reorientation, cultures and language, and concentrate on how our actions will affect customers – both internal and external.

Overall, we need to consider the following issues for the global materials management network:

- the structure of the materials management network;
- clearly defined roles for each centre;

- growth of centres of excellence;
- integration mechanisms designed around businesses' specific needs;
- knowledge of the requirements of other businesses;
- dissemination of information about the services we provide;
- a comprehensive performance tracking system;
- a sophisticated information technology infrastructure;
- consistent use of best practices;
- transfer of skills across the whole materials management network;
- clear development paths and career paths for staff.

These instruments must be used sensibly, and in a way that will allow us to achieve our business objectives.

PREPARING TO INTEGRATE THE SUPPLY CHAIN

Materials managers, purchasing managers, logistics managers and all those involved in the logistics chain must prepare for the future, and in particular must understand the total cost involved in the chain. Titles do not matter, but support at senior level is a key factor for success; teamwork is crucial if the changes are to succeed, as is the active involvement of the coach/manager or mentor. Then the needs of the supply chain, and the fulfilment of these needs, must be addressed. All staff must prepare and plan for the future by looking at the roles of managers, the organization and service.

Managers

They must:

- understand the business intimately by having managed more than one function;
- clearly communicate the mission, objectives and actions of the organization;
- manage the supply chain effectively;
- develop team building, motivation and leadership;
- work and be flexible in situations of novelty, ambiguity and uncertainty;
- encourage employees to be ready for change;
- have a portfolio of skills including:
  - developed individual career plans,
  - an appreciation of all relevant problems faced by the organization;
  - encouragement of personal development,
  - the ability to see a broader global and societal perspective,
  - a second language,
  - information technology skills.

Organizations

In a broader sense, the whole organization should:

- behave in ways that support the policies and objectives it wishes others to adopt;
- support the whole value chain, in line with the organization's infrastructure;
- create objectives and realistic prospects that give managers a challenging role and fulfil their potential;
- implement strategy and policy;
- use central policies for giving direction, continuous improvement and strategies for key item and supplier relationships;
- develop a 'P' model for continuous improvement – with the right blend of central strategies and local execution that minimizes bureaucracy.

The 'P' model for continuous improvement has:

- *Power:* to be used effectively in the organization.
- *People:* who must communicate, be involved, enabled and developed.
- *Process:* to find the best practice.
- *Place:* which asks if the chain is in the right place.
- *Purchasing:* to maximize buying power.
- *Positioning:* which asks where we are in our market.
- *Potential:* which is used for the short-, medium- and long-term plans, measures and performance.
- *Political:* both internal and external.
- *Product:* to market and promote our unique selling points.
- *Profile:* to build and maintain for each country and location.
- *Price:* with costs as the key.
- *Problem:* to solve, and take responsibility for decision making.

Service

This is a measure of success – the vision for the future.

INTERNATIONAL PARTNERSHIPS

How can we manage these areas when looking at international partnerships? One of the key concepts – and engines for change – is efficient customer response (ECR), which applies just-in-time (JIT) principles to the whole supply chain. But without careful implementation JIT might come to mean just-in-trouble, -traffic, -transit or some other problem which needs to be overcome by effective management. It is clear from my experience that, despite the huge body of literature concerning JIT, many people do not practise or understand the concept in full. It relies on effective partnership – and this means effective management, effective communication and continuous improvement. But this does not mean a shift in power from one part of the supply chain to another, as all parts must work together from initial sourcing to final marketing.

The supply chain can be viewed as comprising different elements – including tasks, individuals, organizational structure, and both informal and formal data. Each element must relate to the others, and the way they do this forms the patterns of communication, power, influence, values and norms that are characteristics of the supply chain. To introduce changes in the management of the chain, we have to look at organizational culture and beliefs, and encourage relevant changes in thinking and approach. Communication and teamwork are vital in this. However, to make changes, we also have to examine our requirements in the context of a much wider network. Although the best approach delegates decision making to the lowest possible level, such changes are difficult, and we must have the courage to stand out and apply the best techniques available.

Some other key issues for international operations include:

- price transparency and stability within the eurozone;
- wider currency values and fluctuations;
- terms and conditions of trade – internationally and within the European Union;
- dual pricing, supply and marketing;
- environmental issues, including waste and packaging;
- customers and partnerships;
- available information technology;
- business transformations of various kinds;
- scenario, change and other analyses.

In responding to these issues an organization must:

- use global best practices – taking a wider perspective and changing organizational culture;
- emphasize time – to speed communications and optimize the flow of goods through the supply chain;
- encourage free trade;
- positively make change happen.

The aim should be to break down any barriers between functions and parts of the supply chain, particularly avoiding departmentalized views and job protection. Global best practices need a united view, with everyone in the same team. Then global cooperation should be established, so that the organization looks outwards and not inwards – and with understanding and respect of different cultures.

CONTINUOUS IMPROVEMENT

Whatever changes are made, existing customers and long-term competitiveness must be maintained. This means that the supply chain must keep its traditional objective of providing a continuous flow of materials, with acceptable costs. However, this is not easy, especially with many companies struggling to cope with the speed of change, and having to produce ever-higher outputs with slimmer and smaller organizations.

Without proper coordination, things can go badly wrong in the supply chain, resulting in higher costs and worse service. So companies in a fiercely competitive market are forced continually to review and reorganize the resources in their supply chain, as they try to increase competitiveness and profitability. They can start this by asking some basic questions:

- What are our traditional methods?
- Can these be improved?
- What is the market structure – and how much influence do we have?
- How are our finances?
- How are our cycle times, lead times and service levels?
- What information is available and what can be exchanged?
- What are our working conditions like?
- What is our organizational culture?
- Are any legislative or other changes likely in the future?

Whatever the current answers to such questions, they are likely to change in the future – so organizations must make continuous improvements to compete. Figure 21.1 shows a general model for continuous improvement of the supply chain.

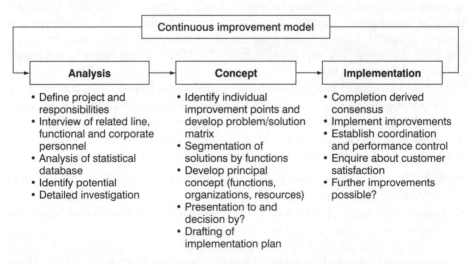

Figure 21.1 Continuous supply chain improvement model

CULTURAL DIFFERENCES

Working internationally shows the range of cultural differences – even between closely related countries. It is generally felt that German workers are highly skilled and responsible, and do not necessarily need a manager to motivate them; they expect their boss to assign tasks and to be the expert in resolving technical problems. American workers are more familiar with managers who emphasize motivation. Experience in this area – particularly with mergers and joint ventures between organizations – demonstrates a definite change in style and approach between, say, Swiss, French and other European countries.

However, there are many similarities. Managers may be very well organized and extremely structured, but some are reluctant to change. When there has been a steady improvement in performance, it is especially difficult to accept the need for change. But when this is accepted, the ensuing approach should be relaxed and take easy steps towards progress. This is rather like the difference between the Chinese and Japanese approaches, and it will be interesting to see how these develop in the future.

The process of communicating change is more difficult than it seems. Changing one area of the organization – for example in customer services – will affect another area, so it is important to concentrate on the needs of customers. It is important to recognize both external and internal driving forces for change, to emphasize the role of strategic planning, and to redefine tasks. The political dynamics must be so shaped that organizations benefit from a highly developed supply chain management – irrespective of whether it belongs to European, American or Asian cultures.

One important issue that comes with international operations is the amount of centralization and decentralization needed, which largely depends on the size of the organization. The problem with decentralization is that the volume of activities may fall below a critical level. Although it is flexible to needs, it lowers the amount of coordination across countries and has little authority. It is important that the best level of centralization is found so that no leverage is lost.

Another point is that purchasing and supply staff have to take into account the implications of legislative changes both locally and globally – as well as the rate of change. At the same time, they must keep a grip on the basic concepts of purchasing and supply, which really have not changed in many areas.

It is possible to define six different attitudes towards change:

- *Negative.* Do nothing, wait and see if problems will go away. This negative approach may be short term.
- *Defensive.* Conduct preliminary research to identify threats and hope that the present position can be maintained.
- *Active.* Undertake research and planning to deal with likely scenarios. If we are dealing with internal customers as well as external customers, there should be sufficient knowledge of the marketplace.

- *Strategic.* Develop coherent and dynamic responses to all aspects of management systems. Challenge the thinking and ensure best practices are upheld. Act on the 'P' model previously discussed.
- *Creative.* Think ahead, and develop ideas about all possible scenarios.
- *Positive.* Make it happen! Communicate, involve and manage the team.

BALANCING PRICE, QUALITY AND SERVICE

It is very important that local arrangements dovetail with global agreements, the implications of which obviously have a worldwide impact. It is not in anyone's interest for global agreements to be used to negotiate separate agreements locally, even in a country with fairly wide price variations. If comparisons of products and specifications show that a lower price can be offered, this must be taken up with the people negotiating the global agreements, otherwise it does not lead to fairness and it also raises questions about ethics. Most organizations still treat their data, terms and conditions as being confidential, and they should be treated as such by local operations, but at the same time they should not embarrass the global operations. However, if there are inconsistencies and variations these might lead to adjustments to the approved list of global suppliers.

An obvious feature of local operations is that they try to provide a local focus and indicate that they are doing a better job than would be offered by a global player. This is particularly noticeable in countries that give preference to domestic products, which seems to be a part of human nature. Unless there is satisfactory team work, globalization will not work.

CONCLUSIONS

Businesses are changing very rapidly, particularly in their approach to supply chain management. They need managers of the highest calibre to deal with – and exploit – these changes.

Improved performance comes from integration and cooperation. Global operations, linked with a sound knowledge of markets and competitive analysis, are essential for sustainable long-term success. This chapter has looked at the implications of this integration in the supply chain, and has described how skilled managers must embrace change, and use all available business skills and resources.

In aiming to be competitive in a changing environment, people must be enabled for change. Effective leadership and good communication are key success factors. Opportunities must be exploited and all skills employed for the full benefit of the organization.

Concentrating on the basics of logistics is essential, while customers expect to have:

- products matching specifications;
- at the right price and agreed quality;
- in the right quantity;
- delivered on time;
- with appropriate certification/documentation;
- and with the ability to solve any problems effectively and efficiently.

Indeed, these customer needs must be met if an organization is to succeed.

The level of centralization is interesting, and European managers tend to be more centrally based than global managers. The infrastructure should be provided to enable operations to continue efficiently through differences in organization and culture.

In conclusion, organizations must concentrate on flexibility, added value and customer benefits. Skilled teams must manage the entire supply chain. This needs partnerships that work, and that ensure continuously improving operations, service levels and profitability for all businesses.

22

Developments in Western European logistics strategies

Michael Browne and Julian Allen
University of Westminster

INTRODUCTION

Several political initiatives have taken place during the last decade that have had major implications for logistics services throughout Western Europe:

- On 1 January 1993, border controls and customs arrangements within the EU were lifted following the creation of the Single European Market (SEM) under the Treaty of Maastricht.
- On 1 January 1995, Austria, Finland and Sweden joined the European Union (EU), increasing the number of Member States to 15.
- On 1 January 1999, the euro was launched as an electronic currency and it became legal tender on 1 January 2002. It has been implemented in 12 of the 15 EU Member States (Austria, Belgium, Finland, France, Germany Greece, Italy, Ireland, Luxembourg, the Netherlands, Portugal and Spain).

Central to the logic of creating the European Union free from unnecessary trading restrictions has been the desire to encourage the development of European companies able to compete on a global basis. It is often claimed that fragmented national economies within Europe have resulted in too many small companies in certain key industrial sectors. Dismantling barriers to trade and opening up new market opportunities allow companies to grow and become more competitive. Inevitably this is also likely to result in the relocation of certain economic activities, as some companies become larger and others fail. The collapse of communism in the former Soviet Union and the countries of Central and Eastern Europe, and the subsequent reorientation of these countries towards the free market have also opened up new avenues of trade which extend beyond the borders of the EU.

This chapter addresses the ways in which company business strategies and manufacturing and retailing operations have been developing within Europe during this time of political, economic and geographical change, and the effect that this is having on the demand for logistics services. The extent to which logistics providers have been meeting these needs is also discussed. These developments, and the similarities and differences in suitable logistics strategies for different European countries, are illustrated by reference to the European grocery industry. The impacts of these emerging logistics services on freight transport patterns and activity levels within Europe are discussed, together with the policy initiatives and responses being generated at the national and European levels. Finally, future European logistics strategies are considered, and the question of whether logistics service providers are able to match their customers' requirements is examined.

CHANGES IN THE DEMAND FOR LOGISTICS SERVICES

An enlarged and more integrated Europe has influenced the demand for logistics services. Indeed, markets for goods and services in Europe have become much less fragmented over the past 10 years, and at the same time, for many companies, there has been a discernible shift away from a mainly national approach to a more unified European strategy. In general, companies increasingly regard the EU as their home market, rather than restrict their trading horizons to a single country. This in turn has important implications for logistics services. For example, increased trade between Member States creates new demands for logistics services such as transport and warehousing. However, the transition to a European pattern of operation has not been as smooth as many commentators expected, and in some cases the benefits have been slow to emerge.

Market developments and retailer/manufacturer strategies

Increasing market integration enables large companies to pursue a number of strategies designed to take advantage of their size. The scope to concentrate production at a small number of carefully selected locations is one that has a special importance within Europe. Until recently the strategy followed by many companies was based on production for separate national markets. The requirement to produce product variants for different markets, the complexity of border crossing formalities and the added costs of international trade transactions led, typically, to a rather fragmented approach to production. Although for many companies the changes in strategy have been part of a broader response to growing global opportunities and increased international competition, the abolition of border controls and the simplification of trading procedures have undoubtedly encouraged plant and warehouse rationalization.

Since the business ambitions of many companies are not confined to the existing EU, the scope for inventory rationalization has grown as Europe becomes more commercially integrated. Dismantling trade barriers has allowed firms to reduce the number of warehouses within their logistics systems, which in turn has important longer-term implications for transport patterns. Instead of looking at Europe on a country by county basis, firms have been able to consider more natural market demand patterns and adapt their warehousing accordingly.

Significantly, these developments are not confined to the EU: many firms have already adopted a very wide definition of Europe in developing their logistics strategies. For example, Bosch-Siemens (manufacturers of domestic appliances with a head office in Munich) took its first steps in cross-market distribution by rationalizing its Scandinavian warehousing operations and consolidating stocks for Finland, Norway and Sweden in one regional centre located between Stockholm and Malmö, distributing to other Scandinavian countries from that single location (O'Laughlin, Cooper and Cabocel, 1993). There are many examples of this type of initiative as companies have changed their traditional views about the best way to serve markets. The sports equipment firm Nike has adopted a completely centralized strategy for storage within its European supply chain, despite increasing diversity of sourcing and continued demands for fast response to customer requirements (Kemp, 1997). Geest, the prepared food company, announced plans to consolidate production in 2001, with dressed salads being produced at one rather than two sites (European Logistics Management, 2001a). The French food group Danone also announced a restructuring plan for its biscuit production business in 2001, in which six of its 36 factories in Europe would be closed, with production levels increasing at the remaining factories (European Logistics Management, 2001b). The trend to centralization has taken a firm hold on management thinking, and there are still many companies seeking further opportunities to reduce the number of stockholding points. Whether these initiatives can be justified against a background of pressure to develop more sustainable logistics strategies remains to be seen.

Many large companies now take a supply chain view when considering new ways to, first, integrate their own operations, and second, seek to extend this integration to their supply chain partners. Growing integration has profound implications for the role of external service providers, since in many cases the physical flow of materials is one of the first areas of change when a supply chain view becomes more clearly developed. When companies start the process of considering the supply chain as a whole, it often becomes evident that there is scope to rationalize the number of service providers, in much the same way as it may become possible to reduce the number of stock-holding points.

In their drive to maintain and increase profit levels, retailers and manufac-turers are trying to achieve more with less. This is epitomized for many companies by the application of the just-in-time (JIT) philosophy. A JIT approach emphasizes the reliance on logistics partners. But service providers need to be able to match the increasingly demanding expectations of their customers not just in terms of speed but in terms of reliability, service moni-toring and consignment tracking. Only by doing this will the benefits of a JIT approach really become apparent.

Market concentration has been occurring in the vast majority of European retail and manufacturing markets in recent years. In grocery retailing, for example, the market share of the top five national retailers in several European countries including the United Kingdom, the Netherlands, Belgium, Germany and France is between 50 and 70 per cent (Mintel, 2002). However, it is important to recognize that the degree of market concentration varies significantly between industries in any one country, and that the general degree of market concentration varies from one country to another.

Limitations on European integration

Despite growing similarities, there are still many differences between European countries; retailing is a case in point. The retail format used in different European markets varies significantly between countries, with very large stores playing the biggest role in some countries (eg hypermarkets selling food and non-food in France and out-of-town supermarkets in the United Kingdom) and small food stores and traditional grocers far more common in others (such as Spain and Italy). As a result of these different retail formats, the total number of stores operated by retailers varies between European countries; for example there are approximately 120,000 grocery stores in Italy, compared with only 33,000 in the United Kingdom (WARC, 2002). In addition patterns of consumption vary widely between European countries for a range of cultural, demographic, and economic reasons. If one argues that we are now operating within an integrated European market-place, this ignores the special distinguishing features of Europe and in particular: market complexity, market size, maturity of the market, density of population spread, number of separate nation states, and many languages. It must be acknowledged that in many cases these factors have acted as a brake on the introduction of European-wide supply chains and logistics systems to serve them.

However, many companies will continue to strengthen their European initiatives, resulting in further examples of corporations making dramatic changes to their European logistics networks. This in turn places new demands on logistics managers and logistics services. We need to be aware that there are often conflicting tensions within large organizations, and in some instances initiatives to implement changes at a European scale will be overtaken by the desire to have in place a framework allowing global coordination of supply chains. Changing priorities can make it difficult to determine the most appropriate way to develop logistics management structures, and this in turn has implications for the relationship with service providers (Hindson, 1998).

MARKET STRUCTURE OF LOGISTICS SERVICE PROVIDERS

Recent changes in the demand for logistics services in Europe pose a problem for logistics service providers, as they are working with a range of companies all moving at different speeds towards what may well be rather varied objectives. Out of this challenge comes an advantage for the bigger organization that can match these requirements across and within different markets.

Company size and response to international opportunities

As we have noted, European deregulation, the abolition of internal frontiers and harmonization of fiscal and technical standards, and the introduction of the euro will all help to boost trade within an enlarged EU and make it simpler for all logistics service providers to participate in that activity. Many factors will influence the response of logistics companies to these opportunities. Among the most important are:

- company culture and background (for example, the size of the company and its ability to absorb the financial and management consequences of rapid change);
- customer profile (industry, speed of reaction to European opportunities);
- customer culture (for example, the customers of the logistics service provider could either purchase services at the European level or purely on a national basis).

Company size is likely to have a special significance in determining the response to the opportunities created by an enlarged EU. For example, in the case of larger logistics providers there will be the opportunity to continue to internationalize their activities in order to provide full national distribution services in more than one country. For smaller companies the impact of an enlarged EU may appear initially to be far more limited, and it is clear that, for example, the road freight industry has a preponderance of small companies. Many small companies operate at a local level, serving local industry, and will expect to go on working in this way. Although these smaller companies predominate in terms of numbers within the third-party sector, it is the larger companies that dominate the market in terms of the total vehicle fleet and, therefore, capacity. In the United Kingdom, for example, 7 per cent of hire or reward companies operate 56 per cent of the vehicles, and this is a trend that can be identified, albeit in some cases to a lesser degree, right across the EU (Reed Business Information, 2002).

Internationalization among larger carriers

One way in which logistics service providers can enter into foreign markets is through the establishment of operating centres in other countries and gradually increasing their networks. However, rather than follow this evolutionary and somewhat slow route to growth in foreign markets, some firms prefer the prospect of mergers, takeovers or strategic trading alliances with operators based in other European countries as a means of becoming more international.

The growing internationalization of business has forced companies providing logistics services to consider their own strategies to meet these new needs. Service providers need to determine the extent to which they can meet all the service requirements of a European business, or whether they can realistically meet only part of those needs. In many cases there remains at present a potential mismatch between the logistics demands of European companies and the ability of any single service provider to meet these demands. This often results in disappointment, when a manufacturer decides to rationalize its logistics network and seeks to reduce the number of service providers it deals with at a European level. In many cases the manufacturer finds that there are few logistics service providers that wish to take on the commitment of handling all its European activities (*Distribution*, 2002).

Providers of logistics services need to be concerned with two dimensions to their activities in the first instance: geographical scope and range of services. A consideration of these two dimensions highlights how challenging it really is for the logistics service company to be able to provide 'one-stop shopping' for a European company. Some companies already provide what can be described as European services, in the sense that they are the long-distance links in a network used by manufacturing companies. This provision of services is evident in the case of airlines, shipping lines, freight forwarders and integrators. It is clearly at the level of local and national distribution that Europeanization of service provision has been slowest to develop.

A broad range of logistics activities can be provided by logistics service providers. Freight transport and warehousing services have been widely available for many decades, together with documentation services to support the flow of these products (eg delivery and customs documentation). However, in recent years, logistics service providers have begun to offer an ever-expanding range of services such as final assembly of products, inventory management, product and package labelling, product tracking and tracing along the supply chain, order planning and processing, and reverse logistics systems (which tackle the collection and recovery of end-of-life products and used packaging in the supply chain).

Despite a period of uncertainty about the benefits of scale for logistics service providers, there have been some important developments in the last few years. Larger logistics service providers have grown mainly through merger and acquisition, and appear to be committed to developing more European and global capabilities. The box below provides details of the ways in which three major logistics service providers have expanded their services and geographical coverage in the last five years through organic growth, mergers and acquisitions and alliances.

Examples of logistics service providers expanding their scope

Deutsche Post

Deutsche Post AG is the former state department responsible for German postal services. In 1995 it became a private company owned by government, and it was partly privatized in 2000 with 31 per cent of stock made available. Since becoming a private company, Deutsche Post has pursued a strategy of extending its geographical coverage in the mail and express sectors, as well as expanding the range of logistics services offered.

Most of this growth has been achieved through acquisitions. Over a five-year period it has spent US $4.9 billion purchasing other businesses (Harnischfeger, 2002). Companies that have been either wholly or partly acquired include many express companies with national and global networks (including DHL (global), Securicor Distribution (UK), and Ducros (global)), and forwarders and distribution companies (such as Danzas (Europe's largest ground forwarder), ASG (Nordic countries), AEI (global forwarding) and Nedlloyd ETD (European coverage)) (Datamonitor, 2002).

The aim of the company is to become an international player capable of offering an extensive range of mail, express and logistics services, and thereby of providing one-stop shopping for national and international customers. It is currently in the process of integrating these newly acquired businesses. This is a significant task, and involves the integration of the companies' internal structures, products, brands, sales and IT systems.

Exel

The merger between Exel Logistics and Ocean Group in May 2000 led to the formation of Exel, the largest logistics service provider in the United Kingdom, and one of the largest in the world. The merger was viewed as highly appropriate, bringing together the contract logistics capabilities of Exel Logistics with the freight forwarding strengths of Ocean Group. Both companies had been active in the acquisition market over recent years, which had led to Exel Logistics' presence in several European countries, and to Ocean's services in both Europe and America. Bringing together these two companies has expanded the range of services offered as well as the geographical coverage (Datamonitor, 2002).

Kuehne and Nagel

Kuehne and Nagel is a major logistics service provider. It has 17,500 employees based at 600 locations in 90 countries. Traditionally the company was a significant presence in the sea and air freight markets. Recently it has been expanding its contract logistics expertise through acquisition.

The German conglomerate Viag held a 33 per cent stake in Kuehne and Nagel. However, Viag withdrew in 1999, and an alliance was reached with SembCorp Logistics of Singapore. This has helped to increase Kuehne and Nagel's presence in Asia. The acquisition in 2001 of USCO, a large logistics service provider in the United States, has helped to increase the company's strengths, with warehousing and distribution becoming part of Kuehne and Nagel's service offering.

The company is currently examining how best to improve its trucking capability in Europe. This could be achieved either by acquisition or by an alliance with existing carriers. However, the company acknowledges that most existing European trucking networks are already working closely with its rivals, and it may therefore have to team up with several regional operators (King, 2002).

LOGISTICS STRATEGIES IN THE EUROPEAN GROCERY INDUSTRY

Developments in the grocery industry provide good examples of many of the points raised in the first sections of this chapter. These include issues such as efforts to achieve greater efficiency in logistics operations, concentration of retail outlets and stockholding facilities, the development of a supply chain perspective, and general market concentration. The grocery industry also helps to illustrate that while there is growing similarity between supply chain and logistics organization in different European countries, important differences still remain that require different logistics solutions. The grocery industry is one of Europe's largest industries, requires substantial transport and logistics services, and has been subject to many interesting developments.

Scope and scale of the European food industry

The European food industry is very important economically. In the United Kingdom, France, Germany, Italy and the Netherlands, for example, between

10 and 20 per cent of household expenditure is on food. It is considered to be a mature market with a relatively static total market size. This has meant that individual firms tend to improve their performance at the expense of other companies' market share and profitability. Trends in both food retailing and manufacturing/processing in recent years have reflected the growing level of competitiveness in the industry.

Grocery retailers and consumer needs

Market concentration has been occurring in all European retail markets in recent years, with concentration in the grocery retailing sector often greater than in non-food retailing. The market share of the top five national food retailers in many European countries including the United Kingdom, the Netherlands, Belgium, Germany and France is between 50 and 70 per cent. However in some countries there is far less market concentration: the top five food retailers in Greece, Italy and Spain only account for 23 per cent, 28 per cent and 41 per cent of the market respectively (Mintel, 2002). The more highly concentrated retail markets exhibit a greater degree of segmentation of retail formats, capitalization, supply chain integration and implementation of information technology.

Retail formats used in different European markets vary significantly between countries, with very large stores playing the biggest role in some countries (eg hypermarkets selling food and non-food in France, and out-of-town supermarkets in the United Kingdom) and small stores and traditional grocers far more common in others (such as Spain and Italy). Figure 22.1 shows the number of grocery stores per 10,000 population in a number of European countries, while Figure 22.2 shows the relative importance of different sizes of store in terms of grocery turnover.

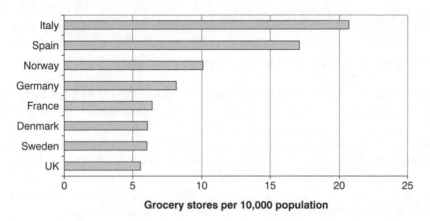

Figure 22.1 Grocery stores per 10,000 population in selected European countries

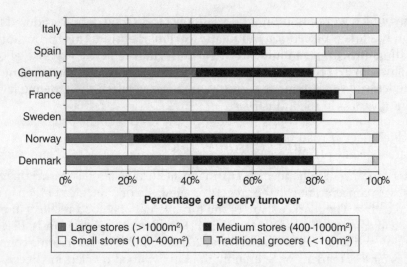

Figure 22.2 Grocery turnover by store type in selected European countries

A characteristic of the European grocery industry is the way in which it responds rapidly to changes in consumer taste and demand by introducing new products at a very fast rate. For instance, the demand for convenience foods, non-domestic foods and other more exotic products has been met by an ever-increasing variety of new products. Patterns of food consumption vary widely between European countries for a range of cultural, demographic, and economic reasons.

Manufacturers are increasingly producing own-label food products rather than branded products for the retailers. This has changed the nature of their role, responsibilities and power within the supply chain. While the European food manufacturing industry contains a small number of very large organizations, it should be noted that there are many relatively small firms.

Transport and logistics in the grocery industry

In European countries with an advanced food retailing structure, large food retailers have taken increasing control over the distribution and logistics of food supply during the last two decades. Even if they do not carry out the transport and warehousing functions directly themselves, they have a high degree of involvement in planning and coordinating these operations.

This involvement has had a marked impact upon the structure of the distribution networks serving retail stores. In the United Kingdom, for instance, the food distribution networks for retailers tend to comprise a small number of large national or regional distribution centres located along motorway corridors (in comparison with networks of numerous small, local distribution centres which were common until relatively recently). Centralization of distribution has taken place for a number of reasons, including retailers' desire to gain discounts from manufacturers for full-load deliveries, the reduction in total stock levels achievable when stock is held in fewer warehouses, and the greater ease of stock management and monitoring when it is held in relatively few locations.

The logistics service companies serving the food retailers usually operate a dedicated fleet of road transport vehicles displaying the retailer's livery, and operate logistics planning systems to help coordinate the food supply chain from the manufacturers to the distribution centres. These distribution companies are usually solely responsible for transport of food products from the distribution centres to the retail store, and are also increasingly responsible for moving food products from the point of manufacture to the distribution centres. The delivery of food to the retail store is tightly planned, and drivers are assigned precise schedules of when to arrive at the shop.

These initiatives and developments in the distribution of food products have had a number of objectives, including:

- to speed up flow of food products through the supply chain;
- to improve the reliability of deliveries to retail stores;
- to reduce stock levels held in distribution centres and retail stores (and thereby the costs associated with stockholding).

The development of a comprehensive food retail and supply strategy is often referred to as 'efficient consumer response (ECR)'. This is defined by the US Council of Logistics Management as 'ensuring that replenishment shipping activities are executed, based on constant forecasting of consumer demand at the item level, using point-of-sale data'. As the CLM notes, these procedures result in 'tremendous pressure on the vendor to support timely, accurate and responsive supply chain management' (CLM, 2002). Service providers need to be able to match the increasingly demanding expectations of their customers, not just in terms of speed but in terms of reliability, service monitoring and consignment tracking. Only if this is done will the benefits of an ECR approach really become apparent.

In more traditional grocery retail markets in Europe, while the logistics arrangements are becoming more like those above, the pattern is still somewhat different. Warehouses are often operated in-house, whilst the transport operation is often contracted out, but on a shared or common user basis rather than as a dedicated operation.

Supply chain relationships in Europe

Supply chain control is linked to the degree of market concentration in the retail sector and the split between retailers' own label and manufacturers' brands. Where own label products are extremely important and multiples dominate the retail market, these large retailers are able to take control of the supply chain. This is in contrast to a manufacturer-driven supply chain. When retailers control the supply chain, they typically organize the logistical network so that the vast majority of products flow through distribution centres run by themselves (or on their behalf by a third-party logistics provider), and they then organize dedicated full-load deliveries to retail stores themselves.

In countries where manufacturer control of the supply chain is still the norm, such as Spain, Greece and Italy, common-user distribution services are standard, with a distribution company delivering to a number of retail customers on behalf of the manufacturer from the manufacturer's warehouse.

There have also been increasing developments in Central and Eastern Europe, with a number of Western European retailers both establishing stores and taking over existing companies. Manufacturers are also establishing production facilities in Central and Eastern Europe. Clearly this geographical region will offer significant opportunities to Western European food retailers, manufacturers and transport and logistics providers in the coming years.

Therefore, as this section has illustrated, several important developments have been taking place in the European grocery industry, including market concentration, internationalization, efforts to take a supply chain perspective and improve logistics efficiency, and concentration in the number of stock-holding facilities. However, it is important to recognize that these changes are occurring at varying rates in different European countries, and that the supply chain structure of the grocery industry varies between European Member States. Differences are noticeable in consumer preferences, and in the importance and power of the different supply chain parties. The major differences include:

- the degree of market concentration in food retailing;
- the market penetration of retailers' own-label products;
- the importance of the retailer in the supply chain: the retailer is less dominant in many food markets outside the United Kingdom, and in some countries including Italy and Spain the supply chain is controlled/led by the manufacturer;
- the sophistication and specialization of distribution and logistics services offered by logistics providers: dedicated logistics services are less generally available in other European countries than in the United Kingdom.

If, as seems likely, the European food industry becomes increasingly international in the future, this will present a new set of logistics challenges in terms of product sourcing, the location of distribution centres and the area they should serve, and how to undertake and organize the transport of products.

TRANSPORTATION IN EUROPE

European road freight activity

The changing demand for logistics services in Europe outlined in the previous sections has had a significant impact on transportation patterns and activity within Europe. Europe's economic growth has gone hand in hand with a growing flow of goods. The growth in freight transport in Western European countries between 1970 and 2000 is shown in Figure 22.3. During this same period there was an ongoing shift towards road transport (see Table 22.1). There is also an integration effect – for example, the EU countries trade four times more foodstuffs than other countries with identical production and consumption levels – and this has important implications for logistics demands.

Although there are some important differences between individual countries, it is evident that road freight dominates the movement of goods within Europe, and that road freight activity has increased in recent years. As

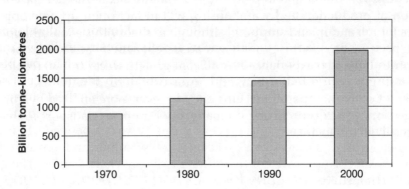

Figure 22.3 Freight transport in Western Europe

Table 22.1 Trends in market share of freight transport modes (tonne-kilometres)

	1970	1980	1990	2000
Road	50%	60%	68%	73%
Rail	30%	22%	16%	14%
Inland waterways	12%	9%	7%	6%
Pipeline	8%	9%	9%	7%
Total	100%	100%	100%	100%

Source: ECMT (2002)

already discussed, the prospect of a Europe free from internal borders has spurred many companies to review and then reconfigure their logistics systems (Cooper, Browne and Peters, 1994). This has resulted in a rationalization of both production and stockholding sites among some large companies operating across Europe, thereby increasing the demand for national, and especially international, transport services. At the same time there has been a trend to reduce stock levels by managing production much more carefully and implementing just-in-time (JIT) production techniques. Both these developments led to an increase in the consumption of transport services within the supply chain. This can occur as a result of either increasing trip length (as is the case with the concentration of production and storage) or greater frequency of deliveries (as occurs in a JIT system). In addition, there is greater pressure on transport services to achieve high levels of reliability.

Many developments in modern logistics tend to increase road transport (see Table 22.2). The growth in international trade and sourcing, as well as the relevance of new business strategies, will make policies aimed at reducing road transport difficult to implement. It is still not clear whether the concentration of production and warehousing will in fact open up new opportunities for rail and inland shipping, although in theory this should happen.

At the same time as this growth in road freight activity across Europe, most countries have also experienced significant growth in car traffic, resulting in increasingly congested urban and inter-urban road networks. Freight transport costs and operational efficiency are ever more affected by this road congestion, which is occurring on many key European transport routes and especially in urban areas.

Policy measures affecting logistics and transport in Europe

The European Commission White Paper on Transport published in 2001 has identified many potential policy measures that, if introduced, would have significant effects on freight transport and logistics services in the EU. The White Paper has identified that lack of fiscal and social harmonization in the transport market has led to several key problems in transport within the EU:

- Unequal growth in different modes of transport. This reflects the facts that not all external costs have been included in the cost of transport, and that some modes have adapted better to the needs of a modern economy than others.
- Congestion on the main road and rail routes, in urban areas and at airports. Growth in the demand for goods transport is due to the shift from a 'stock' economy to a 'flow' economy.
- Harmful effects on the environment and public health.

Table 22.2 Developments in logistics and the impact on transport and traffic

Main development	Impact on transport and traffic
Modal shift towards road	More road vehicle trips
Spatial concentration of production and warehousing	Longer distances, increase in transport volumes on key routes
Adoption of JIT in manufacturing	Smaller shipments, faster transport (road), decrease in load factors
Adoption of quick response and ECR in retail distribution	Smaller shipments, faster transport (road), decrease in load factors
Wider geographical sourcing of supplies	Raw materials and components transported over greater distances
Wider geographical distribution of finished product	Finished products transported over greater distances
Supply chain integration	Decrease in number of suppliers and transport providers, increased road transport in the case of more outsourcing
Decrease in order cycle time	Demand-driven flows lead to increased number of trips, decrease in transport efficiency
Increase in assortments	Smaller shipments, increased number of trips
Reverse logistics	Additional transport of waste materials and end-of-life products
Retail market concentration	Fewer, larger out-of-town stores; encouraging the use of car journeys for shopping

Source: adapted from NEA, quoted in Dutch National Spatial Planning Agency (1997); Technical University of Berlin et al (2001).

In the view of the European Commission, 'sustainable development offers an opportunity, not to say lever, for adapting common transport policy. This objective, as introduced by the Treaty of Amsterdam, has to be achieved by integrating environmental considerations into Community policies.' (European Commission, 2001: 14). The White Paper proposes 60 specific measures to be taken at Community level as part of the transport policy, grouped under four main objectives. It includes an action programme extending to 2010. The proposals that are likely to have most impact on goods movement are shown in the box on page 376.

Proposals in the European Commission White Paper

Shifting the balance between modes of transport

- Harmonize inspections and penalties by the end of 2001 to promote uniform interpretation, implementation and monitoring of existing road transport legislation; establish liability for employers for certain offences committed by their drivers; and harmonize the conditions for immobilizing vehicles.
- Increase checks that Member States are required to carry out on compliance with driving times and drivers' rest periods.
- Harmonize the minimum clauses in contracts governing transport activity to allow tariffs to be revised should costs increase (eg fuel price rise).
- Gradually open up the railway market in Europe (cabotage, interoperability etc).
- Support the creation of new infrastructure and in particular rail freight freeways.
- Launch debate on the future of airports to make better use of existing capacity, review charging systems and improve integration between air and other modes of transport.
- Develop the infrastructure needed to build 'motorways of the sea'.

Eliminating bottlenecks

- Eliminate bottlenecks on the trans-European network by encouraging corridors with priority for freight, a rapid passenger network and traffic management plans for major roads.

Placing users at the heart of transport policy

- Propose a framework directive setting out the principles and structure of an infrastructure-charging system and a common methodology for setting charging levels, offset by the removal of existing taxes and allowing cross-financing. This must encourage the use of modes of lesser environmental impact.
- Make the tax system more consistent by proposing uniform taxation for commercial road transport fuel to round off the internal market.

Managing the effects of transport globalization

- Improve access to outlying areas.
- Link future member states to the EU's trans-European network by means of infrastructure of quality with a view to maintaining modal share of rail transport at 35 per cent in the candidate countries in 2010.

There are several other policy measures that are either already having or will in future have a significant impact on road-based freight and logistics services, and may also affect the location of logistics and other industrial activities:

- The EU Working Time Directive (WTD) will be applied to the freight transport sector in all EU member states by late 2003 or early 2004. It will reduce the average weekly working hours of a goods vehicle driver from 55 hours to 48 hours (a 13 per cent reduction) (Pott, 2001). Self-employed drivers will be exempt from the WTD for at least a further two years after its introduction for company-employed freight vehicle drivers. The WTD is likely to result in companies needing to employ more drivers in order to maintain the total hours their vehicles are driven each week. Even prior to the introduction of the WTD there have been concerns about the shortage of drivers in the freight transport industry.

- Time- or distance-based road-user charging for goods vehicles. Several EU countries have already implemented these charging schemes in place of annual licence fees for lorries. These schemes aim to relate the charge to the usage of the vehicle, and therefore better reflect the costs that they impose when using roads. Time-based road-user charges already exist in Belgium, Luxembourg, Germany, the Netherlands, Denmark and Sweden. Switzerland currently uses a distance-based road-user charge. Germany intends to switch from time-based to distance-based road-user charges at the end of 2002. The UK government is currently proposing a series of changes to modernize the taxation of road haulage, and is likely to switch to a time- or distance-based charging system by 2006 (HM Treasury, 2002).

- Goods vehicles operating in urban areas are finding themselves subject to a growing number of policy measures in different towns and cities in Europe. These measures are being implemented by policy makers in response to congestion, pollution and safety issues. As well as time and weight restrictions, other measures including low emission zones (LEZs) and road pricing schemes may well become more common in future. The LEZ concept reduces the emission levels in a particular location by restricting goods vehicle access (and potentially other types of vehicle as well) to those vehicles that meet certain emission criteria. Such zones already exist in Holland and Sweden and may well be introduced in the United Kingdom in the near future (Transport and Travel Research, 2000). Some urban areas may be subject to congestion charging schemes in future. Such a scheme is proposed for London in February 2003. Goods vehicles (as well as other road vehicles) will have to pay a daily fee in order to enter the city centre during the working day. Although the price charged by such a scheme will increase road freight operating costs, goods vehicles may benefit from reduced traffic levels and hence faster and more reliable journeys as a result of the scheme.

OPPORTUNITIES AND PRESSURES FOR LOGISTICS PROVIDERS IN A NEW EUROPE

It is evident that many multinationals are rationalizing the number of logistics service providers they deal with across Europe, in much the same way as they have rationalized their production and warehousing operations (there is, of course, a link between these developments). This, together with the growth in intra-European trade, is leading to greater demand for transport and logistics services. Political changes have opened up new geographical markets, for both production and consumption. Devising and implementing the right logistics strategies lies at the heart of successfully capitalizing on these commercial opportunities available in Europe. Many of these changes are of significance to logistics service providers, especially those concerned with international markets.

The very different nature of European markets means that logistics providers wishing to provide for this growing demand for European services must adopt suitable and appropriate approaches for different markets. International transport companies engaged in cross-border European work already understand that strategies may need to be tailored to the particular country of operation.

Naturally, what is right for one company will not be right for all. In particular there are important differences between the sort of strategies and initiatives that need to be devised by larger companies and those of smaller ones.

Strategies for larger logistics service providers

In deciding how to take advantage of the new European opportunities, logistics service providers need to be clear about which of the following strategies they wish to adopt:

- *Strategy A (pan-Europeans):* providing a Europe-wide service offering distribution both within and between a number of European countries.
- *Strategy B (multidomestics):* providing national services which are in several European countries.
- *Strategy C (Eurolinkers):* providing a network (or part of a network) of mainly international services between major European markets.

The network implications of each strategy are illustrated in Figure 22.4.

Clearly the most ambitious strategy is the first, to provide a truly pan-European service. Several major logistics service providers are working towards achieving this, but it is a challenging goal. The foundations for the multi-domestic strategy appear to lie in the successful duplication of domestic services in other countries. The original services are, of course, adapted as required.

Strategies for small and medium-sized service providers

The smallest logistics service providers tend either to operate at a local level or to work for a few companies. The scope for these companies to develop

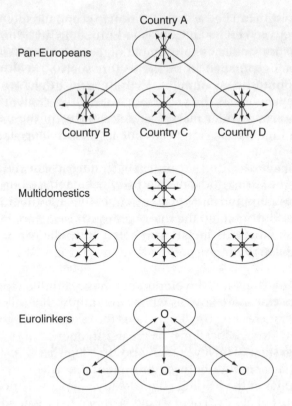

Figure 22.4   Strategy options for providers of logistics services

strategies to take advantage of European opportunities are rather limited. For medium-sized companies, and especially those already operating in the international marketplace, there are undoubtedly ways in which they can develop initiatives to take advantage of the growing opportunities in the EU. However, it is evident that many multinationals are seeking to rationalize the number of logistics providers that they deal with across Europe, and therefore in response to this, medium-sized providers should find ways to tie their operations into those of their customers, so they become a vital part of their customers' distribution operation.

CONCLUDING REMARKS

Cost-effective systems of goods distribution are often argued to be an essential prerequisite for competing in international markets and for delivering a good standard of living at a national level. Efficient distribution of goods and services influences market diversity, consumer choice, jobs and prosperity. Logistics can be viewed as critical to economic success in manufacturing, retailing and service industries in Europe. In addition, the scope for improved logistics strategies to promote higher service levels and reduced costs is also being pursued in public sectors such as health and defence. Logistics contributes to economic growth by, first, extending market reach, thereby giving firms access to a wider range of raw materials and supplies and providing access to a wider market; and second, reducing waste. Concepts such as just-in-time have a significant impact on reducing stock held within supply chains.

Logistics management and supply chain strategies play a critical role in the competitiveness of firms. Indeed it has been argued that increasingly competition is between supply chains rather than between individual enterprises. Within logistics management the role of transport is an important one, and is frequently the aspect of logistics affected by policy interventions (for example deregulation of transport markets, or decisions about infrastructure expenditure).

A number of logistics developments have tended to increase the consumption of transport services within the supply chain. This can occur as a result of either increasing trip length (as is the case with the concentration of production and storage locations) or greater frequency of deliveries (as can occur in a JIT system). However, many positive logistics initiatives have also taken place that combine both environmental and commercial benefits. Clearly companies at the leading edge already enjoy the benefits of this and contribute to sustainability. There would be much to be gained by improving the efficiency of companies that are not at the forefront of these initiatives. Therefore ways need to be found to encourage more companies operating in Europe to use logistics approaches, and to ensure that those approaches that contribute to sustainability become more widely disseminated.

REFERENCES

Browne, M, and Allen, J (1994) Logistics strategies for Europe, in *Logistics and Distribution Planning: Strategies for Management*, ed J Cooper, Kogan Page, London

Cooper, J, Browne, M, and Peters, M (1994) *European Logistics: Markets, management and strategy*, 2nd edn, Blackwell, Oxford

Council for Logistics Management (CLM) (2002) *Logistics Terms and Glossary*, CLM [Online] http://www.clm1.org

Datamonitor (2002) *Consolidation in the European Logistics Industry*, Datamonitor (June)

Distribution (2002) Europe yet to become a single entity, interview with Steve Allen, Managing Director of Securicor Omega Logistics, *Distribution*, **15** (3) (Jun), p 17

Dutch National Spatial Planning Agency (1997) *Spatial Patterns of Transportation: Atlas of freight transport in Europe*, Dutch National Spatial Planning Agency

ECMT (2002) *Trends in the Transport Sector 1970–2000*, ECMT, Paris

European Commission (2001) *European Transport Policy for 2010: Time to decide*, White Paper, Office for Official Publications of the European Communities, Luxembourg

European Logistics Management (2001a) Geest accelerates French acquisition, *European Logistics Management* (19 Feb), pp 9–10

European Logistics Management (2001b) Danone's plan to revamp biscuit business includes closure of six manufacturing sites, *European Logistics Management* (17 Apr), p 9

Harnischfeger, U (2002) Deutsche Post out to prove its gusto, *Financial Times* (20 Sep), p 30

Hindson, D (1998) *The Pressure for Pan-European Logistics*, Pan-European Logistics Conference, London, 20–21 Jan

HM Treasury (2002) *Modernising the Taxation of the Haulage Industry*, Progress Report One (Apr), London

Kemp, D (1997) *Competitive Supply Chain Structure: Nike – A case study*, World Logistics Conference, London, Dec

King, M (2002) 'We can be king of the jungle', *International Freighting Weekly* (1 Apr), p 7

Mintel (2002) *Food Retailing in Europe* (Jun), Mintel

O'Laughlin, K, Cooper, J, and Cabocel, E (1993) *Reconfiguring European Logistics Systems*, Council of Logistics Management, Oak Brook, IL

Pott, R (2001) *Working Time: Part One*, Croner's Road Transport Operation Bulletin 53 (May)

Reed Business Information (2002) *Road Transport Market Survey 2001*, Reed Business Information, prepared by NOP Research Group

Technical University of Berlin *et al* (2001) *SULOGTRA: Analysis of Trends in Supply Chain Management and Logistics*, SULOGTRA Deliverable Report D1, Workpackage 1

Transport and Travel Research (2000) *Key Local Authorities and Implementation Issues*, Low Emission Zone Fact Sheet2, Cleaner Transport Forum

World Advertising Research Centre (WARC) (2002) *The Retail Pocket Book 2002*, WARC, Henley

23

Logistics strategies for Central and Eastern Europe

Grzegorz Augustyniak
Warsaw School of Economics

INTRODUCTION

The fall of communism in Central and Eastern Europe (CEE) at the turn of the 1990s has begun a fascinating period of systemic transition. This period of transformation has coincided with unprecedented economic integration in Europe that, on the one hand, creates enormous opportunities and advantages, but, on the other, needs great – often-painful – changes. CEE has to adapt quickly to European Union (EU) standards at a time of complex and strained economic and political conditions, illustrated by the recent crises in Asia and Russia. One may easily conclude that the development and implementation of logistics strategy – or any strategy – in this region is fraught with difficulty.

When analysing the situation in CEE countries we should not forget that, despite their numerous similarities – resulting from their common fate as Soviet satellites – each is significantly distinct. The most often quoted differences between them include:

- the size of the respective markets (measured by population and per capita income);
- the size of territories and their geographical configuration (determining their logistics systems);

- different starting positions for reforms (determined, for example, by ownership and industry structures and foreign indebtedness);
- cultural and historical differences;
- different ways, degree and effectiveness of reforms implemented (from a shock-therapy approach, through evolutionary progress, to almost giving up);
- degree of integration with NATO and the EU.

For these reasons, this description of logistics strategies for CEE is focused on those countries that are the most advanced in the transition process, and whose logistics strategies are the most similar. This primarily refers to the Czech Republic, Hungary and Poland. These three countries share similar political strategies that are based on integration with NATO (as new members accepted in 1999) and the European Union (recommended to join the Union on 1 January 2004).

While focusing on those three, we should not forget that EU integration also affects other CEE and Baltic states, including Estonia, Latvia, Lithuania, Slovakia, and Slovenia. All of these are similar in size but differ in per capita GDP, with Slovenia being the richest of all CEE countries. When talking of NATO expansion (or enlargement as it is preferred) we should mention states that are less advanced in the reforms, but becoming strongly Western-oriented, such as Bulgaria and Romania, which also aspire to join the EU in the future.

In other words, the CEE region constitutes a mosaic that is struggling with internal logistics problems, while aiming at integration of its logistics systems both with the EU and within CEE. The latter, which creates an important north–south transit area, is under the umbrella of political cooperation of the 'Visegrad Group' supported by the economic organization CEFTA (Central European Free Trade Agreement).

It would be hard to overestimate the impact of this integration on the countries' logistics strategies. However, the current conditions determining the development of logistics in CEE are the result of the communist legacy, so it is necessary to take a brief overview of the 'old' system of working practices.

CONDITIONS OF ECONOMIC DEVELOPMENT OF CEE COUNTRIES BEFORE 1990

After the Second World War, the economic development of CEE countries focused on their reconstruction. This was accompanied by rapid industrialization, based on heavy industry and mining. However, this industrial structure did not reflect the real needs of the economies, but rather was dictated by the prevailing 'cold war' doctrine. As a result, in the 1960s, while the West was experiencing its first consumer revolution, COMECON countries were still developing enormous industrial potential, with almost complete disregard for actual consumer needs.

The problems were exacerbated by the measures of organizational effectiveness. The most common was based on the maximization of assets employed. In other words, the more you use resources (ideally, the entire amount assigned by the relevant central plan) the better. When economies were faced by shortages of supplies, the focus was shifted towards maximization of output – but abandoning any measures of quality.

Other measures of performance were meaningless, since permanent shortages of consumer products – sold at fixed price – gave producers absolute power in the market. Such ways of 'doing business' in the CEE countries stimulated waste and corrupted workers, whose intuitive efforts at rationalization were not only ignored but were, in many ways, punished (Kisperska-Moron, Kapcia and Piniecki, 1996).

Paradoxically, the wave of Western credit in the 1970s, when East–West relations were relaxed, deepened the economic crisis in the CEE countries. Money was wrongly spent or consumed, and this resulted in huge indebtedness. Moreover, industrial plants built on Western technology made countries dependent on imports of spare parts, and when these became too expensive they could only be replaced by low-quality substitutes produced locally. Consequently, the efficiency and lifespan of production lines were significantly reduced. Further attempts at reform in the 1980s brought nothing but economic slump, proving that the socialist economy was bankrupt. Soon, the political system that enforced the 'economic fictions' collapsed, and since 1989 CEE countries, one after another, have moved towards a market economy.

THE LOGISTICS SYSTEM OF CEE BEFORE 1989

In centrally planned economies, a knowledge of logistics and other modern management concepts and techniques was practically useless. The only exceptions were found in those companies whose export orientation exposed them to operations in the West. In other companies, monopolistic producers, whose distribution was also in the hands of monopolies, dominated the quasi-market. The government set prices for products and services (with few exceptions where higher prices were allowed) and fixed the currency exchange rates. In these circumstances, the only business goal was to exist – at the expense of the state, which covered any loss.

The only concern of logistics was to obtain scarce resources from suppliers to secure the execution of centrally set plans (which means the logistics in CEE had a very strong supply orientation), and to deliver goods produced to customers. This sounds similar to those tasks of logistics in the West, but with the significant difference that the logistics system was not focused on quality. None of the logistics systems objectives (well known from the '7 Rs' definition) had to be fulfilled, and both effectiveness and customer satisfaction could be ignored without penalty. Ineffectiveness was officially explained in propaganda terms as a result of 'objective reasons', or sometimes by firing or imprisoning selected managers, employees or 'speculants'. This approach led to enormous waste and technological obsolescence of companies, which treated investments and customer service as costs to be avoided rather than sources of potential improvement and revenue.

The above-mentioned facts indicate that the logistics system of CEE countries was extremely expensive, especially because of high transportation and inventory-carrying costs. The transportation system consisted of a relatively dense, but low-quality, infrastructure serviced by obsolete and inefficient fleets. Another major factor contributing to the high cost of transportation was the commercially ridiculous (but politically motivated) location of production plants and other logistics facilities. The criteria for location were based on a theory of balanced development for all regions in a country. This meant that a factory could be erected anywhere, regardless of its proximity to suppliers or consumers, existing transportation, telecommunication infrastructure and the profile of the labour force available (Kisperska-Moron, Kapcia and Piniecki, 1996).

In practice, every investment of this kind required huge investments in new roads and a social infrastructure, such as workers' hotels, heating plants and sewage systems. This was rarely shared with any other local infrastructure. To make the story even worse, the lack of money often meant that the infrastructure provided was incapable of efficiently serving the needs of the facility. The result of these poor location – and supporting infrastructure – decisions was that distances travelled by transport were far greater than necessary, for both supply and distribution. This often had an impact on the quality of goods carried. While the fixed cost of investment was very high, the system generated a lot of pollution, and other environmental threats were totally ignored. Another major drawback for CEE countries lay in the poor telecommunications infrastructure, which came with a lack of incentive to improve information flows.

Shortages of supplies, combined with inefficient transportation, forced all companies in CEE to carry huge amounts of inventory to secure smooth production. This meant that inventory was treated more like an investment than a necessary evil. The quality aspect again had no impact on the system, since eventual waste was added into the cost of production. Final product defects did not harm the producers, since chronic shortages meant that customers were forced to accept any products they could find.

Overall, the 1990s found CEE countries with inefficient, fragmented and out-of-date logistics systems that did not meet their requirements as they moved towards a market economy. The system was generally characterized by:

- a lack of customer focus;
- the underdevelopment of a transportation and telecommunications infrastructure;

- wrongly located, ineffective, and obsolete industrial plants and related logistics infrastructure (especially low-standard warehouses);
- a lack of specialized, integrated logistics services;
- inadequate and poor management education, especially in logistics and quality management across all levels;
- a lack of reverse logistics systems, as there were no environmental policies for, say, the reuse and recycling of packaging and hazardous waste;
- low employee morale and job satisfaction.

This leads to the clear conclusion that the logistics system inherited from communism was a fundamental barrier to the transformation of these economies and their subsequent competitiveness. This statement is supported by an analysis of the cost of logistics as a proportion of the GDP of these countries, which is estimated at more than 20 per cent, even as much as 30 per cent. This is at least twice as high as typical values in the West. Thus, poor logistics is a major counterbalance for the few advantages of the regions, such as:

- low cost and a technically well-educated workforce,
- incentives for investment in selected regions;
- the relatively low cost of land acquisition;
- favourable geographical conditions (eg proximity to the EU market and its transit location);
- the size of the market and its potential, accompanied by rapid economic growth.

On the other hand, it is logistics where the huge potential for significant improvements and savings exists, and successful transformation in this area might be a key to success for CEE countries and investors involved in this process.

DEVELOPMENT OF LOGISTICS IN THE PERIOD OF TRANSITION

At the beginning of reforms all CEE countries suffered from similar problems, though on different scales. The major effort in the early 1990s concentrated on stabilizing the macroeconomic condition of these countries. It focused on curbing inflation (or hyperinflation, as it was in Poland), high unemployment (a term that never existed in the centrally planned economy) and social security. The simultaneous removal of most barriers and curbs on entrepreneurship – accompanied by privatization of government-run indus-tries – led to the rapid, but also chaotic, development of market economies. Government efforts to gain some sort of control over these changes were made on a trial-and-error basis. However, in general – regardless of the many limitations, mistakes and high social costs – those CEE countries that followed more radical approaches to reforms have become leaders in the transition to a market economy.

Soon, the development of market economies and the need to compete globally raised new challenges for politicians and entrepreneurs, who realized that:

- the transition to a market economy means that CEE markets will gradually shift towards Western patterns;
- the relaxation or abandonment of trade barriers forces these countries to radically improve their productivity;
- the major impediments to the transition will be the underdeveloped banking, telecommunications and transportation systems, which are heavily dependent on the state, or are hard to privatize.

Unfortunately, the shaky political situation in CEE countries (both during the creation of democratic institutions and habits, and caused by changing governments), and the need to pursue tough financial policies (based on IMF guidelines), were major obstacles in implementing reforms. These problems were magnified by the sudden fall of production and replacement of local products by imports. This created an unfavourable trade balance with the West that could not be compensated for by trade with the East, since the COMECON system no longer existed and internal ties had been broken. Lower incomes for governments and inherited indebtedness (despite substantial reductions) limited the scope for investment in the logistics infrastructure. While it was not a major problem at the beginning of transition, after a few years of rapid development of CEE economies, the significant deterioration of the logistics infrastructure, or its too slow rate of improvement – especially in transportation – became the major obstacle for future development. To better understand the reasons that led to this situation, it is worth describing the major factors that stimulated the rapid growth in logistics and related areas. Among the most important were:

- the rapid growth of trade;
- productivity improvements, especially in inventory management;
- deregulation and liberalization processes in selected modes of transportation;
- the development of telecommunications and information infrastructure;
- the development of management education.

The general area of trade is recognized as the first area that fully adapted itself to the market economy. The main reason was that the consumer market was the weakest element of the previous system, and attempts to deregulate it were implemented before the systemic changes of the 1990s. Trade was also the first area in which private capital was invested and entrepreneurship appeared. Growth of the sector was especially high in the retail industry. In

Poland, the number of retail outlets (mostly small shops) tripled between 1989 and 1995, excluding the number of pedlars who covered the streets of cities and villages. Of course, this growth reflected the great underdevelopment of these services during communist times.

Along with retail trade, wholesaling companies were reorganized and many new ones entered the market. At the beginning these were local firms or family business units. But they were soon confronted with aggressive competition from large wholesaling and retailing companies from the West (including large supermarket chains like Casino, Carrefour, Tesco and Metro), which also brought new technology. These new entrants had an inherent advantage, since the collapse of the old system caused paralysis in the former centralized and state-owned companies.

Another sign of the gradual unification of CEE markets with the West is a behavioural change among consumers, who now prefer shopping at large supermarkets and department stores during weekends (Rutkowski, 1996). This, in turn, has forced small shops to search for consolidation opportunities to enable them to compete with the large supermarket chains. It also means that the total number of retail outlets, especially in grocery and fashion, has decreased.

Significant improvements in customer service, along with better (but still not matching European standards) consumer legal protection, encourage more sophisticated systems of delivery (often aimed at achieving just-in-time, QR and ECR). However, suppliers are still mostly local, largely because of the congestion at borders. This also applies to the suppliers and distributors of industrial products, with the automotive industry being a prominent example.

When talking about the positive changes in CEE logistics systems, especially the rationalization of costs, one should mention significant progress in the areas of stock levels and turnover. According to available statistics, better turnover has reduced the average cost of inventory by around 20 per cent. The biggest improvement is in food products and other perishable items. This was achieved despite – as is typical in an emerging market – shifts of inventory from distributors and retailers to producers. Now the producers have to apply innovative ways of production and distribution, and this is a challenge, since flexible manufacturing systems and more advanced computers in manufacturing (CIM) are still scarce in the region.

Along with inventory-carrying improvements, warehousing is a dynamically developing process. There was an initial fall in numbers resulting from the bankruptcy of old, multi-storey and small warehouses. But then many companies, both local and foreign, started to develop modern and well-equipped warehouses, and provide services that go beyond the standard inventory-carrying function. The first state-of-the-art logistics platforms were created at the end of the 1990s, with many new logistics production centres already planned or constructed. Most of these centres are run by large, well-known companies. Such platforms not only improve services, but also create new employment opportunities. Logistics becomes a vital element of the whole economy and the demand for logistics specialists – as a new profession in CEE – is very high (Rutkowski, 1996). Along with the advent of Western know-how, Polish companies (both producers and distributors) also joined the process of rapid infrastructure modernization and (when appropriate) automation of warehousing operations.

All these developments in logistics require parallel development of the transport network and services that bind together the logistics system. After decades of state monopoly, transportation became a hot topic during liberalization and even deregulation. The first mode to be substantially deregulated was road transport. Domestic services can be offered by almost anybody who holds a driver's licence and registers their activity. In terms of international transport some restrictions do apply. and there are still quotas set by bilateral intergovernmental agreements.

The liberalization of road transport led to the establishment of thousands of small and private carriers, and the prices for these services decreased significantly, taking most of the business away from the railways. That, however, created some negative impact on safety, environmental protection and profitability of the sector. The rush for catching more and more orders for transport services and maximization of load resulted in violation of transport procedures, especially for the rest time of drivers and overloading of trucks, which further damaged the existing road network.

In other words, the dynamically developing and deregulated road transport system surpassed the ability of the governmental agencies to provide safety standards. This gap, especially in Poland, forced the authorities to take some radical measures to reorganize the system, by investing in more truck weigh stations (including mobile ones, enforced by the police) and the creation of a specialized agency – Road Transport Inspection – empowered to penalize any deviation from technical, legal and humanitarian (such as the movement of livestock) standards. Of course, all these measures, along with the introduction of new legal acts, are part of the harmonization of regulations in the CEE countries to EU requirements, so the training process is very much supported by EU specialists and police representatives.

These changes are associated with a programme of construction of new roads and motorways. This is a better solution than periodic limitations (typically during hot periods) on truck traffic to protect the roads' surface – and make logistics even more costly and inefficient. These limitations were also ineffective, as they could easily be bypassed by including some perishables that are exempted from these limitations as part of the load.

Despite the rise in hazards on the road cased by uncontrolled development of road transport services, tough competition resulted in a drastic decrease in the profitability of these services, and eventually the lowering of service standards. Realizing that, companies began to quit the 'cheapest-and-first-come' system of carrier selection and to look for more integrated, dedicated transportation services offered by more respected and well-established transport or logistics companies. Some of these are still independent, local, but country-wide companies (having log time experience in international transport services) or have emerged from forwarding agencies into contract logistics companies, who are part of global companies like Schenker, P&O and others.

The railways in CEE countries are still run by the state, and the restructuring process is not as advanced as for other modes opf transport. Each country is searching for the best solution for the eventual privatization of railways, but because of high employment levels and the high cost of modernization, the transformation changes are only gradually being implemented. In Poland, for example, the first step was to separate all services (such as maintenance facilities, construction companies, etc) from the railways. This has already allowed a few other than state-run railway companies to act as a carrier, paying for the use of the rail track, and hopefully foster competition and allow better allocation of resources for modernization and upgrading. At the moment, however, we see the liquidation of certain local connections, and keeping vital commuter lines in large cities with management of local authorities alone, or in cooperation with the former monopoly.

More progress has been achieved in restructuring the railways in terms of separating cargo and passenger operations, and within passenger operations to establish specialized, fully-owned state railways focusing on, for instance, inter-city connections. The major obstacle in faster process of restructuring comes from the trade unions; they realize that applying market principles to the railways will mean that tracks will close (as happens) and there will be further reductions in employment. The need for such a reduction paradoxically reflects the relatively high density of rail track (with the majority of the network electrified), but much of this is used exclusively for commuter passenger services, or has minimal use because of competition from road transport. It is also important to note that most of the existing tracks have to be upgraded for high-speed transport and heavy load cargo movement.

We should also remember that most of CEE railways currently offer limited intermodal services – and there is a major opportunity for them to compete with road transportation (or to support its transit traffic) provided there are financial resources to finance such programmes. Finally, we should also note that the climate around railway privatization (influenced by the poor results from the United Kingdom) is not encouraging, and we should expect more efforts towards the commercialization of state-owned railways, rather their privatization, especially in larger CEE countries.

Ownership changes in air transport are also slow, but the modernization process is well advanced. Former flag carriers are still major players in this regulated market, but they have to compete aggressively with Western carriers on international routes. Domestically and on regional routes, new airlines have emerged and might become strong niche carriers in the future.

An important aim of all CEE airlines is to replace their outdated Soviet-built aircraft; LOT Polish Airlines were the first to operate exclusively Western-built aircraft. With the Hungarian MALEY and Czech CSA airlines, governments were able to pursue privatization (but with control in state hands) by finding foreign airlines to become shareholders (Alitalia and Air France, respectively).

These changes initially had no significant impact on their development, but after the 11 September 2001 tragedy and the spectacular bankruptcy of well-established airlines (led by Swissair), these airlines began a more intensive search for strategic partnerships with members of global alliances like Star Alliance, One World or Sky Team. Such a search is definitely a global trend rather than a CEE-specific process, but with the advent of the 'open-skies' policy and integration of these countries with the EU, it is the 'last call' for them to become partners in such alliances. This should help them to survive on the market (even if it means some marginalization in terms of the number of connections served) and to improve their effectiveness.

Some CEE airlines, like LOT Polish Airlines, have been exposed to enormous turbulence, but fortunately (mostly due to the recognized high quality of their services) this did not lead to their disappearance. By selling 35 per cent of its stock to SAir Group, LOT became a member of the Qualiflyer alliance, which – after the bankruptcy of it leader, Swissair – has now been dissolved. Fortunately the majority stock remained in state hands, and money from the sales of stocks to Swissair has been reinvested into LOT. Currently, LOT has signed an agreement with Lufthansa and on 1 January 2003 it became a member of the Star Alliance. It is expected that sooner or later, if that alliance survives, Lufthansa will become a major stakeholder in LOT and will participate in its privatization.

The current shaky economic situation in the region and the threat of terrorism have slowed down privatization, but not the investments and improvements in CEE airlines' management. These actions are essential as – despite higher productivity and an increased number of passengers, not drastically limited by the attack on the World Trade Center – the revenues are mostly consumed by the costs of leasing newly acquired equipment, and by tighter security precautions and installations in the airports and on board aircraft. Along with airline modernization, the air traffic control infrastructure is undergoing radical changes. New passenger and cargo terminals have been built, and air traffic control systems have been upgraded to improve safety and services in the increasingly crowded skies of the region. Some of these projects are supported by EU structural financial aid and European Bank for Reconstruction and Development (EBRD) credits.

As with other modes of transport, the pipeline system is expanding as a result of new sources of natural gas and crude oil supplies. At present, there is a decline in sea and inland water transportation because it is not being used to its full potential. This is largely because of the lack of proper terminals and underdevelopment of waterways, especially in Poland.

Some progress has taken place in the development of telecommunication and information networks. In the case of Hungary, the Czech Republic and Poland, the monopolistic service providers have already been privatized (with the state as major shareholder), but in other countries they are still under the control of the state. Economic recession and over-optimism about the demand for the latest technological advancements in telecommunications have slowed down the progress in privatization of the sector. Some of the large European telecom companies have indicated financial instability and a lack of resources for further acquisition of stocks offered by the CEE governments.

As far as the services are concerned, these are far from perfect, and charges, although decreasing (especially long-distance ones), are among the most expensive in Europe. The introduction of new tariff plans and services (including ISDN and the Internet) makes a change, but consumer perception of telecoms is still of low quality for high prices. A different situation exists in the mobile phone market, where there is more competition. The underdevelopment of land lines, along with the greater availability and lower prices of mobile services, make CEE one of the most dynamically developing regions. But even here one can observe some indications of saturation, which has forced mobile network companies to focus on effectiveness and more diversified services. To some extent, but not as obviously as in some Western companies, the financial situation of mobile service providers has worsened due to investment in UMTS technology concessions. These were, however, relatively cheap and the government regulatory agencies are flexible about its introduction, which has been postponed for several years. Thus, the impact of UMTS failure to start is not crucial, though some major stakeholders in CEE mobile businesses have already sunk a lot of capital into such concessions in the West.

The use of information networks (with greater use of fibre optics) is also increasing, and the first applications of electronic data interchange (EDI) in accordance with UN/EDIFACT standards are being introduced. In addition, an increasing number of companies are using integrated management information systems, but with mixed results. That is not, however, unique to the CEE, but value for money seems to be lower there, and more advanced management systems are needed that use the technology as a support tool and not a solution in itself.

Regardless of the economic transformation and improvements in logistics infrastructure, statistical data – supported by everyday experience – shows that the logistics system in CEE is still too costly and inefficient. The gap with the West is still at the same level as 20–30 years ago, and in the case of road infrastructure that gap may even be increasing. Some hope to reverse the process when most of the CEE countries become members of the EU, provided they can use effectively the financial resources offered.

There are various reasons for such poor conditions of CEE transport systems, including:

- Road transport was deregulated, while there was slower transformation in other modes of transport (mainly railways). This caused a shift of transport – including bulk – onto trucks. The rapid increase of road traffic, together with an insufficient rate of road modernization, led to the devastation of existing roads. At the same time, railways were losing their business, making reforms of this more ecologically sound mode of transport even harder.

- The rapid increase in car sales (the effect of postponed demand from communist times) combined with higher cargo traffic has resulted in huge congestion and more accidents.

- Time-consuming, postponed and weakly prepared programmes of express and motorway development in CEE countries, along with the inherited lack of bypasses around cities, are contributing to the further collapse of transportation systems in this region.

- CEE countries developed ambitious plans for the construction of motorways, but these were never implemented, or just fragments of them were built. Today, the major problem is who should finance such investments. Initial attempts to involve private companies in financing such projects and let them charge tolls for the use of highways were very unpopular. In Hungary, for such a project linking Budapest and its border with Austria, the charges proved to be too high to attract enough traffic to bring a return on investment over the time of interest to private businesses. In Poland the same question was raised, and similarly to its Czech and Slovak neighbours, the government decided to introduce fees (annual and short-term) for using existing major roads in the form of 'vignette', which most Europeans are familiar with while travelling in Austria or Switzerland. The income from these fees is supposed to support the financing of motorway construction without private involvement.

- Too slow a development of border and other logistics terminals raises doubts about the possibility of introducing operations based on JIT or ECR systems.

- A low proportion of goods use intermodal transport, because of the underdevelopment of the relevant infrastructure and the uncompetitive pricing of such services.

- The rapidly growing need for telecommunications and information networks are hindered by too slow a development and the low level of services offered. This is primarily because of the monopolistic structure in most CEE countries, along with incompatibility of equipment (manual and analogue systems coexist with the high-tech solutions that are gradually replacing old equipment). Fibre-optic technology is still scarce.

- The limited use of information technology by businesses is creating 'islands of information' that are hard to integrate.

Summarizing the situation in CEE countries, one may say that the current logistics system is a result of both advantageous and disadvantageous factors, which indicate the direction of logistics strategy development in these countries at both macro and micro levels. The advantages of the current state of logistics are:

- the increasing recognition and application of modern logistics solutions in both manufacturing and services;
- the increasing efficiency and effectiveness of logistics systems in companies;
- more investments in modern logistics infrastructure;
- the advent of logistics services providers (mainly from the West) promoting state-of-the-art logistics solutions;
- significant progress in customer service and rapid development of the service sector.

The disadvantages are:

- the unsatisfactory progress in implementing modern management concepts and techniques, magnified by insufficient or too formal implementation of quality assurance systems (eg ISO 9000 series);
- the too slow development of a new transport infrastructure (especially roads) to upgrade the existing, and often very poor, system;
- the too high cost of logistics activities (resulting from the conditions described earlier), which lowers the attractiveness of CEE for potential foreign investors in industries requiring effective logistics;
- the shortage of integrated logistics services (too few exist on the market);
- the fragmentation of logistics activities (resulting in constant suboptimization of decisions) and not fostering a holistic approach to supply chains.

A full understanding of the problems and their causes is a key requirement for the development and successful implementation of logistics strategies in these countries. Despite the continuing process of assimilation of Western standards, this awareness is especially important to potential investors in the region, for whom the experience and challenges of CEE countries may still be new.

LOGISTICS STRATEGIES IN CEE COUNTRIES

This description of the existing logistics system in selected CEE countries indicates that it is affected by:

- the dynamics of their economic growth and the inflow of foreign investments (which have slowed down because of the recent global economic downturn and the threat of terrorism);
- the development of the economic and political situation, especially in other CEE countries;
- the progress of CEE countries in adapting to EU and NATO standards;

- global trends;
- a focus on environment protection policy.

Obviously, all these factors are dependent one on another, since it is impossible to separate the internal situation of CEE countries from direct and indirect changes. Besides, a common opinion exists that the logistics system of CEE has to adapt and reach EU standards, otherwise the creation of an integrated and pan-European logistics system will only be wishful thinking, making further economic expansion eastwards unrealistic. One should not neglect the impact of rapidly developing consumer markets in CEE already shaping customer service standards.

The main thrust of economic development is that the recent recession will soon end (as seems to be currently observed), and the legacy of the communist system, mainly in the defective infrastructure and social conditions, will be removed. This aim is encouraging the further inflow of modern technology and management methods, which should result in the higher productivity and improved competitiveness of CEE countries, despite their losing their traditional advantages, such as low-cost labour. We have already emphasized that the high costs of logistics compared with Western standards is a major limitation on the development of CEE economies, so investments in logistics – improving infrastructure, attracting logistics companies and developing logistics education – should be one of the major priorities of economic policies (Rutkowski, 1996). Of course, all these hopes might be crushed by a turbulent global political situation and acts of terrorism, but that is one reason why the whole region is so eager to reintegrate with the rest of Western Europe and to reach the standards set by the NATO.

The key objectives of logistics strategies for CEE countries are determined by the major challenges that await the region at the turn of the 20th century, namely:

- an emphasis on the development of integrated supply chains;
- the implementation of modern tools of forecasting and designing logistics systems in companies;
- a focus on achieving further synergy between cost reduction and customer service levels, especially in delivery times, reliability and flexibility;
- a need for the development of flexible manufacturing systems (FMS) supported by relevant information technology (CIM), provided that companies first begin to build process-oriented management systems;
- the acceleration of improvements to the transport, information, banking and customs infrastructure;
- the adaptation of CEE logistics systems to EU requirements;
- a need for the recognition and development of logistics in service industries, especially in health care, banking, telecommunications and tourism.

To successfully meet these challenges over the next 10 years seems impossible for those countries in the region working on their own. They need external support

– mainly from the EU, which most CEE countries should have joined by the end of 2003. Any government investment has to compete with other very important reforms of administration, education, health care and pension schemes, as well as restructuring heavy industry, agriculture and so on. Unfortunately, with economic recession, such investments sometimes lose out to short-term goals. One example is the recent Hungarian government's proposal to shift some resources from motorway construction into social expenditure. In such complex situations, the logistics strategy implemented by the state should:

- focus on key investments that the private sector is unable to make;
- create a favourable climate for other investments to improve the logistics system;
- work out a joint strategy with NATO and the EU aimed at directing more structural aid for the development and integration of CEE logistics systems with the rest of Europe.

This is why the logistics strategy at the macroeconomic level should focus on:

- expanding the liberalization/deregulation processes in transport;
- accelerating the privatization processes in the banking and telecommunication sectors, complementary to the proper organization of material and services flows;
- more active involvement of CEE governments in the construction of motorways and bypasses, along with modernization of border infrastructures;
- actively supporting environmental solutions in logistics by enacting the relevant legal acts and incentives for companies dealing with reverse logistics and intermodal transport systems.

At the micro level, logistics strategies should reflect global trends and focus on:

- the orientation towards, development of and participation in supply chains – aimed at continuously improving performance and similar to those that meet customer needs in the West;
- investments in modern management education, which emphasizes the development of human resources and knowledge-based management;
- the implementation of outsourcing strategies for logistics, as the development of owned operations is too expensive and risky – a process that must be accompanied by the development of specialized and dedicated logistics services based on modern logistics centres;
- the development of FMS and JIT/QR/ECR systems in manufacturing and services;
- further investments in information technology, linked with radical changes in managing companies.

All these strategies have to be implemented simultaneously to bring maximum effect, and significantly improve the ability of these countries to become strong and attractive partners in a united Europe. Any further delay in this sphere may destroy the whole effort and waste the sacrifices made during the transition process, especially in those countries that will remain for some time outside the EU.

CONCLUSIONS

CEE countries are at different stages in their move towards a market economy, but they are all still a long way from their desired targets. Logistics and the related infrastructure were the most neglected elements of the previous system. To upgrade and develop a modern logistics system, CEE countries must use a significant part of their financial and human resources. They must realize that after fixing the financial system, the second step is to significantly improve logistics. This would give enormous savings to help the economies of CEE gain further momentum in their development. Such reforms seem to be gaining support from societies experiencing the negative aspects of underdeveloped logistics infrastructures – especially in form of worsening their quality of life.

Another important element of successful reforms concerns the development of human resources – and the change of 'inherited' thinking. The emerging market economies inspired individualism and entrepreneurship, but the simplest ways of improving productivity in the region have been almost exhausted. Further development requires more teamwork, a holistic view of enterprise and better education.

Modern logistics, along with developed management concepts, offers a variety of solutions. These challenges have now been recognized in CEE countries. The logistics associations have reached maturity, and more and more universities and companies offer logistics training and consultation. In technology, state-of-the-art solutions are becoming available, and companies are making better use of them. These initiatives are a prerequisite for the rapid development of both internal markets and the external environment. Only effective implementation of the strategies presented will ensure that this region becomes an attractive platform linking the West with the East.

Finally, it is worth emphasizing that regardless of some criticism and real problems faced by the region in its path to join the EU, enormous progress has already been made. This relates especially to those countries that are near the end of negotiations to join the EU, and have a good strategic benchmark for formulating their policies. Even if politicians prefer shortcuts and focusing on elimination of consequences to the prevention of causes, the effort and resources are shifted more towards the future – towards better infrastructure and management of resources.

Not all the countries have used their time of transition effectively. It is also true that the prospective EU members fall below some standards (as was the case with Spain, Greece, Portugal and Ireland at the time of their joining), but they remain a very attractive place for investment, with most of the market rules and institutions already functioning. CEE is still a place that more people should discover, but this region is no longer unknown and unpredictable. We hope that in coming years, progress in CEE will mean that future editions of this book will not need this chapter, as logistics will be discussed exclusively in the context of an overall EU logistics network.

REFERENCES

Kisperska-Moron, D, Kapcia, B and Piniecki, R (1996) Badanie kwalifikacji kadry logistycznej w polskich firmach (Evaluation of logistics staff qualifications in Polish enterprises), *Zeszyty Naukowe*, **5**, pp 117–24, TNOiK Poznan,

Rutkowski, K (1996) Tendencje rozwojowe logistyki w Polsce – od dezintegracji do integracji (Logistics development trends in Poland – from fragmentation to integration), *3rd International Conference 'Logistics '96 on Logistics Systems as Key to Economic Development*, Polish Logistics Association, Poznan

FURTHER READING

Bagchi, P K and Skjott-Larsen, T (1995) European logistics in transition: some insights, *International Journal of Logistics Management*, **6** (2), pp 1–24

Chikan, A (1996) Consequences of economic transition on logistics: the case of Hungary, *International Journal of Physical Distribution and Logistics Management*, **26** (1), pp 40–48

Handfield, R B and Withers, B (1993) A comparison of logistics management in Hungary, China, Korea and Japan, *Journal of Business Logistics*, **14** (1), pp 81–109

24

Route-to-market for Western consumer goods in Asia

Bill Galvin
Kurt Salmon Associates

Donald Waters
Richmond, Parkes and Wright

This chapter looks at the way in which Western consumer products reach markets in Asia. It focuses on food, grocery and fashion brands in the growing economies of the Pacific Rim, and outlines some likely trends. The contrasting situation in Hong Kong and China is used to exemplify route-to-market differences. The chapter starts with a brief look at the economic background.

ECONOMIC BACKGROUND

Asia covers a vast area, with more than 60 per cent of the world's population and around a quarter of its trade. With exports and imports running around US $1.5 trillion (WTO, 2002), it is easy to see the importance of international logistics. As this is a major trading area it is not surprising that economic performance generally follows – but is more variable than – the broader global picture. Figure 24.1 shows the annual change in international trade for the region over the past few years, compared with world trade.

The dominant area for the Asian economy is the southeast, particularly those countries in ASEAN (Association of South East Asian Nations). This area

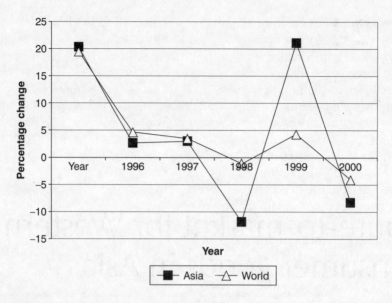

Figure 24.1 Changes in international trade

of the Pacific Rim has some of the world's most dynamic economies, and ones which are putting new demands on logistics. These include the 'Tiger economies' – which are variously taken to include some of Hong Kong, Indonesia, Malaysia, Singapore, South Korea, Taiwan and Thailand. This labelling of groups of countries tends to hide their diversity. People often concentrate on small prosperous states, such as Singapore with a population of 4 million and a GDP per capita of US $23,000 (making it more prosperous than Germany). These states have well-developed infrastructure, manufacturing and logistics systems. Much of their logistics aims at shipping high-value manufactured goods to their main customers in Japan, the United States and Europe. However, the region consists of predominantly less prosperous countries, such as Indonesia with its population of 220 million and GDP of US $723 per capita. Here the infrastructure is poor, and any form of logistics can be difficult.

Apart from its diversity, another problem with the region is that the economies are generally noted for their volatility and uncertainty. Japan is clearly a dominant economy, and for many years pulled along its neighbours with continuing rapid growth. Then in the 1990s it started a period of stagnation which lasted well over a decade. During this time GDP barely moved (falling by 0.7 per cent in 2001 and 1 per cent in 2002), the trade surplus with the United States fell by 40 per cent, unemployment and the national debt rose to record levels, share prices fell by three-quarters, commercial property prices in major cities fell by over 80 per cent, and so on (*Economist*, 2002a). Other economies in the region suffered in similar ways. In the financial crises of 1997/88 the Tiger economies saw their GDPs fall (by more than 10 per cent in some cases) before returning to growth around 2000, and then stagnating in 2001–02. Optimistically, these variations may be seen as 'blips' on underlying trends; some observers take a more pessimistic view and question the sustainability of such rapid industrialization and growth.

Underlying problems within national economies have been exacerbated by outside factors beyond the region's control. Terrorist attacks on the World Trade Center in 2001 had obvious effects on the global economy, while the bombing of Bali in 2002 brought problems nearer. Tourism provides 3.4 per cent of Indonesia's GDP and suffered badly (*Economist*, 2002c); Singapore's economy declined sharply because of its dependence on troubled high-technology industries; unemployment in Hong Kong rose to almost 6 per cent (Lee and Cheng, 2002; see also Web site at http://www.asiaweek.com); guerilla groups in some areas limited investment and growth. Even the Chinese economy, which is to some extent insulated by its large domestic market, affects the region by sucking in foreign investment – around US $50 billion in 2002 – which might otherwise go to other countries. The strength of many smaller countries in the region depends on their larger neighbours rather than any inherent fiscal management skills.

CONSUMER MARKETS IN SOUTHEAST ASIA

Table 24.1 shows the population and GDP per capita for some countries in the region, and clearly shows why the region's consumer market is attractive to Western multinationals. It gives a combination of high income in some countries, with high population in others. If we take a more stable period – covering the late 1990s – we get the picture shown in Figure 24.2. More recently the 'bubbles' in this graph have been jostled around, but the underlying principles remain sound.

Table 24.1 Population and GDP per capita of selected countries

	Population (millions)	GDP per capita (US $)
China	1,294.4	866
Hong Kong	7.1	23,709
Indonesia	217.5	723
Japan	127.5	37,494
Malaysia	23.0	4,035
Philippines	78.5	988
Singapore	4.2	22,959
Taiwan	23.6	13,300
Thailand	64.3	1,945

Sources: UN (2002a, 2002b); see also Web site at http://www.un.org

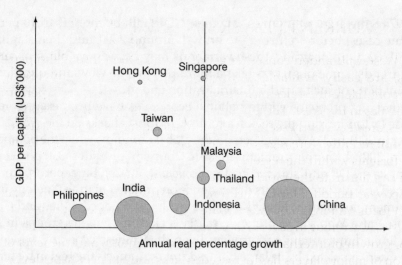

Figure 24.2 Consumer market analysis

Government statistics in much of Asia are neither timely nor especially accurate, but some other indications are positive. For example, Maersk Line, a dominant container carrier for trade between Asia and the West, has reported some increase in traffic. At the same time, the CEO of one of the region's leading export facilitators reports that regional devaluations against the US dollar have led to generally low prices. This has led to higher volumes, but with problems that come when buyers have to finance raw materials and work-in-progress in US dollars. The message is that some prospects for trade are positive, and in the longer term should encourage a return to at least modest growth. (There is a clear parallel here with Mexico's dramatic recovery from its severe economic crisis in the mid-1990s.)

For consumer goods imported to Asia, both currency movements and consumer sentiment have hit the luxury end particularly hard, with many regional retailers in Singapore and Hong Kong being severely squeezed by the combination of high operating costs and low income. Pessimists – who claim that they are more realistic in current circumstances – see the downturn lasting at several more years. Nevertheless, the longer-term outlook for trade between Southeast Asia and the West, driven by population and growth potential, seems set to increase. This underlying trend is reinforced by two more subtle facts: Asia's population is generally much younger than in the West, while urbanization has surged. The latter tends to encourage market growth for more expensive goods, even when spending power is static or growing more slowly.

CURRENT PLAYERS IN SOUTHEAST ASIA

Most Western branded consumer goods, from fashion through to perishable foods, are easily available in the region, particularly Hong Kong and Singapore. Here the sales of luxury goods have tended to outperform per capita sales in the West. These countries are regional and international tourist centres, are very clearly seen as high-end 'shopping malls' for the rest of Asia, and until recently were regarded as the proving grounds for new brands and retail formats within the region.

We can illustrate the rapid growth of international retailers by looking at one six-year period. During this time sales from 'foreign format' retailers – which focus on foreign brands – soared. Wal-Mart opened branches in three countries, Carrefour in seven, Ahold in five, and so on (see Figure 24.3).

The growth of international retailers has continued, and the level of penetration of major players has increased. Marks and Spencer have developed a significant presence, as have Makro, Toys 'R' Us, IKEA, JC Penney and so on. By 2002 Tesco had opened 50 hypermarkets employing 24,000 people. Many of these businesses are operated as joint ventures, franchises, or technical assistance partnerships, as these combine the advantages of new methods of working with local knowledge. As always in the retail sector, there is continuing change, with, for example, Yaohan expanding rapidly and then going bankrupt in 1998, while Marks and Spencer significantly reduced its international operations from 2001.

Supermarkets and other multiple outlets have at least 65 per cent of sales for imported brands in Hong Kong and Singapore, while elsewhere in Asia the

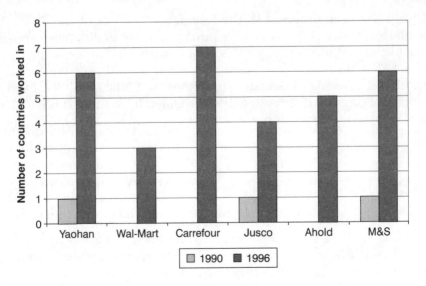

Figure 24.3 Retail expansion in Southeast Asia

traditional 'mom and pop' shops enjoy a much higher share. Table 24.2 shows the situation in three distinct countries, with typical coverage for a leading brand.

Table 24.2 Typical distribution coverage for a leading brand distributor

Type of outlet	Hong Kong	Taiwan	Philippines
Supermarkets	570	380	390
Personal care chains	180	170	In above
Convenience store chains	610	2,200	In above
Tertiary	0	0	15,000
Population (million)	7.1	23.6	78.5
GDP per capita (US$)	$23,700	$13,300	$988

Note: tertiary are small outlets generally supplied direct by brand owners or agents, ie excluding those supplied through wholesalers.

There are clearly contrasting situations here. Even basic factors – such as the availability of centralized distribution systems – vary, as these are sophisticated and used extensively in Hong Kong but only emerging in the Philippines. Perhaps more important is the presence of large operators. Just two companies (Dairy Farm Group and AS Watson Ltd) operate an overwhelming majority of supermarkets, personal care chains and convenience stores in Hong Kong in terms of both square footage and turnover, while President Foods in Taiwan dominates the FMCG retail market. Brand owners wishing to enter the market through retailers in these two countries have few doors on which to knock.

Things are very different in the less developed countries. There it is essential for Western brands to make inroads into the traditional channels in order to succeed, even though this is very difficult. Underscoring this is the fact that there are few logistics companies offering Western-style services and capabilities outside Hong Kong and Singapore. For even the essentials of physical distribution, there is generally limited choice for 'plug and play' market entry, compared with, say, launching a UK brand in the US market.

CHOOSING ROUTES FOR ENTRY TO ASIA'S MARKETS

In the West, market entry for companies hinges upon access to the major retailers. In Southeast Asia, this is true only for Hong Kong, Singapore, and to a lesser extent Taiwan. Elsewhere the major retailers fall far short of forming a critical mass for food and grocery brands, and are only just workable for high-end fashion goods or for hypermarket formats in a handful of major urban areas. 'Own retail' solutions in the fashion sector are rare outside the Hong Kong, Singapore and Taiwan markets, and then only for retailers who have very fixed views on the merchandise they will carry – usually selected from an in-house supply chain determined in the West. Joint-venture retail options exist for fashion goods, but need meticulous country-by-country research to identify a viable niche. Various route-to-market options are illustrated in Table 24.3, using Hong Kong and China as examples.

Leaving aside direct entry via own or joint-venture retail models, a variety of options exist. The route-to-market in most of Asia is heavily dependent upon assistance from third parties, with the first decision being whether to manufacture in the country or the region, or to import. The contrast between Hong Kong and China is a useful illustration of how different things can be from the brand owner's perspective.

Route-to-market in Hong Kong

The real-estate and labour expense of manufacturing in the Hong Kong SAR deters most brand owners from this option, though other regional options are often selected, such as factories in Malaysia or Thailand to serve various regional markets. At least in the initial stages of regional market entry, usually initiated in Hong Kong or Singapore, brand owners are content to import from the West. Indeed, some of the major distribution services companies in Hong Kong built their businesses as agencies, bringing overseas brands into the market.

Significant structural pluses for Hong Kong (and with the exception of sales tax, for Singapore), are:

- a total absence of tariffs, duties, VAT or sales taxes on food and grocery and fashion goods, apart from duties on alcohol and tobacco;
- a good selection of distributors with whom Western brand owners would feel comfortable doing business;
- affluent consumers who are more homogenous than in most other parts of Asia, and who value Western brands;
- a Western commercial and legal model;
- free flow of capital and profits in and out of the region;
- low tax structure for companies and employees;
- sophisticated advertising and marketing services, with ample media selection to reach target consumers.

The question of whether there is a market for a brand may initially be resolved by finding a distributor who will launch the brand on mutually agreeable terms. The major investment to be negotiated will normally be advertising and promotion.

Table 24.3 Western consumer product route-to-market models for Asia

Models		ADVANCED ASIA MARKETS (HONG KONG EXAMPLE)		
		Trade sales by	Revenue trigger	Comments
1	Own retail	n/a	Cash register	Rare: eg M&S (in Hong Kong only); or very specialized outlets
2	Joint venture (JV) retail (incl. franchise etc)	n/a	Fully negotiable	Typically 'fashion' goods and strong retail formats, eg IKEA, Body Shop
3	Own logistics resources to serve retail	Brand owner (BO)	Delivery	Some dominant brands, eg Colgate-Palmolive, Philip Morris
4	Full agency distributor	Distributor	FOB or landed	May not always be fully effective for BO. Examples include Cadbury. Frequent mode for initial market entry.
5	Direct export to key account retailers, rest via local distributor	BO for key accounts, other accounts variable	Normally FOB for key accounts and distributor	Many examples for major brands, eg United Biscuits, with a combination of import from the West and China manufacture. BO sometimes handles all sales
6	100% via local distributor	Mainly by distributor	FOB or landed	Frequently used for lower volume brands
7	Wholesalers	Variable	Delivery	For major brands, used to serve smaller accounts via main distributor
8	Direct marketing	Agents	Supply to agent	Examples include Avon for door-to-door, and TV for direct response

Notes:
a   This table ignores models for brand marketing
b   Revenue Point data excludes credit terms, typically 30 to 60 days, with strong trade compliance
c   Local manufacturing option for very high volumes only (eg San Miguel beer). Final packing in-market is sometimes adopted

DEVELOPING ASIA MARKETS (CHINA EXAMPLE)

	National distribution models	Trade sales	Revenue trigger	Comments
1	Own or JV retail (including franchise etc)	n/a	n/a	No examples yet of national retail representation
2	Own logistics resources to serve retail trade	n/a	n/a	No examples as legal barriers to in-house distribution have only recently been relaxed
3	JV logistics resources to serve retail	BO/JV partner	Delivery	Most common type of arrangement
4	Freight carrier direct to key accounts	BO/JV partner	Delivery	Commonly used to complement the above services
5	Wholesaler network (incl. state-owned)	Wholesaler	Delivery	Model has highly variable degrees of success
	Provincial distribution models	**Trade sales**	**Revenue trigger**	**Comments**
6	Own retail	n/a	Cash register	Very few examples
7	Retail with local JV partner	n/a	See comments	PRC law defines the boundaries of JV arrangements
8	Direct export to key account retailers	BO	FOB/other	Uncommon for food and grocery: supply lead-times plus tariff barriers
9	Local manufacture, in-house/contract delivery	BO	Delivery	Conventional method of market entry by larger MNCs with dominant brands
10	Local manufacture, then via wholesalers	BO/WS	Delivery	Option for smaller and more remote accounts
11	Full agency distributor	Distributor	FOB/ex works if PRC made	Conventional model for many less dominant brands, but strengths vary between distributors both overall and geographically
12	Mix-and-match of 8–11 across provinces	Variable	Variable	An untidy model into which many brand owners have evolved
13	Direct marketing	Agents	Supply to agent	'Personal contact' marketing has recently been limited by law

Notes

a This table ignores models for brand marketing

b Credit performance of wholesalers and retailers is highly variable, with terms normally between 45 and 90 days

Route-to-market in China

Things could hardly be more different north of Hong Kong. The first question is the extent to which Western brand owners or their service providers – especially international firms – can earn profits in China. A product that enjoys spectacular success in Hong Kong may take many years to gain a significant share of expenditure from more affluent consumers in China, while none of the advantages cited for Hong Kong are particularly true for China. However, China has changed dramatically over the last 20 years, and is still changing rapidly, particularly since its entry to the World Trade Organization (WTO) in 2001. In theory, this should open its markets – and 'bind China's economic reforms with the norms of international business' (*Economist*, 2002b). Trade barriers have been reduced in sectors ranging from agriculture to banking, but real changes are likely to continue very slowly. The official growth in GDP has risen by over 8 per cent a year for two decades, with peaks of 15 per cent in 1984 and 14 per cent in 1992; however, this official rate (which is widely held to be an exaggeration) has fallen to around 7 per cent. Industrialization means that the country needs to create 8–9 million new jobs a year to keep unemployment under control, with at least 150 million people moving from the countryside into cities.

Brand owners from the West typically make three strategic errors, which account for many instances of weak performance in China:

- Over-estimating market size. To this day one sees market forecasts based upon a top-down share of spending by the total population (the 'billion pairs of socks' error). Fiducia did a survey of European firms in China, and over 60 per cent of the sample admitted to this error.
- Under-estimating the sheer scale of expenditure on advertising and promotion needed not merely to persuade consumers to buy, but to convert strongly rooted affinities to traditional goods. For example, the concept of mixing toasted cereals with milk is conventional in the West but a curiosity in China.
- Setting up factories in southern China (perhaps because of the sense of geographical comfort in proximity to Hong Kong), whereas the more brand-receptive and trend-setting markets are far away in Shanghai and Beijing.

Another negative factor is protection of brand rights. In the survey by Fiducia mentioned above, 55 per cent of companies found their products being counterfeited, and 71 per cent of these were unable to find any remedy. Moreover, 60 per cent of those companies manufacturing in China encountered parallel imports (unauthorized imports of their own brand). One insight into such problems is that they partially reflect distribution inefficiencies. Local entrepreneurs 'piggy back' the efforts of brand owners by operating a more effective route-to-market.

Part of the difficulty for overseas brand owners wishing to take advantage of the economic growth is a classic problem for logistics: affluent consumers form a small proportion of a very large population, and outside definable urban communities they are very widely scattered. Distribution is, therefore, often the most important factor – and challenge – for market success in China, over-riding what can be a far more esoteric question about whether to manufacture locally or import. Since China entered the WTO, the question of where to manufacture has at least becomes a financial rather than regulatory issue.

Table 24.4 summarizes a study for a prominent international FMCG brand in China. The table identifies the scale of 'reach' required to achieve a given level of coverage ('being there') for the estimated total available market measured in numbers of outlets. The figures give weighting to likely sales yield of different retail formats in different types of location.

Table 24.4 Retail representation needed to yield given market coverage

Cumulative coverage (%)	Number of cities	Number of retail outlets
40	Top 35	77,000
70	Next 230	225,000
80	Next 550 (incl. urban areas)	170,000

To achieve 40 per cent coverage, a personal care brand needs 77,000 outlets – which is only 16 per cent of the estimated total number of outlets in China, but would be expected to yield 40 per cent of overall sales. The plain fact is that no single distributor or distribution channel can sustain this kind of reach, for several reasons:

- China is in effect 24 different countries, based upon its provincial structure. Inter-provincial transport is fraught with logistics and administration challenges, and the choice of freight mode is complex, including road and rail, and waterborne by inland or coastal vessel. Air transport is a limited option.
- Few major Western-style distribution companies operate across the major cities in China, and have on-tap service capacity for major new customers. Many would need to bring new resources on stream (and amortize these resources over a lengthy contract), while few have the capital strength to invest in resources without immediate revenue flow. This may change when local players – including those with roots in Hong Kong and Taiwan – move into the logistics service sector when there is evidence of potential profits.
- Entry to the wholesaler network that dominates service to most outlets – and in turn a very large proportion of achievable volume – means establishing a large and complex patchwork of relationships generally

segmented by geographical area. These wholesalers (whether state-owned or privately owned) can more aptly be described as trade finance companies with distribution services tagged on. A key concern for brand owners is receivables from the network.

These difficulties spell out the need for overseas brand owners to have a very strong commitment to the consumer market in China. The majority of existing entrants have incurred losses for many years. This would not be tolerated unless they had a very optimistic view of the glittering prizes ahead in what – irrespective of regional recession today – may well prove to be the largest economy in the world before very long. Improved logistics will have to play a major part in this transformation.

AN EXAMPLE OF ENTERING THE MARKET: TESCO

Tesco plc is the largest retailer in the UK with 729 stores, sales of £25 billion in 18.8 million square feet of space, and 195,000 staff. It has expanded into a variety of financial services, and is the world's largest online supermarket (Tesco, 2002). Since the 1990s, it has followed a policy of rapid expansion in Southeast Asia.

Tesco's strength is in highly efficient operations, with a history of successful innovations in supply chain management. Its move to Southeast Asia is an important development. The company clearly sees opportunities to expand into new markets. The local economies benefit from a new retail format, substantial employment (24,000 by 2002), and a range of benefits that come from such developments. They also benefit from the introduction of state-of-the-art logistics which give a model for other local operators. Tesco uses worldwide sourcing, with hubs in Bangalore, Hong Kong, Bangkok and Prague linking back to the UK head office. This system enables the organization to buy products from anywhere in the world, and track progress and costs of orders to delivery in any country in which it works. A summary of its turnover in the region is given in Table 24.5.

Table 24.5 Turnover of Tesco in Southeast Asia

Year	Turnover (£million)
1999	156
2000	464
2001	860
2002	1398

This expansion has often been through joint ventures or purchase of local stores in the main markets of Thailand, South Korea, Taiwan and Malaysia.

- *Thailand.* In 1997 Tesco bought a chain of 13 'Lotus' hypermarkets, and is now the market leader with 33 hypermarkets employing 16,000 people. This was Tesco's first entrance to the region, and it has grown particularly strong around Bangkok. There are plans for 16 more stores to open in 2002/3.
- *South Korea.* Tesco entered this market in 1999 by acquiring two high-turnover stores in partnership with Samsung. It now runs 14 stores, with 9 more planned for 2002/3 and plans for considerable growth.
- *Taiwan.* The first hypermarket was opened in 2000, followed by two more in 2001, and plans for another in 2002/3.
- *Malaysia.* In 2002 Tesco announced a joint venture partnership with Sime Darby and opened its first store. Four more are planned with this partnership for 2002/3.
- *China and Japan.* Tesco does not yet work in either of these markets, but it is actively looking at opportunities.

CONCLUSIONS

Countries in Southeast Asia form a diverse group. Their economies have had a rough ride over the past decade, and this seems likely to continue for some years to come. However, the region has immense potential, and we should view the long-term prospects with some optimism. At present, logistics in the region ranges from almost non-existent to very sophisticated. As the economies continue their growth, logistics will become increasingly sophisticated to meet new demands. Even the current recession may bring changes – as those with long memories may reflect upon the dramatic growth in logistics' efficiency that came with recession in the United Kingdom. In China and the rest of Southeast Asia, foreign retailers are already undercutting traditional retailers' prices on locally produced staples. This is a sure sign of supply chain management beginning to have a revolutionary effect upon the lives of ordinary people.

REFERENCES

Economist (2002a) What ails Japan?, *Economist* (18 Apr) [Online] www.economist.com

Economist (2002b) A dragon out of puff, *Economist* (13 Jun) [Online] www.economist.com

Economist (2002c) Counting the cost, *Economist* (17 Oct) [Online] www.economist.com

Lee C S and Cheng M (2002) A false bottom, *Asiaweek* (30 Nov) [Online] www.asiaweek.com

Tesco (2002) *Annual Report*, Tesco plc, Cheshunt [Online] www.tesco.co.uk

UN (2002a) *Indications on Income and Economic Activity*, Statistics Division, United Nations, New York [Online] www.un.org

UN (2002b *Indicators on Population*, Statistics Division, United Nations, New York [Online] www.un.org

World Trade Organization (2002) *International Trade Statistics* [Online] www.wto.org

25

Logistics strategies for North America

Trevor Heaver and Garland Chow
University of British Columbia

INTRODUCTION

At one time, it may have been reasonable to discuss the strategies followed by firms in physically acquiring inputs or distributing products without reference to the broader aspects of corporate strategy. This is no longer true. Logistics strategies have become an integral part of corporate strategy. Porter (1985) recognized that inbound logistics and outbound logistics are vital parts of the value chain, that is, the means by which firms create value for their customers.

Integration of logistics strategy with global manufacturing and marketing strategies is becoming vital. Many firms have found that logistics costs and service levels have increased in importance, as brand loyalty has become a lesser factor in consumer choice and product differences between the goods of alternate producers have diminished. By applying the principles of integration, long the essence of logistics management, on wider, more strategic levels, firms have often been able to provide better services at less cost. It is no wonder that logistics strategies are increasingly an integral component of corporate planning.

The increased importance of logistics is a part of broad developments in industry. Logistics strategies in North America have to be considered in the context of forces for change that are common to most developed countries. The success of the Japanese application of just-in-time (JIT) manufacturing methods provided a wake-up call to the North American and European automobile industries to reappraise their strategies. The lessons learnt from this experience contributed to the popularity of benchmarking and re-engineering. Businesses are being exposed to more foreign approaches to management as a result of direct foreign investment. The overseas investments of Japanese companies, notably in the automobile trans-plants in North America and in Europe, have been important in this regard.

The realities of global competition have made it essential to strive to be world-class. ISO standards that are required by major corporations of their suppliers are extending the reach of world-class pressures down to even small producers. Domestic markets are so exposed to imports and to domestic firms adopting new methods that the effects of global competition are felt by firms serving local consumers as well as those serving international clients. It is no surprise that a survey of manufacturing in the *Economist* (20 June 1998) uses captions such as 'The world as a single machine' and 'No factory is an island'. It also draws on Richard Schonberger's *World Class Manufacturing: The next decade* to show the impact of Japanese 'lean manufacturing' methods on industries around the world. Japanese methods were comprehensive and included features such as JIT and total quality management (TQM) that have significant implications for logistics activities and strategies. Reductions of inventory levels and other improvements in logistics performance have been pronounced. In the United States, logistics costs have been estimated annually by Delaney (1997). His surveys show a reduction of logistics costs as a percentage of GDP from 17.2 per cent of GDP in 1980 to 10.5 per cent of GDP (or US $791 billion) in 1996.

The concepts and most of the technologies that play a key role in logistics strategies have no geographic boundaries. For example, in North America, the German-developed SAP software enjoys a significant market penetration as the architecture on which corporate information systems are built. The survey of firms judged as world-class in logistics by the Global Logistics Research Team at Michigan State University (1995) found that the capabilities of those firms are universal. A survey of European logistics trends and strategies concludes that the 'state of the art' in manufacturing industries in Europe, the United States and Japan is the same (Hessenberger, Seiersen and Straube, 1997). Therefore, the distinctive features of leading logistics strategies among developed regions are the result of local conditions affecting the application of strategies that are found universally. The combination of geographic, economic and institutional (private and public) conditions may give rise to particular features of logistics strategies in different places.

This chapter focuses on what the authors judge to be the most significant feature of logistics strategy in North America, which is its greater attention to managing the supply chain. Our view is supported by the considerable attention given to supply chain management in the literature and by the results of surveys. For example, Closs *et al* (1997) reported on the substantial shift of the world-class firms surveyed in 1995 from a process-oriented strategy in 1995 to a channel-focused strategy in 1997.

A supply chain is the collection of all producers, suppliers, distributors, retailers and transportation, information and other logistics providers that are involved in providing goods to end consumers. A supply chain includes both internal and external participants for the firm. More of the supply chain is internal for a firm that is vertically integrated than for one which is not. The management of a supply chain has moved from one in which relationships are separate, sequential and transaction-based to one that emphasizes collaborative-based strategies to link cross-enterprise business operations under a shared vision (adapted from Bowersox, 1997). However, the efficient management of a supply chain does not preclude the existence of certain transaction-based relationships as conditions warrant. Supply chain management involves planning the number and role of participants in the creation of form, time and place utilities consistent with cost-effective, high-service product availability. It involves planning and managing activities to optimize the roles of short- and long-term business relationships. In general, the management of supply chains has resulted in the simplification of supply chain structures and processes, with greater reliance on long-term relationships among fewer participants.

The prominence given to supply chain management reflects its prominence in North America and the effects of the distinctive features of the North American economy on the features of emerging supply chains.

DISTINCTIVE NORTH AMERICAN CONDITIONS

The geographic and economic size of the United States means that companies there have long been accustomed to continental-scale logistics strategies. The strategies are more established in the United States than are pan-European strategies in the EU, where the cultural diversity of Europe continues to be an important factor. The influences of changing technologies on the centralization of inventories and the development of supply chains on a continental scale are well established in the United States. However, the very self-sufficiency of the economy has meant that American managers have often been less involved with international relationships than those from countries in which foreign trade is more important.

Institutionally, this is reflected in the lesser development of freight forwarding in North America than in Europe. It is not surprising that the freight-forwarding industry is dominated in most parts of the world by European-based forwarding firms. A feature of the influence of global sourcing and marketing strategies in the United States is the rapid expansion of American freight-forwarding and related logistics services companies through internal growth and acquisitions, for example Fritz Companies and Circle International. The absence of an established freight-forwarding sector may also have contributed to the success of American transportation companies setting up domestic and international logistics service operations. Both American President Lines (APL) and Sea-Land have logistics services (ACS Logistics and Buyers, respectively) that have been particularly successful in providing logistics services for their clients in Asia.

In spite of the constraints imposed by economic regulation, in the United States until the early 1980s and somewhat later in Canada, the large size of the two countries' economies has supported efficient and large trucking and rail freight companies. The efficiency of the rail freight services has provided the base for the development of reliable intermodal transport arrangements. Intermodal services form one of the fastest-growing segments of the transportation market. The services have aided shippers in developing effective and geographically extensive supply chains.

The North American Free Trade Agreement of 1993 (NAFTA) contributed to the redesign of supply chains. It has been particularly effective in increasing trade with Mexico, as both the physical and tariff barriers to trade with that country were the most pronounced prior to the agreement. However, it is important to remember that NAFTA is a much more limited agreement than the single market of the EU. The continued existence of different standards for some products supports instances of national production. Nevertheless, the removal of tariffs and lessening of other barriers to trade have led to a shift away from nationally based subsidiaries. In some cases, such subsidiary plants have been closed. In many instances, plants now specialize in products for continental or global markets. However, as expected, the location of plants and distribution facilities has been guided more by underlying economic forces as barriers to trade have been reduced.

The closure of nationally based subsidiaries has led to a greater concentration of strategic functions. As strategic functions shift to head office, they are most likely located in the United States, the home of many multinational companies. This has implications for the logistics of logistics education, as the presence of immigration barriers limits recruiting non-American students into head-office positions. Fortunately for Canadian students, logistics management is a growth field, so that growth can offset the effects of this international shift in employment opportunities to the United States.

Finally, the North American economy has long been recognized as a consumer-driven economy in which the power of advertising is strong. This did not preclude the development of business strategies based on manufacturers producing product and pushing it through distribution channels to retailers. However, it is consistent with the rapid revision of channel power, in which large retailers have determined the patterns in supply chains based on product being pulled through chains in response to consumer demand.

Most of these characteristics contribute to the particular importance of supply chain management as the dominant strategic approach to improving the contributions of logistics to productivity and profitability.

SUPPLY CHAIN MANAGEMENT STRATEGIES

Supply chain management programmes of leading-edge companies display certain common characteristics, the most significant of which are described here. The design of supply chains involves consideration of internal and external relationships among logistics processes and with manufacturing and marketing processes. Indeed, the lack of integration among internal processes is one of the most significant obstacles to achieving true supply chain integration. Therefore, the review of actual supply chain strategies commences with the types of integration and means of achieving integration among internal processes.

Integration of the internal supply chain organization

Leading firms are committed to integrating logistics, production and marketing strategy and to blending traditional logistics activities such as transportation, warehousing, order processing and inventory together into a seamless process. Different firms take different approaches to achieving supply chain integration depending on their circumstances.

Integration through centralization

Companies competing on the basis of cost often find it advantageous to consolidate and centralize decision making. An example is the Vancouver-based Methanex, the world's largest producer of methanol. It sought a strategy to ensure low costs but excellent service levels, as it faces a commodity market driven by cost. The company has concentrated the bulk of production at a limited number of world-scale production hubs, and developed excellence in supply chain management to ensure efficient delivery to customers (*Methanex Annual Report*, 1997). The supply chain group assumed responsibility in 1996 for identifying opportunities and managing the supply chain, from the purchase of feed stock through production scheduling to the delivery of methanol to customers. The group has success-fully maintained high customer service levels with sustained low inventory levels. In 1997, the firm implemented a global logistics information system to improve efficiency in its delivery network. The centralization of supply chain management at Methanex has enabled the company to achieve a high level of integration across a global network.

Integration of the internal supply chain across business units

Many companies are organized with separate business units that may have operations in common geographic markets. In such businesses, there is the potential for great synergies in supply chain management across the business units. These synergies include serving shared customers, the development of a shared supply base, the sharing of assets and resources. The chemical company Arco, which previously managed logistics activities in separate organizations, has created a new supply chain organization which will consolidate worldwide supply chain activities, including purchasing, raw materials supply, production planning, customer support and logistics (*Chemical Market Reporter*, 1997).

It is expected that significant working capital savings and a more efficient process to satisfy customers' needs at the lowest cost will be achieved by putting responsibility for the supply chain into one organization and redesigning the process. However, the integration of logistics activities does not necessarily imply a new functionally oriented group concerned only with logistics performance. Some leading organizations seek to develop horizontal organization structures.

Developing internal horizontal organizations or cross-functional teams

'Re-engineering' argues for a focus on business processes rather than functional departments. It argues that work should be organized around outcomes or business processes or workflow, not tasks or functions. The major advantages of this horizontal organization are coordination across tasks and the focus on the customer, while leveraging expertise is a benefit of specialization by function. Such an organizational structure is often termed the 'horizontal organization' since most workflow processes that directly create value cross traditional functional lines.

Where a typical organization might today be separated into manufacturing, logistics and marketing, each working independently and often at cross purposes, the horizontal organization has 'process teams', consisting of experts from procurement, manufacturing, marketing, finance and distribution. Kraft Foods adopted this approach by creating 'interlocking' cross-functional teams, overlaid on the existing functional structure, to focus on a critical element of the company's value delivery process (Boehm and Phipps, 1996). One of the three teams was the supply chain process team responsible for the production and delivery performance for major product categories. It consisted of representatives from manufacturing, procurement, distribution, quality and engineering.

However, whether process or functionally structured, an internal service unit may be less responsive to the needs of internal customers than desired. One approach to overcome this is to use the shared-services structure.

The shared-services structure

Under this market-oriented model, the internal service provider is fully accountable for its costs and charges its internal customers for its services. The internal service provider and the internal customers negotiate a service agreement that specifies the service levels to be produced. The internal customers are free to choose external suppliers as well as produce the service themselves. In some instances, the internal supplier is free to serve other external customers. The shared-services model seeks to provide market incentives to both the service provider and the internal customer. Internal suppliers must be cost- and service-competitive. Internal customers no longer receive free or underpriced services. Companies implementing this concept at the corporate-services level are Houston Lighting and Power, Shell Services Company and British Columbia Telephone. The model is an alternative to establishing an independent subsidiary.

The independent subsidiary approach

Bell Canada is an example of a company following the 'independent subsidiary' approach to providing supply chain services to core operating divisions and to external customers. Logistics is considered a 'non-core' function for Bell. It is mission-critical but not strategic to telecommunications. Bell has established subsidiaries for other 'non-core' functions as well.

In 1995, Bell considered various options for managing logistics. A decision was made to create a wholly owned subsidiary, Progistix-Solutions, to act as a fast-track change agent (Eckler and Farrell, 1997). It was believed that the newly created subsidiary would allow Bell to make a quantum leap into new supply chain management techniques, rather than simply manage the old systems and attempt to bring change to such systems. Bell considered the subsidiary option to be a 'paradigm buster'. The subsidiary option was chosen because it facilitated fast change with least disruption to the existing logistics system, brought in a new customer-service-oriented culture, improved flexibility with labour, and leveraged people and information technology across multiple Bell customers.

Progistix-Solutions has a master contract with Bell Logistics (the internal division of Bell Canada responsible for purchasing, inventory management and fleet management) to operate the physical distribution system. The services to be provided by Progistix include inventory management, order processing, warehousing, transportation, returns management and supply chain advisory services. The first five of these are considered tactical roles for Progistix. The latter is a strategic role. Effectively it is the vehicle by which Progistix can act as an internal consulting service in supply chain management to individual Bell units as well as to Bell corporate management.

The number one priority of Progistix is to provide competitive service for Bell. However, other clients can be served when requirements complement the primary mission of serving Bell. A medium-term objective is to be a fully competitive third-party logistics provider for the communications industry with above-average service capability. Within two years of its establishment, Progistix had reduced Bell Canada's logistics costs by 30 per cent.

The use of an independent subsidiary has characteristics close to the use of a wholly independent logistics service supplier, a so-called third-party logistics service supplier. This strategy is considered as one of the elements of integration of the external supply chain.

External supply chain integration

Two aspects of the integration of external supply chain relationships are considered here. The first aspect is the outsourcing of logistics services. However, many of the general arguments about the outsourcing of logistics apply to any other purchasing decision. The second aspect is the general role of partnerships and alliances in the establishment of a supply chain structure.

Outsourcing logistics

Logistics outsourcing is the decision to purchase logistics services externally instead of producing them in-house or through a subsidiary. Like other structural changes, it is often the result of re-engineering studies. Outsourcing is much different today from a decade ago. Up to the deregulation era in transportation, most outsourcing involved a single logistics service such as transportation or warehousing, and was primarily for the physical performance of the service. Today, third-party logistics companies offer an array of bundled logistics services including medium- and long-term planning, as well as control of the integrated logistics processes. Outsourcing may involve the elimination of the total logistics operating capability in the firm.

The attractiveness of outsourcing is evidenced by the rapid growth of the third-party logistics industry. It is estimated to have grown from US $10 billion in 1992 to US $25 billion in 1996, and is forecast to expand to US $47 billion in 2000 (Harrington, 1998). Some of the leading suppliers have grown up as subsidiaries of transportation companies such as Ryder Logistics, TNT Logistics and Menlo Logistics (controlled by Consolidated Freightways). Most large transportation companies offer a comprehensive logistics service, although the strategy is least developed in the rail sector. Firms that commenced in Europe have also expanded successfully in North America, for example Excel Logistics, and Tibbett and Britten.

Third-party logistics providers may benefit from economies of scale and of specialization, economies of scope (benefits arising from complementary logistics services such as those with different seasonal peaks), or more favourable access to particular resources, perhaps for local reasons: for example, labour. During the initial development of third-party services, successful firms were seen as developing the business from an asset base, such as trucking facilities. However, the value of a knowledge base is seen as increasingly important, as information technology plays an ever-greater role in supply chain integration, and as operations research models become more sophisticated. Peter Metz of MIT has noted that while the concepts of supply chain management are 'eminently understandable', at its core are many 'rocket science-like' technical tools (Metz, 1997).

Third-party logistics is found in many industries. One in which it is now common but in which the importance of safe, high-quality transport was once seen as a reason for private transportation, is the chemical industry. Chemical producers are now commonly farming out logistics services. Dow Chemical, for example, has a third-party contract with Menlo Logistics that assigns all Dow's shipments to carriers. Dow now benefits from the extensive, computerized distribution tracking system operated by Menlo.

The process of outsourcing requires the very careful analysis of the business and identification of logistics service needs. Indeed, the requirement of this process, too often ignored for 'in-house' activities, can be an important source of benefit. Outsourcing may be conducted with or without formal contracts, as is true for any strategic alliance or partnership.

Strategic alliances and partnerships

To realize a supply chain's full competitive and market potential, companies need to link their organization with external participants of the supply chain, creating an extended team. These 'partners' include suppliers, vendors, distributors and customers. Under the supply chain approach, the emphasis of competition to serve end-consumers is less between companies and more between groups of partners working together to serve the consumer better.

Organizations that have successfully created a cross-functional supply chain extended to the outside partners consistently enjoy a competitive edge, according to the authorities. For example, Mercer Management concludes, 'There is definitely a strong correlation between companies that are paying attention to the integrated supply chain and business success' (Quinn, 1997).

The nature of the relationship between supply chain partners can take many forms. The traditional transactions-based relationship will continue to exist, but as more and more companies seek the benefits of coordination and collaboration, more partnerships and alliances will evolve. Cooperative relationships are characterized by sharing of risks and gains, long-term commitments, and commingling of operations and information. These actions can result in customer service enhancement and cost reduction from redesigning processes across the whole supply chain instead of one part of it, from specialization building on each partner's strengths, and from better planning resulting from increased information flow among the partners.

Communication and information sharing characterize successful partnerships. They allow all participants to plan and coordinate their operations more effectively. One mechanism for communication is JIT II. Under JIT II, a supplier places its own employee in the plant or facility of the customer, and actively manages the ordering of the supplier's product as if the person were part of the customer's organization. This is quite frequently done in transport, where the transport company manages inbound or outbound transportation for the customer. GATX Logistics attributes the level of information about Mitsubishi's production schedule as an important factor in its ability to keep the assembly lines running during last winter's severe weather (Minahan, 1996). 'Knowing the production schedule allowed us to work with Mitsubishi and its suppliers to accelerate some auto part deliveries when we knew bad weather was coming', says Tom Scanlin, vice-president of marketing at GATX. He adds that GATX, which is linked with Mitsubishi's 360 suppliers via electronic data interchange, leverages the schedule to utilize carriers more efficiently and to reroute trucks as supply or production needs change. The logistics provider has also set up three cross-dock facilities near Mitsubishi's suppliers in the Midwest. These supply chain tactics save the auto maker about US $1 million a year.

In summary, the supply chain concept recognizes that, for optimum efficiency, logistics needs to be designed and managed in the context of the whole supply chain, including internal and external aspects. Further, to work effectively, supply chain management requires partnerships and alliances. Collaborative decision making among partners in a supply chain is a new business model characterized by the building of relationships, collaboration, shared knowledge, more certainty, less guessing, and ultimately better planning. The implementation of supply chain management is associated with a number of common system design features.

FEATURES OF SUPPLY CHAIN PROCESSES

The design of efficient and effective supply chain processes is guided by a number of core concepts. Implementation of the concepts requires compatible business philosophies among the participants and appropriate tools.

Concepts and tools of supply chain management

A basic principle of integrated logistics management has always been the total cost approach to decision making. This recognizes cost and service trade-offs between different activities. The same principle has to be applied among companies in a common supply chain. They seek to maintain competitive advantage by optimizing costs across the entire manufacturing and distribution system rather than seek cost reduction in each company.

A related concept derived from the purchasing field is the total cost of ownership. Leading firms adopt a total cost of ownership approach, also known as lifecycle value optimization, in making procurement decisions within the supply chain. This requires managing all processes that affect the total cost, from developing specifications and determining sourcing arrangements, through forecasting and planning requirements, to procuring, distributing, and ultimately salvaging the components. America Electric Power Company followed this concept to reduce total costs when preparing itself for industry deregulation in 1995 (Anderson and Heninger, 1996).

Network simplification and rationalization often reduce total costs in supply chains. This can be achieved in many ways. Product design may be changed to enable the use of more standard components across products, thereby enabling fewer processes and the concentration of production. Flows through a network may be simplified by the reduction of intermediaries and the use of strategically located hubs, taking advantage of new communications technologies and new approaches to carrier selection and vehicle routing. Consolidation of purchasing across business units, including the purchase of logistics services, reduces the number of vendors used and combines the buying power of supply chain members. These examples of network simplification reduce the number of processes and facilitate achieving economies of scale and volume leverage in procurement. However, consolidation of different activities to achieve economies of scale, asset sharing and other synergies is pursued only when customer service is not compromised.

The successful practice of supply chain management requires certain tools. Three are identified here: information technology, effective costing and performance metrics.

The successful supply chain needs real-time or close to it, point-of-purchase information to be provided to all participants, to help everyone manage more closely to actual market demand. This takes costly excess inventory out of the pipeline. Ideally, a supply-chain-wide information technology strategy is developed to support multiple levels of decision making. First, there are the short-term systems that can handle routine day-to-day transactions like order processing and shipment scheduling. Then, from a longer-term perspective, the technology must facilitate such activities as demand planning and master production scheduling. Finally, information systems must enable strategic analysis by providing modelling and other tools that synthesize data for use in high-level 'what if' scenario planning. These forward-looking systems help managers evaluate distribution centres, suppliers and third-party service options.

Information about the actual level of costs by product and channel activity is important to good management. Such information is provided by activity-based costing (ABC), which tracks those processes and costs formerly treated as overheads so that they can be logically and corrected identified with products and consumers. It assigns costs based on how resources actually are used, tagging them directly to the activities and customers consuming them. ABC enables firms to properly cost the services provided to internal and external customers.

An important feature of good supply chains is that they use a variety of performance measures. Their existence is evidence of careful planning and analysis in the design of the supply chain relationships The measures cover more than internal functions. They include channel-spanning performance measures and those that apply to every link in the supply chain. These measurement systems embrace both service and financial metrics, such as each account's true profitability. The importance of measuring supply-chain-wide performance is exemplified by the development of the supply chain operations reference model developed over an 18-month period by 75 leading manufacturers. It contains standardized supply chain process definitions, standard terminology, standard metrics, best practices and enabling information technology functionality requirements (Supply-Chain Council).

Evolving supply chain process designs

The design of supply chain systems reflects commodity characteristics, customer needs and consequently corporate strategy. Increasingly, reducing inventory investment and associated costs through cycle time reduction has become a primary thrust of many firms.

The first and best-known approach to cycle time and inventory reduction is just-in-time management (JIT), which has been adopted widely in manufacturing. The logistics system is designed to ensure product and service reliability and timely availability consistent with JIT manufacturing needs. The JIT concept has been adapted to serve the retail, grocery and healthcare sectors in the form of quick response, continuous replenishment and stockless inventory respectively. The tools used to implement these approaches include bar coding of product, point-of-sale capture of sales information, electronic data interchange and vendor-managed inventory.

Pioneers like Procter and Gamble (P&G) and Wal-Mart lead the way with systems geared to quick response and continuous replenishment. Information on product sales is captured instantly from bar-coded product by point-of-sale scanners, and the information on the stock sold at the retail level is transmitted electronically to the manufacturer on the same day or in real time. P&G replenishes Wal-Mart's inventory automatically under agreed rules, typically within a day or two, in small lot sizes. These are really obvious approaches to using real-time sales data available through robust information systems to take time and, therefore, inventory out of the supply chain.

Quick response emphasizes the speed of delivery, while continuous replenishment focuses on the small but frequent lot size dimension. The real challenge comes in taking the next step of either direct store delivery (which involves bypassing the retailer's distribution center (DC)) or cross-docking. Cross-docking is a process that prevents products from coming to rest as static inventory at the retailer's DC. The manufacturer makes up individual store orders and delivers this store-ready merchandise to the retailer, who simply offloads it at the DC and cross-docks it to waiting delivery trucks. Few retailers, however, have been able to achieve anything close to true cross-docking, as it requires incredibly complex planning and coordination. Perhaps its greatest weakness is that few manufacturers are equipped to create store order quantities efficiently. Partial pallet loads can seriously reduce the cube utilization of the retailer's fleet. However, the effectiveness of the retailer's DCs can be made more efficient for a wider variety of products by equipping them with sortation and case-handling equipment.

The concept of quick response is fundamental to the implementation of the so-called mass-customization strategy. Making product is postponed until orders are received. Cost-effective production is made possible by new flexible manufacturing systems. Cost-effective delivery is possible because of improved supply chain systems. Postponement of production occurs in instances where the nature of customer demand allows a time window before product availability is expected. That is the case with bed sets, with which most buyers are willing to wait a few days for actual delivery. Taking advantage of this, Sears and Bedford Industries set up a quick response system for manufacturing bed sets to order. A less likely example (perhaps common in the 21st century) is the strategy of Levi Strauss to sell women's personal made-to-size jeans over the Internet.

The practice of some firms such as Home Depot is to operate to a large extent with limited distribution centres, preferring to manage the flow of products directly to their own retail outlets. Cosmetics, bakery products, snack foods and beverages are also frequently delivered direct to stores. But the vast majority of products flow from manufacturers to retail distribution centers to the stores, and this situation is not likely to change in the foreseeable future. Inventories will be squeezed by new procedures, but full cross-docking is an elusive goal.

A concept that focuses on improving supply chain performance through more efficient inventory management is 'vendor-managed inventory.' This involves the supplier, not the customer, tracking customer needs and replenishing inventory. The concept is relevant to any supply situation, but most notably it is a recent innovation in supply chain relationships in manufacturing and service organizations such as telephone or power companies. Under this method, a supplier has direct links to a customer's manufacturing or maintenance schedule and has responsibility to supply goods based on that schedule. The advantage to this approach is that it reduces cost and time from a customer's inventory management programme. To implement this process, the customer's and supplier's information and decision systems need to be well integrated. Also, it is essential that pricing and the terms of supply be specified carefully at the beginning of the contract.

The supply chain processes such as quick response, continuous replenishment and vendor-managed inventory reflect the evolution of logistics management. It has shifted from a focus on internal integration within a functional approach to a cross-functional approach with an external orientation. Logistics must complement and work with other business processes internally, and with customers and suppliers in the supply chain. Logistics management is becoming less about managing the flow of goods and of inventory. It is becoming more about managing relationships within the organization, with suppliers and most importantly with customers. It is about the whole supply chain, which must be designed and managed to deliver what customers want, when they want it.

CONCLUSION

Examples have been given of firms managing the supply chain as an important component of competitive strategy, from product-based companies such as Methanex to retailers such as Wal-Mart. Where successful supply chains exist, particular firms in the channel have played a leadership role. However, the successful creation of efficient supply chains has required a favourable environment and the participation of many parties. North America is fortunate that the tradition of competition on a continental scale, the effective role of each of the modes of transport, and the availability of advanced information systems have contributed to a favourable environment. While the forces affecting North America and the concepts of logistics management are similar to those elsewhere, the prominence of managing supply chains on a continental scale is the foremost strategy affecting the development of logistics systems.

REFERENCES

Anderson, M and Heninger, W (1996) Transforming the supply chain: a case study in the utilities industry, *Logistics! Candid insights for supply chain leaders*, Mercer Management Consulting (Fall), pp 36–38

Boehm, R and Phipps, C (1996) Flatness, *McKinsey Quarterly*, 3, pp 128–43

Bowersox, D J, (1997) Integrated supply chain management: a strategic imperative, *Council of Logistics Management Annual Conference Proceedings*, pp 181–90

Chemical Market Reporter (1997) Arco launches cost initiative after lackluster first quarter, *Chemical Market Reporter*, **252** (Jul), p 9

Closs, D et al (1997) World class logistics: a two-year review, *Council of Logistics Management Annual Conference Proceedings*, pp 191–202

Delaney, R (1997) CLI's 8th annual 'state of logistics report', remarks to the National Press Club, Washington DC (2 Jun), pp 3–6

Eckler, J and Farrell, J (1997) Making connections: redesigning Bell Canada's supply chain for a competitive extended enterprise, presentation before the Council of Logistics Management Annual Meeting (7 Oct), Chicago, IL, mimeo

Global Logistics Research Team (1995) *World Class Logistics*, Council of Logistics Management/Michigan State University, Oak Brook, IL

Harrington, L H (1998) Quality and the outsourcing decision, *Distribution Magazine* [Online] www.fedex.com (accessed Sep 1998)

Hessenberger, M, Seiersen, N and Straube, F (1997) European logistics trends and strategies, *Council of Logistics Management Annual Conference Proceedings*, pp 123–42

Metz, P J (1997) Demystifying supply chain management: accomplishments and challenges, *Council of Logistics Management Annual Conference Proceedings*, pp 237–55

Minahan, T (1996) What drives the supply chain? *Purchasing*, **120** (11), p 54

Porter, M (1985) *Competitive Advantage: Creating and sustaining superior performance*, Free Press, New York

Quinn, F J (1997) The payoff! Benefits of improving supply chain management, *Logistics Management*, **36** (12)

Supply–Chain Council [Online] www.supply-chain.org

Index